"Leeman's well-argued book is a welcome reminder that the full reality of the church is to be found in the local congregation. I cannot imagine that his book will not become a standard work in this area of theological inquiry."
**Stanley Hauerwas,** Duke University

"This is a very important book. Impressive in the depth and breadth of its sources, *Political Church* offers a fresh, cogent and well-informed model that deserves wide attention. Situating his arguments in past and present debates, Leeman formulates a unique paradigm for understanding simultaneously the nature of the church and its relation to the kingdoms of this age. *Political Church* is an example of a new level of evangelical reflection and serious engagement."
**Michael Horton,** Westminster Seminary California

"Difficult issues related to church, state and religious freedom arise on a daily basis and fill our newspapers and inboxes. In *Political Church*, Jonathan Leeman offers a way forward that we would do well to read and consider. The virtues of this book are considerable, ranging from its institutional reading of Scripture and the larger society to its trenchant critique of liberalism, with the latter's exaltation of the expansive self and its wants."
**David T. Koyzis,** Redeemer University College

"Jonathan Leeman is one of the most careful, intelligent and skilled theological minds of our day, particularly in matters of ecclesiology. This new volume is a courageous defense of the centrality and indispensability of the local church. *Political Church* is a model for sound exegetical, biblical and systematic theology that makes a powerful argument. For anyone thinking seriously about ecclesiology, local church ministry, the relationship between church and state, or even religious liberty, this volume is a brilliant resource."
**R. Albert Mohler Jr.,** president of The Southern Baptist Theological Seminary

"The church, we are sometimes told, is a fellowship, not an institution. Jonathan Leeman makes us think again. Broad-ranging, deeply biblical, widely informed both theologically and politically, *Political Church* is a fine and statesmanlike contribution that deserves our careful attention. We need to capture the vision of the local church as an embassy of Christ's rule. This is just what the author enables us to do."
**Stephen N. Williams,** Union Theological College

"An incisive and distinctly evangelical contribution to political theology, Leeman's *Political Church* supplants the tired dichotomies of classical liberalism by recapturing the church's unique political ontology as a community with a message that is also at the same time an institution with keys to the kingdom. To bear witness to the rule of Christ is also to represent him publicly to the world. Leeman's account is impressively well-judged and advances a conception of church as embassy that those who take the rule of Christ seriously cannot afford to overlook. Essential (and edifying!) reading."
**Matthew Arbo,** Oklahoma Baptist University

"Jonathan Leeman in this profound and important work argues that Christ is Lord of all, that he rules both in the church and in the public square. At the same time, Leeman unpacks for us the differences between the political sphere and the realm of the church. The implications for our ecclesiology are spelled out in a noteworthy way. Here we find robust biblical and systematic theology deftly applied to our role as citizens and church members."
**Thomas R. Schreiner,** The Southern Baptist Theological Seminary

# POLITICAL CHURCH

*The Local Assembly
as Embassy of Christ's Rule*

◆◆◆◆◆◆◆◆◆◆◆◆◆◆◆◆◆◆◆◆◆◆◆

Jonathan Leeman

An imprint of InterVarsity Press
Downers Grove, Illinois

InterVarsity Press
P.O. Box 1400, Downers Grove, IL 60515-1426
ivpress.com
email@ivpress.com

©2016 by Jonathan Leeman

All rights reserved. No part of this book may be reproduced in any form without written permission from InterVarsity Press.

InterVarsity Press® is the book-publishing division of InterVarsity Christian Fellowship/USA®, a movement of students and faculty active on campus at hundreds of universities, colleges and schools of nursing in the United States of America, and a member movement of the International Fellowship of Evangelical Students. For information about local and regional activities, visit intervarsity.org.

Scripture quotations, unless otherwise noted, are from The Holy Bible, English Standard Version, copyright © 2001 by Crossway Bibles, a division of Good News Publishers. Used by permission. All rights reserved.

Cover design: Cindy Kiple
Interior design: Beth McGill
Image: St. Peter's statue by Giuseppe de Fabris, St. Peter's Square. / Photo © Tarker / Bridgeman Images

ISBN 978-0-8308-4880-5 (print)
ISBN 978-0-8308-9904-3 (digital)

**Library of Congress Cataloging-in-Publication Data**
Names: Leeman, Jonathan, 1973-
Title: Political church : the local assembly as embassy of Christ's rule / Jonathan Leeman.
Description: Downers Grove : InterVarsity Press, 2016. | Series: Studies in Christian doctrine and scripture | Includes index.
Identifiers: LCCN 2015040197 (print) | LCCN 2015042609 (ebook) | ISBN 9780830848805 (pbk.) | ISBN 9780830899043 (eBook)
Subjects: LCSH: Christianity and politics. | Church.
Classification: LCC BR115.P7 L3264 2016 (print) | LCC BR115.P7 (ebook) | DDC 261.7--dc23
LC record available at http://lccn.loc.gov/2015040197

| P | 23 | 22 | 21 | 20 | 19 | 18 | 17 | 16 | 15 | 14 | 13 | 12 | 11 | 10 | 9 | 8 | 7 | 6 | 5 | 4 | 3 | 2 | 1 |
| Y | 34 | 33 | 32 | 31 | 30 | 29 | 28 | 27 | 26 | 25 | 24 | 23 | 22 | 21 | 20 | 19 | 18 | 17 | 16 | | | | | |

To my patient and loving wife. Thank you, Shannon,
for supporting this project from beginning to long-awaited end.

# Contents

| | |
|---|---|
| Outline of the Book | 9 |
| Preface | 13 |
| Acknowledgments | 19 |
| Introduction | 21 |
| 1 What Is Politics? | 55 |
| 2 What Is an Institution? | 98 |
| 3 The Politics of Creation | 142 |
| 4 The Politics of the Fall | 172 |
| 5 The Politics of the New Covenant | 239 |
| 6 The Politics of the Kingdom | 294 |
| Conclusion | 389 |
| *Name Index* | 393 |
| *Subject Index* | 395 |
| *Scripture Index* | 399 |

# Outline of the Book

| | |
|---|---|
| Introduction | 21 |
|     Need #1: A Better Institutional Conceptuality | 25 |
|     Need #2: A Better Political Conceptuality | 27 |
|     What Others Have Said | 31 |
|     A Covenantal Approach | 39 |
|     Combining Political and Institutional Conceptualities | 47 |
| 1 What Is Politics? | 55 |
|     What Is Politics? | 56 |
|         *The Line Between Public and Private* | 56 |
|         *Public-Wide and Coercive Governance* | 59 |
|         *What Is the State?* | 60 |
|         *Conclusion* | 62 |
|     Separating the Political and the Spiritual | 62 |
|     Spirituality of the Church | 68 |
|     Freedom of Religion as Freedom of Conscience | 71 |
|     A Broader Religious Conceptuality and a View from Somewhere | 76 |
|     A Broader Political Conceptuality | 82 |
|     How Religious Freedom Destroys Religious Freedom | 86 |
|     Conclusion | 94 |
| 2 What Is an Institution? | 98 |
|     Community and the Relational Turn | 99 |
|     What Is an Institution? | 105 |
|     What Is a Political Institution? | 112 |
|     What Is a Political Community and Its Membership? | 114 |
|         *Political Community and Territory* | 117 |
|         *Political Rebellion and Other Complexities* | 119 |
|         *Other Kinds of Unity* | 120 |
|     A Community of Subjects or Citizens? | 121 |
|     Biblical and Theological Institutionalism | 126 |

    *Not Just a Secular Concept*     127
    *An Institutional Hermeneutic*     128
    *More than a Political Hermeneutic*     133
  Biblical Wisdom     137
  Conclusion     139

**3 The Politics of Creation**     142

  The Politics of God     144
    *Divine Sociality*     146
    *Human Sociality*     149
  The Politics of Creation     153
    *The Creator Is King*     154
    *The Archetypal Body Politic and Citizenship Mandate*     158
    *Two Classes of Political Membership*     163
    *Political Worship, the Priestly Mandate*
        *and the Archetypal Sanctuary*     165
  Absolute Versus Mediate Authority and Conscience     168
  Conclusion     171

**4 The Politics of the Fall**     172

  God's Universal Rule and the Noahic Covenant     182
    *The Justice Mechanism and the Foundation of Government*     185
    *Religious Tolerance—Part 1*     199
    *Seven Lessons from the Noahic Covenant*     206
  The Political/Religious Accountability of the Nations     209
  Modeling God's Universal Rule Through the Special Covenants     214
    *Abrahamic Covenant*     215
    *Mosaic Covenant*     222
    *Deputized in God's Name*     226
    *Davidic Covenant*     227
  Institutional Change, Naming Names and Visible Rule     228
    *Institutional Relativity and Change*     229
    *The Execution of Rule in Salvation and Judgment*     231
  Conclusion     235

| | |
|---|---|
| 5 The Politics of the New Covenant | 239 |
|    A Political People | 245 |
|    The New Covenant | 247 |
|       *Deuteronomy* | 247 |
|       *Jeremiah* | 247 |
|       *Ezekiel* | 249 |
|       *Isaiah* | 250 |
|       *A Mutually Affirmed Covenant?* | 252 |
|       *Conclusion: The Fulfillment of the Previous Covenants* | 254 |
|    Politics of the Heart and Spirit | 254 |
|       *Totalitarianism and the New Covenant* | 255 |
|       *Four Lessons for a Political Theology* | 257 |
|       *Conclusion* | 278 |
|    Politics of Forgiveness | 278 |
|       *Who Has the Authority to Forgive?* | 280 |
|       *What Is the Basis of This Authority in Light of Retributive Justice?* | 280 |
|       *What Does Forgiveness Mean in Political Terms?* | 284 |
|    Reinvoking Creation's Citizenship Mandate | 290 |
|    Conclusion | 292 |
| 6 The Politics of the Kingdom | 294 |
|    The Politics of Jesus and His People | 296 |
|       *Jesus* | 298 |
|       *Church* | 301 |
|       *Recommissioned in Adam's Office* | 302 |
|    Matthew (Part 1): A Heavenly Citizenship | 305 |
|       *Covenantal Fulfillment* | 305 |
|       *Heaven and Earth* | 307 |
|       *Regime Change* | 309 |
|       *New Covenant* | 311 |
|       *Righteous Office, Righteous Community* | 312 |
|    Paul and Justification | 316 |

|    |    |
|---|---|
| *Present Justification and Covenantal Inclusion* | 317 |
| *The Forensic Is Political* | 323 |
| *By Faith Alone—The Unexpected Basis for Political Unity* | 325 |
| *Future Justification According to Works* | 328 |
| *Conclusion* | 330 |
| Matthew (Part 2): Keys of the Kingdom | 332 |
| *Still Needed: Public Recognition, Assurance, Reauthorization and Authoritative Interpretation* | 332 |
| *Matthew 16 and the Keys of the Kingdom* | 334 |
| *Matthew 18 and the Local Church* | 344 |
| *Who Holds the Keys: Congregations or Elders?* | 348 |
| *Matthew 28 as Deputization Ceremony* | 359 |
| A Church, Its Members and the Ordinances | 362 |
| *Church Membership and the Ordinances* | 362 |
| *What and Where Is a Church?* | 365 |
| A Heavenly and Eschatological Embassy and Signmaker on Earth | 365 |
| *A Political Assembly* | 365 |
| *An Embassy and Signmaker* | 366 |
| *Religious Tolerance—Part 2* | 370 |
| *An Embassy on the International Map* | 374 |
| Conclusion: The Unity of the Church | 385 |
| **Conclusion** | **389** |
| The Political Hope of the Nations | 391 |

# Preface

THIS BOOK HAS TWO MAIN GOALS. The first is to replace the map of politics and religion that many Christians have been using since the democratic revolutions of the eighteenth century with a more biblical one. The second is to explain where the local church fits onto this redrawn map as a political institution or embassy of Christ's rule.

I'm not the first to attempt either task. Yet it's striking to me how many Western Christians continue to take the Enlightenment assumptions of classical liberalism for granted and then find themselves flustered when those assumptions undermine the principles they value or even cramp the space to practice their beliefs.

The most obvious example of this may be in our theories of religious freedom. We often rest the case for religious liberty on the publicly accessible and nonsectarian idea of "freedom of conscience" but are then surprised when a court employs "the right to define one's concept of existence" to uphold abortion, or the right to make "certain personal choices central to individual dignity and autonomy, including intimate choices defining personal identity and beliefs," to justify marrying same-sex couples. Aren't these latter formulations simply other ways of describing the free conscience? Why then should Christian consciences prevail over non-Christian ones when the two come into conflict?

This whole conversation about religious freedom rests on assumptions about the relationship between the political and the religious—namely, that they occupy separate, if sometimes overlapping, domains. Generally, we think of the public square as the place for politics, while the private domiciles of home and church are reserved for religion, even if we maintain that the boundary between them is porous.

This is the map I want to help throw out. Church and state are separate institutions with different jurisdictions. Neither should confuse itself for the other. One bears the sword, while the other bears the keys of the kingdom. Yet the work of each is set on a landscape where politics and religion are wholly coterminous, like two circle lenses placed perfectly on top of one another. The public square is nothing more or less than a battleground of gods. And the church is a political institution inhabited by citizens of heaven who bear a distinctly political message: Jesus is king.

The division between politics and religion, I dare say, is an ideological ploy. Imagine an airport security metal detector standing at the entrance of the public square, which doesn't screen for metal but for religion. The machine beeps anytime someone walks through it with a supernatural big-G God hiding inside of one of their convictions, but it fails to pick up self-manufactured or socially constructed little-g gods. Into this public square the secularist, the materialist, the Darwinist, the consumerist, the elitist, the chauvinist, and, frankly, the fascist can all enter carring their gods with them, like whittled wooden figures in their pockets. Not so the Christians or Jews. Their conviction that murder is wrong because all people are made in God's image might as well be a semiautomatic. What this means, of course, is that the public square is inevitably slanted toward the secularist and materialist. Public conversation is ideologically rigged. The secularist can bring his or her god. I cannot bring mine because his name starts with a capital letter and I didn't make him up.

Meanwhile, churches err in one of two directions. Either they falsely claim to be spiritual, not political, and so fail to take the stands that they should. The Church of England in South Africa's refusal to address the matter of apartheid is one such example. Or they convince themselves that political advocacy in the public square is their most important work and distract themselves from their primary mission: being the church.

Others have said it before me, but the church's most powerful political activity is being the church and proclaiming its unique message. After redrawing the map of politics and religion, *that* is the main work of this volume—presenting the local church as an embassy of Christ's breaking-into-history rule. The church wields the keys of the kingdom in order to speak for heaven on earth by affirming the *what* and the *who* of the gospel. And the church's life is held together by justification by faith alone, the most powerful political force in the world today for flattening hierarchies and uniting one-time enemies.

To put it another way, the state is an earthly platform builder while the church is a heavenly signmaker. The state's work is to build a platform of peace and order and protection for God's people so that churches can get on with their business. And the church's business is to hang signs with Jesus' name over right beliefs, right practices, and right people—the repenting and believing citizens of Christ's kingdom. Through baptism and the Lord's Supper, a church hangs signs on God's people that say, "Jesus Representative." That is surely not the work of the state, just as employing coercive force for the sake of peace is surely not the work of the church.

I worked hard in this book to dig deep biblical foundations, particularly by working through the Bible's covenantal storyline. And I dare say that what readers might be tempted to find the most tedious parts of the book, the long discussions of Scripture's storyline in the middle chapters, are in fact the most important parts, at least for reframing how we think about religion and politics and the work of the church.

Every writer is tempted to make his audience as broad as possible so that more people might benefit from his or her labors. Yet there is enough of what's called anti-modernism in me that I'm convinced each of us can only write *within* our own traditions of justice and rationality, to borrow from Alasdair MacIntyre. My point here is not the relativist's one, that any tradition is as good as another because everything's relative. My point is the presuppositionalist's one. We are all building on our own presuppositions and first principles, and the various traditions of justice and rationality possess incommensurable starting points. As such, it seems most honest to say that I am writing as a Christian to Christians. And my primary goal is to edify Christians and strengthen churches. If that's achieved, it will have the added benefit of serving our non-Christian neighbors and possibly even blessing the public square. But the order and emphasis here are crucial. If Christian political theologians or political philosophers try first to convince their non-Christian counterparts even before they convince themselves and their fellow believers, they will have to build on common ground, which invariably means compromising their own foundations, which is where I began a moment ago. (In that sense, the theologian's work is different than the apologist's.)

If you happen to be a non-Christian reader, I propose that you might gain a better understanding of one Christian perspective by my writing to fellow

Christians than by writing to you. It's like sneaking into a house and eavesdropping on a family's conversation. You just might get a better sense of what they *really* think. Within an anti-modernist framework, in fact, I'm even inclined to think this is the better approach to public conversation, whether political or philosophical: let me climb into your tradition to see what I can see, and then you climb into mine.

In general, much recent political theology as a discipline seems to incline in this anti-modernist direction, or at least it does among those who call themselves political theologians. Not only that, this recent strain of political theology tends to have more interest in understanding and describing the church, while those who self-style as political philosophers tend to be interested in the state and then treat the church as an afterthought. Think of Thomas Jefferson or James Madison from yesterday, or John Rawls or Michael Sandel from today. They all have theories about the relationship between church and state. But can any of them offer a biblically rigorous description of what the church is? I think the answer is obviously no. To my knowledge, Thomas Jefferson never grappled with the relationship between the biblical covenants or how Jesus typologically fulfills the Adamic office of priest-king before establishing a people as new-creation priest-kings. All that to say, Christians who claim to care about the relationship between church and state would do well to pay slightly less attention to the standard cast of philosophers popular in political theory departments (though I interact with some of them here) and more attention to the theologians who work to unpack what Scripture says about the church. I believe Luke Bretherton is correct when he writes,

> Consequent upon . . . the church being the church is the refusal to allow the state [*or the political philosopher, I would add*] to set the terms and conditions of entry into the public square: if the church, to be authentically itself, is a public political body which speaks its own language, then so be it. The state oversteps its proper limits when it seeks to determine when, where, and in what voice the church may speak. Conversely, the church falsely limits itself when it only acts and speaks within conditions set for it externally.[1]

---

[1] Luke Bretherton, *Christianity and Contemporary Politics: The Conditions and Possibilities of Faithful Witness* (Maldan, MA: Wiley-Blackwell, 2010), 54.

My prayer for this book is that it would give you, the reader, a better understanding of what the Bible says about church as well as how it describes the political map on which the church serves the purposes of Christ's kingdom. And I pray that it might equip you in the work of building up your local congregation in holiness and love for Christ's kingly purposes.

# Acknowledgments

A SPECIAL WORD OF THANKS is owed to advisors, conversation partners and opportunity providers. Stephen Wellum, Johannes Hoff and Maurice Dowling advised me throughout the project, helping to sharpen arguments and point me to unexamined perspectives. Wellum especially is responsible (or to blame?) for my theological methodology. Hoff, who comes from a fairly different theological perspective than my own, humbly engaged the project on its own terms, thereby modeling the open-mindedness, fairness and dedication to understanding that characterizes the most humane and reasonable teachers. I am also indebted to Stephen N. Williams, who read the entire work at least twice and perceived a number of cracks in the cement that I had not discerned.

Bobby Jamieson probably deserves pride of place for being the friend who gave hours of conversation to working over some concept with me—like two squirrels collaborating on a stubborn nut. David Koyzis and Tom Schreiner also read the volume and provided feedback that improved it.

Michael Haykin originally launched me on this project. Matt Schmucker, Mark Dever and Ryan Townsend generously provided the sabbatical space and general support to study and write. Kevin Vanhoozer and Dan Treier, remarkably, took an interest in the book and offered the kind opportunity for publishing it in their series. And David Congdon helpfully shepherded it through the publication process at IVP. Thank you to each of these friends and partners.

Most of all, my wife, Shannon, owns my deepest gratitude and love for the countless late nights and early mornings, stolen weekends and holidays, and many prayers involved in a work that has been nine years in the making. A book dedication is a wholly inadequate repayment, but she deserves it more than any.

# Introduction

Political science professor Robert Putnam, in a well-known 1995 essay titled "Bowling Alone," observed that "more Americans are bowling today than ever before, but bowling in organized leagues has plummeted."[1] Putnam's project, which focused on declining levels of American participation in voluntary organizations, was aided by dozens of research assistants who poured over countless city directories, Masonic Lodge yearbooks, membership statistics for the General Federation of Women's Clubs, Rotary Club files, Episcopal Church reports, and more. Indeed, one year of my own life was spent in the Library of Congress, Harvard's Widener Library, and the offices of many national and local organizations searching out those very membership figures.[2] Not, perhaps, the *most* riveting year of my life.

A foundational assumption of all this neo-Tocquevillian analysis, and an assumption of many democratic Westerners, is that local churches are one more voluntary organization, something to be classified with the likes of Little League and the Sierra Club. Few people would deny that local churches are *politically significant*, not least Putnam, who argues that participating in voluntary organizations is instrumental in "making democracy work," as he puts it in another book by that title. But that is qualitatively different from saying that local churches are political associations outright, as one would with, say, the US embassy in London, England.

---

[1] Robert D. Putnam, "Bowling Alone: America's Declining Social Capital," *Journal of Democracy* 6 (January 1995): 70.
[2] I had nothing to do with bowling league research. What I worked on can be found in Gerald Gamm and Robert D. Putnam, "The Growth of Voluntary Associations in America, 1840–1940," in *Patterns of Social Capital: Stability and Change in Historical Perspective*, ed. Robert I. Rotberg (New York: Cambridge University Press, 2001), 179-80; see also Robert Putnam, *Bowling Alone: The Collapse and Revival of American Community* (New York: Simon & Schuster, 2001), 507.

Yet the primary claim of this book is that the local church is just such a political assembly. Indeed, the church is a kind of embassy, only it represents a kingdom of even greater political consequence to the nations and their governors. And this embassy represents a kingdom not from across geographic space but from across eschatological time.

In other words, this book is concerned with the biblical and theological question of what constitutes a local church. The answer, it will argue, is that Jesus grants Christians the authority to establish local churches as visible embassies of his end-time rule through the "keys of the kingdom" described in the Gospel of Matthew. By virtue of both the keys and a traditional Protestant conception of justification by faith alone, the local church exists as a political assembly that publicly represents King Jesus, displays the justice and righteousness of the triune God, and pronounces Jesus' claim upon the nations and their governments.

Does this mean I am charging my former employer with a methodological error, that churches are not really voluntary organizations after all? From the standpoint of the state, to be sure, church membership should be voluntary. The state has no authority here, or so I will maintain. The question is, how do the Christian Scriptures present the local church, and where do they fit onto a political landscape of the nations as the Bible conceives of that landscape? Should churches be classified as institutions of state, voluntary organizations or something else altogether? The prosaic picture of a slump-shouldered research assistant typing membership statistics into Excel spreadsheets offers a useful "reality check" for any claim that the local church is a "political" institution, lest we fall into useless theological abstraction. How then would the Bible's prophets and apostles instruct a political scientist's research assistant to classify the local church? Answering that question requires two things then: describing what the local church is and also sketching out the political landscape of the nations as the Bible conceives of it, which may be the harder part.

Of course, it is not just political scientists who classify a church as a club-like organization. Christian historians of the first century, too, look for affinities between churches and the public religious associations and voluntary associations of the Greco-Roman world. Such historians tell us that these organizations, like churches, employed initiation rites for membership;

collected membership dues; exercised discipline over their members; used kinship language, calling one another "brother" or "father"; and even gave their leaders titles like *episkopos* and *diakonos*.³ These historians do not necessarily mean to say that churches were merely one more such organization; and I personally do not mean to deny that analogies between the two types of entities exist, any more than I would deny that analogies exist between the church and the household, an analogy that is biblical (e.g., 1 Tim 3:15; 1 Pet 4:17; cf. Eph 2:19).⁴ Many such comparisons and analogies make for useful avenues of theological inquiry and formulation.

Still, my purpose here is to argue that the institutional essence of the local assembly is a political unity. A church's members are united in more ways than politically. But what binds the local church together as a distinct body of people, distinct from the nations *and* distinct from Christians united to other churches, is the fact that Jesus Christ's universal lordship gets exercised *there*—among *them*. *Here* is where the keys of the kingdom are exercised in membership, discipline, and doctrinal affirmation. Christ's political rule may be "not of this world," meaning it has its source or origin not in the world but in heaven (Jn 18:36).⁵ And his rule unites all Christians everywhere invisibly. But this universal rule is visibly and institutionally manifest in history through the proclamation of the gospel and the binding and loosing activity of the local church, the two activities that constitute an otherwise unincorporated group of Christians as a particular church. To become a member of a church is to be declared a citizen of Christ's

---

³Richard S. Ascough, "Greco-Roman Philosophic, Religious, and Voluntary Associations," in *Community Formation in the Early Church and in the Church Today*, ed. Richard N. Longenecker (Peabody, MA: Hendrickson, 2002), 3-19; see also Wayne A. Meeks, *The First Urban Christians: The Social World of the Apostle Paul* (New Haven, CT: Yale University Press, 1983), 77-80; Philip A. Harland, *Associations, Synagogues, and Congregations: Claiming a Place in Ancient Mediterranean Society* (Minneapolis: Fortress, 2003) and *Dynamics of Identity in the World of Early Christians: Associations, Judeans, and Cultural Minorities* (New York: T&T Clark, 2009). See also Robert Louis Wilken's discussion of how the Romans viewed churches, as with Pliny the Younger's description of Christian groups as *hetaeria*, which might be translated "political club" or "association." Wilken, *The Christians as the Romans Saw Them*, 2nd ed. (New Haven, CT: Yale University Press, 2003), 32-35.
⁴E.g., Meeks, *First Urban Christians*, 75-77; Joseph H. Hellerman, *The Ancient Church as Family* (Minneapolis: Fortress, 2001).
⁵D. A. Carson, *The Gospel According to John*, Pillar New Testament Commentary (Grand Rapids: Eerdmans, 1991), 594; J. Ramsey Michaels, *The Gospel of John*, New International Commentary on the New Testament (Grand Rapids: Eerdmans, 2010), 922-23; Raymond E. Brown, *The Gospel According to John XIII-XXI*, Anchor Bible (Garden City, NY: Doubleday, 1970), 852.

kingdom. It is a local church's politically authorized corporate existence that constitutes a group of Christians as a visible embassy of Christ's kingdom on earth and that, in turn, formally authorizes every individual within that assembly to represent the King's name before the nations and their governors as an ambassador.

That is not to say that the authority exercised in a local church bespeaks its own self-contained politics and that I am using the term metaphorically, as when one speaks of "office politics" or "university politics." Rather, the local church's rule is but one bolt of fabric in the larger roll of cloth that makes up Christ's rule among the nations and their governments. The state and the church both mediate the rule of God, and unlike the mediate authority of, say, a parent, they both make an authoritative claim on the whole of a society, one by the sword and one by gospel proclamation. And backing up both claims is God's own sword, even if that sword won't show itself until the eschaton. The proto-liberal Thomas Hobbes observed, "The Kingdome therefore of God, is a reall, not a metaphoricall Kingdome."[6] What's therefore needed, says present-day political theologian Oliver O'Donovan, is a much "fuller political conceptuality," one that "pushes back the horizon of commonplace politics and opens it up to the activity of God."[7]

---

[6]Thomas Hobbes, *Leviathan*, ed. Richard Tuck, Cambridge Texts in the History of Political Thought (Cambridge: Cambridge University Press, 1991), chap. 35, para. 219. Hobbes may seem like an unlikely candidate for making this point, but he did affirm the literal existence of the kingdom of God. Yet this does not affect his theory of the state the way one might expect because he (more or less) placed this kingdom entirely into the eschaton: "the Kingdome of Christ is not to begin till the generall Resurrection" (ibid., chap. 41, sec. 262; see also sec. 263 and 264). His seal between the present and future, however, was not hermetic. Though he argued that "the Kingdome hee claimed was to bee in another world," he also acknowledged that "the Godly are said to bee already in the Kingdom of Grace, as naturalized in that heavenly Kingdome" (ibid., chap. 41, sec. 243). In short, Hobbes offered a precarious balance. On the one hand, he wanted to say "there is nothing done, or taught by Christ, that tendeth to the diminution of the Civill Right of the Jewes, or of Caesar" (ibid.). On the other hand, Hobbes wanted to reserve a place for civil disobedience when a government calls an individual to defy God's law: "But if the command [of the civil sovereign] be such, as cannot be obeyed, without being damned to Eternall Death, then it were madnesse to obey it, and the Counsell of our Saviour takes place, (*Mat. 10.28*) *Fear not those that kill the body, but cannot kill the soule*" (ibid., chap. 43, sec. 321; see also chap. 31, sec. 186; chap. 42, sec. 271). Whether or not Hobbes's system was wholly consistent on these points is not for this book to decide.

[7]Oliver O'Donovan, *Desire of the Nations: Rediscovering the Roots of Political Theology* (New York: Cambridge University Press, 1996), 2. See also David Miller and Sohail H. Hashmi, introduction to *Boundaries and Justice: Diverse Ethical Perspectives*, ed. David Miller and Sohail H. Hashmi (Princeton, NJ: Princeton University Press, 2001), 13.

## Need #1: A Better Institutional Conceptuality

It is tempting to jump directly to Matthew's discussion of the keys of the kingdom in chapters 16, 18 and (implicitly) 28. We will do this in chapter six to argue that Jesus authorizes the local church to act as this embassy from the future. But if our political and institutional conceptualities are formed by the ideologies of the day more than by the biblical storyline, the lenses of those ideologies just might warp our investigation of these passages. Therefore, I am going to spend the first five chapters of the book—the bulk of it—trying to get the wrong lenses off and the right ones on. After that we'll look at the key texts.

That means this book, before we ever get to the ultimate goal of defining the local church, will first build a political theology from the ground up. Arguing that the church is a "political institution" requires us to get our heads around the idea of the "political" as well as the idea of an institution. I'm convinced we need a better political conceptuality and a better institutional conceptuality. Let me say a bit about each, starting with the latter.

A theme that will surface throughout this book is institutional specificity. The problem with much theology these days, I believe, is a lack of institutional understanding and specification.

Consider, for instance, how the generally remarkable Bible scholar George Eldon Ladd describes Jesus' promise to build his church and give Peter the keys of the kingdom. This statement, says Ladd, "does not speak of the creation of an organization or institution" but instead stands in direct continuity with the Old Testament tradition of "building a people."[8] When Ladd pits building an institution and a kingdom people against one another, one only wonders what he means by "institution." Keys are symbols of institutional authority. And "building a people" is by definition to institutionalize those people. It is to place them within a construct of rules, beliefs, or norms that will shape their behavior relative both to one another and to outsiders while also providing them with a measure of social stability, identity and meaning.[9] In other words,

---

[8] George Eldon Ladd, *A Theology of the New Testament*, rev. ed. (Grand Rapids: Eerdmans, 1993), 107-8.

[9] The very Old Testament texts to which Ladd looks to prove his point contain precisely these kinds of institutional elements within Old Testament Israel (e.g., structures of authority;

the concepts described in Matthew 16:18-19 practically point to the definition of an institution. Why does Ladd not see that?

Yet this lack of institutional understanding and specificity is common. It is easy and popular to talk about the virtues of "community" and "fellowship" and even "kingdom," but leave questions like "who is in charge" or "are there membership boundaries" unasked, unmentioned. Think of that phrase of Abraham Kuyper overused by young preachers and bloggers everywhere: "There is not a square inch in the whole domain of our human existance of which Christ, who is Sovereign over all, does not cry 'Mine!'"[10] Such a statement rightly affirms the universal nature of Christ's lordship, but it remains institutionally underspecified.[11] Does Christ the king require the same thing of all people and institutions? The same thing of the father as of the president? And of the president as of the pastor? Or does he delegate one kind of authority here and another kind there? The same lack of institutional specification shows up in vague talk of "holistic salvation" or "the church's mission" or the idea that Jesus came as king with "a different kind of power."

The same problem occurs in discussions of religion in the public square. Theologians and lawyers alike inveigh against "legislating morality" and "establishing religion," but doesn't all legislation have some moral basis and, behind that, a religious worldview? And what exactly counts as *establishing* religion? I very much like the US Constitution's language about making no law with respect to "an establishment of religion," but I'm not convinced that many theologians or lawyers perceive the difference between "establishing religion" and "an establishment of religion." Every law could be said to establish some religion or set of religions, at least if we're defining religion

---

membership boundaries; laws that are applicable only to members): Ruth 4:11; 1 Chron 17:12-13; Ps 28:5; 118:22; Jer 1:10; 24:6; 31:4; 33:7; Amos 9:11.

[10]Quoted in James E. Bratt, *Abraham Kuyper: Modern Calvinist, Christian Democrat* (Grand Rapids: Eerdmans, 2013), xx.

[11]My point here is not to indict Kuyper's system generally, or even to suggest that he should have more carefully qualified that statement in its original context. One cannot say everything all the time. John Halsey Wood Jr. argues that Kuyper eventually recognized this lack of institutional specificity and saw the confusion it caused in the relation between church and state. Wood, "Theologian of the Revolution: Abraham Kuyper's Radical Proposal for Church and State," in *Kingdoms Apart: Engaging the Two Kingdoms Perspective*, ed. Ryan C. McIlhenny (Phillipsburg, NJ: P&R, 2013), 164-65. See also John Halsey Wood Jr., *Going Dutch in the Modern Age: Abraham Kuyper's Struggle for a Free Church in the Nineteenth Century Netherlands* (New York: Oxford University Press, 2013), 147-48.

*functionally* and not *substantively*.¹² But that is different than institutionally organizing a religion, its members and its statements of belief or behavior. Again, the conversation suffers from a lack of institutional conceptuality.

To remedy this problem, chapter two will introduce the "new institutionalism" that has emerged among political scientists and sociologists over the last several decades. Hopefully this institutional revival tour will help us develop a better institutional conceptuality, which in turn will enable us to discern what an institutional church is in the pages of Scripture. Just to make the tour sound even more exciting, I conclude chapter two by developing an "institutional hermeneutic."

### NEED #2: A BETTER POLITICAL CONCEPTUALITY

The larger question at stake in claiming that the church is a political institution, of course, is whether the "political" category is an appropriate one to bring to bear on New Testament interpretation or the nature of the church. Scholars over the past few decades have been happy to characterize the church as the "community of the kingdom," to use Ladd's description.¹³ And the New Testament word "kingdom," observes New Testament scholar N. T. Wright, is nothing if not a "thoroughly political concept."¹⁴ So, too, the term *ekklēsia*. Another New Testament scholar, Mark Seifrid, notices "it is striking that the earliest Christians chose a distinctively political . . . term for their collective existence, speaking of themselves as an *ekklēsia*, a public assembly, rather than as a 'religious gathering' ('synagogue')."¹⁵

---

[12] I am taking this distinction from William Cavanaugh, which I will discuss (along with a third "constructivist" way) in chapter one.

[13] Ladd, *Theology of the New Testament*, 109. He then expounds this relationship under five points: the church is not the kingdom; the kingdom creates the church; the church witnesses to the kingdom; the church is the instrument of the kingdom; and the church is the custodian of the kingdom (ibid., 109-17).

[14] N. T. Wright, "Paul and Caesar: A New Reading of Romans," in *A Royal Priesthood: The Use of the Bible Ethically and Politically* (Grand Rapids: Zondervan, 2002), 173.

[15] Mark Seifrid, *The Second Letter to the Corinthians*, Pillar New Testament Commentary (Grand Rapids: Eerdmans, 2014), 7; see also Bernd Wannenwetsch, *Political Worship* (New York: Oxford University Press, 2004), 137-38. The term *ekklēsia* (from *ek-kaleō*, or "called out") can be found from the time of Euripides and Herodotus in the fifth century BC, before the Hebrew Bible was translated into Greek, as a term that referred to the gathering of full citizens in the Greek *polis* for making decisions, often by vote, on matters of judicial and political import. Every citizen was able to speak or propose items for discussion. The term *ekklēsia* then occurred about one hundred times in the Septuagint (including the Apocrypha) as a translation of the Hebrew term *qāhāl* and represented the people in a specially summoned or convened capacity such as hearing

Still, it is my assumption that most Westerners today (Christian and non-Christian) have a secular and liberalized understanding of "politics" or the "political." The political sphere is treated like its own sacred realm that must be kept clean from the profane world of religion. The two spheres are separated, says Oliver O'Donovan, by a carefully guarded cordon sanitaire.[16] William Cavanaugh similarly remarks, "Politics has been emancipated and properly differentiated from theology. Politics takes place in an autonomous, secular sphere, and is established on its own foundations."[17] Though Hobbes did not so cleanly separate the political and the spiritual, he did anticipate what would eventually become the sacred nature of the political sphere when he described a (ironic) parallel between the *holiness* of God's kingdom and the *publicness* of an earthly kingdom.[18]

Formally, this separation between the political and the religious or spiritual can be attributed to philosophical liberalism. And liberalism, a number of thinkers have remarked, is "the overarching mythos of the modern age"[19] and the "political philosophy by which we live."[20] When people today think about politics or citizenship, they tend to think within a liberal framework, whether they mean to or not. Another political philosopher writes, "So thoroughly has this liberalism come to suffuse our political culture, especially in the Anglo-Saxon world, that virtually all of us can be said to be liberals in some sense, even if we explicitly repudiate the label."[21] Liberalism is

---

God's word from Mount Sinai or to assemble three times a year on Mount Zion. Adapted from Peter T. O'Brien, *Colossians, Philemon*, Word Bible Commentary (Waco: Word, 1982), 57-58; and Lothar Coenen, "Church," in *Dictionary of New Testament Theology*, vol. 1 (Grand Rapids: Zondervan, 1975), 291-93.

[16]O'Donovan, *Desire of the Nations*, 2.

[17]William T. Cavanaugh, *Migrations of the Holy: God, State, and the Political Meaning of the Church* (Grand Rapids: Eerdmans, 2011), 123.

[18]Hobbes writes, "Out of this literal interpretation of the *Kingdome of God*, ariseth also the true interpretation of the word HOLY. For it is a word, which in Gods [sic] Kingdome answereth to that, which men in their Kingdomes use to call *Publique*, or the *Kings*. The King of any Countrey is the *Publique* Person, or Representative of all his own Subjects. And God the King of Israel was the *Holy one* of Israel." Hobbes, *Leviathan*, chap. 35, para. 220.

[19]Cavanaugh, *Migrations of the Holy*, 2.

[20]Michael Sandel, *Democracy's Discontent: America in Search of a Public Philosophy* (Cambridge, MA: Belknap Press of Harvard University Press, 1996), 4. Alasdair MacIntyre similarly writes, "The contemporary debates within modern political systems are almost exclusively between conservative liberals, liberal liberals, and radical liberals." MacIntyre, *Whose Justice, Which Rationality?* (London: Duckworth, 1988), 392.

[21]David T. Koyzis, *Political Visions and Illusions: A Survey and Christian Critique of Contemporary Ideologies* (Downers Grove, IL: InterVarsity Press, 2003), 45.

not without its critics, but I mention all of this because I believe that liberalism and its dualisms remain the inarticulate assumption for many Christians and non-Christians in the West. And it is these assumptions that present the biggest hindrance to conceptualizing the "community of the kingdom" in political terms (presuming, for a moment, that this is what the Bible teaches). As such, I believe that it is worth beginning this book by retracing the outlines of liberalism, which is a significant part of what chapter one will do. If the whole book is devoted to developing a more biblical political conceptuality, chapter one is necessary for recognizing our default conceptuality. The words *politics* or *political*, for most Westerners today, are simply understood in liberal terms. That at least is my working assumption.

At the same time, some argue that the seeds of liberalism were planted with Martin Luther's doctrine of *sola fide* and its political counterpart, his doctrine of the two kingdoms.[22] After all, Luther arguably introduced to the history of political thought the picture of the lone individual standing before the judgment seat of God, not finally accountable to prince or priest, not declared just for one's obedience to them or to God, but accountable to one's conscience and justified and made (internally) free as a gift of grace through faith alone. The best a prince can do, therefore, is to regulate the outer person, leaving the church to address the inner person or conscience with

---

[22]James Madison drew the connection between Luther and liberalism when he referred in a personal letter to "the excellence of a system which, by a due distinction, to which the genius and courage of Luther led the way, between what is due to Caesar and what is due to God, best promotes the discharge of both obligations. The experience of the United States is a happy disproof of the error so long rooted in unenlightened minds of well-meaning Christians, as well as in the corrupt hearts of persecuting usurpers, that without a legal incorporation of religious and civil polity, neither could be supported. A mutual independence is found most friendly to practical Religion, to social harmony, and to political prosperity." *Letters and Other Writings of James Madison*, vol. 3 (Philadelphia: J. B. Lippincott, 1865), 242-43. More critically, Jean Bethke Elshtain practically draws a straight line from Luther to the Kantianism of John Rawls when, in a critique of *sola fide*'s inner/outer distinction, she observes, "One can readily see Immanuel Kant emerging out of this Lutheran chrysalis." Elshtain, *Sovereignty: God, State, and Self* (New York: Basic Books, 2008), 81. Also, Quentin Skinner helpfully recounts the movement from Luther's theology, particularly his doctrine of justification by faith alone, through to its ecclesial and political implications. Skinner, *The Foundations of Modern Political Thought: The Age of the Reformation*, vol. 2 (Cambridge: Cambridge University Press, 1978), 3-19; see also W. D. J. Cargill Thompson, *The Political Thought of Martin Luther* (Sussex: Harvester, 1984); J. W. Allen, *A History of Political Thought in the Sixteenth Century* (1928; repr., New York: Barnes & Noble, 1960), 15-30.

God's Word.[23] Reading Luther's *On Secular Authority*[24] and John Locke's *Letter Concerning Toleration*[25] back to back does show a striking number of similarities.[26] Both divide the outer and inner person. Both place a secular[27] government over one and a spiritual government over the other. Both insist that the two governments must remain distinct. Both argue that secular authority cannot reach the inner person or conscience but only reaches to outward things, and that faith cannot be coerced. Locke was no Lutheran, but not a small number of scholars have argued that his work depended upon a Protestant theological rationale.[28] And Luther was no philosophical

---

[23]Political scientist Timothy Lomperis connects the dots between Luther and liberalism in succinct fashion: "Luther's belief in a justification by faith alone, and not by good works (especially those prescribed by the church), gave Christians the fundamental freedom of their souls. Outside institutions, like the church, the state, or even the pope himself, could not determine the internal condition of the souls of believers or their social standing as moral beings in the community. . . . There was, then, in this internal freedom of the soul, and of external professions of faith, a justification for the freedom of the conscience above any claims by religious or political institutions that became a central tenet of Lutheran theology—and of modern liberalism." Lomperis, "Lutheranism and Politics: Martin Luther as Modernizer, but for the Devil," in *Church, State, and Citizens: Christian Approaches to Political Engagement*, ed. Sandra F. Joireman (New York: Oxford University Press, 2009), 37.

[24]For introductions to Luther's two-kingdoms doctrine, see William J. Wright, *Martin Luther's Understanding of God's Two Kingdoms: A Response to the Challenge of Skepticism* (Grand Rapids: Baker, 2010); also Bernard Lohse, *Martin Luther's Theology: Its Historical and Systematic Development* (Minneapolis: Fortress, 1999), 153-56, 314-24; Oswald Bayer, *Martin Luther's Theology: A Contemporary Interpretation*, trans. Thomas H. Trapp (2003; repr., Tübingen: J. C. B. Mohr, Grand Rapids: Eerdmans, 2008), 309-25, esp. 313-17; David VanDrunen, *Natural Law and the Two Kingdoms: A Study in the Development of Reformed Social Thought* (Grand Rapids: Eerdmans, 2010), 55-62; W. D. J. Cargill Thompson, "The 'Two Kingdoms' and the 'Two Regiments,' Some Problems of Luther's *Zwei-Reiche-Lehre*," *Journal of Theological Studies* 20, no. 1 (April 1969): 164-85; James M. Estes, "Luther on the Role of Secular Authority in the Reformation," in *The Pastoral Luther: Essays on Martin Luther's Practical Theology*, ed. Timothy J. Wengert, Lutheran Quarterly Books (Grand Rapids: Eerdmans, 2009), 355-80, esp. 363-68.

[25]A series of helpful discussions of Locke's letter can be found in *John Locke—A Letter Concerning Toleration in Focus*, ed. John Horton and Susan Mendus (New York: Routledge, 1991), especially the essays by J. W. Gough, Maurice Cranston and Jeremy Waldron in that volume.

[26]Compare, for instance, parts one and two of Martin Luther, *On Secular Authority*, in *Luther and Calvin on Secular Authority*, trans. Harro Höpfl, Cambridge Texts in the History of Political Thought (New York: Cambridge University Press, 1991), with the first third or so of John Locke, "Letter," in *Two Treatises of Government and a Letter Concerning Toleration*, ed. Ian Shapiro (New Haven, CT: Yale University Press, 2003); see also "On the Difference Between Civil and Ecclesiastical Power," in *The Life and Letters of John Locke*, comp. Lord Peter King (London: Henry G. Bohn, 1858), 300-306.

[27]"*Weltlich*" in Luther's German. See Höpfl, "Glossary," in *Luther and Calvin on Secular Authority*, xxxviii.

[28]See Ian Shapiro, introduction to Locke, *Two Treatises*, xiii; John Dunn, *The Political Thought of John Locke: An Historical Account of the Argument* (New York: Cambridge University Press, 1969), 33, 99; James Tully, *A Discourse Concerning Property: John Locke and His Adversaries* (New York:

liberal, particularly as he pointed to God's will and ordinance as expressed in Romans 13 as the ground of government, not the public's consent. But he arguably put the necessary anthropology, ecclesiology, and aspects of governmental authority in place for liberalism to follow.[29] In the centuries after Luther, a more developed doctrine of a spiritual (not political) church was tied to a decidedly spiritual gospel. Such a viewpoint seems to correspond, furthermore, with the liberal idea that the public square must or at least might hypothetically remain neutral between various religious or spiritual concerns, and that the state cannot coerce the conscience. So while chapter one examines our default political conceptuality, it will also, at least briefly, sketch out a religious conceptuality.

### What Others Have Said

Is this the first book to argue for the political nature of the church? Students of political theology know the answer to that question is no. And for the sake of such students I assume it is useful to locate myself on the landscape,

---

Cambridge University Press, 1980); John Marshall, *John Locke: Resistance, Religion and Responsibility* (New York: Cambridge University Press, 1994); Jeremy Waldron, *God, Locke, and Equality: Christian Foundations of Locke's Political Thought* (New York: Cambridge University Press, 2002); and Greg Forster, *John Locke's Politics of Moral Consensus* (New York: Cambridge University Press, 2005).

[29] Referring to the medieval idea that the pope and emperor were parallel and universal powers, Quentin Skinner observes that Luther effectively "destroyed 'the metaphor of the two swords; henceforth there should be but one, wielded by a rightly advised and godly prince.'" Skinner, *Foundations of Modern Political Thought*, 15. Skinner then recounts examples of how the reformulation of who possessed the swords began to instantiate itself in the policies of European governments. In particular, the governments of many German cities, Denmark, Sweden, and England repudiated "the separate legal and jurisdictional powers hitherto exercised within their territories by the Papacy and the Catholic Church," changes "legitimated by way of appealing to an essentially Lutheran conception of the church as a purely spiritual body, the sole duty of which was to preach the word of God without laying claim to any other powers" (ibid., 84). It was at this point, says Skinner, that "a distinctively modern concept of political obligation begins to emerge" in which "it became possible for the secular authorities to legitimate the claim that they should be regarded as the sole jurisdictional power within their own territories, and thus that they should be recognized as the sole appropriate object of a subject's political allegiance" (ibid., 89; see also Elshtain, *Sovereignty*, 86). For all these reasons, it is hardly surprising that another historian would write, "Modern politics is unimaginable without the redefinition of the relation between politics and religion that Martin Luther . . . demanded and obtained. It was the Reformation that made the separation of religion, law, and history from politics inevitable." Constantin Fasolt, *The Limits of History* (Chicago: University of Chicago Press, 2004), 49. Fasolt further remarks, "Whoever wishes to improve our understanding of early modern political thought should therefore read more than Machiavelli, Hobbes, and Locke" (ibid., 50).

which I will attempt to do in this section and the next. These two sections may be the most technical sections of the book, and nonspecialists should feel free to skip them. Consider this a "get out of jail free" card.

In response to the traditionalist's *spiritual* gospel and *spiritual* church, a first generation of twentieth-century "political theologians," "liberation theologians" and "public theologians" sought to draw out the political meaning of the gospel and to consider what kind of church such a political gospel creates.[30] For instance, the Protestant Jürgen Moltmann, who with the Roman Catholic Johann Baptist Metz is counted among a movement of political theologians, argued,

> 'Liberation' is an 'open concept' which permeates and embraces the different dimensions of suffering. It runs from the economic abolition of exploitation which results from the rule of particular classes, or the political vanquishing of oppression and dictatorship and the cultural elimination of racialism, down to faith's experience of liberation from the compulsion of sin and the eschatological hope of liberation from the power of death.[31]

From this more holistic concept of salvation emerged a so-called political church: "A logical and consistent Christian discipleship always has logical political consequences. . . . The expression 'political church' therefore does not mean a politicizing of the church. On the contrary, it means the Christianization of the church's politics according to 'the yardstick and plumbline of Christ.'"[32] Moltmann and Metz, in turn, proved very influential among the South American liberation theologians like Gustavo Gutiérrez and Leonardo Boff. We will glance at some of these ideas as Gutiérrez expresses them in chapter five.

While the so-called political and liberation theologians explored the political significance of Christianity on the theological and political left, several conservative thinkers such as the Roman Catholic Richard John Neuhaus or the Reformed Max Stackhouse argued for the public significance of Christianity on the center or right by arguing that Christian

---

[30]This tripartite characterization comes from Daniel M. Bell Jr., "State and Civil Society," in *The Blackwell Companion to Political Theology*, ed. Peter Scott and William T. Cavanaugh (Malden, MA: Blackwell, 2004), 428-33.
[31]Jürgen Moltmann, *The Church in the Power of the Spirit: A Contribution to Messianic Ecclesiology* (Minneapolis: Fortress, 1993), 17, see also 87-93.
[32]Ibid., 15.

doctrines bore an attendant "public theology."[33] Neuhaus famously argued that the public square should not be naked or bare of religious speech.[34] Stackhouse, observing the threat to human rights coming from various secular quarters, argued that "human rights," a so-called liberal concept, "is essentially a matter of religious ethics."[35] Broadly, the point among such thinkers is that Christianity or religious thought generally provides the foundations and moral capital necessary for democratic and liberal institutions to flourish.

Following this first generation of political theologians came a second generation, who are sometimes characterized as post-liberal and anti-modernist and who sometimes self-characterize as Augustinian.[36] To this second generation belong names like the neo-Anabaptists Stanley Hauerwas and John Howard Yoder as well as the Radical Orthodoxy writers like John Milbank, Daniel Bell, and William Cavanaugh. Charles Mathewes perhaps belongs to this second generation.[37] And some lump the harder-to-classify

---

[33] Bell, "State and Civil Society," 431-33. For a broader discussion of public theology that goes beyond the characters and characterization offered in Bell, see the multi-essay volumes *Public Theology for a Global Society: Essays in Honor of Max Stackhouse*, ed. Deirdre King Hainsworth and Scott R. Paeth (Grand Rapids: Eerdmans, 2010), and *Theology and Public Philosophy: Four Conversations*, ed. Kenneth L. Grasso and Cecilia Rodriguez Castillo (Lanham, MD: Lexington Books, 2012).

[34] Richard John Neuhaus, *The Naked Public Square: Religion and Democracy in America*, 2nd ed. (Grand Rapids: Eerdmans, 1988). See also Stephen Carter, *The Culture of Disbelief: How American Law and Politics Trivialize Religious Devotion* (New York: Doubleday, 1993).

[35] Max L. Stackhouse, *Creeds, Society, and Human Rights: A Study in Three Cultures* (Grand Rapids: Eerdmans, 1984), 6. See also Nicholas Wolterstorff, *Justice: Rights and Wrongs* (Princeton, NJ: Princeton University Press, 2008), which argues for the pre-Enlightenment and even Old Testament basis of natural rights and a concept of justice grounded in those rights.

[36] Oliver O'Donovan remarks of the school of thought that self-identifies as Augustinian, "They are a heterogeneous crowd, assertive of the Augustinian identity because they had to find it for themselves, but diverse in their interpretation of it and inclined to disagree with each other over almost everything." O'Donovan, "Book Review: Charles Mathewes, *A Theology of Public Life*," *Political Theology* 12, no. 4 (2011): 616-20. See also Eric Gregory's survey of the Augustinians, *Politics and the Order of Love: An Augustinian Ethic of Democratic Citizenship* (Chicago: University of Chicago Press, 2008), 1-2.

I am loosely following what Bell characterizes as the movement from the "dominant tradition" to an "emerging tradition," in "State and Civil Society," 428-37. The same basic distinction is found in Peter Scott and William T. Cavanaugh, introduction to *Blackwell Companion to Political Theology*, 3; also Michael Kirwan, *Political Theology: An Introduction* (Minneapolis: Fortress, 2009), 4-9. Eric Gregory offers a four-part division in "Christianity and the Rise of the Democratic State," in *Political Theology for a Plural Age*, ed. Michael Jon Kessler (New York: Oxford University Press, 2013), 99-101.

[37] See his *A Theology of Public Life* (New York: Cambridge University Press, 2007).

Anglican theologian Oliver O'Donovan into this camp.[38] What unites this somewhat disparate group is that they hold modernist suppositions at arm's length and disavow Enlightenment dualisms, such as a strong separation between faith and reason or politics and religion. John Milbank, for instance, has argued that all the supposedly neutral, rational, and objective social sciences—sociology, psychology, economics, political science, and so on—"are themselves theologies or anti-theologies in disguise." All such secular disciplines and theories (like liberalism) are built on covert idols, which points to "the practical inescapability of worship." You are always worshiping *something*. And the secular theories of the West are either Christian heresies or Neopagan rejections of Christianity—in both cases being derivative.[39] Along these lines, it is not difficult to think back to Augustine's *City of God*, which attributes all human activity to one of two loves, to idolatry or to worship.[40] William Cavanaugh draws out the implications of Milbank's ideas for the post-Hobbesian or modern state, which claims to possess imperium over against the church: such a state offers an "alternative soteriology to that of the church"; but it is "a simulacrum, a false copy, of the Body of Christ."[41] Radical Orthodoxy, says Daniel Bell similarly, "begins with the recovery of the Augustinian insight that politics as statecraft is but a secular parody of the true politics that is the fellowship of the saints."[42]

This critique of Enlightenment social theory is accompanied by a critique of any correlationist (read "modern") theology—liberal or conservative, Moltmann or Neuhaus—which is bamboozled by the neutral and rational

---

[38]Useful comparisons between O'Donovan and Hauerwas can be found in William T. Cavanaugh, "Church," 393-406 in *Blackwell Companion to Political Theology*, 403-4, as well as from Hauerwas himself in his *War and the American Difference: Theological Reflections on Violence and National Identity* (Grand Rapids: Baker Academic, 2011), xii.

[39]John Milbank, *Theology and Social Theory: Beyond Social Reason*, 2nd ed. (Maldan, MA: Blackwell, 2006), 3.

[40]Augustine, *The City of God Against the Pagans*, ed. and trans. R. W. Dyson, Cambridge Texts in the History of Political Thought (New York: Cambridge University Press, 1998), e.g., 634 (XV.1) and 632 (XIV.28).

[41]William T. Cavanaugh, "The City: Beyond Secular Parodies," in *Radical Orthodoxy: A New Theology*, ed. John Milbank, Catherine Pickstock and Graham Ward (London: Routledge, 1999), 182; also Cavanaugh, *Migrations of the Holy*, 42-43.

[42]Daniel M. Bell Jr., *Liberation Theology After the End of History: The Refusal to Cease Suffering* (London: Routledge, 2001), 72; Bell, "State and Civil Society," 427-28; also Stanley Hauerwas, *After Christendom? How the Church Is to Behave If Freedom, Justice, and a Christian Nation Are Bad Ideas* (Nashville: Abingdon, 1991), 40-44.

pretense of social theory: "Contemporary theologies which forge alliances with such theories are often unwittingly rediscovering concealed affinities between positions that partake of the same historical origins." That is, they do "Christian" theology on heretical or Neopagan foundations.[43] Case in point: "the main proponents of 'political theology' in Germany, and 'liberation theology' in Latin America . . . remain . . . trapped within the terms of 'secular reason,' and its unwarranted foundationalist presuppositions." Specifically, these political and liberation theologies embrace Marxism "as a discourse which supposedly discloses the 'essence' of human beings and a 'fundamental' level of human historical becoming."[44] The Radical Orthodox and post-liberal perspectives eschew philosophical foundations but profess instead to depend epistemologically either upon a concept of revelation and illumination[45] or upon discipleship into a particular narrative.[46]

Though Stanley Hauerwas does not formally belong to the Radical Orthodoxy movement, he is sympathetic with these points. The problem, says he, is that "contemporary Christians allow their imaginations to be captured by the concepts of justice determined by the presuppositions of liberal societies. For example, we simply take for granted distinctions between fact and value, public and private, that these societies privilege."[47] In the process, Christians let their faith become "privatized" and domesticated to the liberal cause. This means shearing off all those troublesome Christian distinctives ("e.g., the nature of God, the significance of Jesus, the eschatological fate of the world") and turning the faith into an inoffensive civil religion, neutered of any real public significance. Which is to say, the Christian partnership with liberalism reduces one's faith to one more private "opinion" as opposed to a proclamation of what is true, thereby undermining it both inside and

---

[43]Milbank, *Theology and Social Theory*, 3.
[44]Ibid., 207-8.
[45]John Milbank, Catherine Pickstock and Graham Ward, introduction to *Radical Orthodoxy: A New Theology*, ed. John Milbank, Catherine Pickstock and Graham Ward (London: Routledge, 1999), 2; see also John Milbank, "Knowledge: The Theological Critique of Philosophy in Hamann and Jacobi," in the same volume, 21-37; and Milbank, *Theology and Social Theory*, 384-91. A helpful overview of the epistemology of Radical Orthodoxy can be found in James K. A. Smith, *Introducing Radical Orthodoxy: Mapping a Post-secular Theology* (Grand Rapids: Baker Academic, 2004), 143-83.
[46]Stanley Hauerwas, *The Peaceable Kingdom: A Primer in Christian Ethics* (Notre Dame, IN: University of Notre Dame Press, 1983), 1-34; *After Christendom?*, 93-111.
[47]Hauerwas, *After Christendom?*, 63.

outside the church.⁴⁸ Scientific verification, instead, becomes the evaluator of truth. "We thus live in a time where Christians in the name of being socially responsible try to save appearances by supplying epistemological and moral justifications for social arrangements that made and continue to make the church politically irrelevant."⁴⁹ Hauerwas therefore urges Christians to stop underwriting the liberal project but instead seek, above all else, to be themselves—an alternative society that gives up coercive violence but lives out the politics of the cross and the resurrection, the kind of political witness powerfully enacted through the martyrs.⁵⁰

In short, the first generation of political theologians may have spoken of a "political gospel" and a "political church," but the second generation effectively suggests that the first generation remains stuck within a liberal, Enlightenment paradigm and that they still view the political and the spiritual too separately. At the risk of oversimplification, it is as if the second generation accuses the first generation of *saying* that the gospel and the church are "political," but it argues that what the first generation *means* is that the gospel merely has political "implications" and that the church is not much more than politically "significant,"⁵¹ somewhat like Robert Putnam does. The Augustinians and post-liberals, on the other hand, insist that the church actually is a political entity.⁵² Cavanaugh therefore points us back to the word *ekklēsia*, and in so doing brings us back to our earlier conversation about voluntary associations:

> In Greek usage, *ekklesia* named the assembly of those with citizen rights in a given polis. In calling itself *ekklesia*, the church was identifying itself as fully public, refusing the available language for private associations (*koinon* or *collegium*). The church was not gathered like a *koinon* around particular interests, but was concerned with the interests of the whole city, because it was the

---

⁴⁸Hauerwas, *Peaceable Kingdom*, 12-16; Hauerwas, *After Christendom?*, 23-44.
⁴⁹Hauerwas, *After Christendom?*, 27.
⁵⁰Ibid., 35-39; Hauerwas, *Peaceable Kingdom*, 87-91; Hauerwas, *A Community of Character: Toward a Constructive Christian Social Ethic* (Notre Dame, IN: University of Notre Dame Press, 1981), 83-86.
⁵¹See Arne Rasmusson, *The Church as Polis: From Political Theology to Theological Politics as Exemplified by Jürgen Moltmann and Stanley Hauerwas*, rev. ed. (Notre Dame, IN: University of Notre Dame Press, 1995), 12.
⁵²Of course, Milbank would be quick to insist that we would use the term "is" analogically, not univocally.

witness of God's activity in history. At the same time, the church was not simply another polis; instead, it was an anticipation of the heavenly city on earth, in a way that complexified the bipolar calculus of public and private.[53]

Cavanaugh also observes that the word *ekklēsia* was used in the Septuagint for significant public gatherings of the nation of Israel (e.g., Deut 4:10; 1 Kings 8:14; Neh 8) and that the early Christians used the Greek term to identify themselves with the nation of Israel as God's public representative on earth.[54] Hauerwas, too, pushes the political significance of the Christian message and the church beyond talk of "implications" to what the things *are*. "Jesus' salvation does not have social and political implications," says Hauerwas, "but it is a politics that is meant as an alternative to all social life that does not reflect God's glory."[55] The church does not just *have* a social ethic, Hauerwas is well known for saying, but the church *is* a social ethic.[56] And this ethic, this politics, witnesses to the kind of social life possible for those who have been formed by the story of Christ. The church's challenge has always been "to be a 'contrast model' for all polities that know not God."[57]

Arne Rasmusson describes the movement from the first generation to the second generation as a movement from political theology to theological politics, and he narrates this movement in the persons of Moltmann and Hauerwas. His summary of the differences is clarifying:

> For Moltmann the political of the national and world communities, and more precisely power over the national (or future world) state, has priority. His concern is the participation of Christians in this political struggle. Hauerwas, on the other hand, sees the church, the called people of God, as the primary locus for a new politics. The church as an alternative *polis* or *civitas* is thus a carrier of a specifically theological politics; that is a politics determined by the new reality of the kingdom of God as seen in the life and destiny of Jesus. He therefore understands the politics of the world, and relates to it, in the light of this new politics.... Moltmann makes God's activity in the world,

---

[53]Cavanaugh, *Migrations of the Holy*, 43.
[54]Ibid., 42-43.
[55]Hauerwas, *After Christendom?*, 58; also Hauerwas, *Community of Character*, 12.
[56]Hauerwas, *Peaceable Kingdom*, 99-102; Hauerwas, *Community of Character*, 10-11, 37, 40-52; Hauerwas, *In Good Company: The Church as Polis* (Notre Dame, IN: University of Notre Dame Press, 1995), 26.
[57]Hauerwas, *Community of Character*, 84.

understood as the political struggle for emancipation, the horizon in which the church's theology and practice are interpreted, while Hauerwas makes the church's story the "counter story" that interprets the world's politics. In this difference we find the most decisive parting of ways between Moltmann's political theology and Hauerwas' theological politics.[58]

Though the distinction is ontologically artificial,[59] perhaps we can capture the differing emphases by suggesting that the first generation almost uses "political" as an adjective, while the second uses it as a noun.[60] Does the church merely have political qualities, or is it a Spirit-filled *polis*?

This second generation, too, has its critics, who are typically of a liberal bent.[61] Whether we say they belong to a third generation or the first, I'm not sure. But they, like a number of other Christian writers, are not convinced the liberal project has given up the ghost. A number of academic and popular books in the United States respond to the present-day cultural wars by urging us to "go back to the Founders" or even to John Locke. Not to be confused with the Religious Right's call for a Christian America, such writers point to Locke as offering a nonsectarian "moral consensus" among different religious groups, and to the broadly theistic Founders as conciliating religious belief and liberal ideals.[62]

---

[58]Rasmusson, *Church as Polis*, 187-88.

[59]I say it's ontologically artificial because any adjective that describes an essential (not accidental) attribute of something must be a constituent part of that something. And I assume that Moltmann would say that the political nature of the church is an essential attribute of it.

[60]That said, Hauerwas observes that "ethics always requires an adjective or qualifier—such as, Jewish, Christian, Hindu, existentialist, pragmatic, utilitarian, humanist, medieval, modern—in order to denote the social and historical character of ethics as a discipline." Hauerwas, *Peaceable Kingdom*, 1.

[61]E.g., Jeffrey Stout, *Democracy and Tradition* (Princeton, NJ: Princeton University Press, 2004), 118-79; Wolterstorff, *Justice*, 96-98; also James Davison Hunter, *To Change the World: The Irony, Tragedy, and Possibility of Christianity in the Late Modern World* (New York: Oxford University Press, 2010), 150-66, though I don't know how sympathetic with the liberal project Hunter is.

[62]Forster, *John Locke's Politics*, e.g., 1-7; Nicholas P. Miller, *The Religious Roots of the First Amendment: Dissenting Protestants and the Separation of Church and State* (New York: Oxford University Press, 2012), esp. 168-71; Jon Meacham, *American Gospel: God, the Founding Fathers, and the Making of a Nation* (New York: Random House, 2006). Though I don't know that these authors profess to be Christians, the same hope is expressed in Waldron, *God, Locke, and Equality*, and Steven Waldman, *Founding Faith: Providence, Politics, and the Birth of Religious Freedom in America* (New York: Random House, 2008).

## A Covenantal Approach

My own view is that Christians should not be beholden to any one ideology, since doing so invariably leads to idolatry,[63] but instead become "fluent in the idiom of multiple ideologies," as a friend of mine put it. We can pick and choose according to principles of wisdom. That means I am not a wholesale critic of liberalism, or at least a liberal polity, as some belonging to the second generation might claim to be. Even the severest critic of liberalism, I assume, agrees that both church and state have limited jurisdictions, and that there are some questions that both institutions do not have the authority to answer while the other does, such as "what should a church believe about the atonement" for one or "who should the prime minister designate as the home secretary" for the other. And as soon as we accept a limitation on jurisdictions, we have embraced a certain kind of institutional neutrality in those areas beyond an institution's jurisdiction.[64] So against the critics I would say that everyone but the most thoroughgoing (and probably imaginary) theonomist adopts some form of neutrality, that hallmark of liberal institutions, whether they mean to or not. But this need not be the incoherent neutrality of liberal antiperfectionism[65] or the far-reaching secularism of a France or a Turkey.[66] Neutrality can "vary in both its conceptual scope and field of application."[67] And just because church and state should both remain neutral on certain questions that fall within the other's jurisdiction does not mean the church is politically neutral or the state religiously neutral in general. In fact, this book, together with these same critics, bears an Augustinian posture insofar as it argues that there is in fact no such thing as spiritual or political neutrality. Everything the state does is spiritual or religious, and everything the church does is political, though neither has permission to step beyond the authorizations God has given it. The phrase "Yahweh is king," observes O'Donovan, is a "liturgical act in which political and religious meanings were totally fused."[68] So with "Jesus is Lord." And

---

[63] See Koyzis's excellent *Political Visions and Illusions*.
[64] Andrew Koppelman, *Defending American Religious Neutrality* (Cambridge, MA: Harvard University Press, 2013), 15.
[65] See ibid., 26, 148.
[66] See Jocelyn Maclure and Charles Taylor, *Secularism and Freedom of Conscience* (Cambridge, MA: Harvard University Press, 2011), 14; Koppelman, *Defending American Religious Neutrality*, 27.
[67] See Koppelman, *Defending American Religious Neutrality*, 26.
[68] O'Donovan, *Desire of the Nations*, 32.

this book's thesis, on the surface, lines up with the second generation's basic point: the church is a political entity.

But my primary goal is not to engage with these authors or their movements, largely because I arrive at this conclusion by a different means. Open up the machine and you will find different wiring inside. My hope instead is to present a case for the political nature of the local church using a theological methodology that individuals and churches within my own evangelical tradition would find compelling—specifically, a theological method driven by the biblical covenants. And this leads to different implications and conclusions.

For those who are familiar with this second generation of political theologians (henceforth, I will use the phrase "political theology" more generically and not just in reference to the movement of Moltmann and others), here are a few points of comparison and contrast, points which should help every reader locate the perspective of this book on the theological landscape (again, this section not only can but probably should be skipped by non-specialists!):

*Ontologically*, like Radical Orthodoxy, I believe we should begin with the "interpersonal harmonious order" of the Trinity[69]—that Christianity must place "in the *arche* (the Trinity) a multiple which is not set dialectically over against the one, but itself manifests unity."[70] And I agree that creation, in some sense, "participates" in the life of God (see Acts 17:28), even while affirming that we can only speak of God analogically. What's more, human participation in the life of the triune God is the direct counter to violence.[71] But following Michael Horton, I believe we need a covenantal ontology, not the Neo-Platonic ontological participation called for by Radical Orthodoxy.[72] Milbank, Catherine Pickstock and Graham Ward argue that there is

---

[69]Milbank, Pickstock and Ward, *Radical Orthodoxy*, 2.
[70]Milbank, *Theology and Social Theory*, 381.
[71]In general, James K. A. Smith's *Introducing Radical Orthodoxy* is extremely helpful for discerning the strengths of the movement while raising good questions and challenges.
[72]Michael Horton, *Covenant and Salvation: Union with Christ* (Louisville, KY: Westminster John Knox, 2007), 153-216, esp. 181-215; cf. Bruce L. McCormack, "What's at Stake in Current Debates over Justification? The Crisis of Protestantism in the West," in *Justification: What's at Stake in the Current Debates*, ed. Mark Husbands and Daniel J. Treier (Downers Grove, IL: InterVarsity Press, 2004), 113-17. See also James Smith's critique of a Radical Orthodoxy's participationist ontology, which he attempts to improve with a "creational ontology." Smith, *Introducing Radical Orthodoxy*, 197-229.

no "territory independent of God,"⁷³ which is a statement I would be happy to make too, but I would make it covenantally and politically, not ontologically. Radical Orthodoxy is anxious not to separate or unhook creation from the Creator, for fear of creating a conceptual independency and autonomy, a good motive to be sure. But it is hard to see how it avoids a Platonic ascendancy of being that blurs the Creator/creature distinction and that, Horton observes, "seems to represent a different kind of univocity . . . since created being participates ontologically in uncreated being as such."⁷⁴ Hans Urs von Balthasar's critique of any Platonic concept of ascendency makes the point well: "Thus one finds in one's human nature a place—perhaps only a point, but this point suffices—where one can, as it were, traffic with God 'religiously,' on the same footing, a place where a mystical *identity* obtains between Creator and creature."⁷⁵ The separation between God and humanity, a separation which began at the fall, is overcome not by ontological tinkering but by the work of God: "This union we [Christians] enjoy is effected for and in us not by an impersonal process of emanations, by a ladder of participation, or by infused habits, but by the Holy Spirit, who gives the ungodly the faith both to cling to Christ for justification and to be united to Christ for communion in his eschatological life."⁷⁶ In short, Radical Orthodoxy is right to seek an ontology that celebrates political unity in diversity in the face of the violence of univocal concepts of being and truth, and right to seek it in the Trinity, but the solution, I believe, is covenantal, not Neo-Platonic.

*Epistemologically*, like the post-liberals, I believe we should eschew an Enlightenment foundationalism that employs pure reason to build Babel-like edifices of universal truth or morality. Further, it strikes me as unavoidable—following Hauerwas, who follows Alasdair MacIntyre—to say that every theological truth claim (e.g., interpretive statements about what the Bible means) exists within a historically situated narrative and tradition of rationality. Christian Scripture, too, is historically situated, being authored by human beings. However, insofar as the post-liberals, Hauerwas,

---

⁷³Milbank, Pickstock and Ward, *Radical Orthodoxy*, 3.
⁷⁴Horton, *Covenant and Salvation*, 205.
⁷⁵Quoted in ibid., 206.
⁷⁶Ibid., 183.

MacIntyre and others of a communitarian bent are unwilling to affirm that the authorship of the Bible is no less that of God than it is of humans, at least as rendered by a traditional doctrine of concurrence which affirms that what God says the author says (see 2 Pet 1:20-21), but adopt instead something like a Barthian doctrine of the Word, then we part ways. In addition to being a deeply human document, drafted by human personalities fully engaged in the emotional and intellectual processes of research, lamentation, argument making and so forth, I take the Bible to be the Word of God, which is to say, a divine speech-act through which the Spirit of God communicates a true understanding of the divine Father and Son.[77] On the matter of how an individual begins to believe or understand, Hauerwas speaks of "conversion" as the process of being appropriated into a new narrative by acquiring the skill of living according to the ethics of that narrative, much like a new bricklayer apprentices himself or herself to an old master.[78] I think that is true so far as it goes. But the emphasis here, like it often is in modern and postmodern epistemology, remains on the subjective knower, as it has been ever since Descartes. But this emphasis, remarks theologian John Webster, "eclipses what in fact is most interesting, about what happens when Christians read the Bible: that the Bible as text is the *viva vox Dei* addressing the people of God and generating faith and obedience."[79] Along these lines, I am content to conclude with Horton, "when one reads this text [the Bible], one encounters God speaking so clearly by the Spirit's work both in inspiration and in the illumination of the reader, that having to justify that God has spoken here and now is equivalent to having to justify that one has heard one's spouse this morning at breakfast."[80] A Tolstoy character might even be

---

[77] See Michael Horton, *Covenant and Eschatalogy: The Divine Drama* (Louisville, KY: Westminster John Knox, 2002); also Kevin J. Vanhoozer, *Is There a Meaning in this Text: The Bible, the Reader, and the Morality of Literary Knowledge* (Grand Rapids: Zondervan, 1998), and Vanhoozer, *The Drama of Doctrine: A Canonical Linguistic Approach to Christian Theology* (Louisville, KY: Westminster John Knox, 2005). See also John Calvin's doctrine of illumination in *Institutes of the Christian Religion*, 2 vols., ed. John T. McNeill, trans. Ford Lewis Battles, Library of Christian Classics 20-21 (Philadelphia: Westminster, 1960), 1:580-81 (bk. III, chap. 2, sec. 33).

[78] Hauerwas, *After Christendom?*, 103.

[79] Quoted in Horton, *Covenant and Eschatalogy*, 201. In light of my comment a moment ago concerning the distance between Barth's doctrine of Scripture and my own, it does occur to me this statement represents a place where a Barthian and an evangelical doctrine of Scripture do overlap.

[80] Ibid., 201.

said to have captured the point more concisely: "I know not by reason, but it has been given to me."[81] On the subjective side of knowing, John Frame usefully combines normative, situational and existential perspectives all within the framework of a covenantal relationship. Speaking of the covenant relationship, he says,

> Above all, we must recognize that human knowledge of God is covenantal in character, as all human activities are. Knowing is the act of a covenant servant of God. That means that in knowing God, as in any other aspect of human life, we are subject to God's control and authority, confronted with His inevitable presence.... We dare not aspire to the kind of knowledge that God has of himself; we must be satisfied with the kind of knowledge that a servant may have of his Lord, even when that knowledge is a knowledge of mystery or of our own ignorance.[82]

In short, just as I adopt a covenantal ontology, so I adopt a covenantal epistemology.

One last point of relevance and possible contrast here concerning epistemology: a covenantal epistemology can make room for a concept of common grace since all humanity belongs to God's Adamic and Noahic covenants. That means there is much space, in my view, for borrowing discerningly from political scientists, sociologists, and other social scientists in the work of theologizing—even modernist ones! Radical Orthodoxy is correct to question the foundations of philosophical thought, but that does not mean people cannot partake in the structure of philosophical thinking. Throughout chapters one and two, I will borrow from secular thinkers, and it is not obvious to me that I necessarily compromise theological foundations by doing so.[83]

*Hermeneutically*, two comments are in order. First, reading the biblical text for political significance requires a measured ability to read "behind the text," "within the text" and "in front of the text," to borrow the tripartite methodology of Old Testament scholar Gordon McConville.[84] Taking them

---

[81]Konstantin Levin in Leo Tolstoy, *Anna Karenina*, trans. Constance Garnett (New York: Barnes & Noble Books, 1997), 721.
[82]John Frame, *The Doctrine of the Knowledge of God* (Phillipsburg, NJ: P&R, 1987), 40, see also 73-75.
[83]Cf. Luke Bretherton, *Christianity and Contemporary Politics: The Conditions and Possibilities of Faithful Witness* (Malden, MA: Wiley-Blackwell, 2010), 19-20.
[84]J. G. McConville, *God and Earthly Power: An Old Testament Political Theology* (New York: T&T Clark, 2006), 6-11. See also Richard Bauckham, *The Bible in Politics: How to Read the Bible*

one at a time: It is difficult to grasp the meaning of texts without some awareness of the world *behind* them. Clear examples relevant to our purposes include the Old Testament question of ancient vassal treaties or the New Testament meaning of "binding and loosing." That said, I believe McConville is right to argue that we should not be "unduly influenced by overconfident theories of the text's origins, and by an excess of 'suspicion' about the motives for its production."[85] A number of things could be said about reading *within* the text. My concern lies with recognizing that the text, as I said a moment ago, is a human and divine speech-act, whose interpretation depends on sensitivity to genre, authorial intent and a text's location in the canonical horizon. A text should be understood on its own terms before its significance for the contemporary reader can be ascertained. That said, because the text presents itself to God's covenant people, God's covenant people can read *in front of* the text, trusting it has political significance for today (see 1 Cor 10:6). In short, the goal here is to offer a reading of the biblical text "which a) learns from historical setting, b) reads the text in its integrity and interconnectedness, and c) aims to hear it in relation to modern issues."[86]

Second, reading the biblical text for political significance means accounting for the covenantal structure of the canon as a whole. Strangely, political theologies too often fail to closely heed Scripture's covenantal drama but instead rely on a proof-text methodology. I agree with Bible scholar Peter Gentry and systematician Stephen Wellum—among others—when they argue that "the covenants form the backbone of the metanarrative of Scripture and thus it is essential to 'put them together' correctly in order to discern accurately the 'whole counsel of God' (Acts 20:27)."[87] That is to say, the manifold characters, authorities and episodes of the Bible must be viewed in light of *the structure* of the canonical plot line in order to help us properly understand "the metanarrative of Scripture and not a marriage of

---

*Politically* (Louisville, KY: Westminster John Knox, 1989).
[85]McConville, *God and Earthly Power*, 6.
[86]Ibid., 11.
[87]Peter Gentry and Stephen Wellum, *Kingdom Through Covenant: A Biblical-Theological Understanding of the Covenants* (Wheaton, IL: Crossway, 2012), 21, 57. See also Michael Horton, *God of Promise: Introducing Covenant Theology* (Grand Rapids: Baker, 2006), 13-14; Horton, *Covenant and Eschatalogy*, 16-17.

biblical data and secular worldviews";[88] the major biblical covenants afford us with just this *structure*. Something like Radical Orthodoxy, for all its attempts *not* to marry revelation and secular philosophy, does exactly this (I would argue) because it does not appear to pay heed to Scripture *on its own terms and within its own covenantal framework*. You might as well try to convince your spouse that you are "really listening" even though you don't let her (or him) explain what she means on her terms. Chapters three, four and five will be devoted to delineating the covenantal structure.

*Institutionally*, it is necessary for this book to give some attention to the state, because one's views on the jurisdiction and authority of the state influences one's views on the jurisdiction and authority of the church, and vice versa. And here we find two other places of contrast between the aforementioned thinkers and myself, both of which fall under the "institutional" banner. First, these authors don't seem to take much interest in institutional questions. Their focus (not a bad one) is on explicating Christian practice, not static structures. For instance, Milbank says that he does not "subscribe to the rather ahisoricist and static division of human life into distinct 'spheres.'"[89] I am sympathetic with this point insofar as the language of "spheres" can be institutionally imprecise. Still, if God has established different institutions with different jurisdictional boundaries, then we should be able to use a concept of "spheres" that accords with those different jurisdictional lines. To put it the other way around, doing away with spheres is only conceivable if you have a weak view of institutional authority in the first place, and this latter weakness will lead to confusion over the precise nature of the church's authority relative to the state's authority.[90]

---

[88] Gentry and Wellum, *Kingdom Through Covenant*, 226.

[89] John Milbank, foreword to James K. A. Smith, *Introducing Radical Orthodoxy*, 13.

[90] I am sympathetic with Cavanaugh's point, discussed above, that the supposedly neutral liberal state offers itself as an alternative soteriology (see footnote 41). My sense is that liberal states often have. The messianic content of American presidential speeches presents one obvious example. That said, Cavanaugh's critiques may overreach. The church does not exist by permission of the state, yet God *has* given the state authority over the church within its domain (e.g., I would argue that churches exceed their biblical authorization by trying to deal with child abuse themselves behind closed doors without notifying the public authorities). Hobbes's subjection of the church to the state—which Cavanaugh criticizes—is appropriate within the state's authorized jurisdiction. Yet even Hobbes acknowledged that the state's sovereignty is not absolute, which is why he reserved a place for civil disobedience, as we saw a moment ago: "But if the command [of the civil sovereign] be such, as cannot be obeyed, without being damned to Eternall Death,

Second, I am not convinced that Scripture views all acts of coercive and even destructive force as wrong, whether in the present or the eschatological age. And this appears to put me slightly at odds with Milbank's "ontology of peace"[91] and even more with Hauerwas and Yoder's pacifism. For instance, Yoder's interpretation of Romans 13 claims that the function of government to bear the sword is "not the function to be exercised by Christians." Non-Christians might bear this function, but they do so in the same way that "divine providence can in its own sovereign permissive way 'use' an idolatrous Assyria (Isa. 10)"[92]—as if to say God can mysteriously use even bad for good. But it is not clear to me why one would restrict the government's use of the sword to non-Christians unless a further assumption is at play, namely, the assumption that all coercive and destructive force is wrong or ungodlike.[93] But why this assumption when there are so many texts that speak of God's wrath and judgment? I do not intend to pursue this train of thought much further, except to say that one's view of the state profoundly relates to one's view of God's judgment. Does God have the right to destroy as an act of judgment or to authorize humans to use destructive force, whether for proleptic or restraining purposes, since this is where a theory of government begins? What's more, could it not be that God's judgment is a property of his love and goodness as much as it is of his righteousness and holiness? That he will destroy all evil *because he is good and loving*? It is my sense that, as a general principle, one who possesses an underspecified doctrine of divine judgment will, to the extent that that person is consistent, possess a doctrine of the state that is anemic, wobbly and underspecified. And a wobbly, underspecified concept of the state will, in turn, affect one's concept of the church.

*The doctrine of justification* is one more place where my own views depart from the thinkers cited above. Where most of these thinkers adopt

---

then it were madnesse to obey it, and the Counsell of our Saviour takes place (*Mat. 10.28*)." Hobbes, *Leviathan*, chap. 43, sec. 321.

[91]Milbank says that all evil "converts" to violence, but he acknowledges that not all violence "converts" to evil. He then distinguishes his position from pacifism in *Being Reconciled: Ontology and Pardon* (New York: Routledge, 2003), 26-43.

[92]John Howard Yoder, *The Politics of Jesus*, 2nd ed. (Grand Rapids: Eerdmans, 1994), 198.

[93]I certainly agree with Hauerwas when he writes, "Because Christians believe we are what the world can be, we act in the hope that the world can and will positively respond to the witness of peace. That witness begins with Christians refusing to kill one another in the name of lesser loyalties and goods." Hauerwas, *War and the American Difference*, xiii.

either some Roman Catholic or New Perspective view on justification,[94] I will propose in chapters five and six that the best way to establish the local church as a model political society is through a traditional Protestant conception of *sola fide*, albeit with a covenantal emphasis. A properly covenantal conception of justification involves a corporate component. I will argue that being declared righteous before a judge means, as an intrinsic property of that declaration, being declared righteous before an entire populace. Furthermore, justification *by faith alone*, I will contend, provides the only true basis for a just political unity. Whereas Isaiah Berlin famously employed his positive and negative conceptions of liberty as the grand divider in the history of political philosophy, I would propose that history's real division lay between those political philosophies grounded in some form of self-justification and those political societies grounded in justification by faith alone. And of course that is nothing more than the division between the "wisdom of this world" and a gospel-preaching local church. Behind every flavor of tyranny, oppression and social stratification in history is some form of justification grounded in the self and its works: "I'm more righteous, more ideologically correct, more freedom-loving, more tolerant, more inclusive, more wise, more white, more wealthy than you. Therefore, I should rule over you." Such self-justification leads invariably to injustice. *Sola fide*, however, undermines all such self-justifications and is therefore the only source of a just political unity and liberty (see Acts 24:15). And it is in the local church that we should witness this new and true unity that yields a right liberty, as one-time enemies learn to love one another and beat their swords into plowshares and spears into pruning hooks.

## Combining Political and Institutional Conceptualities

In short, this book will present a covenantal approach to political theology for the sake of establishing the political essence of the local church.

---

[94]Milbank et al. characterize a traditional concept of guilt, atonement and justification as "univocalist-nominalist." John Milbank, "Alternative Protestantism," 25-42 in *Radical Orthodoxy and the Reformed Tradition: Creation, Covenant, and Participation*, ed. James K. A. Smith (Grand Rapids: Baker Academic, 2005), 28. For a response and critique, see Horton, *Covenant and Salvation*, 158-74; see also Smith, *Introducing Radical Orthodoxy*, 151n28. Yoder and Hauerwas adopt something closer to the New Perspective on Paul. See Yoder, *Politics of Jesus*, 212-27; Hauerwas, *Peaceable Kingdom*, 93-94. Cf. Wolterstorff, *Justice in Love* (Grand Rapids: Eerdmans, 2011), 260-66, 271-76.

Covenants provide the "constitutionalization" and "institutionalization" of human relationships, says Jewish political philosopher Daniel Elazar.[95] He elaborates,

> The Bible necessarily holds that the covenantal relationship is the only proper basis for political organization—that is, the structured allocating of authority and power among humans. . . . In a political sense, biblical covenants take the form of constituting acts that establish the parameters of authority and its division without prescribing the constituting details of regimes.[96]

In other words, covenants constitutionalize or institutionalize relationships, and this is the basis of a political society. Covenants bring together both a political and institutional conceptuality, which, to return to the earlier discussion, is what's lacking in so much theology today.

To oversimplify the current state of play, some emphasize the Oneness of God's political rule. Think perhaps of the neo-Kuyperians (the "not one square inch" crowd), the post-liberals, the Augustinians, the theonomists, those who claim the mission of the church is to transform culture and so forth. These are the thinkers who, like me, want a "fuller political conceptuality" that explores the impact of Christ's rule in all of life. And their political conceptuality helpfully attends to both divine and human actors and their power. But these writers tend to stop short of institutional questions such as who has authorized whom to do what, where the lines of jurisdiction and membership fall, and how these structures in turn shape the identities of the actors.

Meanwhile, others emphasize the Twoness of the institutions of state and church, for instance, by arguing that God rules through one institution as creator and through the other as redeemer. Here I'm thinking of two-kingdom writers and those sympathetic with the liberal tradition. These writers, like me, insist on institutionally distinguishing the Two in one fashion or another. But their political conceptuality of the One can remain underdeveloped. Does Scripture actually distinguish God's creation rule from his redemptive rule, or does it simply declare him to be king and judge over all nations, now licensing one institution one way and another

---

[95]Daniel J. Elazar, *Covenant and Polity in Biblical Israel: Biblical Foundations and Jewish Expressions*, vol. 1, *Covenant Traditions in Politics* (New Brunswick, NJ: Transaction Publishers, 1995), 24.
[96]Ibid., 68.

institution another way? Yes, God grants one institution the sword of coercion and another institution the key of declaration. Yes, we could even say he rules the two institutions differently. But isn't that like saying a prime minister rules over his personal staff in one way and the average citizen on the street in another way? Or like saying a CEO delegates one kind of authority to his vice president of marketing while he deputizes his lawyer with another kind of authority (power of attorney)?[97] Would we then refer to the "two rules" of the prime minister or the "two kindoms" of the CEO? Such characterizations would seem a bit overwrought.

In short, it's as if those emphasizing the One are responding to a brand of political concerns (re actors), while those emphasizing the Two are responding to a number institutional concerns (re structures), such that conversations between them can occur at cross-purposes. It reminds one of how Charles Taylor once characterized the liberal-communitarian debate in the late twentieth century.[98] One side of that older debate, Taylor suggested, traded in the coin of sociological, anthropological and epistemological *description*; the other side in the currency of political and institutional *advocacy*; and the two, to some extent, missed one another.

How then do we bring a political and institutional conceptuality together? And the One and the Two together? First, by looking to where God's political rule is given institutional expression: the Bible's common and special covenants. Elazar again: "The basis for political authority is invariably covenantal, and political obligation flows from a covenantal base. Covenanting makes Divine sovereignty concrete and human self-government possible in the world."[99] A full political conceptuality contains *within it* an institutional

---

[97]The distinction between delegated and deputized authority, which we will pick up in chapter four, comes from Nicholas Wolterstorff, *The Mighty and the Almighty: An Essay in Political Theology* (New York: Cambridge University Press, 2012), 50; and Wolterstorff, "'The Authorities Are God's Servants': Is a Theistic Account of Political Authority Still Viable or Have Humanity Accounts Won the Day?" in *Theology and Public Philosophy: Four Conversations*, ed. Kenneth L. Grasso and Cecilia Rodriguez Castillo (Lanham, MD: Lexington Books, 2012), 63-65.

[98]Charles Taylor, "Cross-Purposes: The Liberal-Communitarian Debate," in *Liberalism and the Moral Life*, ed. N. Rosenblum (Cambridge, MA: Harvard University Press, 1989). See also John R. Wallach, "Liberals, Communitarians, and the Tasks of Political Theory," *Political Theory* 15, no. 4 (1987): 592; Amy Gutmann, "Communitarian Critics of Liberalism," *Philosophy and Public Affairs* 14, no. 3 (1985): 318; Don Herzog, "Some Questions for Republicans," *Political Theory* 14, no. 3 (1986): 481-82, 484, 487.

[99]Daniel J. Elazar and Stuart A. Cohen, *The Jewish Polity: Jewish Political Organization from Biblical Times to the Present* (Bloomington: Indiana University Press, 1985), 5.

conceptuality, which is what the biblical covenants provide. In chapter four, I will define politics as *the mediating of God's covenantal rule*.[100]

But there is a second place for us to look for the institutionalization of God's authority: in the power of the sword and in the keys of the kingdom. The sword is God's authorized gift to humanity for protecting life under the Noahic covenant. The keys of the kingdom are Jesus' authorized gift to the members of the new covenant for the purpose of administering that covenant by establishing churches. We will spend a little time on the former, but more on the latter. The keys, I will argue, both affirm new covenant doctrine and new covenant citizens, thereby constituting the visible, institutional church on earth—the local church. The state, I will argue, is a platform builder, while the local church is a signmaker. The latter has the authority to hang signs over the *what* and the *who* of the gospel. A church can declare on behalf of heaven, "that is the true gospel, that is a false gospel" and "he is a Christian, she is not." It is an authority, quite simply, to write statements of faith and to affirm church members and so constitute itself as a local church, actions that the state must not undertake. That said, the state is accountable to the judgment of precisely the same heavenly king; and every action taken by the state, invariably, affirms God's rule over humanity or the rule of some other god. The state must remain formally neutral on matters outside of its jurisdiction, as I said above, but, ironically, within its jurisdiction no law and no constitution is religiously neutral, even if it's called the "godless constitution," as the US Constitution sometimes is because it never names God. Within the state's jurisdiction and within the public square generally, there is religious overlap and religious imposition, nothing more. Not only shouldn't the public square be naked, it cannot be. It's nothing more or less than a battleground of gods, each vying to push the levers of power in its favor. Which means, there are no secular states, at least in terms of what the basis is for a nation's laws. There are only pluralistic states.

---

[100]This definition captures the basic relationship between kingdom and covenant articulated in the title of Peter Gentry and Steve Wellum's book *Kingdom Through Covenant*—namely, God establishes his kingdom throughout redemptive history through covenants. G. K. Beale, too, writes, "Covenant is the primary means by which God, the suzerain, governs his people, the vassal." Beale, *A New Testament Biblical Theology: The Unfolding of the Old Testament in the New* (Grand Rapids: Baker, 2011), 174.

The political theology developed in this book will not depend upon an anthropological division, say, between the inner and outer person, or between a religious portion of our lives and a political portion. Rather, it depends on a "doctrine of the two" or "doctrine of two ages" as Oliver O'Donovan has explained it. Institutions like the state and family have authority over the whole person in one age, within the limits of their mandates; while the church has authority over the whole person for another age, within the limits of its mandate. The state's authority is one of *temporal coercion*; the church's is one of *eschatological declaration*. But both must attend to the inner and outer person. Both are political, and both are spiritual.

All this, of course, requires us to rethink our doctrine of religious freedom. I don't believe that Scripture endorses any one form of government. But I do think that Scripture requires every governor, whether a monarch or a constitutional democracy, (1) to be religiously tolerant, upholding what a number of democratic constitutions refer to as "free exercise," based on the fact that God, in the Noahic covenant, did not authorize human beings to prosecute crimes against himself such as idolatry. And it requires every governor (2) to prohibit making a law "respecting an establishment of religion," as the US Constitution puts it, precisely in those places where the keys of the kingdom give authority to the church—over statements of faith and church members. In fact, I will argue that the tension that abides between the free exercise and establishment clauses of the First Amendment is analogous to a tension found in Scripture's approach to religious tolerance.

Quite a few cans of worms here. To chart out the whole terrain, then, chapters one and two provide this book with a prolegomenon—or language—for a political and an institutional conceptuality, respectively. Chapter one will consider the reigning liberal paradigm and how it is reinforced by a concept of the church's spirituality, while chapter two will provide a more precise institutional language and hermeneutic for understanding Scripture's institutional landscape. Chapters three through six, which provide the book's biblical argument, put this political and institutional language to work through the course of redemptive history. Chapters three and four examine the Old Testament landscape and conclude that politics is a mediating of God's covenantal rule. It's here that we will inquire briefly into a concept of the state's authority and offer the first part of an alternative account of religious tolerance over against the more common conception of religious freedom. Chapter five follows the covenantal storyline into the new covenant and raises the question of a politics of forgiveness. Chapter six concludes this question by examining the politics of *sola fide* and then offers an institutional and political reading of Matthew's Gospel, especially the texts that pertain to the keys of the kingdom. It is here in the final chapter that I will argue that the church is an embassy of God's international rule, which in turn requires us to consider where the church sits in the landscape of the nations and to conclude the book's recurrent discussion of religious freedom or tolerance.

To call a church "political," no doubt, immediately raises questions about how the church should engage the public square. Those are important questions, but they come second. The church's political nature begins with its own life—with its preaching, evangelism, member oversight and discipline. To put real flesh on the idea, it begins with the two crumpled old women sitting over there in the church pew. Do you see them? Both have persevered in the faith for decades. Both have listened carefully week after week to their King's words heralded from a pulpit. And year after year, decade after decade, through the ebb and flow of seasons, through the raising of children and the temptation to compare whose children rise higher, through the petty jealousies of friendship and maybe even an injury inflicted, through the divergent paths of financial prosperity and the attendant threats of covetousness and condescension, through ethnic contrast and conflict, through hasty words and hurt feelings, through times good and bad, those two old women, unrelated by blood, enemies by birth, have, by the power of the Spirit, found their worth and justification in a vicarious righteousness. And so, relieved of the burdern to boast in themselves, they have discovered the freedom to forgive one another's hasty words, to surrender the desire to compete and compare, to outdo one another only in showing honor, to fight for sisterly love and justice amidst everything that would have torn them apart. Here between these two old women is where we find a model political life, one that confronts, condemns and calls the nations.

Is the local church a voluntary association? From the standpoint of the state, yes. The state possesses no authority over church membership. But from the standpoint of Christ's overarching kingdom, no—in two respects.

First, Christians must be united to a local church. Second, the local church is not an association; it is an office. And the work of this office includes confronting the peoples, parliaments and princes of history with the justice and righteousness of the king who will one day judge them. One might as well have told the prophet Jonah that his office was "voluntary," even as he pulled the seaweed out of his hair.

# What Is Politics?

**B**OTH THIS CHAPTER and the next serve the purpose of developing a vocabulary, a prolegomenon. Here the goal is a political prolegomenon; there an institutional one.

The project begins with a little reporting work: What do people mean when they refer to "politics" or the "political"? How are they using the concept? Then, with scribbled notes in hand, we can turn to the Scriptures in subsequent chapters and see how the popular answers stack up against a "fuller political conceptuality" that "pushes back the horizon of commonplace politics and opens it up to the activity of God."[1]

If philosophical liberalism is indeed "the overarching mythos of the modern age" and the "political philosophy by which we live," as advanced in the introduction, then our reporting work should be enhanced by a little background research into the idea of liberalism, particularly the manner in which it divides the political and the spiritual. Further, it is worth exploring how Christians have complemented talk of liberal neutrality toward religion with a spiritual neutrality toward politics, as well as with a concept of religious freedom grounded in the inviolable conscience.

I will also offer some of the incisive criticisms of liberalism that have been leveled by communitarians such as Michael Sandel, as well as feminist and minority-rights theorists. What we will discover along the way is that there is a role for both a narrow and a broad conception of politics.

---

[1] Oliver O'Donovan, *Desire of the Nations: Rediscovering the Roots of Political Theology* (New York: Cambridge University Press, 1996), 2.

## What Is Politics?

Were we to ask the average Westerner both inside and outside the church "What is politics?" I assume that most would answer by pointing to the activities surrounding the institutions of the state that concern the distribution of power. Harold Lasswell's oft-mentioned book captures this idea in its title, *Politics: Who Gets What, When, How.*

***The line between public and private.*** If we continued to probe, I assume that both the average citizen and church member would eventually make some type of distinction between our "public" and our "private" lives. Somewhere deep down inside, the Western person "just knows" that the government shouldn't stick its nose into all of a person's business.[2] "Politics is the activity by which the framework of human life is sustained; it is not life itself," says political theorist Kenneth Minogue.[3] And this is "why despots do not belong in politics."[4] In the totalitarian regimes of the twentieth century, says Minogue, "everything in society was the private property of the despot."[5]

This cultural instinct is captured in William Butler Yeats's 1938 poem "Politics." At the top of Yeats's poem is an epigraph of Nazi refugee Thomas Mann's famous line, "The destiny of man presents its meaning in political terms." Mann, staring into the ugly face of fascism in Spain, Italy and Germany, as well as communism in Russia, couldn't help but conclude that everything that people used to call "private" was becoming political. But Yeats didn't like it. His poem's narrator concedes that "maybe what they say is true" about all of life being political; but still, "How can I, the girl standing

---

[2] Hanna Pitkin usefully describes three ways of understanding the concept "public." Something may be publicly accessible, publicly consequential or publicly controlled. She writes, "First, something may be public in the sense that it is accessible to all, open to scrutiny by anyone, visible as a focus of attention.... Second, something may be public in the sense that it affects all or most of us, public in its consequence or significance.... [And third is] public direction or control. This is the publicness of government, public administration, and collective action." Hanna Pitkin, "Justice: On Relating Public and Private," *Political Theory* 9 (August 1981): 329-30. Our discussion is concerned with the third category.

[3] Kenneth Minogue, *Politics: A Very Short Introduction* (New York: Oxford University Press, 1995), first page of foreword.

[4] Ibid., 1. Some conceptions of liberalism define the very idea of politics to exclude the coercive activities of dictators and despots. Politics, it is said, is a property of persuasion, and therefore a despot's acts of coercion in policy making are, by definition, not "politics." See Bernard Crick, *In Defense of Politics*, 2nd ed. (Chicago: University of Chicago Press, 1972), 18-22.

[5] Minogue, *Politics*, 5.

there, / My attention fix / On Roman or on Russian / Or on Spanish politics?"[6] The narrator wants assurance that there is more to life than politics. What about art, literature, religion or romance?

The assumption that Minogue, Yeats and my stock Westerner share, the assumption that makes them opposed to the totalitarian regimes of Hitler and Stalin, is the basic assumption of philosophical liberalism: human beings are fundamentally self-governing or autonomous.[7] They are fundamentally free to reexamine all their relationships and ends,[8] as well as the structures of power and authority in which they find themselves as a matter of historical accident. Further, they should be free from political interference to fix their attention on things other than politics, like art, literature, religion and romance. The autonomous, nonpolitical individual exists hypothetically prior to the state and prior to the person in his or her political capacity. Classically, this prior position is Hobbes, Locke and Rousseau's "state of nature." More recently, it is John Rawls's "original position."[9]

Politics in the liberal vision is what happens when this prepolitical person steps out of the private realm and into the public realm where

---

[6]William Butler Yeats, "Politics," in *Selected Poems and Three Plays of William Butler Yeats*, ed. M. L. Rosenthal, 3rd ed. (New York: Collier Books, 1986), 199-200.

[7]Not all liberals would grant this statement since it implies a comprehensive doctrine of the good. The "political liberalism" of John Rawls, for instance, attempts to limit its claims to the "political" person and not to the person fundamentally. See esp. Rawls, *Political Liberalism*, expanded ed. (New York: Columbia University Press, 2005), 78. See also Richard Rorty's foundationless liberalism in *Contingency, Irony, and Solidarity* (New York: Cambridge University Press, 1989); and Rorty, "Priority of Democracy to Philosophy," in *Objectivity, Relativism, and Truth: Philosophical Papers* (New York: Cambridge University Press, 1991), 175-96. Stephen Mulhall and Adam Swift helpfully separate the "non-perfectionist" liberals (like Rawls and Rorty) from the "perfectionist" liberals (like Joseph Raz), in Mulhall and Swift, *Liberals and Communitarians* (Oxford: Blackwell, 1992), 229-31, 249-88.

[8]In response to the communitarian objection that people are defined by their relationships and ends, Will Kymlicka replies, "What is central to the liberal view is not that we can *perceive* a self prior to its ends, but that we understand our selves to be prior to our ends, *in the sense that no end or goal is exempt from possible re-examination*" (italics original). Kymlicka, *Liberalism, Community, and Culture* (Oxford: Clarendon Press, 1991), 52. In Kymlicka's defense, the communitarian's legitimate sociological observation does not necessarily produce a normative political principle. "Is" does not produce "ought." A biblical worldview, however, does not always permit the freedom of reexamination. Certain relationships and commandments have been instituted by God, and individuals are *not* free to reexamine them (e.g., "Children, honor your parents"; "What God has joined together, let no man separate").

[9]The state of nature and the original position are not precisely the same, as we will see in a moment, but John Rawls writes that his original position "corresponds to the state of nature in the traditional theory of the social contract." Rawls, *A Theory of Justice* (Cambridge, MA: Belknap Press of Harvard University Press, 1971), 12, see also 136-42.

political activities occur. He does this because, as much as he enjoys his privacy, he can't keep his neighbor from raking her leaves into his yard. He recognizes the need to establish rules for regulating their interactions. Liberal thinkers view the state of nature differently: Hobbes pessimistically as a state of war, Rousseau optimistically as a state of freedom. But in either case a social contract is formed and the individual's political life begins. John Locke writes, "Whenever therefore any number of men are so united into one society, as to quit every one his executive power of the law of nature, and to resign it to the public, there and there only is a political or civil society."[10] The contract among the classical thinkers is "emphatically not a pact between rulers and ruled . . . but a pact to *establish* rule. It marks the transition from the 'state of nature' to the 'civil state.'"[11] It is the act by which separate individuals, who conceive of themselves as equals or at least are mutually interested in treating one another as equals, "transform themselves or incorporate themselves into an acting unity."[12] Authority or rule must be agreed upon and entered into. Legitimate government is based upon the consent of the governed since, says Locke, people are "by nature all free, equal and independent."[13] The contract for a contemporary Kantian liberal like John Rawls is a little different. It is a hypothetical agreement for establishing the rules of justice, which themselves are the grounds of legitimate political rule.[14] The emphasis here is not so much on the origins of politics as on the legitimate basis for politics, which is the consent that all free and rational persons would give in an initial position of equality.[15]

---

[10] John Locke, "A Second Treatise of Government," in *Two Treatises*, section 89 from the second treatise, 137-38.

[11] Murray Forsyth, "Hobbes's Contractarianism: A Comparative Analysis," in *Social Contract from Hobbes to Rawls*, ed. David Boucher and Paul Kelly (London: Routledge, 1994), 37 (italics original).

[12] Ibid., 38.

[13] Locke, "A Second Treatise of Government," in *Two Treatises*, sec. 95 from the second treatise, 141.

[14] Rawls, *Political Liberalism*, 136-37, 217.

[15] Rawls, *Theory of Justice*, 11, 15, 136-50; Rawls, *Political Liberalism*, 22-28, 271-75. Michael Sandel provides an exceptionally helpful description (and the beginning of a critique) of the sense in which John Rawls is a contractarian, particularly in comparison to the classical contractarians, in *Liberalism and the Limits of Justice* (New York: Cambridge University Press, 1982), 104-32. For a description of the difference between classical contractarianism and Kant's version, see Wolfgang Kersting, "Politics, Freedom, and Order: Kant's Political Philosophy," in *The Cambridge Companion to Kant*, ed. Paul Guyer (New York: Cambridge University Press, 1992), 353-55; Michael Sandel, *Justice: What Is the Right Thing to Do* (New York: Farrar, Straus and Giroux, 2009), 139.

Either way, liberalism validates Yeats's hope for life beyond politics (never mind for the moment that "autonomous" is a politically laden term). Liberalism says that there is a public area of our lives, an area in which we are somehow related to the institutions of the state, whether as citizen, judge, soldier, policy maker or executioner, and that this public area is where "politics" transpires. But it also says that there is a private area of our lives, an area which should remain protected from the institutions of the state and its politics. The private nonpolitical world "is that of the family, and of individual conscience as each individual makes his or her own choice of beliefs and interests."[16] Political theorist Chandran Kukathas summarizes all this when he writes, "A political community is essentially an association of individuals who share an understanding of what is public and what is private within their polity. A matter is of public interest if it is something which is generally regarded as an appropriate subject of attention by the political institutions of the society."[17]

***Public-wide and coercive governance.*** If politics in the liberal view describes what happens in the public domain, how do we describe the nature of that activity? Political activity involves several components. First, it involves collective decision making or governance, as comes through in Hanna Pitkin's definition of politics. She writes that politics is "the activity through which relatively large and permanent groups of people determine what they will collectively do, settle how they will live together, and decide their future, to whatever extent this is within their power."[18] Political activity first and foremost is about governance.[19]

Second, political activity refers to that governance by institutions that are capable of making decisions that bind an entire society, the whole public or population. Another political scientist, Guy Peters, sounds very similar to

---

[16]Minogue, *Politics*, 5.
[17]Chandran Kukathas, "Liberalism, Communitarianism, and Political Community," in *The Communitarian Challenge to Liberalism*, ed. Ellen Frankel Paul, Fred D. Miller Jr. and Jeffrey Paul (New York: Cambridge University Press, 1996), 86-87.
[18]Pitkin, "Justice," 343.
[19]I do appreciate and am inclined to agree with Nicholas Wolterstorff's more precise description of government as "the power to make judicial declarations." But I think that may be too refined for the discussion here. Wolterstorff, "'The Authorities Are God's Servants': Is a Theistic Account of Political Authority Still Viable or Have Humanity Accounts Won the Day?" in *Theology and Public Philosophy: Four Conversations*, ed. Kenneth L. Grasso and Cecilia Rodriguez Castillo (Lanham, MD: Lexington Books, 2012), 53-54.

Pitkin when he writes that politics refers "to that complex set of processes whereby governments come to choose between a variety of collective goals for society and seek to implement them." But then Peters adds a necessary elaboration: "It follows that 'politics' presupposes, at the very least, the existence of a set of institutions of government which is in principle capable of taking and implementing such decisions for the whole of society. Families take decisions like that, as do schools or churches or companies. But they make decisions for themselves, not for whole societies."[20]

Yet there is one more element that needs to be added to these first two, which is the idea of legitimate coercive force, at least in a fallen world. Liberals sometimes speak this way only with red faces,[21] but

> what makes the government's actions political . . . is not that they are general and public and may or do affect everyone in the society; after all, so are a manufacturer's decisions when he fixes the prices of his products. The distinctive mark of political action is that it can be enforced, because the government can coerce people into obedience by the threat of physical force, and ultimately by using it.[22]

For the purposes of this book, force is something that separates a metaphorical use of "politics" like "university politics" from a literal one. Hence, "we therefore exclude from the discipline of Politics the study of the running of such groups and institutions as businesses, trade unions, schools, universities, banks, churches and families, because in none of them may force play a role except with the permission of the state."[23]

To sum up, political activity involves a noun characterized by two adjectives: politics involves public-wide and coercive governance.

**What is the state?** Does this mean that a band of armed robbers are acting "politically" when using force? No, their force is not public-wide or legitimate. A private party cannot legitimately use force apart from the state's permission. The modern state alone has a monopoly of legitimate violence, as Max Weber famously put it. It is this monopoly of coercive power, in fact,

---

[20]B. Guy Peters, "Politics Is About Governing," in *What Is Politics? The Activity and Its Study*, ed. Adrian Leftwich (Cambridge: Polity Press, 2004), 25.
[21]See Rorty, *Contingency, Irony, and Solidarity*, ix.
[22]Peter P. Nicholson, "Politics and the Exercise of Force," in *What Is Politics?*, 45.
[23]Nicholson, "Politics and the Exercise of Force," 48.

that gives definition to the state. The state, said Ernest Gellner building on Weber, "is that institution or set of institutions specifically concerned with the enforcement of order." It is an "order-enforcing agency."[24] Political theorist Simon Roberts, being even more explicit about the power over life and death, defines the state as

> the presence of a supreme authority, ruling over a defined territory, who is recognized as having power to make decisions in matters of government [and] is able to enforce such decisions and generally maintain order within the state. Thus the capacity to exercise coercive authority is an essential ingredient: the ultimate test of a ruler's authority is whether he possesses the power of life and death over his subjects.[25]

In a word, the difference between the power of a band of armed robbers and the power of the state is that the state's power is *authorized*.[26] The state is said to have *authority*, which is the right to do things or to demand that things be done.[27] Authority in the simplest terms is power legitimately exercised.[28] To the modern state belong the legislatures and the courts, the police force and the army; and to all such institutions belong legitimized power for enforcing their will upon all other associations and assemblies within their collective dominion.[29] The modern state, says historian of

---

[24]Ernest Gellner, *Nations and Nationalism* (Ithaca, NY: Cornell University Press, 2006), 4.

[25]Quoted in Stuart Hall, "The State in Question," in *The Idea of the Modern State*, ed. Gregor McLennan, David Held and Stuart Hall (Philadelphia: Open University Press, 1984), 1.

[26]Sociologist W. Richard Scott defines authorization "as the process by which norms supporting the exercise of authority by a given agent are defined and enforced by a superordinate power. Authority is legitimated power; legitimated power is normatively regulated. When an organization's use of power is authorized it is, presumptively, both supported and constrained by the actions of the officials superior to it and in a position to oversee its appropriate use." W. Richard Scott, "Unpacking Institutional Arguments," in *The New Institutionalism in Organizational Analysis*, ed. Walter W. Powell and Paul J. DiMaggio (Chicago: University of Chicago Press, 1991), 176.

[27]See R. S. Downie, "Authority," in *The Oxford Companion to Philosophy*, ed. Ted Honderich (New York: Oxford University Press, 1995), 68-69.

[28]Hence, professor of government James L. Gibson writes, "'Authority' is sometimes used as a synonym for legitimacy. Institutions perceived to be legitimate are those with a widely accepted mandate to render judgments for a political community." Gibson, "Judicial Institutions," in *The Oxford Handbook of Political Institutions*, ed. R. A. W. Rhodes, Sarah A. Binder and Bert A. Rockman (New York: Oxford University Press, 2006), 525.

[29]"Regulating and controlling them all, defining and delimiting their rights, is the modern state, which has itself wholly or partly absorbed many functions formerly performed by other associations ... an over-riding allegiance is made on its behalf." S. I. Benn and R. S. Peters, *Social Principles and the Democratic State* (London: George Allen & Unwin, 1959), 255-56.

political thought Quentin Skinner, is "the sole bearer of *Imperium* within its own territories, all other corporations and organisations being allowed to exist only with its permission."[30] It possesses the power of the sword.

**Conclusion.** Later in this chapter we will expand on this definition of politics, and in chapters three through six we will open it up to a theological and covenantal conceptuality, which will allow us to see that the church surely does not exist by the state's "permission," even if Skinner believes it does. Here we have identified three elements that offer a good starting point for what people mean when they speak of politics. Politics refers to (1) the institutional activity of governance (2) over an entire population (3) backed by the power of coercion, which in varying degrees will be regarded as legitimate.[31]

This definition has been drawn mostly from theorists working within the liberal tradition and the context of the modern state, but I believe it serves, with various adjustments and qualifications, for both liberal and non-liberal polities, as well as across states, empires and tribes. The coercive, public-wide institutional activity in the totalitarian body politic, we might say, extends from the head all the way down to the toes. The state determines which gods to worship, which books to write, which crops to grow and which borders to line with barbed wire. In the liberal body politic the state's institutional activity does not incorporate so much of the body—only down to the shoulders.

## Separating the Political and the Spiritual

To draw the microscope in more closely on liberalism's division between public and private, what quickly appears is how a political/spiritual divide maps over the public/private divide. A liberal state aims to avoid controlling—and being controlled by—its citizens' spiritual or religious commitments.

---

[30]Quentin Skinner, *The Foundations of Modern Political Thought: The Age of the Reformation*, vol. 2 (Cambridge: Cambridge University Press, 1978), 352. In context, Skinner is referring to the modern, post-sixteenth-century nation-state. But I would contest the description is applicable, with qualifications, to government generally; e.g., a vassal state within an empire is not the "sole bearer" of imperium because the empire possesses a final imperium.

[31]See Locke's definition of politics, which incorporates these three elements, in "A Second Treatise of Government," in *Two Treatises*, chap. 1, sec. 3, p. 101.

This political and spiritual divide comes in harder and softer versions. Everyone's favorite example of the harder version is the "political liberalism" of John Rawls.[32] Rawls's liberalism portends to be an anti-perfectionist political liberalism, as opposed to a perfectionist's comprehensive liberalism, which would rest on a conception of the good.[33] In this slightly reworked version of the liberalism espoused in his original *A Theory of Justice*, which he self-critically concedes was sustained by a "comprehensive philosophical doctrine,"[34] Rawls attempts to rest the entire edifice of the original position and the principles of justice on "the idea of public reason." He acknowledges that many people do in fact "regard it as simply unthinkable to view themselves apart from certain religious, philosophical, and moral convictions."[35] And so he means not to ask them to do so, at least from the standpoint of their "noninstitutional or moral identity." But Rawls goes on to argue that people also possess a "public" or "political identity" that is in fact capable of entering—and indeed must enter—the political arena, maintaining neutrality between different conceptions of the good.[36] This is where "public reason" enters in. Citizens must set aside their moral and religious convictions when acting politically, whether in the legislative arena, the courtroom or the ballot box. Instead, they must act according to political values that everyone can endorse no matter their religious or moral background:[37] "Public reason—citizens' reasoning in the public forum about constitutional essentials and basic questions of justice—is now best guided by a political conception of the principles and values of which all citizens can endorse. The political conception is to be,

---

[32]Nicholas Wolterstorff refers to this brand of liberalism as public reason liberalism and interacts with some of its most prominent voices, including Rawls, in part one of *Understanding Liberal Democracy* (New York: Oxford University Press, 2012), 11-110.

[33]Contemporary theorists who hold to a comprehensive or what is sometimes called a "perfectionist" liberalism include Joseph Raz, *Morality of Freedom* (New York: Oxford University Press, 1986); Ronald Dworkin, *Justice for Hedgehogs* (Cambridge, MA: Harvard University Press, 2011); also Dworkin, "Foundations of Liberal Equality," in *Equal Freedom: Selected Tanner Lectures on Human Values*, ed. Stephen Darwell (Ann Arbor: University of Michigan, 1995), 190-230. Brian Barry also describes himself as "putting forward a universally valid case in favour of liberal egalitarian principles," in Barry, *Justice as Impartiality* (Oxford: Clarendon Press, 1995), 3.

[34]Rawls, *Political Liberalism*, xvi.

[35]Ibid., 31.

[36]Ibid., 29-35.

[37]Ibid., 9-11, 15-16, 215, 224-25.

so to speak, political and not metaphysical."[38] In a proposal that subtly echoes Kant's categorical imperative, albeit shorn of the explicit appeal to universal reason, Rawls advises citizens to enter the public arena always using a Supreme Court litmus test: "How would our argument strike us presented in the form of a supreme court opinion?"[39] The ultimate foundation for approaching the political arena with the supposed neutrality of a supreme court justice is not any conception of the good but the fact that citizens in Western democracies can assume there is an "overlapping consensus of reasonable comprehensive doctrines." That is to say, people of differing (and reasonable) moral and religious convictions can endorse the politically liberal principles of justice, each from their "own point of view."[40] Christians have one reason to treat people equally; Hindus another; atheists still another.[41]

Rawls illustrates the distinction between the moral person and the political person with the example of one very famous religious convert: Saul of Tarsus become Paul the apostle. Saul was a Roman citizen, and so was Paul. His relationship to Caesar and the Roman Empire before and after conversion was the same: "Such a conversion implies no change in our public or institutional identity."[42] As such we can say that Paul the apostle's Roman citizenship did not depend upon his Christianity. Paul the citizen therefore had room to act apart from the dictates of Christianity. In a modern democratic society that is characterized "by a pluralism of incompatible yet reasonable comprehensive doctrines,"[43] this citizen should then adopt a position of neutrality for the sake of preserving his freedom of religion and belief.

---

[38] Ibid., 10.
[39] Ibid., 254. Kant's categorical imperative is, "Act only according to that maxim whereby you can at the same time will that it should become a universal law." Immanuel Kant, *Grounding for the Metaphysics of Morals*, trans. James W. Ellington, 3rd ed. (Indianapolis, IN: Hackett, 1993), 421.
[40] Rawls, *Political Liberalism*, 134. For a good explanation and critique of *Political Liberalism*, see Michael Sandel's review in *Harvard Law Review* 107, no. 7 (May 1994): 1765-94.
[41] It is worth noticing the implicit contradiction in Rawls's idea of an "overlapping consensus." On the one hand, citizens must leave their moral and religious beliefs behind. On the other hand, citizens are expected to affirm liberal principles on the grounds of their beliefs. For a helpful clarification on Rawls's concept of "overlapping consensus," see Wolterstorff, *Understanding Liberal Democracy*, 308.
[42] Rawls, *Political Liberalism*, 30-31.
[43] Ibid., xvi.

Rawls's public reason liberalism, as I said, offers a harder version of the separation between politics and religion, meaning he not only assumes that the political and spiritual *can be* separated; he avers they *should be*. He reifies what he takes to be an existential division with an ethical norm. Softer versions of this division occur among those critics of Rawls, including Christian ones, who still want to hold onto some form of liberalism.[44] Such critics presume that the political/spiritual division is real and that one can, at least in principle, keep religious causes outside. Yet they argue strenuously that religious and moral claims should sometimes be allowed to enter the political sphere, and they concede that sometimes the church must speak politically. Their division between the political and spiritual might be called softer because they maintain a *descriptive* division but jettison the *normative* injunction to keep the two entirely separate.

Philosopher of religion Jeffrey Stout, for instance, argues, "The notion of state neutrality . . . should not be seen as [the democratic tradition's] defining mark. Rawlsian liberalism should not be seen as its official mouthpiece." Stout posits instead that "modern democratic reasoning is secularized, but not in a sense that rules out the expression of religious premises or the entitlement of individuals to accept religious assumptions." After all, "religion is not essentially a conversation-stopper, as secular liberals often assume. . . . Neither, however, is religion the foundation without which democratic discourse is bound to collapse, as traditionalists suppose."[45]

Stout's call to embrace democratic tradition but not a Rawlsian liberalism bears at least a passing resemblance to the conclusions of Nicholas Wolterstorff. Wolterstorff argues that Christians have good reasons to support a *liberal political structure* even if they disavow *liberal political theory*. After all, "the theory and the structure [can] be distinguished," and "one can support liberal democracy without being a liberal theorist."[46]

---

[44]E.g., Wolterstorff, *Understanding Liberal Democracy*; Jeffrey Stout, *Democracy and Tradition* (Princeton, NJ: Princeton University Press, 2004), 3-9; Greg Forster, *John Locke's Politics of Moral Consensus* (New York: Cambridge University Press, 2005), 26-27.
[45]Stout, *Democracy and Tradition*, 3, 10-11.
[46]Wolterstorff, *Understanding Liberal Democracy*, 305.

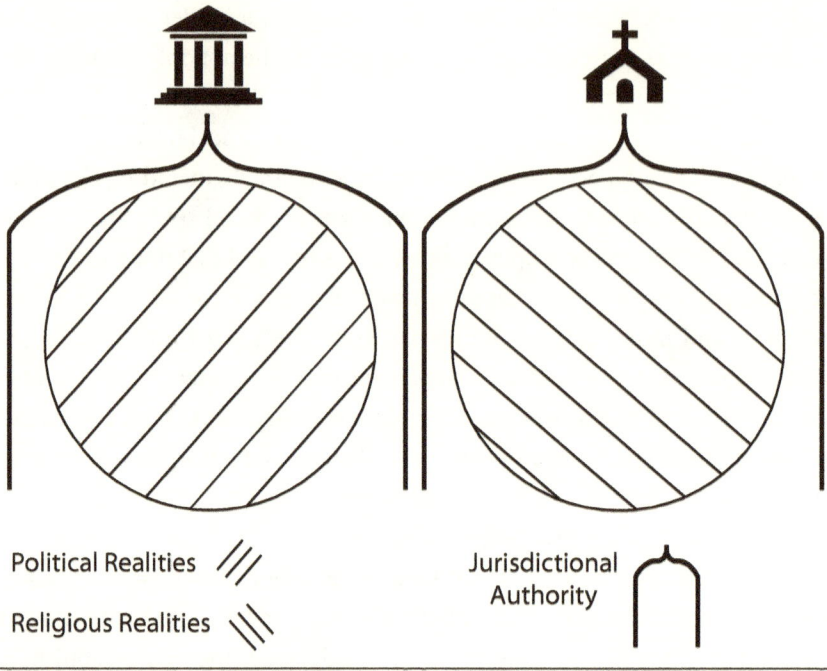

**Figure 1.1.** Hard separation

If the harder version envisions two nonoverlapping circles, one called "political realities" and one called "spiritual" or "religious realities," the softer version pushes those two circles closer together so that they partially overlap. Figures 1.1 and 1.2 picture both perspectives. Wolterstorff's labels for the "inclusivist" and "exclusivist" positions capture the distinction.[47] The softer version *includes* religion in the public square. The circles overlap. The harder version attempts to *exclude* religion. No overlap. In both the harder and softer versions, furthermore, the basic idea is that the state has institutional or jurisdictional authority over the political domain, while the church has such authority over the spiritual or religions domain. (This institutional authority is the topic of chapters two through six.) Culture wars, not surprisingly, occur whenever there is overlap. The contrast to both of these views, at least in purely conceptual terms, would be a theonomic vision that combined church and state and gave it dominion in matters spiritual and political, as seen in figure 1.3.

---

[47]Ibid., 11.

*What Is Politics?*

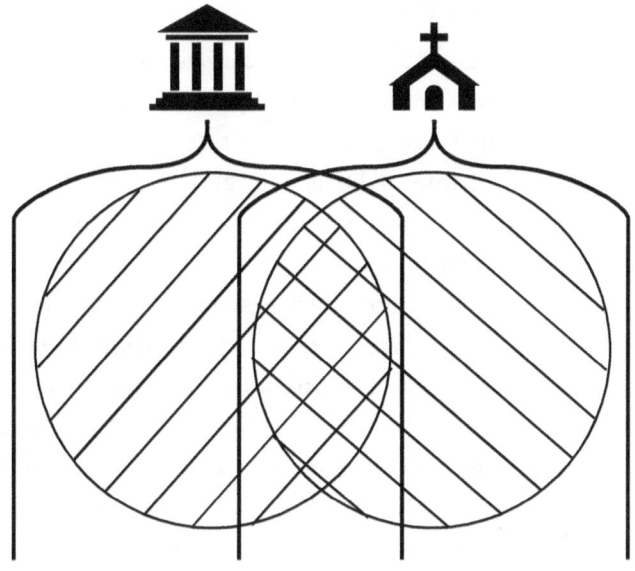

**Figure 1.2.** Soft separation

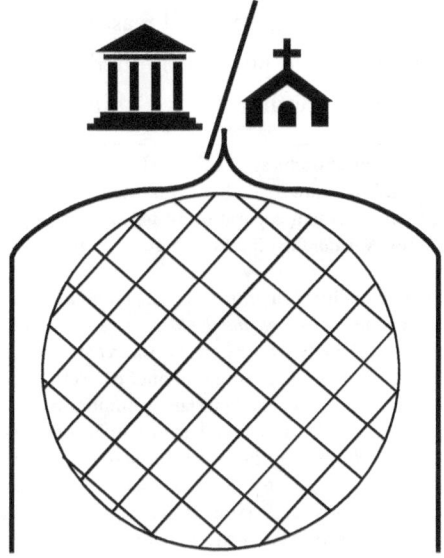

**Figure 1.3.** Theonomy

## Spirituality of the Church

We have not yet said anything about the church side of things. If Rawlsian liberalism represents a "harder" spiritual neutrality in the political sphere, the nineteenth-century Presbyterian doctrine of "the spirituality of the church" represents a harder political neutrality in the church.[48] If the first asks citizens to divest themselves of their moral or spiritual commitments when entering the public square, the second tells Christians to divest themselves of their political opinions when standing in a church's pulpit or planning a church budget. Like liberalism, the doctrine of the church's spirituality characterizes religion and politics as two separate domains of life, rather than as distinct but inseparable domains (as I will maintain). And like liberalism, it makes the church the domain of the spiritual and the state the domain of the political.[49] Nineteenth-century pastor and theologian Stuart Robinson wrote, "The scope and aim of civil power is only things *temporal*; of the ecclesiastical power, only things *spiritual*. *Religious* is a term not predicable of acts of the state; *political* and *civil*, not predicable of acts of the church."[50] Robinson distinguished the ecclesiastical and civil power in five ways: (1) the civil power derives its authority from the "Author of nature," while the church derives its authority from "Jesus the Mediator"; (2) the civil power is guided by "the light of nature and reason," while the church looks to Christ and his word; (3) civil power is limited to "things seen and temporal," while the church has authority over "things unseen and spiritual";

---

[48] I understand the doctrine of the church's spirituality to be one possible formulation of the doctrine of the two kingdoms. There are formulations of the two-kingdoms doctrine that do a better job of avoiding such a strident separation of political and spiritual, e.g., David VanDrunen, *Living in God's Two Kingdoms: A Biblical Vision for Christianity and Culture* (Wheaton, IL: Crossway, 2010).

[49] Classic statements of the spirituality of the church can be found in Stuart Robinson, *The Church of God as an Essential Element of the Gospel, and the Idea, Structure, and Functions Thereof* (Philadelphia: Joseph M. Wilson, 1958); J. H. Thornwell, *The Collected Writings of James Henley Thornwell*, vol. 4, *Ecclesiastical* (1875; repr., Edinburgh: Banner of Truth Trust, 1974); R. L. Dabney, *Lectures in Theology*, 4th ed. (Richmond: Presbyterian Committee of Publication, 1890), 873-87, esp. 879. Contemporary introductions include David VanDrunen, *Natural Law and the Two Kingdoms: A Study in the Development of Reformed Social Thought* (Grand Rapids: Eerdmans, 2010), 247-67; D. G. Hart, *Recovering Mother Kirk: The Case for Liturgy in the Reformed Tradition* (Grand Rapids: Baker, 2003), 51-65; cf. Preston D. Graham Jr., *A Kingdom Not of This World: Stuart Robinson's Struggle to Distinguish the Sacred from the Secular During the Civil War* (Macon, GA: Mercer University Press, 2002).

[50] Quoted in Thomas E. Peck, "Church and State," in *The Writings of Thomas E. Peck*, vol. 2 (Carlisle, PA: Banner of Truth, 1999), 287, italics original.

(4) the civil employs the sword with force, while the church employs the keys for ministerial purposes and (5) civil power may be exercised by a magistrate "severally," while all ecclesiastical power must be exercised "jointly." For Robinson, the two domains are utterly separate: "*Religious* is not a term predicable of the acts of the state; *political* is a term not predicable of the acts of the Church."[51] Advocates of the church's spirituality such as Robinson recognized that "the claims of the moral law made some overlap necessary," but they still maintained that the church "was to stay out of political matters, strictly defined."[52]

Many of the doctrine's advocates were writing in the years leading up to and through the American Civil War, and they shared the concern that too many churches and pulpiteers had allowed themselves to be domesticated by one partisan cause or another, whether Northern or Southern, pro-slavery or antislavery. Robinson, a border-state pastor, lamented that "the vulgar fire of secular politics" had corrupted too many churches, and that too many church courts had "meddled with civil affairs."[53]

The issue of political commitment came to a head for the Presbyterian Church at its Philadelphia General Assembly in 1861, when, after much debate, the Assembly affirmed an "unabated loyalty" to "the integrity of these United States," "the Federal Government in the exercise of all its functions" and "our noble Constitution" with 156 ayes and 66 nays.[54] Charles Hodge, an advocate of the church's spirituality, protested the decision: "We deny the right of the General Assembly to decide the political question, to what government the allegiance of Presbyterians as citizens is due, and its rights to make that decision a condition of membership in our Church." He described the Assembly's action as a lamentable break from the Presbyterian precedent of neutrality: "We have, at one time, resisted the popular demand to make total abstinence from intoxicating liquors a term of membership. At another time, the holding of slaves." But by siding with the Northern Federal Government against the Southern Confederate Government, the

---

[51] Robinson, *Church of God*, 85-86.
[52] Hart, *Recovering Mother Kirk*, 62.
[53] Quoted in Graham, *Kingdom Not of This World*, 168.
[54] From "Transcript of the Minutes of the 73rd General Assembly, Pertaining to the Gardiner Spring Resolution," May 16, 1861, PCA Historical Center: Archives & Manuscript Repository for the Continuing Presbyterian Church, www.pcahistory.org/documents/gardinerspring.html.

Assembly "descended from this high position, in making a political opinion a particular theory of the Constitution" and in so doing "endangered the unity of the Church."[55] New Orleans pastor and theologian Benjamin Palmer, too, lamented the fact that the Assembly had missed "the splendid opportunity ... of demonstrating the purely spiritual character of the Church, as the 'kingdom which is not of this world.' It would have been a superb triumph of Christianity, if the Church could have stretched her arms across the chasm of a great war, preserving the integrity of her ranks unbroken." Alas, "The golden vision was not to be realized."[56]

One contemporary advocate of the spirituality of the church is Darryl Hart, who refers to himself as a "Christian secularist." He summarizes his conception of the relationship between religion and politics succinctly: "Christianity is an apolitical faith." Politics concerns itself with "life, liberty, and the pursuit of happiness," but Christianity—"with the major exception of its American expression"—is about "salvation from sin and death."[57] To employ the institutional church for political ends would fundamentally distort Christianity because Christianity "is essentially an otherworldly faith."[58] The church is a "spiritual institution with a spiritual task and spiritual means for executing that task."[59]

Hart appears to recognize the overlap between his own views and philosophical liberalism, yet he observes that they have different foundations: "For Christian secularists, the work of government lacks any overtly religious or spiritual purpose. This is not because Christian secularism has a certain political philosophy that involves government's religious neutrality.... Instead the reason for keeping Christianity out of the hands of government stems from a particular understanding of the Christian religion and the institutions that bear responsibility for its propagation." Specifically, the Christian God works by the Spirit and not by the sword, from the inside out, not outside in.[60] And coupled with the doctrine of God's unilateral work in

---

[55]Ibid.
[56]B. M. Palmer, *Life and Letters of James Henley Thornwell* (Richmond: Whittet & Shepperson, 1875), 501.
[57]Darryl Hart, *A Secular Faith: Why Christianity Favors the Separation of Church and State* (Chicago: Ivan R. Dee, 2006), x.
[58]Ibid., 16.
[59]Hart, *Recovering Mother Kirk*, 63.
[60]Hart, *Secular Faith*, 15.

salvation are "the doctrines of the lordship of Christ over individual conscience and Christian liberty."[61] All this leaves Hart concluding that "the most intimate and sacred acts of religious devotion, those that fulfill the Christian's duty to love God, take place in either personal (the home) or private (the church) settings."[62]

I agree with Hart that the Bible shows God working from the inside out, as we will consider in chapter five's discussion of the new covenant. But a person changed on the inside is changed everywhere, including when he or she steps into the public square. So how is it that Christianity is "apolitical"? If we define "sacred" as "consecrated to God," it would seem that a Christian's public acts should be no less consecrated to God than his or her private acts. In what sense then are a person's "most" sacred acts in private? I, at least, want to simultaneously affirm a number of things that Hart says and yet say the overall picture is missing something.

### Freedom of Religion as Freedom of Conscience

Furthermore, I assume that few Christians or the citizens of Western democracies would go as far as Rawls in evacuating the public square of all religion or adopt a doctrine of the church's spirituality as strident as Robinson's or Hart's. The British public, for instance, at least tacitly accepts the place of Church of England bishops in the House of Lords. Still, most Christians and Westerners believe that political and religious realities belong to at least partially non-overlapping domains, as if politics and religion were separate rooms you could walk into or out of, and that the church should remain mostly neutral in the political room and the state mostly neutral in the religious room. And so the very same British public becomes outraged when a prime minister uses his office to encourage Christians to become more "evangelical," as one did not too long ago.[63]

---

[61] Hart, *Recovering Mother Kirk*, 62.
[62] Hart, *Secular Faith*, 16.
[63] See Steven Swinford, "David Cameron Says Christians Should Be 'More Evangelical,'" *The Telegraph*, April 16, 2014, www.telegraph.co.uk/news/religion/10770425/David-Cameron-says-Christians-should-be-more-evangelical.html; "David Cameron Fosters Division by Calling Britain a 'Christian Country,'" *The Telegraph*, Letters, April 20, 2014, www.telegraph.co.uk/comment/letters/10777417/David-Cameron-fosters-division-by-calling-Britain-a-Christian-country.html.

A primary goal for Christians of this separation, whether hard or soft, is to maintain a space for religious freedom. Christians might criticize Rawls's naked public square, but they often describe the moral universe in similarly bifurcated terms. After all, "Rawls and other neutralists," observes law professor Andrew Koppelman, "thought that their move to neutrality was a generalization from the idea of freedom of religion."[64] At least this is the case with the formulation of religious freedom that emerged from the two-kingdoms tradition and that was eventually embraced by the US Founders, a formulation that historian Nicholas P. Miller characterizes as a "consilience . . . between dissenting Protestant thought and Enlightenment thought."[65]

In the traditional liberal and two-kingdoms formulation, freedom of religion begins with a distinction between the inner and outer person, and then it treats freedom of religion interchangeably with the freedom of conscience. The state's jurisdiction is limited to the outer person, the inner belonging to God and the individual. Legal theorists have arguably never worked out this relationship between freedom of religion and conscience or even sought to justify their equation.[66] Yet Miller traces it back to Martin Luther's "to go against conscience is neither right nor safe" from the famed "Here I Stand" speech, as well as the formal protest lodged by Lutheran princes at the Diet at Speyer, at which the term "Protestant" was born.[67]

---

[64] Andrew Koppelman, *Defending American Religious Neutrality* (Cambridge, MA: Harvard University Press, 2013), 16.

[65] Nicholas P. Miller, *The Religious Roots of the First Amendment: Dissenting Protestants and the Separation of Church and State* (New York: Oxford University Press, 2012), 131. Similar views of a synthesis can be found in George Marsden, *The Twilight of the American Enlightenment: The 1950s and the Crisis of Liberal Belief* (New York: Basic Books, 2014), xxiii-iv; Stephen D. Smith, *The Rise and Decline of American Religious Freedom* (Cambridge, MA: Harvard University Press, 2014), 7, 14-47, 105-8; Koppelman, *Defending American Religious Neutrality*, 56-64; Douglass Laycock, *Religious Liberty*, vol. 1, *Overviews and History* (Grand Rapids: Eerdmans, 2012), 91.

[66] Nathan S. Chapman, "Disentangling Conscience and Religion," *University of Illinois Law Review* 2013, no. 4 (2013): 1460.

[67] Miller, *The Religious Roots of the First Amendment*, 19. A fuller statement can be found elsewhere in Luther: "To every ordinance of man we are to be subject . . . so long as it does not bind the conscience and only forbids in respect to outward things. . . . But if it invade the spiritual domain and constrain the conscience, over which God only must preside and rule, we certainly should not obey it, but rather slip our neck from under it." Martin Luther, *Commentary on Peter & Jude*, trans. and ed. John Nichols Lenker (Grand Rapids: Kregel Classics, 1990), 123.

The early Baptists, too, argued for religious freedom by building on a two-kingdoms framework, the inviolability of the conscience and the noncoercive character of faith.[68] John Smyth argued the magistrate was not permitted "to meddle with religion, or matters of conscience, to force and compel men to this or that form of religion, or doctrine."[69] Notice that religion and conscience are placed in parallel position. To bind the conscience, after all, is to bind the soul, and, said Thomas Helwys, "The king . . . hath no power over the immortal soules of his subjects."[70] Universal religious freedom is the natural conclusion: "Let them be heretics, Turks, Jews, or whatsoever, it appertains not to the earthly power to punish them."[71]

Both John Locke and the American Founders placed these two-kingdom and dissenting Protestant formulations inside the larger political philosophy of liberalism, which meant treating the inviolable conscience as a right and government authority as a property of consent. Locke argued that governments should concern themselves with "outward things" such as "life, liberty, health, and indolency of body" as well as "money, lands, houses, furniture and the like."[72] He offered this as a point of contrast with the church, whose jurisdiction he said lies with "the care of souls" and "the inward and full persuasion of the mind."[73] Thomas Jefferson, later on, observed that the "operations of the mind" are not subject to coercion in the same way as "acts of the body."[74] In light of this duality, Jefferson, sounding a bit like Helwys, drew the lesson that "it does me no injury for my neighbor to say that there are twenty Gods, or no God."[75] Baptist minister John Leland made a similar remark a few years later: "Let every man speak freely without fear—maintain the principles that he believes—worship according to his own faith, either one God, three Gods, no God, or twenty Gods; and let government protect

---

[68]Timothy George, "Between Pacifism and Coercion: The English Baptist Doctrine of Religious Toleration," *Mennonite Quarterly Review* 58 (January 1984): 39-43.
[69]Quoted in ibid., 35.
[70]Quoted in ibid., 40.
[71]Helwys in ibid., 40.
[72]Locke, "A Letter Concerning Toleration," in *Two Treatises*, 218.
[73]Ibid., 218, 219.
[74]Thomas Jefferson, *Notes on the State of Virginia*, ed. Frank Shuffelton (New York: Penguin Books, 1999), 165 (Query XVII).
[75]Ibid., 165.

him in so doing."[76] The inward person and the outward person, according to Locke, Jefferson and Leland, are sufficiently separable for the purposes of the public square.

These formulations were soon reflected in the constitutions and declarations of rights that proliferated in the decade following 1776, such as the constitutions of Pennsylvania (1776), Delaware (1776), Maryland (1776), Virginia (1776), New Jersey (1776), Vermont (1777), and New Hampshire (1784).[77] The language of the North Carolina Constitution (1776) is typical: "All men have a natural and inalienable right to worship Almighty God according to dictates of their own consciences." Wolterstorff observes, "One of the things that is strikingly uniform in these declarations is the way conscience is brought into the picture, more specifically, 'the dictates of conscience.'" Such phraseology, he observes, was "truly innovative." Prior to the seventeenth century, theologians would have argued that it is our duty and right "to worship God as God *wants* to be worshipped." But now "an immense change in religious conviction had taken place."[78]

Conscience, clearly, was key. One of the greatest architects of the era's doctrine of religious freedom, James Madison, averred, "Conscience is the most sacred of all property."[79]

Of course, it is not just the documents of the United States that ground religious freedom in the free conscience. The Universal Declaration of Human Rights, similarly, places conscience and religion in parallel position: "Everyone has the right to freedom of thought, conscience, and religion." So, too, does article 25 of the 1949 Constitution of India, and article 44.2 of the Irish constitution, and article 2 of the Canadian Charter of Rights and Freedoms, and on the list goes.

It is not difficult to understand the emphasis given to the conscience. Conscience proves a useful concept for religious freedom because, unlike religion, it seems to be a universal concept—most would agree that they have

---

[76] Quoted in Jon Meacham, *American Gospel: God, the Founding Fathers, and the Making of a Nation* (New York: Random House, 2006), 32.
[77] Wolterstorff, *Understanding Liberal Democracy*, 333-34.
[78] Ibid., 335, 336.
[79] Peter Augustine Lawler and Robert Martin Schaefer, eds., *American Political Rhetoric: Essential Speeches and Writings on Founding Principles and Contemporary Controversies*, 6th ed. (Lanham, MD: Rowman & Littlefield, 2010), 39.

one and would prefer for it to remain unmolested. The conscience therefore provides a convenient, publicly accessible stand-in for religion, which is why so many contemporary theorists favor it.[80] It diminishes the specialness of religion, or at least it doesn't discriminate against the nonreligious by giving the believer something that is not given to the unbeliever. Plus, it provides the believer with a way to ask for religious liberty without appealing to the beliefs of his or her religion. After all, says legal theorist Douglous Laycock,

> The Constitution cannot adopt a Baptist or Deist or Episcopal conception of religious liberty, at least not without deep paradox. . . . Moreover, explanations of religious liberty based on beliefs about religion cannot possibly persuade persons who do not hold the same religious beliefs. . . . The strongest such explanation would make sense of the ratified text [of the US Constitution's first amendment] without entailing commitments to any proposition about religious belief.[81]

If religion is a property of conscience and both believer and unbeliever share one of those, then the believer can convince the unbeliever to respect his or her religion. All told, the conscience provides a place of "overlapping consensus," to use the Rawlsianism. It supposedly gives the liberal formulation an explanation "without entailing commitments to . . . religious belief." Indeed, this is the consummate "view from nowhere." Rawls, like many others, therefore treats the conscience as the umbrella category: the freedom of conscience means the freedom of "fundamental religious, moral, and philosophical interests."[82] And he freely acknowledges where his thinking came from: the "intuitive idea" of equal liberty of conscience "is to generalize the principle of religious toleration to a social form."[83]

---

[80] A few recent theorists who ground freedom of religion in the freedom of conscience (in addition to Rawls, discussed below) include Jocelyn Maclure and Charles Taylor, *Secularism and Freedom of Conscience* (Cambridge, MA: Harvard University Press, 2011); Martha Nussbaum, *Liberty of Conscience: In Defense of America's Tradition of Religious Equality* (New York: Basic Books, 2008); William Galston, *The Practice of Liberal Pluralism* (New York: Cambridge University Press, 2005), 45-71; Amy Gutmann, *Identity in Democracy* (Princeton, NJ: Princeton University Press, 2003), 151-91; Michael J. Sandel, *Democracy's Discontent: America in Search of a Public Philosophy* (Cambridge, MA: Belknap Press of Harvard University Press, 1996), 65-71; cf. Ronald Dworkin, *Religion Without God* (Cambridge, MA: Harvard University Press, 2013), 128-37, who uses the language of the freedom of "ethical independence."
[81] Douglas Laycock, *Religious Liberty*, 58.
[82] Rawls, *Theory of Justice*, 206.
[83] Ibid., 206n6.

In other words, believers might not like Rawls's separationism, but it's made of the same stuff they use to justify religious freedom in the public square.

## A Broader Religious Conceptuality and a View from Somewhere

But can religion and politics really be separated as phenomenological realities, politics quarantined to one part of the person or one part of life and religions quarantined to another part? I am not asking about normative categories, but descriptive ones. Let's start with the spiritual or religious. Is there such a thing as spiritual or religious neutrality? If not, wouldn't we have to say that every law or constitution establishes *some* religion or religions?

Whether spiritual or religious neutrality is possible depends upon what we mean by spiritual or religious. We could employ a sociologist's fairly clinical definition of religion, such as Peter Berger's "the human enterprise by which the human cosmos is established" or Emile Durkheim's "a unified system of beliefs and practices relative to sacred things" or Williams James's "the belief there is an unseen order, and that our supreme good lies in harmoniously adjusting ourselves thereto."[84] Each of these definitions political theologian William Cavanaugh would probably characterize as offering a "substantivist" approach to defining religion—religion as the organized substance of beliefs and practices of a community typically involving the supernatural. This he would compare to a "functionalist" approach—religion understood according to the function it plays in someone's life. A functionalist approach to religion allows for a broader range of ideologies and allegiances to qualify as religion, such as nationalism, Marxism, capitalism and so forth. Thus if a professing Christian spends most of her life devoted to the stock market—Cavanaugh's illustration—then her functional religion is capitalism, "not metaphorically, but really."[85]

---

[84]These three examples are taken from Brendan Sweetman, *Why Politics Needs Religion: The Place of Religious Arguments in the Public Square* (Downers Grove, IL: IVP Academic, 2006), 47.

[85]William T. Cavanaugh, "What Is Religion?" in Michael C. Desch and Daniel Philpott, eds., *Religion and International Relations: A Primer for Research. Report of the Working Group on International Relations and Religion of the Mellon Initiative on Religion Across the Disciplines* (University of Notre Dame, 2013), 63 (http://rmellon.nd.edu/assets/101872/religion_and_international_relations_report.pdf);

Both the substantivist and the functionalist approaches define religion as something "out there," something with a real essence. Cavanaugh then points to a constructivist approach, which is more historical in its orientation. The constructivist argues that the idea of "religion" as we think about it today is a modern, Western construction devised for the purpose of creating the religion/politics divide, thereby legitimating certain practices, delegitimating others and yielding the liberal's preferred political configuration. He observes, "It is not simply that religion and politics used to be mixed, and then modernity sorted them out; the religion/politics distinction was invented, and did not exist before."[86] And the goal of creating this divide was nothing if not ideological: "What counts as religion and what does not in any given context is contestable and depends on who has the power and authority to define religion at any given time and place."[87]

Cavanaugh seems to favor the constructivist approach: "Religion does exist, but as a constructed category. Religion is not simply an object; it is a lens."[88] And while I'm sympathetic to his general project, I would also say we don't need to view these three perspectives as mutually exclusive. The prophet Isaiah seems to combine all three persepctives in his indictment of the idolatry of Israel: A man takes some wood, and "half of it he burns in the fire. . . . He warms himself and says, 'Aha, I am warm, I have seen the fire!' And the rest of it he makes into a god, his idol, and falls down to it and worships it. He prays to it and says, 'Deliver me, for you are my god!'" (Is 44:16-17). Here, it would appear, is a self-constructed set of substantive beliefs and practices functioning as a religious lens.

---

see also Cavanaugh, "The Invention of Religion," in *The Myth of Religious Violence* (New York: Oxford University Press, 2009), 57-122.

[86]Cavanaugh, "What Is Religion?," 65.

[87]Cavanaugh, *Myth of Religious Violence*, 59. Cavanaugh writes elsewhere, "The broader point I am trying to make is that 'religion' as it appears in religious-secular, religion-politics, and other similar binaries, is not a universal feature of all human societies across time and space but is rather a contingent invention that arose from a very particular set of circumstances of early modern Christian Europe. . . . 'Religious' and 'secular' as they have been constructed originally in Europe and subsequently in the rest of the world are not neutral descriptive terms, but are rather prescriptive. They help create the reality they purport to describe. They are . . . 'collective affirmations about what kind of world we want to experience.'" William T. Cavanaugh, "The Invention of the Religious-Secular Distinction," in *At the Limits of the Secular: Reflections on Faith and Public Life*, ed. William A. Barbieri Jr. (Grand Rapids: Eerdmans, 2014), 118, 120-21.

[88]Cavanaugh, "What Is Religion?," 66.

Whether or not Cavanaugh would agree with that (I assume he might), I propose that the religious conceptuality of Christianity can simultaneously accommodate all three perspectives, at least with regard to false religion. Specifically, I believe that Scripture teaches there is no such thing as religious neutrality and that all humanity is inescapably religious, functionally and constructively speaking. Indeed, history's first act of religious construction showed up quite early with the promise, "You will be like God" (Gen 3:5)—a text that well substantiates Cavanaugh's basic point: people define religion in order to legitimate some practices, delegitimate others and yield their preferred political configuration.

Augustine knew there was no such thing as spiritual or religious neutrality. People are for or against the Bible's God. All humanity, he observed, belongs to one of two societies—one city that "lifts up its head in its own glory" and "loves its own strength as displayed in its mighty men," and another city that "says to its God, 'Thou art my glory and the lifter up of mine head'" and "'I will love Thee, O Lord, my strength.'"[89]

Luther's definition of a "god" is also helpful here: "A 'god' is the term for that to which we are to look for all good and in which we are to find refuge in all need. Therefore, to have a god is nothing else than to trust and believe in that one with your whole heart.... Anything on which your heart relies and depends, I say, that really is your God."[90] By this definition, everybody has a god—something that they worship, something that justifies them, something that claims the firstfruits of their income and that commands all their obedience.

Ironically, Augustine and Luther just might be joined by the atheistic and liberal philosopher Ronald Dworkin, who argues that atheists can be religious, too, because they possess "a deep, distinct, and comprehensive worldview" that governs their lives[91] or joined by the US circuit court that defined religion as a belief system that "addresses fundamental and ultimate

---

[89]Augustine, *The City of God Against the Pagans*, ed. and trans. R. W. Dyson, Cambridge Texts in the History of Political Thought (New York: Cambridge University Press, 1998), 634 (XV.1) and 632 (XIV.28).

[90]Martin Luther, "The Large Catechism," in *The Book of Concord: The Confessions of the Evangelical Lutheran Church*, ed. Robert Kolb and Timothy J. Wengert, trans. Charles P. Arand (Minneapolis: Fortress, 2000), 386.

[91]Ronald Dworkin, *Religion Without God* (Cambridge, MA: Harvard University Press, 2013), 1. Brendan Sweetman has observed, rightly I think, that though religions are a subset of

questions having to do with deep and imponderable matters" and "is comprehensive in nature."[92] Functionally (and constructively) defined, everyone has such a religion, and all of life is religious (whether or not people can articulate that comprehensive worldview). Either Jesus rules every square inch, to borrow again that favorite Kuyper line, or some other god does. Everyone has a god or gods, which is one reason why the first commandment forbids worshiping other gods and the second the making of an idol.

Admittedly, the argument against spiritual neutrality here comes from a distinctly Christian point of view, not from liberalism's "view from nowhere."[93] Christianity affirms that this is God's universe, not the philosopher's on his all-seeing mountaintop. Everyone stands somewhere *in relation to God*. Here, in fact, Christianity finds common cause with the late-twentieth-century communitarians who, in their critique of liberalism, affirmed that everyone was standing somewhere—embedded, as it were, in some cultural perspective, identity, and tradition of rationality and justice. Every person and belief is constituted by its social and historical location "all the way down."[94] Christianity's complementary claim, then, is that the triune God is the principle social Other who defines us all the way down, whether as friend or enemy. Which means, the "I" of the Pharisee Saul was transformed all the way down when he became the apostle Paul (see Gal 2:20), contra Rawls. One only need read the book of Acts to see how much Paul changed from Saul *politically*. Doesn't the book conclude with Paul under house arrest, not waging war against Christians?

If this is correct, secular liberalism does not offer some "neutral" brand of justice or "neutral" divide between public and private. It steps into the public square with a "covert religion,"[95] perhaps even a "liberal totalitarianism."[96] It offers a worldview that, like all worldviews, is grounded

---

worldviews, the two terms "can profitably be used interchangeably in the debate concerning religion and politics." Sweetman, *Why Politics Needs Religion*, 47.
[92] Africa v. Pennsylvania, 662 F.2d 1025, 1032 (3d Cir. 1981).
[93] Michael Walzer, following Thomas Nagel, uses the phrase "no particular point of view," and he uses this language to set up his own critique of liberalism in *Interpretation and Social Criticism* (Cambridge, MA: Harvard University Press, 1987), 5.
[94] Sandel, *Liberalism and the Limits of Justice*, 11; see also Taylor, *Sources of the Self*, 36.
[95] Reinhold Niebuhr, *The Children of Light and the Children of Darkness* (1944; repr., Chicago: University of Chicago Press, 2011), 131. Hat tip to Paul D. Miller for this reference.
[96] Robert Benne, *Good and Bad Ways to Think about Religion and Politics* (Grand Rapids: Eerdmans, 2010), 10.

in faith, says philosopher Brendan Sweetman. It depends in part upon beliefs for which it does not have conclusive evidence or proofs. "And so secularism is just as much a religion as any traditional religion."[97] Legal theorist Peter Berkowitz calls Rawls's theory a "liberal faith,"[98] a religion Rawls effectively means to impose. Indeed, this has been the critique of the Rawlsian project from the outset—that it inarticulately and inevitably relies on certain conceptions of metaphysics, morality and man.[99]

Communitarian Michael Sandel, a well-known critic of Rawlsian liberalism, applied this general critique to the questions of abortion or same-sex marriage, exposing their inevitable religious underpinnings. Concerning the former, he argues,

> The "pro-choice" position in the abortion debate is not really neutral on the underlying moral and theological question; it implicitly rests on the assumption that the Catholic Church's teaching on the moral status of the fetus—that it is a person from the moment of conception—is false.... The case for permitting abortion is not more neutral than the case for banning it. Both positions presupposed some answer to the underlying moral and religious controversy.[100]

Sandel's logic on the matter of same-sex marriage proceeds in the same vein: "The case for same-sex marriage can't be made on nonjudgmental grounds.... The underlying moral question is unavoidable."[101]

If Sandel's argument holds—and it strikes me as intuitive—it would seem that there is no such thing as genuine moral or spiritual neutrality in these kinds of political matters.[102] In fact, one could extend the argument beyond cultural moral flashpoints to issues that are less obviously morally

---

[97] Sweetman, *Why Politics Needs Religion*, 86; see also 18. See also Steven D. Smith, *The Disenchantment of Secular Discourse* (Cambridge, MA: Harvard University Press, 2010), 39.

[98] Peter Berkowitz, "John Rawls and The Liberal Faith," *Wilson Quarterly* (Spring 2002): 60-69.

[99] E.g., Alasdair MacIntyre, *Whose Justice? Which Rationality?* (London: Duckworth, 1988), 345; Taylor, *Sources of the Self*, 88-89; Sandel, *Liberalism and the Limits of Justice*, 133-83. For a defense of impartiality and a critique of some of the critics, see Barry, *Justice as Impartiality*, 119-38; also Kymlicka, *Liberalism, Community, and Culture*.

[100] Sandel, *Justice*, 251-52; see also Sandel, "Review," 1778; Sandel, *Democracy's Discontent*, 100-103.

[101] Sandel, *Justice*, 253-54; see also Sandel, "Review," 1786-87; Sandel, *Democracy's Discontent*, 103-8.

[102] See also Richard Ashcraft's helpful critique of the philosophical dominance of political theory, which is tied to his argument that all political theory is political and ideological. Ashcraft, "Political Theory and the Problem of Ideology," *Journal of Politics* 42, no. 3 (August 1980): 687-705; also Ashcraft, "On the Problem of Methodology and the Nature of Political Theory," *Political Theory* 3, no. 1 (February 1975): 5-25.

significant, such as funding for national parks or regulations on fishing licenses. One could argue that any and every position a person might adopt in the political sphere relies upon a certain conception of human beings, their rights and their obligations toward one another, creation and God. Notice, then, that I am proposing something stronger than "religion itself *influences* political commitments," as one Christian author puts it.[103] I am proposing that religion, broadly defined, *determines* or *yields* or *provides the worldview lens through which we come to hold* our political commitments—always. Cavanaugh, I think, is right. In the liberal West we've been trained to view religion and politics as occupying separate domains instead of as coterminous and mutually informing ones.

Now, any given political commitment might be driven by a person's double-minded commitment to several gods at once. And people of the same religion might disagree on a multitude of political decisions. The path from religious principle to policy application is often "complex and jagged."[104] But I would contest that our spiritual commitments, whether godly or ungodly, are always the drivers. How strange, then, was one Christian US senator's quip, "The Lord baptized me, not my voting record."[105] Did he mean his voting record was not free from error? Well enough. But it almost sounds as if he thought he could separate the senator and the baptizee, as if he became "unbaptized" when stepping onto the Senate floor to vote. Tocqueville understood better: "There is almost no human action, however particular one supposes it, that does not arise from a very general idea men have conceived of God, of his relations with the human race, of the nature of their souls, and of their duties toward those like them. One cannot keep these ideas from being the common source from which all the rest flow."[106] Hence, "Next to each religion is a political opinion that is joined to it by affinity."[107]

---

[103]Benne, *Good and Bad Ways*, 69 (italics mine).
[104]See ibid., 71.
[105]The statement is attributed to Oregon Senator Mark Hatfield by his former speech writer Aaron Menikoff in Menikoff's doctoral dissertation, "Piety and Politics: Baptist Social Reform in America, 1770-1860" (PhD diss., Southern Baptist Theological Seminary, 2008), vi.
[106]Alexis de Tocqueville, *Democracy in America*, trans. and ed. Harvey C. Mansfield and Delba Winthrop, 2 vols. (Chicago: University of Chicago Press, 2000), 2:417 (bk. 1, chap. 5).
[107]Tocqueville, *Democracy in America*, 1:275 (bk. 2, chap. 9).

Yet what shall we say about those laws whose content do not intrinsically tied to any one religion? For instance, political and legal theorist Jeremy Waldron wonders if it is possible to "bracket out the religious content" of something like the prohibition against murder. The content of the sixth commandment, he observes, "might be conceived of as issued by any number of commanders (and by commanders of quite different kinds)."[108] As such, we could say there is no intrinsic connection between the content of the law and its purpose or issuer. Perhaps, then, we could consider it to be neutral between various religions. Few people, after all, would say that a law prohibiting murder "establishes religion."

The problem is, this whole argument presumes to speak from a "view from nowhere"—as if we can ethically measure murder apart from any prior commitments about humanity, God, the moral universe and so forth. I would propose that a law against murder does "establish religion." First of all, it establishes the Christian religion because, from a Christian perspective, the law against murder is intimately tied to the image of God in humanity (Gen 9:6; a point acknowledged by Waldron). And such a law simultaneously establishes every other religion that likewise prohibits murder. What a law against murder represents, therefore, is not neutrality but the overlap of any number of religions. Religion hasn't left the public square at least with this law. It's there with multiple faces on—a détente between my God and yours.

If all of life is religious, and *some* god or idol rules every square inch of it, it would seem that inside the public square there is only religious overlap and religious imposition, as suggested in the introduction. The public square is nothing more or less than a battleground of gods, each vying to push the levers of power in its favor. Which means, from one perspective, there are no truly secular states, only pluralistic ones.

## A Broader Political Conceptuality

Matching this broader conception of religion is a broader conception of politics. Like the perspective that would say all of life is religious, some political scientists adopt an expansive view of politics that encompasses all

---

[108]Jeremy Waldron, *God, Locke, and Equality: Christian Foundations of Locke's Political Thought* (New York: Cambridge University Press, 2002), 45-46.

of life. "Politics is everywhere," says one; "no realm of life is immune to relations of conflict and power." Politics in this broader conception is not limited to the institutions of state but instead is "concerned with the struggle over the control and distribution of power across a whole range of sites."[109] Art is political. Sport is political. Family dynamics are political. All of life, it would seem, is political, as in Thomas Mann's famous line quoted earlier. Another political scientist puts it like this: "Politics is a universal and pervasive aspect of human behavior and may be found wherever two or more human beings are in engaged in some collective activity, whether formal or informal, public or private."[110] In this conception, politics is not limited to the domain of the state but is viewed as a process—namely, the process of organizing people, resources and power, whether or not the institutions of public-wide and coercive governance are directly involved.[111]

This broader conceptuality has animated feminist and minority theorists for decades, which has led to critiques of liberalism analogous to Sandel's. The feminist complaint has been that the liberal's "private sphere," which is supposedly pre- or nonpolitical, effectively excludes from the public domain so-called domestic matters like sexuality and family relations that largely affect women—and to the great detriment of women: "The classification of the family as private has frequently worked to hide abuse and domination within familial relations, thereby shielding them and placing them beyond 'political' scrutiny or legal intervention."[112] Just as the Rawlsian liberal uses the excuse of neutrality to exclude moral and spiritual values from the public square while quietly relying upon his or her own, so the feminist and minority theorist charges the liberal with doing the same in the matters of gender or ethnic particularity. In the liberal's attempt to ascend to the realm of universal justice, he or she must ask the woman, the black, the Jew to leave behind those things that make their groups distinct. The liberal's demand to

---

[109] Judith Squires, "Politics Beyond Boundaries: A Feminist Perspective," in *What Is Politics?*, ed. Adrian Leftwich (Cambridge: Polity Press, 2004), 120.

[110] Adrian Leftwich, "The Political Approach to Human Behaviour: People, Resources and Power," in Leftwich, *What Is Politics?*, 100.

[111] Adrian Leftwich, "Thinking Politically: On the Politics of Politics," in Leftwich, *What Is Politics?*, 13-14; also Leftwich, "Political Approach," 101.

[112] Squires, "Politics Beyond Boundaries," 129. Will Kymlicka provides a helpful overview of the feminist political theory, particularly as it intersects with liberalism in *Contemporary Political Philosophy: An Introduction* (Oxford: Clarendon Press, 1990), 238-92.

keep such particularities in the private sphere is criticized, understandably, as an ideological and political ploy to normalize the dominant group's own preferences.[113] Yet ironically, the division between the inner and outer person is now switched from classical liberalism. The Rawlsian (or Kantian) liberal is said to stand for objective reason, which excludes any mention of the body and outer person. The feminist and minority theorist, however, feels discriminated against for not being able to bring considerations of body and difference into the public square.[114]

Just as Cavanaugh observed that political forces will define "religion" in order to yield a certain political arrangement, so all these critics of liberalism argue that the "nonpolitical" private is private because that is what various actors have decided to make private according to their worldview and religious or ideological commitments. Previous generations of Americans and Europeans might have placed legal restrictions on, say, abortion or homosexuality, while ignoring so-called domestic matters like child abuse or marital rape. But today the opposite is true.[115] Ironically, it is the political decisions of each era that make some matters political and some matters nonpolitical and private. "There is, in fact, nothing *more political* than the constant attempts to exclude certain types of issues from politics."[116] And any political philosophy that says otherwise is being political itself.[117]

Turning our gaze to the domain of the church, can we ever say the church is "apolitical"? During the apartheid era, the Church of England in South Africa (CESA) tried to. But as the Truth and Reconciliation Commission

---

[113] Iris Marion Young, *Justice and the Politics of Difference* (Princeton, NJ: Princeton University Press, 1990), 97. See also Carole Pateman, *The Sexual Contract* (Stanford, CA: Stanford University Press, 1988); Charles Wade Mills, *The Race Contract* (Ithaca, NY: Cornell University Press, 1997); Seyla Benhabib, ed., *Democracy and Difference: Contesting the Boundaries of the Political* (Princeton, NJ: Princeton University Press, 1996).

[114] Iris Marion Young writes, "When the dominant culture defines some groups as different, as the Other, the members of those groups are imprisoned in their bodies. Dominant discourse defines them in terms of bodily characteristics, and constructs those bodies as ugly, dirty, defiled, impure, contaminated, or sick. . . . Modern philosophy and science established unifying, controlling reason in opposition to and mastery over the body, and then identified some groups with reason and others with the body." Young, *Justice and the Politics of Difference*, 124, 125.

[115] Minogue, *Politics*, 5.

[116] David Held and Adrian Leftwich as quoted in Squires, "Politics Beyond Boundaries," 121 (italics original). Disputed in Rawls, *Political Liberalism*, 484n91. See also Benhabib, *Democracy and Difference*.

[117] See Ashcraft, "Political Theory"; Ashcraft, "Problem of Methodology."

afterward observed, "Declaring itself 'apolitical,'" CESA "failed to adequately understand the suffering of our many black members who were victims of apartheid." The pretence of neutrality allowed CESA "to be misled into accepting a social, economic and political system that was cruel and oppressive.... The fears of white church members made them vulnerable to propaganda, leading them into sins of omission."[118] CESA's political "neutrality" effectively functioned as an endorsement of the status quo. It was nothing if not political.

So with the antebellum advocates of the church's spirituality. Senate candidate Stephen Douglass claimed in 1858 to be an agnostic on slavery, saying he did not care whether it "was voted up or voted down." His opponent, Abraham Lincoln, responded that a man can claim to be politically neutral "who does not see anything wrong in slavery, but no man can logically say it who does see a wrong in it; because no man can logically say he does not care whether a wrong is voted up or down." In other words, the Lincoln-Douglass debate was not finally about slavery, observed Michael Sandel, but about "whether to bracket a moral controversy for the sake of political agreement," which is impossible, both Sandel and Lincoln concluded.[119]

A number of scholars, including Hart, have sought to rehabilitate the antebellum advocates of spirituality.[120] The trouble is, their arguments for spirituality were deeply political. We saw above that Benjamin Palmer hoped the 1861 Presbyterian General Assembly would affirm "the purely spiritual character of the Church," but he used his 1860 Thanksgiving Day sermon to convince his congregation "to conserve and to perpetuate the institution of domestic slavery as now existing." Speaking against those who "intermeddled" with the South's affairs, he declared, "We know better than others that every attribute of their [African American] character fits them for dependence and servitude.... No calamity can befall them greater than the

---

[118]"Faith Communities and Apartheid: Report Prepared for the Truth and Reconciliation Commission by the Research Institute on Christianity in South Africa," March 1998, 3.2.24, http://web.uct.ac.za/depts/ricsa/commiss/trc/trcr_ch3.htm.

[119]Sandel, "Review," 1779-80; also Sandel, *Democracy's Discontent*, 21-23.

[120]E.g., Graham, *Kingdom Not of the World*; Hart, *Mother Kirk*, chap. 3. Two works that indict the spirituality doctrine for its connection to slavery include Ernst Trice Thompson, *The Spirituality of the Church: A Distinctive Doctrine of the Presbyterian Church in the United State* (Richmond: John Knox, 1961), and Jack P. Maddex, "From Theocracy to Spirituality: The Southern Presbyterian Reversal on Church and State," *Journal of Presbyterian History* 54, no. 4 (1976): 438-57.

loss of that protection they enjoy under this patriarchal system."[121] Palmer then went on to tell his parishioners that "in this great struggle, we defend the cause of God and religion. The abolition spirit is undeniably atheistic."[122] The point isn't just that Palmer was being inconsistent with his spirituality doctrine, which he was. The larger question is raised: Could it be that every argument for a spiritual church is inescapably political, every claim to political neutrality a kind of politics?

It does seem that one's moral and religious stance on an issue like slavery must inevitably affect one's political stance—that an "otherworldly" position will always have "this worldly" consequences. Christians surely don't want to separate "what God thinks" from "how to live." This would nominalize religion, as two-kingdoms critics have often suggested.

No doubt, there is some space between the claim that churches could not help but adopt a political posture over issues like apartheid or slavery and the claim that all that a church does and is, is political. Besides, one wonders if this all-of-life definition of politics is too broad to be useful. Is there no difference between the activity of an artist, a preacher and a congressman?

That said, these examples do make the point that there is a certain vagueness about where political activity "happens." Does a sermon on abortion or tax policy qualify as a "political activity"? Or two members discussing these things privately? What about a church picketing a private abortion clinic? Or a church that preaches that Jesus is Lord, which in turn impels church members to picket? The rest of the book will be necessary for us to understand the political nature of the church, but hopefully it is evident that neither politics nor religion is so easily compartmentalized.

## How Religious Freedom Destroys Religious Freedom

Collapsing the separation between politics and religion no doubt raises questions about the cost to religious freedom. And to be sure, there is a

---

[121]Reprinted in Thomas Cary Johnson, *The Life and Letters of Benjamin Morgan Palmer* (Richmond, VA: Presbyterian Committee of Publication, 1906), 210-11.
[122]Johnson, *Life and Letters*, 212. According to Harry S. Stout, Palmer, in the ensuing years, abandoned all pretentions to a separation of church and state and argued for the establishment of the Confederacy's civil religion—what Stout characterizes as "nation worship." Harry S. Stout, *Upon the Altar of the Nation: A Moral History of the Civil War* (New York: Penguin Books, 2006), 274-75, 415-16.

cost to abandoning liberalism's "view from nowhere" and adopting a distinctly Christian perspective: it deprives us, to some measure, of the traditional liberal formulations for religious freedom. Then again, it may be that the liberal formulation for religious freedom itself is the greater enemy of religious freedom.

The doctrine of religious freedom that, we said earlier, represents a consilience of Enlightenment and dissenting Protestant thought is precisely a formulation that depends on a view from nowhere. It stands here, of course, for the sake of public accessibility and in order to claim impartiality between competing religious demands.

The trouble is, if there really is no such thing as a view from nowhere, and if the liberal doctrine of religious freedom continues to pretend standing there, "religious freedom" is not necessarily free. It is a way of cloaking the gods of the moment in the pretend garb of neutrality. Now, there is an account for religious tolerance that we can and should give *as Christians*, and chapters four and six will offer just such an account. Stay tuned. But one cannot expect this to be persuasive to non-Christians, so it's worth taking a moment to better understand the difficulty with the traditional formulation,[123] three of which are worth highlighting. First, government is very much in the business of binding whole persons, including their consciences. As we'll see in chapter four, God established governments in Genesis 9 precisely because humanity's consciences had become unbound. A person might be conscientiously convicted that a nation's immigration laws are unfair, but he or she is still obligated to obey them, even while simultaneously working to change them. His or her conscientious objection is no measure of the law's legitimacy. An act of disobedience by the Christian can only be justified by demonstrating that the law is not *just* or *right*, not simply that one has a conscientious objection to it.

Second, appealing to the inviolability of the conscience as this publicly accessible stand-in for religion has the ironic effect of removing God from the doctrine of religious freedom, which is why I keep saying it stands on a view from nowhere. In public terms, it invests the conscience with final

---

[123]See Hauerwas's provocative chapter, "The Politics of Freedom: Why Freedom of Religion Is a Subtle Temptation," in *After Christendom? How the Church Is to Behave If Freedom, Justice, and a Christian Nation Are Bad Ideas* (Nashville: Abingdon, 1991), 69-92.

authority. After all, the doctrine must be something both believers and unbelievers can agree to. The two groups cannot agree to God's existence, but they can agree upon their desire for a free conscience. As such, God is removed from the religious-freedom contract, objectively speaking, in spite of whatever pious subjective motivations the believer may quietly harbor. The liberal doctrine of religious freedom, to switch our spatial metaphors, possesses a foundation "from below," not "from above."[124]

Third, the doctrine of religious freedom becomes unaccountable to any standard of right, divine or otherwise. What's to ensure that its philosophical services will be hired only by upstanding and virtuous monotheistic religions? What's to prevent other parties and interests from employing it for ends besides the worship of God? Defenders quickly assert that, of course, no one advocates religious freedom or conscience "without limits." But this misses the point. Where will those limits come from? Establishing limits requires some worldview or religion to draw them, which means that someone's religion must work covertly in the background.[125] And such was the case with the seventeenth- and eighteenth-century classical liberals. They had the backstops of natural law, or something like it. But in their public and legal documents they invested final authority in the individual conscience,

---

[124]In saying this, I do not deny that accounts for the freedom of conscience "from above" can be given—John Locke's entire project in *The Letter Concerning Toleration* and *Two Treatises* perhaps being the most obvious. Christian political theorist Greg Forster presents a fascinating (and I assume historically accurate) picture of Locke as grounding government and religious toleration not merely in consent but in divine law: "Locke's account of natural law is an attempt to ground political action in a source of divine moral authority . . . that can be recognized by members of conflicting religious denominations" (Forster, *John Locke's Politics*, 29; also 167-93). The difficulty for Locke and Forster, simply as a matter of realpolitik, is that it's nearly impossible to imagine a publicly accessible social contract or account of religious freedom today that excludes unbelievers (Locke) or that is grounded in divine law (Forster wouldn't exclude athiests like Locke; ibid., 176-77), as suggested in Laycock's comment above. Indeed, less than a hundred years after Locke, Jefferson and Leland presented the inevitable evolution of Locke's idea by speaking of their political indifference to their twenty gods or no gods, also noted above. As such, my claim that "freedom of conscience" in Western democracies comes "from below" is first of all a descriptive claim, based on the assumption that a godless doctrine of religious freedom stands the greatest chance of broad public accessibility in our secular age. I also think there are theoretical difficulties in Locke's project, which I will address in chapter four.

[125]Stanley Hauerwas writes, "Where one has separation of church and state it is often assumed that Christianity has been disestablished. The irony is, however, that Christian self-understanding of legal disestablishment presumed the continued social and cultural hegemony of generalized Christian presuppositions. You do not need an established church when you think everyone more or less believes what you believe." Hauerwas, *After Christendom?*, 25.

which contradicts any external source of law or *right*. That is, supplanting "religion" with "conscience" because it provides a publicly accessible common ground undermines any backstop you hope your religion might provide. What then happens when all backstops "from above" are removed because the consensus over what they should be has evaporated, as is the case in contemporary liberalism and the Western public of today? Answer: "religious freedom" or the "free conscience" begins to protect all kinds of things that the original architects never intended and to prosecute the architects for some of their religion-driven practices.

To use a famous example from the United States, the Supreme Court affirmed in 1992 that "men and women of good conscience can disagree" about abortion, and that the right to abortion is grounded in "the right to define one's concept of existence, of meaning, of the universe, and of the mystery of human life." The court, in other words, fooled itself into believing that it could refuse to "mandate our own moral code."[126] In 2003, the Massachussettes Supreme Court then borrowed this same self-deceiving language to establish same-sex marriage.[127] Christians, for their part, turn around and argue against nationally sponsored health care programs that cover abortion, or against court-ordered demands to provide services to same-sex weddings, claiming that these requirements burden their conscience. But in so doing they merely pit one conscience's burdens against another's. The "right to define one's concept of existence" *is* nothing other than a contemporary way of saying "freedom of conscience." And why should the believer's conscience count for more? In other words, the terms of debate surrounding abortion and same-sex marriage make them look like the unintended but DNA-tested children of the original consilience between Protestant and Enlightenment thought, as if they were a late-blooming inevitability from the time of the American Founders.[128] Abortion, by these standards, should be protected as a religious freedom; same-sex marriage as

---

[126] Planned Parenthood of Southeastern Pennsylvania et al. v. Robert P. Casey, Governor of Pennsylvania et al., 505 U.S. 833 (1991).

[127] Hillary Goodridge v. Department of Public Health, 440 Mass. 309 (2003). Michael Sandel connects these court cases in Sandel, *Justice*, 256-60, esp. note 29. For his account of the development of the doctrine of neutrality in the high court, see *Democracy's Discontent*, chaps. 2-4.

[128] See Smith, *Rise and Decline*, 47.

a right of conscience. As stated in the introduction, book after book proposes "going back" to the Founders or to Locke as a solution to the culture wars. Yet it's not clear to me we have ever left them. Instead, we're seeing precisely what Founders like Washington and Adams predicted would happen should their philosophy of government be inhabited by an unreligious and unvirtuous people.[129] The so-called consilience or gentlemen's agreement between Protestant and Englightenment thought, which presents itself to our imaginations as Baptist preacher Isaac Backus shaking hands with Thomas Jefferson, should be replaced by a different metaphor: spoiled, substance-abusing, fast-living children of wealthy parents who foolishly squander their parents' inheritance.

It is true that a Christian remains "free" in many places today because there remain many places of consensus in today's Western public squares. But eventually political decisions must also be made in places beyond the boundaries of that consensus. And there, *someone's* gods must prevail. Which is to say, classical liberalism's "freedom of religion," when pushed outside the boundaries of consensus, must remove the sheep's clothing and so prove itself a fake.[130] It lasts only as long as the many gods of a nation do not require anything outside the boundaries of the liberal's religion. So Jefferson and Leland can bluff indifference as to whether their neighbors have twenty gods or none, but they assume their neighbors live within the bounds of their own worldview and spiritual commitments, and that their neighbors do not extol stealing as virtue and paying one's taxes as vice. What a nation's constitution and laws represent is an amalgam of competing values and religious commitments, cobbled together over time by compromise and negotiation. In the battleground of gods called the public square, the law books present a record of which gods won a majority when the vote was taken or which could secure a high court decision.

In short, the traditional liberal formulation simply demands too much for the conscience and too little by way of foundations. Christians will like what it produces only when the vast majority of citizens inhabit a

---

[129] See Os Guinness, *A Free People's Suicide: Sustainable Freedom and the American Future* (Downers Grove, IL: InterVarsity Press, 2012), 93-129.
[130] See Ross Douthat, "Defining Religious Liberty Down," *New York Times*, July 29, 2012.

broadly Christian value system. It's true from a biblical perspective that true worship cannot be coerced, and a biblical perspective on religious tolerance insists on carving out an area for the conscience to freely respond to God, as we will see in subsequent chapters. But this free conscience must remain hemmed in by a concept of *right* and not just *rights*. To argue that "the conscience is entitled to remain free" is an overstatement. It invests too much authority in the individual. It presumes too much about the rightness of the conscience's claim. And in the end it will cave in on itself and undermine true religion because it's accountable to nothing but the whims of whatever ideologies rule the day. All this is the result of asking the publicly accessible "conscience" to stand in for "religion." This trade works just fine in a nation of believers and relatively biblically virtuous people. But in a nation of believers and unbelievers, the unattached, unaccountable conscience will be employed to legitimize the freedom of various religions (institutionally defined) only as long as the consciences of a nation's decision makers value them. When a nation's decision makers decide that the traditional (substantivist) institutional religions are a threat to liberty or equality or tolerance, they will banish them, first from the public square, then from the marketplace, and perhaps, in partial ways, from the home ("No, you may not indoctrinate your children"). Even the religiously sympathetic Charles Taylor seems to succumb to today's reigning ideology. He argues with coauthor Jocelyn Maclure that

> an education in tolerance and pluralism will in certain circumstances justify the denial of parents' requests for exemption [from various forms of public school instruction in sex education, ethics, religious culture or civic education] and the exposure of their children to subject matter at odds with the beliefs transmitted at home. That sort of restriction on freedom of conscience and parental authority is reasonable and justified.[131]

Notice, Taylor and Maclure are not arguing for an utterly unconstrained conscience. Rather, they are arguing that conscience should be constrained (even inside the family unit) by modern conceptions of tolerance and pluralism, two ideas which, in turn, are grounded in nothing other

---

[131] Maclure and Taylor, *Secularism and Freedom of Conscience*, 102.

than the equality of human beings and the demand to respect their free consciences! Inside this tautological merry-go-round, providing the true backstop, are the reigning ideologies of the day—we want to do what we want to do. It might even be a bill of rights, that very thing which is supposed to protect a nation from the tyranny of the majority, that will be employed to suppress the conscience for the sake of conscience. In the end, we will find that "religious freedom is being subverted by . . . religious freedom itself (as currently understood), which through its commitments to equality and neutrality and secular government has effectively deprived itself of its historical reasons for being."[132] A nation of citizens who insist that their consciences must always be free is a nation that will eventually have little patience for the incursions of the minority's religion in public or private.

There is a logic to the persecution of Christians throughout history, and it's easy to see once we recognize that politics and religion are inseparable. A people's strongest desires—the desires they refuse to let go of—reveal their worship. And people will always fight for their idols and gods, their objects of worship. Christianity, then, will be opposed in precisely those places it opposes a people's particular idols. Any Christian who has shared the gospel with a friend knows this much. So it is in the public square. Churches do not need to take up arms against the state in order to pose a threat to the state; they only need to oppose the gods upon which a nation's political and economic institutions depend. And every nation has them.

To oppose unabated sexual freedom in the democratic West today, for instance, is to condemn one of the West's favorite altars of worship. What religious conservatives have been slow to recognize is, sexual freedom *is* religious freedom in a pagan culture, which is increasingly our own. (To understand this equation phenomenologically one need only consider the tight connection between religion and sexuality in everything from the Old Testament's description of idolatry as harlotry, to the historically common practice of shrine prostitution, to brain chemistry, to the typological connection in the Bible between marriage and salvation.) When a nation bows to Ashtoreth, Aphrodite, Hollywood heroines, or pornography, Christians

---

[132]Smith, *Rise and Decline*, 168.

who oppose sexual freedom just might expect to be excommunicated from the sacred public square. And they will be excluded for violating the very principle that grounds their own doctrine of religious freedom: the right of the free conscience.

Let me make three final qualifications to this discussion on religious freedom, the first two of which will be picked up later in the book. First, Christians no doubt possess a duty to be faithful to their consciences, yet I would argue that they possess a higher duty to be right. After all, consciences in the Bible can be misguided and must be instructed. Luther's loyalty to his conscience wouldn't be celebrated by Christians today had he been wrong. What if Arius had made a "Here I Stand" speech in 325? Would Christians celebrate him, too? We will drill down on the question of conscience in chapter three. And in chapter four we'll discover a deeper debate relevant to this whole conversation between "justice as right" and "justice as inherent rights."

Second, I am *not* saying Christians should abandon their support for religious freedom. Others, like the agnostic Koppelman, argue that we should protect religion not because it is interchangeable with the conscience but because it is a distinct societal good[133]—like marriage is a good to be protected, even though not everyone is married. Again, I will present a distinctively Christian formulation for religious tolerance in chapters four and six.

Third, there may be good pragmatic reasons, at any given moment of debate in the public square, for employing the traditional liberal formulations.[134] The point is, this political calculus, like all pragmatic calculuses,

---

[133] Koppelman, *Defending American Religious Neutrality*, see esp. 120-65. See also Robert P. George, *Conscience and Its Enemies: Confronting the Dogmas of Liberal Secularism* (Wilmington, DE: ISI Books, 2013), 118-25.

[134] In *Conscience and Its Enemies*, George builds a case for religious freedom on natural law, both by pointing to the good of religion (see previous note) and by seeking to protect the conscience. He seeks to avoid some of the critiques I offered above by distinguishing between the modern liberal idea of conscience as "writer of permission slips" and an older concept of conscience as "stern monitor," which must be instructed concerning its obligations and matters of human flourishing. I agree with this distinction. The trouble is, his language places this formulation into an "inherent rights" framework: "The right of conscience is a right to do what one judges oneself to be under an obligation to do" (112). Notice, the obligation transposes into a right, which allows George to emphasize the "rights" language so comfortable to Westerners. And I think this is fair so far as it goes. Obligations can be construed to entail rights. But the real concept doing work here to provide a backstop to freedom's limitations is the obligation, an

needs to involve a cost-benefit analysis, and that's hard to calculate if we are blind to the costs. To return to Charles Taylor's observation about the cross-purposes of the older liberal-communitarian debate, it is fine to build a political philosophy geared for *advocacy* in the public square, as liberalism is, but a Christian must take care not to adopt any *description* of the moral universe other than a biblical one.[135]

## Conclusion

Moving forward, both the narrow definition of politics that focuses on the public-wide and coercive power of governance and the broader perspective that incorporates all of life will be useful to keep in mind, particularly as we move in chapter three to incorporate a theological perspective of politics. For the time being, we have discovered a few reasons to be suspicious of liberalism's neutrality toward religion and the so-called spiritual church's neutrality toward politics. Chapters three through six will argue that the activities of the public square are always undergirded by some spiritual or religious worldview and that everything taught inside a church building has political meaning because the church is a political assembly. The two circles of political and religious realities, I hope to show, are not just partially overlapping, as posited by the soft-separationists, but completely and wholly overlapping. Politics and religion are distinct things, but they are coterminous, as if the blue lens of politics is laid completely on top of the red lens of religion or spirituality so that all we see is purple.

Does that mean I am arguing for theonomy, or a fusion of church and state together ruling all of life? By no means. The church and the state are separate institutions, with separate authorities, mandates and jurisdictions.

---

obligation determined by what is *right*. And the question that remains outstanding for George's natural-law approach is whether he can convince people that they have rights, grounded in obligations, which in turn are established by . . . well, not by God as such, but by their own rational sense of human flourishing. It's not clear to me that some collective sense of human flourishing is sufficient to ground a nation's morality, either philosophically or practically. Still, for the purposes of advocacy, George is exactly right to pursue arguments like his that mean to convince people who possess different worldviews. Any challenge I might offer him would be a prudential and strategic one—that is, will this stategy really work for the purposes of political persuasion?

[135]See Charles Taylor, "Cross-Purposes: The Liberal-Communitarian Debate," in *Liberalism and the Moral Life*, ed. N. Rosenblum (Cambridge, MA: Harvard University Press, 1989).

What exactly is an institution? I believe the answer to that question is so important for answering the main question of this book ("What is the local church?") that we will spend a significant portion of the next chapter considering it.

What I will ultimately argue is that a local church's very existence is bound up in one kind of institutional authority (the keys), while the state's existence is bound up in another kind of institutional authority (the sword). All people "worship" in everything they do, whether in public or private. What institutions do, to oversimplify, is proscribe and prescribe which activities appropriately express that worship in different domains. God might command me to worship him in eating and drinking (1 Cor 10:31), but some of the older women in my church would tell me not to worship God *that way* when I want to bring my coffee cup into the church pews! As I stated in the introduction, churches should strive to remain neutral on questions outside of their institutional jurisdiction, and governments the same.

But neutrality obtains not to the categories of "religion" or "politics" but to activities that fall beyond the church's and the state's institutional remits.[136] Speaking of political or religious neutrality is an overreach, even a category confusion, like pointing to a constitutional provision for free speech and concluding that the government must be neutral toward "speech" in general, when in fact there is some speech that it restricts and some that it permits. Figure 1.4 offers the perspective of this book. It attempts to combine the political sensibilities of the neo-Kuyperians, the Augustinians, the theonomists and the communitarians (represented by the fact that there is one circle) with the institutional sensibilities of the liberals and the two-kingdoms advocates (represented by the separate lines of jurisdiction).

In short, we must not confuse separation of church and state with the separation of religion and politics.[137]

---

[136]For useful discussions on different kinds of neutrality, see Koppelman, *Defending American Religious Neutrality*, 15-26, as well as the critique of Koppelman in Smith, *Rise and Decline*, 133-36.

[137]Benne (*Good and Bad Ways*, 55-56) says the same thing, but he is ever so slightly more separationist than I am.

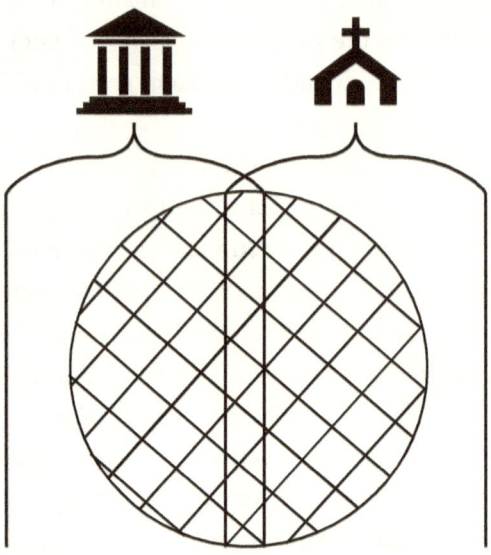

**Figure 1.4.** The perspective of this book

In the final analysis, Christian theology's attempt to reconcile religion and politics might benefit from a Jewish perspective. The Jewish experience of moving in and out of statehood has required theorists of Jewish political thought to grapple with exactly this relationship between religion and politics. Michael Walzer, for instance, has observed that "the association of politics with the state is pervasive in Western thought," but still, "politics is pervasive, with or without state sovereignty."[138] He demonstrates this by pointing to the Jewish communities of the diaspora who, since the Babylonian exile of the sixth century BC, had to organize a common life, albeit under non-Jewish governments, in which political decisions were made about membership in the Jewish community, distributions of power, the enforcement of laws or the taxation of members. "So there arose," he writes, "a tradition of thought, theological and legal rather than autonomously political in form, but political in substance nonetheless. Its point of departure

---

[138]Michael Walzer, "Introduction: The Jewish Political Tradition," in *The Jewish Political Tradition*, ed. Michael Walzer, Menachem Lorberbaum, Noam J. Zohar and Yair Lorberbaum, vol. 1, *Authority* (New Haven, CT: Yale University Press, 2000), xxi.

is always the Hebrew Bible, understood as the revealed word of God."[139] Of course, this exilic brand of Jewish politics did not occur in national bodies capable of making decisions explicitly binding upon all the Jews of a geographic region—there was no state institution. Instead, their politics were discussed in independent assemblies. Walzer writes,

> The most important political structure of the exile emerged only gradually, in western Europe and North Africa: this was the *kahal*, a small autonomous or semiautonomous community (ordinary *kehillot* ranged from ten families to a few hundred in size, although by the early modern period there were much larger urban centers). The miracle of Jewish politics is the persistence of this formation over many centuries—a common regime with a common legal system, reiterated across a wide range of countries, in very different circumstances, without the benefit of (and sometimes in opposition to) state power.[140]

Before the modern state of Israel was established in 1948, these small bodies constituted the body politic of the Jewish "nation," and they were the place where Jewish politics occurred: "The *kahal* is both historically and symbolically important; it is the polis of exilic Jewry—the actual site of an untheorized and undervalued politics that is nonetheless vigorously enacted and endlessly debated."[141]

The goal of this book is to present a fuller vision of God's political authority, one that contains *within itself* both governments and churches, the latter of which are the *polis* of exilic Christianity.

---

[139] Ibid., xxii.
[140] Ibid., xxix. Daniel J. Elazar and Stuart A. Cohen make a similar point in *The Jewish Polity: Jewish Political Organization from Biblical Times to the Present* (Bloomington: Indiana University Press, 1985), 11-12, 15.
[141] Walzer, "Introduction," xxx; Elazar and Cohen, *Jewish Polity*, 12; Noam J. Zohar similarly writes, "Eventually, the Jews established what we might call a *social boundary*. . . . This was the setting in which the institution of *giyyur* . . . was born: a formal procedure deemed both necessary and sufficient for a non-Jew to become a Jew. To the extent that non-sovereign Jewish communities were political units, the *giyyur* procedure—conferring membership in the community—can be seen as akin to naturalization." Zohar, "Contested Boundaries: Visions of a Shared World," in *Law, Politics, and Morality in Judaism*, ed. Michael Walzer (Princeton, NJ: Princeton University Press, 2006), 89.

TWO

# What Is an Institution?

IF WE'RE GOING TO call the local church a political institution, we need to get a good grip on the word *political*. Chapter one began this investigation. But before pressing further, there is another concept to get our heads around, and that is that idea of an institution.

The concept of an institution is both misunderstood and maligned in many theological conversations, particularly in conversations pertaining to the doctrine of the church. Yet one of my side purposes in this book is to help theologians and Christians generally recover the ability to "think institutionally," as political scientist Hugh Heclo has put it (discussed below). In fact, I will argue that we need to learn how to read our Bibles institutionally.

The kind of institution we are particularly interested in here is the institution of a body politic or a political community. Christians in the present-day West are happy to describe their churches with the word *koinonia* or communion, but they become skittish about adding any *politeia* to their *koinonia*. Doing so institutionalizes that communion, and that sounds unsavory. Institutions are cold, impersonal, bureaucratic. The communion of the church, on the other hand, is about love. And is not the triune God himself a communion of love? So give me spirituality, but don't give me institutional religion.[1]

---

[1] I have argued elsewhere that such views among Christians demonstrate our dependency on an eighteenth- and nineteenth-century Romantic worldview. See my *The Church and the Surprising Offense of God's Love: Reintroducing the Doctrines of Church Membership and Discipline* (Wheaton, IL: Crossway, 2010), 45-57.

Interestingly, a "new institutionalism" has emerged among political scientists and sociologists over the last three decades. And it is a revival that is instructive for our ability to discern what an institutional church is in the pages of Scripture. The goal of this chapter, like the last one, is to develop a vocabulary, a prolegomenon, only here it is for institutions. First, we will glance at what my institutional emphasis is set against—namely, a larger relational turn in theology and church life generally. Second, we will attempt to understand what an institution is, at least as it is described by contemporary political scientists. Third, we will attempt to understand more carefully what a body politic or political community is. Finally, we will offer a few tentative hermeneutical suggestions for reading the Bible institutionally.

## COMMUNITY AND THE RELATIONAL TURN[2]

The topic of institutions, as far as I can tell, is not a popular one in theological circles. Instead, theological writers have contended for at least two centuries that churches need to be deinstitutionalized. Liberal Protestants have called for "more community" and "less institutional authority" ever since Friedrich Schleiermacher borrowed language from the Romantics to pit religious experience against what he viewed as the Enlightenment's rationalistic formulations of doctrine.[3] About the same time, an anti-institutional Romantic renewal movement began in earnest among Roman Catholic writers influenced by Schleiermacher and others, a revolution that would eventually culminate in a number of changes made in Vatican II.[4] The mainline Protestants and the Catholics worked within their respective traditions, to be sure, but their doctrines of salvation and the church began to

---

[2]Portions of this section have been adapted from Leeman, *Church and the Surprising Offense*, 26-27, 130-34.

[3]See Roger Haight, *Christian Community in History*, vol. 2, *Comparative Ecclesiology* (New York: Continuum, 2005), 312-13.

[4]Among them, Johann Adam Möhler in particular helped inaugurate a "conceptual revolution" in the doctrine of the church among Catholics in the 1820s with his *Unity in the Church or the Principle of Catholicism: Presented in the Spirit of the Church Fathers of the First Three Centuries* (Washington, DC: Catholic University of America Press, 1995), 355. See also Dennis Doyle's helpful overview, *Communion Ecclesiology* (Maryknoll, NY: Orbis, 2000), and Avery Cardinal Dulles's "The Church as Mystical Communion," in *Models of the Church*, expanded ed. (New York: Image Books, 2002), 39-54. Following after the work of Johann Adam Möhler, key thinkers in the last century of Roman Catholic communion ecclesiology that are commonly cited include Charles Journet, Yves Congar, Henri de Lubac and Jean-Marie Tillard. Both John Paul II and Benedict XVI also made significant contributions.

approximate one another largely because they "share in the same post-Enlightenment Romantic renewal."[5] What resulted is what is sometimes referred to as *communio* or communion ecclesiology. Communion ecclesiology "emphasizes the element of spiritual fellowship or communion between human beings and God in contrast to juridical approaches that overemphasize the institutional and legal aspects of the Church.... In contrast with overly institutional approaches, communion ecclesiology places its primary emphasis on relationships."[6]

Of course the communio impulse is not restricted to those who have been influenced by Romanticism. The neo-orthodox critic of Schleiermacher Emil Brunner argued that "the *Ecclesia* of the New Testament ... is precisely *not* that which every 'church' is at least in part—an institution, a something. The Body of Christ is nothing other than a fellowship of persons ... where fellowship or *koinonia* signifies a common participation, a togetherness, a community life."[7] Conservative evangelicals, meanwhile, have harbored anti-institutional, "essentialist" impulses at least since George Whitefield found the Baptists and Presbyterians in America more amenable to his revival work than his own Anglicans.[8] And it crops up, understandably, whenever nominal Christianity and "cheap grace" become a concern within the church.

Over the last few decades a spate of books aimed at practitioners by evangelical and so-called post-evangelical writers that echo this same call for less institution and more community.[9] Some of them offer compelling

---

[5] Haight, *Christian Community in History*, 356; Doyle, *Communion Ecclesiology*, 23-37.
[6] Doyle, *Communion Ecclesiology*, 13; also Dulles, *Models of the Church*, 39-54. For a trenchant critique of communion ecclesiology, see John Webster, "The Church and the Perfection of God," in *The Community of the Word: Toward an Evangelical Ecclesiology*, ed. Mark Husbands and Daniel J. Treier (Downers Grove, IL: InterVarsity Press, 2005), 75-95; see also Matt Jenson and David Wilhite, *The Church: A Guide for the Perplexed* (New York: T&T Clark, 2010), 21-27, 51-57.
[7] Emil Brunner, *The Misunderstanding of the Church* (1952; repr., Cambridge: The Lutterworth Press, 2002), 10.
[8] A helpful survey of George Whitefield's effect on the evangelical ecclesiological consciousness can be found in Bruce Hindmarsh, "Is Evangelical Ecclesiology an Oxymoron? A Historical Perspective," in *Evangelical Ecclesiology: Reality or Illusion?*, ed. John G. Stackhouse (Grand Rapids: Baker, 2003), 15-37.
[9] Here's a sample of both academic and nonacademic works by evangelicals and post-evangelicals, chronologically listed, which, in varying degrees, call for a greater emphasis on community and less on institution: Colin E. Gunton, "The Church on Earth: The Roots of Community," in *On Being the Church: Essays on the Christian Community*, ed. Colin E. Gunton and Daniel W. Hardy (Edinburgh: T&T Clark, 1989), 48-80; David J. Bosch, *Transforming Mission: Paradigm Shifts in Theology*

and articulate visions, but these more careful volumes bring with them a slew of bastardized and populist works, such as George Barna's *Revolution*, which claims to lead a revolution of making local church involvement optional. The Romantic impulse to downplay doctrine for the sake of experience surges through some of these books as well.

In many respects, it is easy to applaud the renewed attention given to community and relationships among social science and theological writers. Amidst the hustle and bustle of modern urban and autonomous lives, everyone wonders how to "aid a process of healing the fragmentation which is so much a feature of our world."[10] Communitarianism is not the buzzword it was in the 1990s. Still, there is a larger movement here that is sometimes called the "relational turn," according to which the formerly peripheral matter of relationships comes into the substantive center of human existence (ontology).[11] We *are* our relationships and cannot divorce ourselves from them without an identity crisis.[12]

---

*of Mission* (Maryknoll, NY: Orbis, 1991), e.g., 50-51; Paul G. Hiebert, *Anthropological Reflections on Missiological Issues* (Grand Rapids: Baker Books, 1994), 107-36, 159-72; Kevin Giles, *What on Earth Is the Church: An Exploration in New Testament Theology* (1995; repr., Eugene, OR: Wipf & Stock, 2005), 8-22; Darrell L. Guder, ed., *Missional Church: A Vision for the Sending of the Church in North America* (Grand Rapids: Eerdmans, 1998), e.g., 80, 84, 93-94, 221-47; Darrell L. Guder, *The Continuing Conversion of the Church* (Grand Rapids: Eerdmans, 2000), 181-204; Craig Van Gelder, *The Essence of the Church: A Community Created by the Spirit* (Grand Rapids: Baker, 2000), 55-58, 74-75, 125, 157-58; Eddie Gibbs, *Church Next: Quantum Changes in How We Do Ministry* (Downers Grove, IL: InterVarsity Press, 2000), 65-91; Stanley Grenz, *The Social God and the Relational Self: A Trinitarian Theology of the Imago Dei* (Louisville, KY: Westminster John Knox, 2001), 331-36; Doug Pagitt, *Church Re-Imagined: The Spiritual Formation of People in Communities of Faith* (Grand Rapids: Zondervan, 2003), 23-31, 47-48; Stuart Murray, *Church After Christendom* (Milton Keynes, UK: Paternoster, 2004), 135-64; Reggie McNeal, *The Present Future: Six Tough Questions for the Church* (San Francisco: Jossey-Bass, 2003), 26-27, 34-36; Eddie Gibbs and Ryan K. Bolger, *Emerging Churches: Creating Community in Postmodern Cultures* (Grand Rapids: Baker, 2005), 89-115; Neil Cole, *Organic Church: Growing Faith Where Life Happens* (San Francisco: Jossey-Bass, 2005); Peter R. Holmes, *Trinity in Human Community: Exploring Congregational Life in the Image of the Social Trinity* (Milton Keynes, UK: Paternoster, 2006), 1-3; Dan Kimball, *They Like Jesus but Not the Church: Insights from Emerging Generations* (Grand Rapids: Zondervan, 2007), 73-95.

[10]Colin Gunton, *The One, The Three, and the Many: God, Creation, and the Culture of Modernity* (New York: Cambridge University Press, 1993), 7.

[11]For a brief overview of this turn, see F. LeRon Shults, *Reforming Theological Anthropology: After the Philosophical Turn to Relationality* (Grand Rapids: Eerdmans, 2003), 11-36; also Kevin Vanhoozer, *Remythologizing Theology: Divine Action, Passion, and Authorship* (New York: Cambridge University Press, 2010), 112-24; John Franke, "God Is Love: The Social Trinity and the Mission of God," in *Trinitarian Theology for the Church: Scripture, Community, Worship*, ed. Daniel J. Treier and David Lauber (Downers Grove, IL: InterVarsity Press, 2009), 111-17.

[12]Michael Sandel, *Liberalism and the Limits of Justice* (New York: Cambridge University Press, 1982), 179; Charles Taylor, *Sources of the Self* (Cambridge, MA: Harvard University Press, 1989), 27.

In theology, the significance of relationships (the dialectic of I and Thou) reorients every category of systematics.[13] It has been observed that

- God's very being is defined not by the substantive Greek categories of static being but by the fact that he is three persons in community;
- human persons bear a "relational analogy" to God's trinitarian community;
- love is a matter of "mutuality";
- sin is the breaking of community;
- Christ reconciles us to himself and restores us to a relationship with God;
- Christ also restores us to a relationship with his body, the church community; and
- the eschaton will sum up all things in our participation in the divine community.[14]

Perhaps a few concrete examples are sufficient to make the point. William Cavanaugh intentionally mimics Rousseau's famous opening sentence from the *Social Contract* ("Man was born free but is everywhere in chains") when he writes, "Humankind was created for communion, but is everywhere divided."[15] This principle then informs his interpretation of Scripture: "Cain's fratricide, the wickedness of Noah's generation, and the scattering of Babel can be understood only against the backdrop of the natural unity of the human race in the creation story of Genesis 1."[16] The emphasis falls not on breaking God's law but on dividing unity. Theologian Tom Snail offers a similar account of what went wrong with the world: "The wages of sin is death, because, if our life has its basis in our relationship to God and to

---

[13]See esp. Shults, *Reforming Theological Anthropology*, and Shults, *Reforming the Doctrine of God* (Grand Rapids: Eerdmans, 2005).

[14]The titles of a number of key books making these arguments tell the story themselves: *The Trinity and the Kingdom* (1981 in English); *Being as Communion* (1985); *After Our Likeness: The Church as the Image of the Trinity* (1998); *The Social God and the Relational Self* (2001); *Like Father, Like Son: The Trinity Imaged in Our Humanity* (2005); *Trinity in Human Community: Exploring Congregational Life in the Image of the Social Trinity* (2006).

[15]William T. Cavanaugh, "The City: Beyond Secular Parodies," in *Radical Orthodoxy: A New Theology*, ed. John Milbank, Catherine Pickstock and Graham Ward (London: Routledge, 1999), 182.

[16]Cavanaugh, "The City," 183.

other people and if these relationships are corrupted, our very life is threatened to its core."[17] Again, the basic problem with humanity is not the breaking of God's law; it is the breaking of relationship. Theologian Colin Gunton applies the same lesson to the world today: "My contention is that the distinctive failures of our era derive from its failures of due relatedness to God."[18] The trouble with our era is not disobedience but due relatedness.[19] Now, all three authors stand on biblical ground to emphasize the significance of relationships, and I do not want to pit their emphases against an emphasis on breaking God's law. My point is simply that there is a difference between a broken law and a broken relationship. One's an asymmetrical breach, the other a symmetrical one. And—here's the point—the God of the broken relationship feels just a little bit smaller than the God of the broken law. Perhaps all this is captured in the difference between Augustine's characterization of Genesis 3 as "the fall" and Jacques Ellul's "the rupture."[20] Countless other examples could be provided of how theologians are configuring theology in relational rather than hierarchical categories, such as John Zizioulas's Cappadocian conceptions of divine personhood and the community of the church. "Ultimately," says theologian Simon Chan, "all things are to be brought back into communion with the triune God. Communion is the ultimate end, not mission."[21] And so, observes Jürgen Moltmann, the picture of God as Lord will give way to the picture of God as Father, which will then give way to the picture of God as Friend.[22] Relationality replaces lordship.[23]

---

[17]Tom Smail, *Like Father, Like Son: The Trinity Imaged in Our Humanity* (Grand Rapids: Eerdmans, 2005), 238.

[18]Gunton, *The One, The Three and the Many*, 38.

[19]Perhaps Gunton means to pack the absolute asymmetry of divine authority into his flimsy word *due*, but it is hard to imagine the apostle Paul or the prophet Jeremiah putting the matter like this: "Thus says the Lord, 'I have observed a failure of due relatedness, O Israel.'" Gunton's emphasis—the noun—is clearly on this idea of relatedness.

[20]This comparison is observed in Graham A. Cole, *God the Peacemaker: How Atonement Brings Shalom* (Downers Grove, IL: InterVarsity Press, 2009), 56.

[21]Simon Chan, interview by Andy Crouch, "The Mission in Trinity," in *Christianity Today*, June 2007, www.christianvisionproject.com/2007/06/the_mission_of_the_trinity.html.

[22]Jürgen Moltmann, *Church in the Power of the Spirit* (Minneapolis: Fortress, 1993), 114-21, esp. 118.

[23]This is how Stanley Grenz characterizes Moltmann, in *Rediscovering the Triune God: The Trinity in Contemporary Theology* (Minneapolis: Fortress, 2004), 84, citing Moltmann's *Trinity and the Kingdom* and *God in Creation*, trans. Margaret Kohl (Minneapolis: Fortress, 1993), 221.

As theology converts to practice, programmatic consequences for churches follow. Structures, to the extent they exist, should be organic, liquid or natural. The church is a "spiritual organism that has an organic expression."[24] One need only consider the titles of several recent books written at a popular level for church leaders: *Natural Church Development* (1996); *Liquid Church* (2002); *Organic Church* (2005); *Seeds for the Future: Growing Organic Leaders for Living Churches* (2005); *Organic Community* (2007); and *Reimagining the Church: Pursuing the Dream of Organic Christianity* (2008).

A popular phrase bandied about by some church leaders is "belonging before believing."[25] Churches want outsiders to feel the invitation and embrace of a loving community.[26] Boundaries make outsiders feel measured and judged, so let the unchurched, the prechurched, the semichurched, and the dechurched feel like they belong even before they believe. And do not make any demands on the postchurched and the antichurched, because the demands will push them even further away.[27]

A slightly more careful way of talking about belonging before believing is to say that churches should adopt a "centered-set," not a "bounded-set," approach to their lives together. Bounded-set churches create boundaries around what they consider right behavior and right belief, and then they patrol those boundaries. Centered-set churches focus on bringing people into a relationship with the person at the center, Christ. The first model is said to be static and institutional. The second model is said to be dynamic and loving. The first emphasizes organizational purity. The second emphasizes inviting, embracing and growing people. The first requires people to reach a certain standard just to join the club. The second reaches out to everyone, no matter how different or broken people are.[28]

---

[24]Frank Viola, "Why I Left the Institutional Church," *Frank Viola*, accessed December 15, 2012, http://frankviola.org/LeavingInstitutionalChurch.pdf.

[25]See Murray, *Church After Christendom*, 10-23, for a surprisingly elaborate discussion on this topic.

[26]See Dan Kimball's story in this regard, in Kimball, *They Like Jesus but Not the Church*, 160-61.

[27]These categories can be found in Murray, *Church After Christendom*, 25.

[28]Hiebert, *Anthropological Reflections*, 110-36; Murray, *Church After Christendom*, 12-38; Michael Frost and Alan Hirsch, *The Shaping of Things to Come: Innovation and Mission for the 21st Century* (Peabody, MA: Hendrickson, 2003), 47-50; cf. the call by Guder et al. for a congregation that's part bounded-set, part centered-set, in Guder, *Missional Church*, 205-12.

But must a relational conception of life, salvation and the church be pitted against an institutional conception?[29]

## WHAT IS AN INSTITUTION?

Interestingly, similar anti-institutional impulses reverberated through the field of political science in the middle of the twentieth century but then began to reverse course in the 1980s in a burgeoning "new institutionalism." For a time the "behavioral revolution" prompted political scientists to shift their attention away from formal political institutions and toward individual and group behavior, informal distributions of power and the supposed underlying causes of political activity.[30] In the behaviorist vision, both political behavior and governmental institutions have nonpolitical determinants and bases such as class, other forms of group identity and ideology, determinants which cannot be discovered through studying the formal-legal structures of government.[31] To know how politics "really works," one needs to ascertain what motivates the actors themselves. Political activity is conceived as the aggregation of all these self-interested actions working themselves out through the institutions of the state, institutions that actors manipulate with more or less skill to attain their goals.[32] As with the anti-institutional im-

---

[29]Miroslav Volf helpfully argues against pitting the institutional elements against the work of the Spirit, in *After Our Likeness: The Church as the Image of the Trinity* (Grand Rapids: Eerdmans, 1998), 234.

[30]Kathleen Thelen and Sven Steinmo, "Historical Institutionalism in Comparative Politics," in *Structuring Politics: Historical Institutionalism in Comparative Analysis*, ed. Sven Steinmo, Kathleen Thelen and Frank Longstreth (New York: Cambridge University Press, 1992), 4; also W. Richard Scott, *Institutions and Organizations: Ideas and Interests*, 3rd ed. (Thousand Oaks, CA: Sage Publications, 2008), 7. For a more thorough discussion, see James G. March and Johan P. Olsen, *Rediscovering Institutions: The Organizational Basis of Politics* (New York: The Free Press, 1989), 1-19.

[31]James G. March and Johan P. Olsen, "Elaborating the 'New Institutionalism,'" in *The Oxford Handbook of Political Institutions*, ed. R. A. W. Rhodes, Sarah A. Binder and Bert A. Rockman (New York: Oxford University Press, 2006), 5. See also March and Olsen, "The New Institutionalism: Organizational Factors in Political Life," *The American Political Science Review* 78, no. 3 (September 1984): 734-37.

[32]Walter W. Powell and Paul J. DiMaggio, "Introduction," in *The New Institutionalism in Organizational Analysis*, ed. Walter W. Powell and Paul J. DiMaggio (Chicago: University of Chicago Press, 1991), 2. For example, Richard Neustadt's classic *Presidential Power and the Modern Presidents: The Politics of Leadership from Roosevelt to Reagan* (New York: Free Press, 1980), first published in 1960 and lauded by presidents from Kennedy to Clinton and assigned to me as a political science undergrad, is a classic example of behaviorist political science. It begins with the presumption of the presidency's institutional weakness and then examines how individual presidents can amass more power to themselves through persuasion and prestige.

pulse among some theological circles, the anti-institutional campaign among political scientists, says political scientist Hugh Heclo, seemed to derive from the sort of Romantic impulse articulated in Rousseau's *Emile*: "Civil man is born, lives, and dies in slavery. At his birth he is sewed in swaddling clothes; at this death he is nailed in a coffin. So long as he keeps his human shape, he is enchained by our institutions."[33]

Moving into the 1970s and '80s, however, political scientists increasingly discovered that the behaviorist explanations of political activity could not explain divergent activities among similarly situated groups in different countries.[34] One author asked, for instance, why British and American labor unions sought similar objectives until the late nineteenth century and then radically diverged in the nature of their work. Another wondered why France, Switzerland and Sweden have such different national health care policies even though politicians sought national health insurance in all three.[35] By asking these kinds of questions, the new institutionalists have begun to observe that a nation's formal and informal political institutions dramatically affect not just the strategies of political actors but also their ideas, attitudes, preferences and goals, which in turn account for the differences of political outcomes from one nation to another.[36]

In short, institutions matter. They influence an actor's "definition of his own interests"[37]—what he (or she) thinks he wants. It is not that the new institutionalists deny the various forces that animate behaviorist conceptions of politics, or that they claim institutions are the sole cause of political outcomes.[38] But they no longer treat those forces separately from the institutions, believing that institutions and actors implicate and shape one another:

---

[33]In Hugh Heclo, "Thinking Institutionally," in *The Oxford Handbook of Political Institutions*, ed. R. A. W. Rhodes, Sarah A. Binder and Bert A. Rockman (New York: Oxford University Press, 2006), 732.

[34]Thelen and Steinmo, "Historical Institutionalism," 5.

[35]See Victoria C. Hattam, "Institutions and Political Change: Working-Class Formation in England and the United States, 1820-1896," and Ellen M. Immergut, "The Rules of the Game: The Logic of Health Policy-Making in France, Switzerland, and Sweden," in *Structuring Politics*, 155-87 and 57-89.

[36]Thelen and Steinmo, "Historical Institutionalism," 27.

[37]Peter Hall, *Governing the Economy: The Politics of State Intervention in Britain and France* (New York: Oxford University Press, 1986), 19.

[38]Thelen and Steinmo, "Historical Institutionalism," 4.

"Institutions constitute actors as well as constrain them."[39] That's not to say the self is utterly dissolved as in some radical post-structuralist vision, but the new institutionalists recognize that, while humans give shape to the institutions which bind them, those institutions in turn shape humans and their sense of identity and purpose.

As such, it is important to think of institutions as not only constraining but also commissioning.[40] They offer "bounded innovation."[41]

What exactly are institutions? Different schools of thought answer that question differently according to the questions they are trying to answer.[42] But to capture the idea in as few words as possible for our purposes, we could call them "behavior shaping rule structures"[43] or "the rules of the game in a society."[44] Two of the pioneers in the new institutionalism, political scientists James March and Johan Olsen, offer this slightly fuller definition:

---

[39] Powell and DiMaggio, "Introduction," 7. As Ronald L. Jepperson puts it, "Institutional accounts ... suggest, typically, that actors ... are highly institutional in their origins and operation and, moreover, that in modern polity forms they are often constructed institutions themselves." In Jepperson, "Institutions, Institutional Effects, and Institutionalism," in *The New Institutionalism in Organizational Analysis*, ed. Walter W. Powell and Paul J. DiMaggio (Chicago: University of Chicago Press, 1991), 158; see also Ronald L. Jepperson and John W. Meyer, "The Public Order and the Construction of Formal Organizations," in the same volume, 204-231.

[40] Jepperson writes, "Institutions are not just constraint structures; all institutions simultaneously empower and control. Institutions present a constraint/freedom duality ... : they are vehicles for activity within constraints. ... All institutions are frameworks of programs or rules establishing identities and activity scripts for such identities." In Jepperson, "Institutions, Institutional Effects, and Institutionalism," 146.

[41] Margaret Weir, "Ideas and the Politics of Bounded Innovation," in *Structuring Politics*, 188-216.

[42] Peter A. Hall and Rosemary C. R. Taylor offered one of the first essays which distinguished three different schools pushing the neo-institutional agenda that "developed quite independently of each other": historical institutionalism, rational choice institutionalism and sociological institutionalism. Hall and Taylor, "Political Science and the Three New Institutionalisms," in *Political Studies* 44, no. 5 (December 1996): 936-57; see also Marie-Laure Djelic, "Institutional Perspectives—Working Towards Coherence or Irreconcilable Diversity," in *The Oxford Handbook of Comparative Institutional Analysis*, ed. Glenn Morgan et al. (New York: Oxford University Press, 2010), 15-40. Colin Hay provides a useful two-page chart comparing four different forms of institutionalism in "Constructivist Institutionalism," in *The Oxford Handbook of Political Institutions*, ed. R. A. W. Rhodes, Sarah A. Binder and Bert A. Rockman (New York: Oxford University Press, 2006), 58-59; Thelen and Steinmo helpfully compare historical institutionalism and rational choice in "Historical Institutionalism," 7-10. Even theorists within these schools subdivide; e.g., Kenneth Shepsle distinguishes two different forms of rational choice institutionalism (institutions as exogenous versus endogenous constraints) in "Rational Choice Institutionalism," in *Oxford Handbook of Political Institutions*, 24-26.

[43] Elizabeth Sanders, "Historical Institutionalism," in *Oxford Handbook of Political Institutions*, 38.

[44] Douglass C. North, *Institutions, Institutional Change, and Economic Performance* (New York: Cambridge University Press, 1990), 3.

> An institution is a relatively enduring collection of rules and organized practices, embedded in structures of meaning and resources that are relatively invariant in the face of turnover of individuals and relatively resilient to the idiosyncratic preferences and expectations of individuals and changing external circumstances.

They then elaborate on the different components of this definition:

> There are constitutive rules and practices prescribing appropriate behavior for specific actors in specific situations. There are structures of meaning, embedded in identities and belongings: common purposes and accounts that give direction and meaning to behavior, and explain, justify, and legitimate behavioral codes. There are structures of resources that create capabilities for acting.

Then they summarize:

> Institutions empower and constrain actors differently and make them more or less capable of acting according to prescriptive rules of appropriateness. Institutions are also reinforced by third parties in enforcing rules and sanctioning non-compliance.[45]

To put all this in a slightly more accessible idiom, institutions tell you how to act, and they give you opportunities to act. They help to define relationships, giving them purpose and direction. They even shape aspects of your identity. Consider just a few examples listed by the sociologists: marriage, the contract, wage labor, the handshake, insurance, the army, academic tenure, the presidency, the vacation, attending college, the corporation, the motel and voting.[46] These are very different kinds of institutions, but all of them, in various ways, contain rules and opportunities for action, shape a relationship, and impinge upon identity.[47]

Notice, also, that institutions can be a set of rules (formal or informal) or they can be an actual organization or polity. An organization is in fact a

---

[45]March and Olsen, "Elaborating the 'New Institutionalism,'" 3.
[46]Jepperson, "Institutions, Institutional Effects, and Institutionalism," 144.
[47]Oliver O'Donovan, in the good intention of placing human authority inside divine rule, pits human *institutions* against human *actions* since he wants to draw a direct line from divine authorization to human action. It is not clear to me, however, why our formulations need to denigrate the role of human institutions in the process. If it is only to make the point that human institutions are relative, then I agree, as I will discuss below. See O'Donovan, *Desire of the Nations: Rediscovering the Roots of Political Theology* (New York: Cambridge University Press, 1996), 20.

fairly elaborate complex of rules and procedures.[48] One sociologist describes the formal organization as "a packaged social technology, with accompanying rules and instructions for its incorporation and employment in a social setting."[49]

Legal philosopher Nick Barber extends this lesson beyond organizations to all forms of social groups. Social rules and social groups are inextricably connected: "Groups can only exist where they are constituted by social rules. But, conversely, social rules can only exist in the context of a social group, a group defined by—at minimum—their common acceptance of the rule, coupled with an awareness of their common acceptance."[50] John Rawls also picks up on the importance of mutual awareness and recognition: "A person taking part in an institution knows what the rules demand of him and of the others. He also knows that the others know this and that they know that he knows this, and so on. To be sure, this condition is not always fulfilled in the case of actual institutions, but it is a reasonable simplifying assumption." The more formal an institution is, the more public its constitutive rules must be: "The publicity of the rules of an institution insures that those engaged in it know what limitations on conduct to expect of one another and what kinds of actions are permissible. There is a common basis for determining mutual expectations."[51]

With this connection between groups and publicly recognized rules in mind, it is worth returning for just a moment to George Eldon Ladd's claim

---

[48]Economists sometimes distinguish institutions and organizations (see for example, Douglass C. North, "The New Institutional Economics and Third World Development," in *The New Institutional Economics and Third World Development*, ed. John Harris, Janet Hunter and Colin M. Lewis [London: Routledge, 1995], 23), whereas political scientists more often treat organizations as one type of institution (see Jean Blondel, "About Institutions, Mainly, but Not Exclusively, Political," in *Oxford Handbook of Political Institutions*, 722-23; also Hall, *Governing the Economy*, 19).

[49]Jepperson, "Institutions, Institutional Effects, and Institutionalism," 146-47.

[50]Nick Barber, *The Constitutional State*, ed. Martin Loughlin, John P. McCormick and Neil Walker, Oxford Constitutional Theory (Oxford: Oxford University Press, 2010), 69. Barber, partially following Joseph Raz, offers a convincing critique of John Searle's attempt to distinguish the nature of constitutive rules from other regulatory rules; yet he still affirms that some rules are used to constitute a group or a practice, while others regulate activities within the group or practice (ibid., 69-70). Incidentally, Rawls also follows Searle in distinguishing the two kinds of institutions; in John Rawls, *A Theory of Justice* (Cambridge, MA: Belknap Press of Harvard University Press, 1971), 56-57.

[51]Rawls, *Theory of Justice*, 56. Rawls is explicitly addressing a society's basic political institutions here (see 54, 57), but I think the principles apply more broadly.

that, in Matthew 16, Jesus' statement about building his church "does not speak of the creation of an organization or institution" but instead stands in direct continuity with the Old Testament tradition of "building a people."[52] To give Ladd the benefit of the doubt, one can only assume that he means to distance Jesus' conception of a church from something very specific, such as episcopalian hierarchies or independent church deacon boards. But Jesus' promise to build an assembly *is* a promise to take an unconnected group of individuals and to institutionalize them—to place them inside "behavior shaping rule structures." Membership in Christ's assembly, whatever that assembly is, implies some rule, some criteria, some expectation that binds or characterizes every member in contradistinction to nonmembers. Both permanent and temporary assemblies are governed by a host of such expectations and rules. And with permanent assemblies, which Jesus promised the church would be, those rules are deeply formalized.[53] Indeed, Jesus said that the gates of hell would not overcome this community. If that's the case, it would certainly seem (to borrow from March and Olsen) that "the idiosyncratic preferences and expectations of individuals and changing external circumstances" would not overcome it either.

This same category confusion between "a people" and "an institution" also plagues the way that communion theology pits communion and institution against one another.[54] It is certainly fair to say that churches can become "overly institutional," as with a church that consists of nothing more than dead rituals and moralistic traditions. Still, communion ecclesiology's overarching critique posits a false dichotomy. A "communion of persons" is itself a kind of institution, a set of people set inside "behavior shaping rule structures," even if the only rules are the rules of love and forgiveness. Nick Barber again: "All social groups are constituted by rules.

---

[52]George Eldon Ladd, *A Theology of the New Testament*, rev. ed. (Grand Rapids: Eerdmans, 1993), 107-8.

[53]Barber writes, "A rule becomes formalized when it is articulated in a definitive fashion. This is a matter of degree. At one end of the scale a social rule may start to become formalized when it is expressed by community leaders whose statements begin to clarify the rule. At the other end of the scale, law provides an example of an extremely formalized set of rules: it contains rules which are frequently written in canonical fashion, coupled with institutions empowered to resolve disputes that may arise over their interpretation." In Barber, *Constitutional State*, 73.

[54]Jenson and Wilhite, *The Church*, 21, 51.

Even the very simplest social group consists of a collection of people bound together by shared rules—though the rules may be so basic, so elemental, that members of the group may be unaware of them."[55] Any and every so-called communion presupposes some set of rules, norms or practices for determining why some people belong to the communion while others do not. Furthermore, it is ill-conceived to pit relationships and institutions against one another. This is why institutionalists speak explicitly about "the 'relational character' of institutions; that is to say, on the way in which [institutions] structure the interactions of individuals."[56] What anti-institutionalism really is, is a preference for one set of rules over another.[57] Such writers want to write their own rules, not adopt the rules of their theological parents or grandparents.

To speak of the relational character of institutions helps us to understand what they are from yet another angle: institutions are the application of authority to a relationship. Institutions exist wherever two or more individuals relate to one another according to some set of binding principles that commission and constrain the nature of their interactions. It is not difficult to see how this applies to everything from the handshake, to a slave/master relationship, to the partnership structure of a law firm, to the rules for passing the baton between members of a relay track team. What is common to each of these examples is that individuals do not relate to one another however they please, but relate within some type of authoritative structure, whether the authority is exercised wholly within the relationship (as between master and slave) or upon the relationship (as with the rules of track and field).[58]

To speak about institutions, in short, is to speak about authority.

---

[55] Barber, *Constitutional State*, 67. The more formalized a group becomes, of course, the more *aware* group members will be of those rules that constitute them as a group.
[56] Hall, *Governing the Economy*, 19.
[57] Cf. Jenson and Wilhite, *The Church*, 21.
[58] The distinction here is analogous to what institutionalists distinguish as exogenous and endogenous institutions. With exogenous institutions, actors are constrained by something from "outside" —by an autonomous, external institution, such as the fixed rules of baseball. With endogenous institutions, the actors establish the rules themselves, as when a group of children playing baseball decide together that a ball which rolls into the creek allows the batter to proceed only one extra base. The distinction between exogenous and endogenous as well as the baseball example is taken from Shepsle, "Rational Choice Institutionalism," 24-25.

## What Is a Political Institution?

If every institution is a behavior-shaping rule structure, what makes an institution "political"? Every institution offers a kind of governance, even the convention of the handshake; but a political institution is one whose reach or jurisdiction extends to the whole body politic, and which the body politic (generally, not necessarily) recognizes as formally possessing the right to govern it through coercive force. One can abstain from handshakes without threat of bodily reprisal; one cannot so abstain from paying taxes.[59]

Of course, political authority can be delegated and departmentalized. The US Department of Agriculture does not possess, by itself, the power of the sword. Rather, its work is backed by the larger structures of government that, taken as a whole, do. Political institutions, like office buildings, are elaborate things, with multiple floors and offices, each office possessing its own mandate and set of keys. And while the occupants of most of these offices can threaten force, few can independently execute it. This is especially the case, for instance, with a nation's foreign embassy. There the threat of force is, at best, delayed and contingent on a host of factors unique to the field of international relations and the interplay of multiple competing sovereigns.

These latter qualifications seem necessary to mention since, as I have been saying since the beginning, the local church comes closest to the embassy model of a political institution, an embassy representing the eschatological future and the rule of a king to whom the nations owe their allegiance now. No, the local church should not exercise force! But, like an embassy abroad, its declarations are backed up by one who does.

A further distinctive of political institutions is that they are concerned with the principles of justice. Feminist political theorist Iris Marion Young has observed that "the concept of justice is coextensive with the political."[60] A government recognizes membership in a body politic according to

---

[59]This is not to say that a political institution is a concrete given and that people are merely actors walking across this concrete, unchanging stage. Rather, "[Political] institutions are sets of rules that emerge from and subsequently structure social and political interaction." Jack Knight and James Johnson, *The Priority of Democracy: Political Consequences of Pragmatism* (Princeton, NJ: Princeton University Press, 2011), 2.

[60]Iris Marion Young, *Justice and the Politics of Difference* (Princeton, NJ: Princeton University Press, 1990), 9.

principles of justice.⁶¹ It extends its reach into people's lives wherever it believes justice requires it.⁶² Furthermore, says John Rawls, a well-ordered society possesses a "shared" and "public understanding as to what is just and unjust."⁶³ The rules of justice should have been publicized and agreed to. As we will see in chapter five's discussion of the new covenant and chapter six's discussion of *sola fide*, a church by definition is united on the matter of justice.

A final thing to note about political institutions is that one of their primary functions lies with establishing unity for the community, not that this does not apply in some sense to all institutions. For instance, institutions involving membership create a unity of identity. And institutions involving governance create a unity of decision-making procedures. Hence, political theorists Jack Knight and James Johnson observe, "Politics, in large part, is a response to diversity." Human populations are divided across "multiple, overlapping dimensions, including material interests, moral and ethical commitments, and cultural attachments"⁶⁴ (to say nothing of what Abraham Kuyper refers to as the "disintegrating force" of sin),⁶⁵ which makes conflict unavoidable. Yet people remain highly interdependent—stuck together. Knight and Johnson continue,

> Thus, despite their diversity and the discord to which it gives rise, they require some means of coordinating their ongoing social and economic interactions. For this, they need, most importantly, social institutions. More specifically, in their efforts to coordinate in mutually beneficial ways, they require a set of institutional arrangements consisting of everything from the

---

[61] Michael Walzer writes, "The idea of distributive justice presupposes a bounded world within which distributions take place: a group of people committed to dividing, exchanging, and sharing social goods, first of all among themselves." Furthermore: "The primary good that we distribute to one another is membership in some human community. And what we do with regard to membership structures all our other distributive choices: it determines with whom we make those choices, from whom we require obedience and collect taxes, to whom we allocate goods and services." Michael Walzer, *Spheres of Justice: A Defense of Pluralism and Equality* (New York: Basic Books, 1983), 31.

[62] Hence, John Rawls began his most famous book on justice by observing, "For us the primary subject of justice is the basic structure of society, or more exactly, the way in which the major institutions distribute fundamental rights and duties and determine the division of advantages for social cooperation." Rawls, *Theory of Justice*, 7; also 54-60.

[63] Rawls, *Theory of Justice*, 56.

[64] Knight and Johnson, *Priority of Democracy*, 1.

[65] Abraham Kuyper, *Lectures on Calvinism* (Grand Rapids: Eerdmans, 1931), 79.

most decentralized institutional mechanisms, like informal norms, practices, and conventions, to a wide range of decentralized (e.g., markets) and centralized (e.g., government) formal institutions.

Politics, these authors conclude, "consists in deep, persistent contests over the contours and distributive implications of these shared institutional arrangements."[66] As philosophical pragmatists, Knight and Johnson unsurprisingly describe politics as a contest and give little attention to the theological, anthropological and sociological background of that contest. Nonetheless, their emphasis on the link between institutions and unity is instructive for theological purposes. Since the break with Rome, there has been a tendency among Protestants to speak about unity in "spiritual" terms while simultaneously downplaying the significance of institutional unity. Yet to quarantine church unity to the spiritual domain fails to acknowledge the fact that Christians and churches must somehow "coordinate [their efforts] in mutually beneficial ways" on planet earth. Somehow the Christians must figure out who "they" are. Somehow they must decide who gets baptized, who receives the Lord's Supper and who can be said to belong to this thing called Christian *koinonia*. No matter how a Christian answers such questions, one must make an "institutional decision" if one wants to coordinate one's practice with anyone else calling himself or herself a Christian. There must be some rule—some institution—by which one Christian recognizes another Christian, amidst all the other points of difference.

## WHAT IS A POLITICAL COMMUNITY AND ITS MEMBERSHIP?

We have already begun to consider the connection between social groups and social rules and the sense in which every social group is a kind of institution. Is there further definition we can give to a political community and its membership? For starters, I propose that a political community or body politic is *a community of people united by a common governing authority*, an authority that possesses imperium for the purposes of justice (as opposed to the authority one finds in lesser organizations like businesses, schools, families or soccer teams). Minimally, members of this commununity are subject to the authority irrespective of their assent, infants and slaves no less

---

[66]Knight and Johnson, *Priority of Democracy*, 1.

than adults and office holders; maximally, they acknowledge this government as "theirs" and even participate in its rule.

This spectrum between the minimal and the maximal, which in a moment we will designate as the spectrum between "subject" and "citizen," pushes us to define the concept of political membership. Political membership, then, is a *relationship in which (1) an individual is subject to the primary governing authority and typically acknowledges that authority in some fashion, and in which (2) the governing authority publicly affirms the individual as belonging to its charge.*[67] This definition, again, tries to accommodate the spectrum between minimal and maximal by making subjectitude the absolute minimum of political membership (for the sake of, say, infants) while granting that some kind of acknowledgment is *typical*, whether the reluctant acknowledgment of a slave or the proud participation of an office holder. Yet other than in the case of infants, political membership is a relationship of formal mutual recognition, ownership and identification. The individual says of the authority, "That government and its work of justice, for better or worse, is mine." And the government says of the individual, "That individual belongs to us." Yet while the recognition is typically mutual, it is also asymmetrical: one party *submits* while the other *takes responsibility*. The individual submits to whatever laws, duties, forms of discipline and general requirements of justice the governing authority requires. The governing authority in turn takes responsibility for the individual by recognizing his or her inclusion within the group, by promising to protect the individual, by granting the individual whatever benefits and rights belong to members of the group and by agreeing to ensure the individual maintains the requisite duties of membership, threatening the individual with punishment for injustice, breeches of duty and transgressions of law.[68]

---

[67]Political theorist Seyla Benhabib defines political membership as "the principles and practices for incorporating aliens and strangers, immigrants and newcomers, refuges and asylum seekers, into existing polities. Political boundaries define some as members, other as aliens. Membership, in turn, is meaningful only when accompanied by rituals of entry, access, belonging, and privilege." In Seyla Benhabib, *The Rights of Others: Aliens, Residents, and Citizens* (New York: Cambridge University Press, 2004), 1.

[68]The homepage for "U.S. Citizenship" at the website for the U.S. Citizenship and Immigration Services reads, "Deciding to become a U.S. citizen is one of the most important decisions in an individual's life. If you decide to apply to become a U.S. citizen, you will be showing your commitment to the United States and your loyalty to its Constitution. In return, you are rewarded with

It is important to notice here the role that identity comes to play in the exercise of authority. I identify myself as "an American," in part, because I recognize the US government as my own. I identify myself as "a Leeman," in part, because the two individuals tasked by God with exercising parental authority over me are both named Leeman. A legitimate authority relationship necessarily involves the identity of both authority figure and subject.[69] The authoritative relationship ties into *who* each party *is*, even when that authority is temporary or voluntarily granted. We accept authority whenever and wherever our self-identification permits, and we give authority whenever and wherever our self-identification insists. This is why the short definition of an institution that I used earlier (a behavior-shaping rule structure) can be slightly improved by adding the concept of identity: an identity- and behavior-shaping rule structure. March and Olsen's longer definition captures the note of identity by observing that institutions entail "structures of meaning, embedded in identities and belongings." Oliver O'Donovan, too, points to the ideas of recognition, ownership and identity in his explanation of political authority:

> *In acknowledging political authority, society proves its political identity.* Acknowledgment is the fundamental relation that obtains between a society and its own political authorities. It recognizes them—not in the constitutive sense of conferring existence on them by recognition, but in the much more basic sense of simply acknowledging that they are *there* and that they are *theirs*. "This government is our government" it acknowledges, with whatever mixture of complacency and ruefulness, simply as a fact about itself.[70]

This connection between institutional authority and identity will prove significant for our purposes as we come to consider what it means to be taken into the institutional church by being baptized "in the name" of the Trinity (Mt 28:19) or what it means to gather "in the name" of Jesus (Mt 18:20; 1 Cor 5:4). In the meantime, let me propose that these two definitions of political community and political membership are broadly applicable to both participatory and nonparticipatory forms of government.

---

all the rights and privileges that are part of U.S. citizenship." Found at www.uscis.gov/us-citizenship, accessed December 13, 2012.

[69]Not surprisingly, rebellion against authority is often justified at the level of identity, whether it is the stepchild who says the father figure is not really "my dad" or the insurrectionist who claims the government is not really "ours."

[70]O'Donovan, *Desire of the Nations*, 47 (italics original).

One more concept is worth defining here: political unity. Where familial unity (at its root) is premised on common biology, and spiritual unity is premised on a common movement of the Spirit, and ethnic unity is premised on a common ethnicity, and professional unity is premised on a common profession, so political unity is premised on a common ultimate authority. *Political unity, more precisely, refers to the formal and institutionalized relationships that abide between subjects of the same governing authority, particularly as that governing authority obligates those individuals toward one another according to its rules of justice.* That, anyhow, is how the term will be used in this book and not as a way of designating partisan or ideological unity, which is another way one might imagine using the concept.

All three of these definitions, which I have devised to hang together logically, require at least five further words of explanation. And for each point of explanation I will forecast why the qualification is relevant for our ecclesiological purposes. First, I mean for these definitions to be descriptive rather than normative, applicable to any kind of government and its community. I do not intend for them to prejudice one form of church government over another.

***Political community and territory.*** Second, a body politic—a community united by a common governing authority—need not be tied to a particular territory. When we are focused on the modern state, it can be difficult to imagine delinking government and geographic territory. For instance, political scientist Stuart Hall has observed,

> Sovereignty is linked in complex ways with "territory." It has proved impossible to use the term "state" in relation to a population without a permanent place of settlement.... "Territory" and "state" are ... not the same. Yet territory matters for the definition of sovereignty, partly because the sense of "belonging"—sentiments of loyalty—are important constituents of being members of a state; but mainly because of the need to establish the boundaries to power and legal rule. There must be some way of defining what parts are unified under the state, how extensive in space is its rule and where the boundaries to its rule end and the jurisdiction of other states begin.[71]

---

[71]Stuart Hall, "The State in Question," in *The Idea of the Modern State*, ed. Gregor McLennan, David Held and Stuart Hall (Philadelphia: Open University Press, 1984), 18.

Yet these observations seem especially tied to the modern nation-state, where one nation and its government are divided from another by ruler-straight lines on a map. Indigenous tribes, especially migratory ones, can hardly be said to be tied to territory in the same way, and yet they possess the necessary criteria for being construed as a "political community" according to the definition above. Medieval monarchies and the empires of the ancient world were also tied to territory differently than the nation-state. Sociologist Benedict Anderson illustrates:

> Kingship organizes everything around a high centre. Its legitimacy derives from divinity, not from populations, who, after all, are subjects, not citizens. In the modern conception, state sovereignty is fully, flatly, and evenly operative over each square centimetre of a legally demarked territory. But in the older imagining, where states were defined by centres, borders were porous and indistinct, and sovereignties faded imperceptibly into one another.[72]

I would argue, based on the examples of a migratory tribe as well as the picture of a kingship with indistinct territorial borders, that we can conceive of a political community as united by a common governing authority whether or not the body politic is tied to a particular territory. The definition of a political community here works for migratory tribes, nation-states, and empires with fuzzy borders. In fact, laws of extradition point to the same idea, though obviously multiple sovereigns are involved.

The point of relevance for our purposes pertains to the historical-redemptive movement from the landed nation of Israel to the unlanded church. With a glance, one might contest that the citizens of the former regime were marked off geographically, but wonder how a landless, borderless kingdom like Jesus' could be political since there are no borders. How can you exercise border patrol when there are no borders? The task, no doubt, is more difficult, but that doesn't mean it cannot be done. The continued political identity of the Jews in exile suggests as much, as we considered at the end of chapter one. The illustration of an embassy is also useful here, particularly if the existence of a local church is tied in some sense to its gathering—which is a kind of territorial phenomenon.

---

[72]Benedict Anderson, *Imagined Communities: Reflections on the Origin and Spread of Nationalism*, rev. ed. (New York: Verso, 1991), 19.

***Political rebellion and other complexities.*** Third, plenty of factors might complicate the picture of a political community. For instance, the citizens of a vassal state set inside of an empire might be uncertain of the boundaries of their community. Was Jesus to be tried by Herod or Pontius Pilate? And what can be said about the multiple classes of citizenship such as slave and free, Greek and metic, passport holders and green-card holders? And if someone holds two citizenships? All such factors surely complexify the picture, but the basic principles of the definition above still apply, even if it means, for instance, that someone belongs to two political communities simultaneously (e.g., Roman *and* Jewish).

But it is especially important for us to give a little more attention to the matter of acknowledgment or assent. An infant offers no assent for obvious reasons; hence I defined political membership as *typically* involving acknowledgment, while subjectitude is the bare minimum. The more difficult conceptual challenge comes with insurrectionists, rebels and slaves. Slaves taken in wartime, for instance, may begrudgingly acknowledge the new government, but they also identify themselves with their former government, will refuse to swear allegiance to the new government, and may act in seditious ways toward it. In such a situation, I think we can say that the slaves occupy two political communities, but they occupy them differently.

To generalize, political rebellion in institutional terms is the rejection of one political authority for another. It is a rejection of the legitimacy or *justice* of that authority's claim and therefore, to some measure, that authority's view of justice. It is a rejection of the political *community* created by the bonds of the rejected authority. Finally, it is an assertion of an alternative *identity* and the prerogatives of that identity: "I am not *yours*, I am *mine/ theirs*, so hands off!" All this will become relevant when we get to a political and institutional analysis of Genesis 3 in chapter four.

In spite of the fact that a political rebel rejects the authority, justice, community and identity-construct of his or her government, the rebel remains a subject of that government until the rebellion successfully supplants one sword holder with another. Which means, affirmation or not, a rebel *remains a member of the original community until the rebellion succeeds and a new sword holder is installed.* The very idea of "rebel" means that the rebel's identity still roots in a kind of relationship with the original authority.

The rebel may reject the authority, but the authority maintains a hold on the rebel.

That said, as long as a rebel does not acknowledge the legitimacy of a government's claim, that political community exists in a precarious state. Its existence is under threat. It is "ruled" not by one concept of justice but by more than one. And it is in the fact that an alternative conception of justice and legitimacy "govern" the rebels that we discover the conflicted identity and something like the seeds of a new community. Therefore, we must say that *time* becomes a significant factor in conceptualizing political rebellion, because this double political identity exists *until* the rebellion is resolved one way or another. (Here, indeed, is why eschatology becomes so significant for political theology.)

It should be clear, then, that rebellion is politically meaningful because it means laying claim to an alternative rule, justice, community and identity. I have a few more comments to make about slaves and insurrectionists in just a moment, but for now it is worth observing that this third qualification will prove important for when we turn to develop our political cartography both for God's kingship over a world of insurrectionists as well as for the relationship of the nations to the kingdom of Christ.

***Other kinds of unity.*** The fourth explanation worth giving to the definitions offered above is that the presence of political unity does not preclude the presence of other kinds of unity, such as a unity that is born of divine election or love. For instance, one can wholly agree with Dietrich Bonhoeffer that God's "community is constituted by the complete self-forgetfulness of love,"[73] and yet also maintain that a community is simultaneously bound together by other kinds of glue. There is no need to pit different forms of union, even union by love and by authority, against one another. Love should indeed *motivate* the formation of a community, but that love might then be called to *act* or *express* itself in an authoritative way, as with a parent who lovingly requires obedience of a child.[74] Along these lines, Jewish

---

[73]Dietrich Bonhoeffer, *Sanctorum Communio: A Theological Study of the Sociology of the Church*, ed. Clifford J. Green, Dietrich Bonhoeffer Works, vol. 1 (Minneapolis: Augsburg Fortress, 1998), 190.

[74]Bonhoeffer seems to imply this in the sentence that follows the above quote. He continues, "I and You face each other no longer essentially in a demanding, but in a giving way, revealing their hearts have been conquered by God's will" (ibid., 190-91).

political thinker David Novak simultaneously alludes to the connection between politics, covenant and divine election when he writes, "A covenantal society is based on God's initiation of a political relationship between Himself and a people. Unlike a contract, it is not the coming together of equal parties, nor do the people have any right of initial refusal or subsequent termination of the covenant."[75] Political authority, election, a covenant and love all work together to unite God's people. The relevance of this point for understanding a local church's unity should be clear: claiming that the local church's unity is political in its essence does not preclude other essential forms of unity.

## A Community of Subjects or Citizens?

There is a fifth explanation of these four generic definitions that is worth an extra measure of attention. It, too, will prove essential to mapping out a political cartography of the Bible post-fall. I earlier defined political membership and community, making room for both the minimum of subjectitude and the maximum of assent and even participation. This spectrum between minimum and maximum is in fact the spectrum between two different kinds of membership, namely, the passive subject and the active citizen.

A classic essay by J. G. A. Pocock, which contrasts conceptions of citizenship in ancient Greece and Rome, is helpful for understanding the distinction. Pocock contrasts the "political" conception that characterized the city-states of ancient Greece and Aristotle's *Politics* with a "legal" conception more characteristic of the Roman Empire and for which the apostle Paul is a symbolic figure.[76] The Greek conception, which is commonly said to have inaugurated the republican tradition of citizenship, envisions the citizen as a political actor who participates in making the rules that bind him or

---

[75]David Novak, "Land and People," in *Law, Politics, and Morality in Judaism*, ed. Michael Walzer (Princeton, NJ: Princeton University Press, 2006), 73.

[76]I do not mean to suggest that these are the only two ways of conceiving of citizenship. For instance, T. H. Marshall's oft-cited essay "Citizenship and Social Class" argues that our modern ideas about citizenship grew from a "civic" to a "political" to a "social" conception through the eighteenth, nineteenth and twentieth centuries, respectively. Marshall's essay has been reprinted in *The Citizenship Debates: A Reader*, ed. Gershon Shafir (Minneapolis: University of Minnesota Press, 1998), 93-111. Cf. Barber, *Constitutional State*, 50-52.

her—"a citizen is one who both rules and is ruled."[77] It aims primarily at a positive concept of freedom that comes from self-determination and participation in government. Beyond Aristotle,[78] this tradition is said to show up in the writings of Cicero, Machiavelli and Rousseau.[79] It has also proven popular in recent decades among communitarian writers,[80] who emphasize how political membership is strongly tied to personal identity.[81] The Roman "legal" conception, on the other hand, does not so much emphasize the freedom of political action as equality before the law—rights more than duties. The apostle Paul, Pocock observes, never would have imagined himself having a hand in joining with Caesar to fashion the laws that bound him,[82] but he did view his Roman citizenship as guaranteeing the protection of Roman law. Citizenship here is conceived of as a legal status, which Pocock observes "is not quite the same thing as a political status and which

---

[77]Pocock's "The Ideal of Citizenship Since Classical Times" has been reprinted a number of times. I have taken it from Shafir, *Citizenship Debates*, 32.

[78]In Aristotle's own words, a citizen is someone who "has the power to take part in the deliberative or judicial administration of any state." Aristotle, *Politics*, in Richard McKeon, ed., *The Basic Works of Aristotle*, trans. Benjamin Jowett (New York: Random House, 1941), 1177, 1275b. At the same time, said Aristotle, "the ruler must learn by obeying." He goes on to write, "It has been well said that 'he who has never learned to obey cannot be a good commander.' The two are not the same, but the good citizen ought to be capable of both; he should know how to govern like a freeman, and how to obey like a freeman—these are the virtues of a good citizen" (ibid., 1181, 1277b).

[79]Derek Heater, *What Is Citizenship?* (Cambridge: Polity Press, 1999), 44-79; Richard Bellamy, *Citizenship: A Very Short Introduction* (New York: Oxford University Press, 2008), 31-38.

[80]E.g., Michael Sandel, *Democracy's Discontent: America in Search of a Public Philosophy* (Cambridge, MA: Belknap Press of Harvard University Press, 1996); Adrian Oldfield, "Citizenship and Community: Civic Republicanism and the Modern World," in *The Citizenship Debates*, ed. Gershon Shafir (Minneapolis: University of Minnesota, 1998), 75-89; cf. Robert P. George, *Making Men Moral: Civil Liberties and Public Morality* (New York: Oxford University Press, 1995), esp. 21-28.

[81]Oldfield writes, "In a political community what is shared is identity, born in part from self-determination and in part from a common history, or language, or continued occupancy of the same territory. Political solidarity and cohesion result from the equality of a shared identity, which is at least in part self-determined and chosen." Oldfield, "Citizenship and Community," 80.

[82]Perhaps it is true that Paul never would have conceived of joining hands to making laws with Caesar per se, but there was still enough Roman *Republic* in the Roman *Empire* at this point in history to envision participating in political activity at a more local level. The councils and the assemblies of old city-state politics did not expire until the late second and early third centuries AD, and "a man who happened to have Roman status, such as Paul at Tarsus, would tend to look for an active political life in the municipal affairs of his own city." A. N. Sherwin-White, *Roman Society and Roman Law in the New Testament: The Sarum Lectures, 1960-61* (1963; repr., Eugene, OR: Wipf & Stock, 2004), 84, 179. The storyline of Acts, for instance, suggests that the *demos* in Thessalonica and Ephesus remained active (ibid., 175; see Acts 17:5-10; 19:24-40).

will, in due course, modify the meaning of the term political itself."[83] These days, it is suggested that philosophical liberalism has joined this tradition insofar as it places a premium on the citizens' equal status, privilege, protection before the law and therefore the ability to move about freely apart from the state's intervention (negative freedom).[84] Yet what is especially important to note for our purposes is that the line between "citizen" and "subject" is often drawn right here in between the "political" and "legal" conceptions of citizenship. The word *citizen*—at least in academic literature—is often used to describe the individual who has a hand in making the rules that bind him or her: "A citizen is both governor and governed," says one writer;[85] and another, "Citizenship has traditionally referred to a particular set of political practices involving specific public rights and duties with respect to a given political community."[86] Citizenship, in short, is a kind of political office or activity, and these ideas ultimately course through the communitarian and liberal traditions alike. A "subject," on the other hand, is a passive recipient or subject of the law, not an office holder or actor per se. Like the Roman conception of citizenship, it is a legal status. So the apostle Paul may have explicitly referred to himself in the book of Acts with the Greek word for "citizen," but, says Pocock, "it would do little violence to our use of language to suppose that Saint Paul claimed to be a Roman 'subject' since by doing so he could claim protection and privilege as well as offering allegiance and obedience."[87] Will Kymlicka's encyclopedia definition of citizenship would yield, no doubt, the same conclusion concerning Paul, namely, that he was a subject, not a citizen: "Within political philosophy, citizenship refers not only to a legal status, but also to a normative ideal—that the governed should be full and equal participants in the political process. As such, it is a distinctively democratic ideal. People who are governed by monarchs or military dictators are subjects, not citizens."[88]

---

[83]Pocock, "Ideal of Citizenship," 37.
[84]Gershon Shafir, "Introduction," in Shafir, *Citizenship Debates*, 10; Bellamy, *Citizenship*, 39-42.
[85]Herman van Gunsteren, "Four Conceptions of Citizenship," in *The Condition of Citizenship*, ed. Bart van Steenbergen (Thousand Oaks, CA: Sage Publications, 1994), 36.
[86]Bellamy, *Citizenship*, 3.
[87]Pocock, "Ideal of Citizenship," 39.
[88]Will Kymlicka, "Citizenship," *The Oxford Companion to Philosophy*, ed. Ted Honderich (New York: Oxford University Press, 1995), 135-36. Pocock himself summarizes the difference between "citizen" and "subject" as follows: "What is the difference between a classical 'citizen'

Pocock himself seems willing to continue using the term *citizen* a little more broadly since the Roman conception in fact brought about "some equation" of the citizen and subject.[89] He says of his own British citizenship, "In terms of protection and allegiance, right and authority, *subject* and *citizen* might be interchangeable terms, and when my passport declares me to be a United Kingdom 'citizen' as well as a British 'subject,' I know that it is offering me rights and protections within the United Kingdom which may be denied to other 'British subjects.'"[90]

With this distinction between subject and citizen in mind, we can return to discussing what role acknowledgment or acceptance plays in a political community, particularly around the question of political rebellion. Nick Barber—we heard above—says that the existence of a social group depends upon the "common acceptance of the rule, coupled with an awareness of their common acceptance."[91] This definition, we also heard, needs to be qualified to account for infants as well as individuals who belong against their will, such as insurrectionists and slaves. What we find in real-life political communities is a range or spectrum: at one end are infants and members by force, while at the other end is participatory membership. And in most political communities, people sit somewhere along that spectrum, involving elements of necessity (force) and decision (participation in governance). For conceptual simplicity, I would like to offer the two ends of the spectrum as representing the subject and the citizen. The subject is a subject whether he likes it or not. He's *subject*. A citizen, on the other hand, exercises her will in belonging. She participates in the group's actions by choice or assent. That is not to say there is no authority over her. It is to say that, wherever rule does exist over her, she happily accedes to it and agrees with it. (The perfect picture of this, we will

---

and an imperial or modern 'subject'? The former ruled and was ruled, which meant among other things that he was a participant in determining the laws by which he was to be bound. The latter could appeal to Caesar; that is, he could go into court and invoke a law that granted him rights, immunities, privileges, and even authority, and that could not ordinarily be denied him once he had established his right to invoke it. But he might have no hand whatever in making that law or in determining what it was to be." Pocock, "Ideal of Citizenship," 40. See also Barber, *Constitutional State*, 48-49.

[89] Pocock, "Ideal of Citizenship," 39.
[90] Pocock, "Ideal of Citizenship," 39-40.
[91] See note 51 above.

see in the next chapter, is the incarnate Son's submission to and shared rule with the divine Father.)

So to ask the question one more time, what exactly constitutes a political community and its members? Is it the presence of a common coercive authority? Yes, at minimum. This would be a community of pure subjects, such as a group of infants, prisoners and slaves. Furthermore, we could describe this community of political subjects as "politically united." But again, we would mean this in a minimal sense. It would be the political unity of subjects. To constitute a society of citizens, on the other hand, requires assent, agreement or voluntary submission to the legitimacy of a coercive authority and its work of establishing justice. Such a society shares the political unity of citizens.

What is the moral of this story for our ecclesial purposes? There are four. First, this book will argue that biblical authority simultaneously involves both ends of the spectrum. This can be seen most clearly in the fact that the Bible offers both "mandatory rules" (which one would do with a subject) and "power-conferring rules" (which one would do with a citizen), to use the language of legal theorists. Broadly speaking, mandatory rules are commands, as in "Worship the Lord your God" or "You shall not steal." And power-conferring rules are commissions, as in "Fill the earth and subdue it" or "You are to me a royal priesthood" or "Whatever you bind on earth will be bound in heaven" or "Go into all nations, preaching and baptizing" or "Serve as overseers."[92] When the two ends of the spectrum are held simultaneously, one perceives that leading always includes following. To be a citizen, a person must be a subject, and godly subjecthood in God's world is part of the commissioned work of displaying God. (Recall Jepperson's description of institutions: "All institutions simultaneously empower and control. Institutions present a constraint/freedom duality.")[93] Hence, God created Adam in his image to obey and to rule (Gen 1:28; 2:14-16), and one of the promises of the eschaton is to coreign with Christ (2 Tim 2:12; Rev 5:10; 22:5). Christ himself is a picture of one *under* authority *with* authority, just as a Roman

---

[92]A mandatory rule obliges a person to act or forbids him or her from acting; a power-conferring rule enables a person to establish mandatory rules for others. Barber, *Constitutional State*, 58-59; Joseph Raz, *Practical Reason and Norms*, 2nd ed. (Princeton, NJ: Princeton University Press, 1990), 85-97.

[93]See note 41 above.

centurion observes and as the Gospel of John testifies again and again (Mt 8:9; e.g., Jn 4:34; 8:28; 15:10). In short, the biblical perspective is very different from Aristotle's, who wrote, "From the hour of birth, some are marked out for subjection, others for rule."[94] The Bible marks out all humanity for both obedience and rule, as we will consider in the next chapter.

Second, this distinction between citizens and subjects will prove useful when we attempt to account for the political status of Adam and Eve before and after the fall. We will see that their insurrection doesn't in fact remove God's rule from over them, but it does change their status from citizens to subjects. Redemption, furthermore, is a recovery of citizenship.

Third, political membership in the Bible necessarily involves a kind of office or vocation or, in popular Christian language, mission. I defined political membership above as an asymmetrical relationship involving the submission of the individual and the affirmation of the authority. Yet a fuller definition would fill out the idea of office even for the "submitting" individual. A person's submission, almost by definition, grants him or her some measure of authority within the body politic. (Even in a tyrannical state like Hitler's a citizen has more authority than a noncitizen.) The question then becomes, how much authority does a member have? Or, to be even more specific, how has the Bible authorized the average church member?

Fourth, the life and foundation of the church, as with every political community, depends on its concern for justice. As we will see in chapter six, the church seeks justice first through the alien justification of the cross, and second in new creation lives given over to justice and righteousness.

### Biblical and Theological Institutionalism

Throughout this chapter, I have treated the institutionalist's vision as applicable to Scripture and to theological concepts. But this raises a question. The neo-institutional movement is a secular one; institutions are perceived as "*humanly devised* constraints that shape human interaction."[95] Furthermore, political scientists and sociologists take an interest in institutions for

---

[94]Aristotle, *Politics*, bk. 1, chap. 5, p. 20.
[95]Douglass C. North, *Institutions, Institutional Change, and Economic Performance* (New York: Cambridge University Press, 1990), 3 (italics mine).

descriptive purposes. Can we legitimately use them to describe divinely devised constraints and then afford them normative status for the lives of people today?

***Not just a secular concept.*** I see absolutely no reason to limit the discussion to institutions of human ingenuity. In fact, a theological perspective would suggest that humans are capable of manufacturing institutions only because they are made in God's image. People are rule making because God is rule making. The Ten Commandments are an institution. The Great Commission is an institution. The kingdom of God is an institution. The universal church is an institution. The Lord's Supper is an institution. The biblical list is long. Each of these things, to borrow from March and Olsen as quoted above, is a "relatively enduring collection of rules [or] organized practices, embedded in structures of meaning and resources that are relatively invariant in the face of turnover of individuals and relatively resilient to the idiosyncratic preferences and expectations of individuals and changing external circumstances."

Should the word *relatively* be omitted from this definition when applied to divinely established institutions? What is crucial to realize is that the answer is no. In orthodox theological perspective, God's nature and character are eternal, and therefore his "law," in some sense of that word, is eternal. Yet the diachronic and episodic nature of redemptive history in the Bible is marked by institutional change from one epoch to the next. In fact, one biblical epoch is differentiated from another precisely by a change in institutions. The command to not eat from the tree of the knowledge of good and evil in Genesis 2 is no longer relevant in Genesis 4. The rule of the judges in the beginning of Samuel has passed away by the end of Samuel. Each of these institutions, to draw again from March and Olsen, "are constitutive rules and practices prescribing appropriate behavior *for specific actors in specific situations*" (italics mine). With a few exceptions, institutions are not eternal, as Paul avers concerning institutions as significant as the Mosaic covenant or the Lord's Supper. The law, Paul says, was "added"; and it came "until" (Gal 3:19-25). Likewise, the Lord's Supper would only be useful "until he comes [again]" (1 Cor 11:26). The institutions of Scripture, then, are relative to God's particular purposes for a particular era.

***An institutional hermeneutic.*** Like the political scientist or sociologist, a Christian theologian will begin with the descriptive enterprise, asking what institutions Scripture describes. But a theologian also assumes that relationship between God and humankind affords normative status to divine institutions,[96] as we will consider more carefully in the next chapter. What is needed, then, is something like an institutional hermeneutic. The goal of such a hermeneutic is not to impose extra-biblical concepts onto Scripture but to employ a more developed "grammar" for interpreting what's in Scripture, much like an understanding of participles and infinitives and verb endings help us understand Hebrew and Greek sentences.

Specifically, an institutional hermeneutic would peel its eyes for those identity- and behavior-shaping rule structures that might be described in one passage but whose jurisdictions must extend into subsequent passages. The challenge lies with determining how far a particular jurisdiction lies and what it means for interpreting a later passage. For instance, how should we interpret the Christian life as it is described in the Epistles in light of the authority of the keys for binding and loosing that Jesus instituted in Matthew 16 and 18? The "keys of the kingdom" are never explicitly mentioned again, but that hardly means they have no relevance for our understanding of the rest of the New Testament.

An institutional reading, in certain respects, looks much like Richard Lints's three horizons of redemptive interpretation. Every biblical text, Lints argues, has three interpretive horizons—textual, ephocal and canonical.[97] Of particular relevance to us is the epochal horizon, since marking off the different biblical epochs is necessary to discern how that text impinges normatively on the Christian's own epoch.[98] Lints has in mind the macroepochs

---

[96]For an inspiring account of biblical authority that is trinitarian and covenantally minded, see Scott R. Swain, *Trinity, Revelation and Reading: A Theological Introduction to the Bible and Its Interpretation* (New York: T&T Clark, 2011), esp. 72-75. Swain helpfully builds on Oliver O'Donovan's conceptions of authority; see 72-73 n. 21. See also Timothy Ward's excellent *Words of Life: Scripture as the Living and Active Word of God* (Nottingham, UK: Inter-Varsity Press, 2009), esp. 22-50 and 129-31.

[97]Richard Lints, *The Fabric of Theology: A Prolegomenon to Evangelical Theology* (Grand Rapids: Eerdmans, 1993), 293-310. To relate Lints to my discussion of Gordon McConville's tripartite methodology in the introduction, I would say that Lints's textual horizon is interested in reading "the text" and "behind the text," in McConville's terms, while the epochal and canonical horizons are necessary for reading "in front of the text."

[98]Lints, *Fabric of Theology*, 301.

of redemptive history, such as the Old and New Testament epochs and their different covenantal administrations. An institutional hermeneutic should certainly begin there, but it would also investigate less obvious microinstitutional structures (such as the keys of the kingdom) in order to consider how they affect later interpretation.[99] Should the Great Commission in Matthew 28 be interpreted through the grid of Matthew 16 and 18, even if that connection is textually unspecified, simply because we assume the disciples still have the authority that Jesus gave them back in chapter 16? That is, should baptisms be performed only by those who possess the power of the keys, or can anyone perform them? And do we then interpret the baptisms in the book of Acts through the lens of Matthew 16 and 18? By analogy, suppose a parent authorizes a babysitter at 6:00 p.m. to keep and instruct the children until the parent returns home. We assume, by virtue of the parent's authorization, that the babysitter can legitimately decide to send the child to bed several hours later, even though nothing was explicitly specified by the parent about the moment of bedtime. The babysitter simply has that authority. Can we interpret disparate biblical texts from different human authors in the same way? It seems that we should be able to if we affirm one divine author, but what is to keep us from unconstrained interpretations?

This brings us to the central point of an "institutional hermeneutic." The question that is always at stake in an institutional hermeneutic is, who is authorized to do what? An institutional hermeneutic views people neither as autonomous agents nor as freely relating members of some vaguely defined community; it views them as citizens in a body politic, both constrained and commissioned by their group membership and governing authority. Indeed, to be a human is to be an office holder. So an institutional reading asks what exactly God authorized Adam to do, and then Noah, then Abraham, then his descendants and so forth.

The question of authorization is at the forefront of an institutional hermeneutic because, unlike philosophical liberalism, an institutional hermeneutic assumes that people are not intrinsically entitled to do *anything*, but must be authorized to act—even to pull a piece of fruit off a tree and eat it

---

[99]For a great example of Jewish political scientists who do this through the Old Testament or Hebrew Bible, see Daniel J. Elazar and Stuart A. Cohen, *The Jewish Polity: Jewish Political Organization from Biblical Times to the Present* (Bloomington: Indiana University Press, 1985).

(Gen 1:29; 2:16). The liberal's "state of nature" story of origins begins with the presumption of individual human authority—executive authority—which the individual may or may not consent to give to the state. The biblical story of origins, on the other hand, offers a more complicated picture, one involving an always-contingent mediated authority.

An institutional hermeneutic also takes care to treat indicatives as indicatives and imperatives as imperatives, while also distinguishing one kind of imperative from another. It is a common evangelical truism, for instance, to observe that "biblical *imperatives* are characteristically founded on biblical *indicatives*."[100] God's indicatives provide the ethical ground of God's imperatives. It's for this reason, says Old Testament ethicist Christopher Wright, that we should take "the indicative and the imperative of the biblical revelation with equal seriousness, and interpret . . . each in light of the other." What that means, says Wright in explaining his so-called missional hermeneutic, is that biblical indicatives have a certain imperatival force, too: "Biblical missiology recognizes that if all this indicative theology is indicative of *reality*, then that carries a massive missional imperative for those who claim this worldview as their own."[101] It is important to Wright for Bible readers to see the imperatival force of indicatives because this allows Wright to then align the mission of God's people with God's mission: "Mission, from the point of view of our human endeavor, means the committed *participation* of God's people in the purposes of God for the redemption of the whole creation. The mission is God's. The marvel is that God invites us to join in."[102] The point is true enough, generically speaking. The difficulty is when Wright begins to point to divine indicatives and treat them as possessing imperatival force for human beings, and then argues that we should not prioritize any one set of imperatives over another:

> A missional hermeneutic of the Bible will not become obsessed with only the great mission imperatives, such as the Great Commission, or be tempted to impose on them one assumed priority or another (e.g., evangelism or social justice or liberation or ecclesiastical order as the only 'real' mission). Rather

---

[100]Christopher J. H. Wright, *The Mission of God: Unlocking the Bible's Grand Narrative* (Downers Grove, IL: IVP Academic, 2006), 59 (italics original).
[101]Ibid., 61 (italics original).
[102]Ibid., 67 (italics original).

we will set those great imperatives within the context of their foundation indicatives, namely, all that God affirms about God.[103]

It is almost as if when Bible readers encounter God doing something *indicatively*, they should assume they are probably responsible to do the same thing *imperatively*.

The problem here is Wright's lack of institutional specificity. An institutional hermeneutic, for this reason, tries to be more careful by letting indicatives behave as indicatives and imperatives as imperatives. The "mission" of a father is not the mission of a president or pastor or church. Nor should we assume the mission of God perfectly maps over the mission of humanity, the Christian, or the church. Instead, we should give careful attention to what imperatives God gives to whom, particularly when they are not just mandatory imperatives but power-conferring imperatives—authorizations and commissions. Also, it is true that imperatives are grounded in indicatives. Yet it remains the case that many biblical indicatives should be evaluated in light of the Bible's power-conferring imperatives. The Old Testament indicatives concerning polygamy, for instance, should be interpreted with the framework of the power-conferring mandate "A man shall leave his wife, and the two shall become one flesh." Wright, to be fair, is more interested in divine indicatives. Yet even here caution is needed before we turn such indicatives into imperatives. I have known married Christians who interpret Psalm 127's indicative concerning the "reward" that children are from the Lord as an imperatival prohibition of birth control. As a result, they have more children than their incomes can support and, in so doing, ironically risk defying Paul's imperative to provide for the members of their household (1 Tim 5:7-8). They fail to treat indicatives as indicatives and imperatives as imperatives.

In short, an institutional hermeneutic is happy to grant that, theologically speaking, imperatives are grounded in indicatives. Yet it would also argue that not all imperatives are created equal. And some imperatives—particularly power-conferring imperatives, authorizations and commissions—do possess a kind of primacy in determining our ethical responsibilities and duties. Determining which ones do, no doubt, is part art, part science, like all interpretation, and Bible readers must inevitably exercise judgment about

---
[103]Ibid., 61.

which commands are the "more important" ones. Jesus seems to have acknowledged that such prioritizations are possible (Mk 12:28-30).

One significant clue, however, can be found in the covenantal structure of the Bible as a whole, which will be explored in chapters three through five. If the life of God's people is structured by covenants, it stands to reason that the commands that play a crucial role in establishing or maintaining a divine-human covenant possess a certain primacy for members of that covenant. Consider the analogy of marriage: those rules that pertain to establishing and formally maintaining the marital covenant ("do not commit adultery") are surely more significant than other kinds of rules for living righteously in marriage ("be considerate"). Violating those covenant rules that establish and solemnize a marriage arguably breaks the marital covenant and provides the grounds for divorce. Other broken rules—being inconsiderate or impatient—do not possess this weight. In case this comparison is unclear, any man might ask his wife whether she would prefer him to be inconsiderate or unfaithful. Her "marital hermeneutic" just might offer a useful guage for knowing which commands are greater and which are lesser.

In the same way, it is not unreasonable to suppose that those biblical imperatives that establish or maintain the covenant community possess a certain primacy. So if the Great Commission extends the reach of the new covenant to places it has never been, might it not possess a certain pride of place in the church's mission?

For our ecclesial purposes, the key question that our institutional hermeneutic will attempt to answer is, *whom* does Jesus authorize to do *what* with the keys of the kingdom? And how can we characterize the biblical differentiation between apostolic authority, elder authority and congregational authority? Whatever the answer is to this particular question, we can generally say that an institutional hermeneutic goes looking for such explicit moments of divine authorization. It changes the way we read texts. It recognizes that once authority has been placed into a person's or a group's hands, other passages pertaining to that person or group must be interpreted in light of that authorization, as with the babysitter analogy above.[104]

---

[104]Elsewhere I have summarized an institutional hermeneutic in five steps: 1. Ask, *who* is authorized to do *what*? 2. Employ wisdom for determining *how* to fulfill an authorization. 3. Heed canonical horizons and covenantal administrations. 4. Be sensitive to different kinds of

***More than a political hermeneutic.*** Let me draw out a bit further what I mean by an "institutional hermeneutic" by comparing it with something similar, namely, Richard Bauckham's political hermeneutic. Bauckham's political hermeneutic attempts to answer the question of how to interpret the Bible politically, which is certainly a complementary goal to my own. Like Lints, Bauckham approaches texts through several layers of interpretation: (1) the text in its linguistic, literary, cultural and historical context; (2) the pre-canonical context; (3) the canonical context; and (4) the contemporary context.[105] These layers don't map over Lints's horizons precisely, but they get us to the same general place—applying ancient texts to today's problems. Bauckham helpfully observes the changing forms and functions of government in Scripture, an important point we will return to. And he argues, correctly in my opinion, that all of what Jesus teaches, even the Sermon on the Mount, is politically relevant: "This being so, it not only follows that the Sermon on the Mount requires political as well as other forms of implementation. It also follows that fundamental New Testament principles for life in the Christian community extend in principle to life in human community as such, and therefore have political relevance."[106] In one sense, I agree with this statement, and my discussion of the relationship between the common covenants and special covenants in chapter four will explain why. But I am unsure of what Buackham means by "political" and "implementation." Just because a matter is "political" does not mean that God has authorized any one institutional agency to implement the matter. Police should not turn the other cheek in their capacity as officers of the law, and churches should not excommunicate members every time a member gets angry.[107] Bauckham presumably agrees with that. My point is merely that we must distinguish between political realities and

---

authority. 5. Treat polity as a subcategory of ethics. Jonathan Leeman, *Don't Fire Your Church Members: A Case for Congregationalism* (Nashville: B&H Academic, 2016), chap. 1.

[105] Richard Bauckham, *The Bible in Politics: How to Read the Bible Politically* (Louisville, KY: Westminster John Knox, 1989), 13-19.

[106] Ibid., 9. Lints affirms the overarching unity of God, God's promises and the storyline of Scripture. Nonetheless he acknowledges the progressive nature of revelation and the fact that God's "redemptive plan does take on different appearances in different periods." Lints, *Fabric of Theology*, 301.

[107] Cf. David VanDrunen, "Bearing Sword in the State, Turning Cheek in the Church: A Reformed Interpretation of Matthew 5:38-42," *Themelios* 34, no. 3 (2009): 322-34.

institutional authorities, and we must give a precise accounting of the latter whenever we assert the presence of the former. "Politics," we saw in chapter one and will consider again in chapter four, admits of both a broad definition that pertains to all of life and a narrow definition that pertains to various institutional entities. So, yes, the Sermon on the Mount has "universal political relevance." But we need to say more than that, institutionally speaking. Whom does Jesus mean to bind and how? And by whom? By analogy, both the sixth commandment and the Russian law against murder are "politically relevant" to me, but neither expressly binds me as an American citizen.[108] In short, I agree utterly with Bauckham that "it is doubtful whether any sharp distinction can be drawn between public and private life" and that "there should be no hermeneutical rule which excludes [Jesus' teaching] from the political sphere."[109] Jesus' teaching is relevant to the whole person, not just to the "spiritual" or "religious" or "Sunday-morning" part of the person. That said, Bauckham's generally salutary political reading requires further institutional specification. Jesus has authorized neither the institutional church nor the state to extend its rule as deeply or broadly as his own rule goes—to implement everything that he has commanded.[110]

Here are two more recent examples of theological authors who employ a reformulated political language (even more than one finds in Bauckham) for theological purposes. First, N. T. Wright rightly rejects "the modern western separation of theology and society, religion and politics,"[111] and therefore he offers a fascinating and in some ways helpful reading of Paul as

---

[108] The fact that the Mosaic covenant is not explicitly binding on anyone who is not a citizen of ancient Israel causes me to be sympathetic with Brian Rosner's treatment of the Old Testament law as "wisdom" for the Christian. The Ten Commandments, technically speaking, do not bind Christians in their Mosaic form. But certainly they point to God's eternal law and wisdom. See Brian Rosner, *Paul and the Law: Keeping the Commandments of God*, New Studies in Biblical Theology (Downers Grove, IL: IVP Academic, 2013).

[109] Bauckham, *Bible in Politics*, 8.

[110] Abraham Kuyper's notion of "sphere sovereignty" comes much closer to my own institutional reading since he conceives of separate spheres of life that are "conscious of the power of exclusive independent judgment and authoritative action, within its proper sphere of action." He begins with the sovereignty of God, who is the source for sovereignty (i.e., authorization) in every sphere. Kuyper, *Lectures on Calvinism*, 78-109, on 96.

[111] N. T. Wright, *Paul: In Fresh Perspective* (Minneapolis: Fortress, 2009), 60, 156-58; also Wright, *The Challenge of Jesus: Rediscovering Who Jesus Was and Is* (Downers Grove, IL: InterVarsity Press, 1999), 21.

confronting the powers of empire.¹¹² So, too, with his understanding of Jesus. As we read Jesus' commands to repent and believe, Wright observes, we must not "screen out these [political] meanings." After all, Jesus' kingdom announcement summoned "people to follow him in the new way of life, the kingdom-way."¹¹³ Wright can make such a claim because he is operating with a reformulated conception of the "political," an appropriate and necessary reformulation that critics miss insofar as they operate from within an Enlightenment paradigm that places too hard a line between the political and the spiritual.¹¹⁴ Yet where their critical noses rightly smell something fishy, perhaps, is in Wright's lack of institutional specification.¹¹⁵ Wright goes on to observe, for instance, that "what Jesus was to Israel, the church must now be for the world. . . . If we are to shape our world, and perhaps even to implement the redemption of our world, this is how it is to be done."¹¹⁶ There is a sense in which that's true, of course. Jesus said he will send his disciples as he has been sent (Jn 20:21).¹¹⁷ But an institutional reading of Scripture demands more specificity. Precisely what did the resurrected Jesus authorize

---

¹¹²Wright, *Paul*, 59-79; Wright, "Paul and Caesar: A New Reading of Romans," in *A Royal Priesthood: The Use of the Bible Ethically and Politically* (Grand Rapids: Zondervan, 2002), 173-193. It *may* be that Wright overreads the significance of the Roman Empire and Caesar in Paul, as if to say that Paul very much has the Caesar cult in mind and not the idolatry of worldly power generally. This, anyhow, is the argument of John Barclay (see his *Pauline Churches and Diaspora Jews* [Tübingen, Germany: Mohr Siebeck, 2011], 363-87). I am genuinely unsure of whether this is a fair critique of Wright. In his defense, Wright extends the significance and challenge of Jesus' rule well beyond the Caesar cult; e.g., "Jesus is Lord and Caesar is not; that Jesus is Lord and Marx, Freud and Nietzsche are not; that Jesus is Lord and neither modernity nor postmodernity is" (Wright, *Challenge of Jesus*, 187). Nonetheless, Barclay's critique does offer an excellent and perhaps more precise articulation of the nature of Jesus' challenge to Caesar: "Paul's gospel is subversive of Roman imperial claims precisely by not opposing them within their own terms, but by reducing Rome's agency and historical significance to just one more entity in a much greater drama. To oppose the Roman empire *as such* would be to take its claims all too seriously: to upstage or outdo Rome would be to accept its terms of reference, even in surpassing them" (Barclay, *Pauline Churches*, 386). I think Barclay is exactly right here; it is just not clear to me that Wright would disagree.
¹¹³Wright, *Challenge of Jesus*, 44.
¹¹⁴Wright correctly perceives that we should not treat the "political" and the "spiritual" as utterly distinct spheres. See Wright, *Paul*, 49. Wright is slightly ambiguous, however, on whether he attributes this same error to the pre-Enlightenment Luther and Luther's concept of the two kingdoms; compare Wright, *Paul*, 49, and *Challenge of Jesus*, 21-22.
¹¹⁵See especially Gilbert Meilaender's incisive critique of Wright's politics in "Wrong from Wright," *First Things*, February 2007, 9-11.
¹¹⁶Wright, *Challenge of Jesus*, 53.
¹¹⁷Wright's discussion of this passage occurs in the final chapter of *Challenge of Jesus*, beginning esp. on 177.

the church to do? Does the church also possess all authority in heaven and earth like Jesus? Should we say that the church holds precisely the same set of office keys that Jesus holds? Wright, to his credit, does differentiate Christ's task from a Christian's task as analogous to a composer and a performer, or an architect and a builder, and hence he summarizes, "our task is to implement his unique achievement."[118] Still, such poetic language in the conversation would be served by a higher degree of institutional specification. For instance, critics hear Wright's talk of Third World debt relief and grow suspicious of ideological foul play. Yet I think this suspicion would be at least partially relieved by clearer demarcations between the local church's joint responsibility and the local church's several responsibility (see chapter six's discussion of joint/several), as well as greater clarity on whether such proposals belong to the category of divine principle or human wisdom, a distinction we will consider in just a moment.[119]

Second, Michael Horton also offers a kind of reconfigured political language in some of his statements. In a discussion of the New Testament's kingdom metaphor in a popular-level work, Horton observes,

> As a minister, I am called regularly by God to make a political speech. A deeply partisan political speech. However, it is not to rally the troops in defense of Christendom against the infidels of various sorts. It divides not between Republicans and Democrats, liberals and conservatives, but between Christ and Antichrist.[120]

Preaching, it would seem, is political. So is evangelism. Both kinds of speech call people to bow before a king whose claims are higher than all other kings. Yet where Horton differs from Wright is that he explicitly distinguishes Christ's authority and the church's authority by referring to Christ's possession of the keys of Death and Hades (Rev 1:18), keys which must not be confused with another set of keys.[121] Horton also observes that the "institution" of the church has a particular and unique charge, not an open-ended one.[122]

---

[118] Wright, *Challenge of Jesus*, 182.
[119] To his credit, Wright *seems* to insinuate the latter. Ibid., 190.
[120] Michael Horton, *The Gospel-Driven Life: Being Good News People in a Bad News World* (Grand Rapids: Baker Books, 2009), 164.
[121] Ibid., 164.
[122] Ibid., 177-78.

## Biblical Wisdom

Back to Richard Bauckham: Bauckham righly points to the "thoroughly historical character of human government" in the Bible, such that "its functions must change and develop in relation to the changes and development of human society."[123] This brings us to one last matter that plays a role in interpreting Scripture institutionally and that should play a role in political theology generally: the distinction between biblical commission or command and wisdom. Many of the arguments Christians have with one another over church and state polity and policy blur these two categories or speeds, which inevitably raises the stakes (and temperature). But our moral and political reasoning needs to be able to operate at both speeds.

Delegated authority, by its nature, is made of stuff that is *fixed*, but it leaves other stuff *flexible*. After all, an authorizing word stipulates an action to be performed, or a goal to be pursued, or a boundary to be kept, but does not always prescribe the precise manner in which the commission must be fulfilled. Inside an authorization, usually, is some measure of freedom, a space where the authorized actor must use wisdom to accomplish the commission's ends. The *who* and the *what* may be specified, but the *how* may be left open. It's like telling a player to take the ball past the goal line, but leaving it to him to figure out how. Broadly speaking, things expressly mandated or commissioned by God are fixed. Things not mandated by God are flexible and subject to wisdom. At the risk of overgeneralizing, this provides us with the relationship between law and wisdom in the Bible: the law establishes the boundaries of the field and the rules of the game; wisdom determines how to best play the game on that field.[124] *That* "whoever sheds the blood of man, by man shall his blood be shed" (Gen 9:6) is divinely fixed. *How* people should go about forming a government is *flexible*.

Within the realm of human rule, then, wisdom becomes vastly important. It begins with the *posture* of fearing the Lord (Prov 1:7), and then it translates into the *skill* of studying the world, the fixed laws of God and the nature of fallen reality, and bringing order to it (e.g., Ex 28:3; 31:6).[125] Biblical wisdom,

---

[123]Bauckham, *Bible in Politics*, 11.
[124]Cf. Walter Brueggemann, *Theology of the Old Testament* (Minneapolis: Fortress, 1997), 337-38.
[125]See "*hakmah*" in *A Hebrew and English Lexicon of the Old Testament*, by Francis Brown, S. R. Driver and Charles A. Briggs (Boston: Houghton Mifflin, 1906); see also Bruce K. Walke, *An*

in two words, is this posture and this skill. It considers the contest (Knight and Johnson's word) of principles and possibilities, and it determines how they all fit together at any given time, all in light of God's overarching rule. Inside the boundaries of his rule and his mandates, biblical wisdom recognizes that there is a time and a season for everything, including "a time to kill and a time to heal, a time to break down and a time to build up" (Eccles 3:3). But what time is it now?

A Christian might therefore argue for liberal political institutions, or a flat tax, or Third World debt relief. Or, on the church side of things, an elder might argue that a church should plant more churches instead of building a bigger building when it's full. What is important to recognize is, none of these institutions, policy applications or practices are biblically prescribed. They fall into the category of wisdom. They are flexible matters, not fixed ones. They might be right in some times and place, but wrong in others. Figuring out which depends on the posture of fearing God and the skill of sorting out how a host of biblical principles uncomfortably collide with the vast multitude of factors that constitute the historical moment. Robert Benne observes, "One must traverse a number of links in an argument to move from those central [biblical] claims to specific public policies. Each link provides an opportunity for Christians of good will and intelligence to disagree on the movement from the center to public policy."[126] Therefore, there is freedom—indeed, a need—for Christians to have good and rowdy debates on these kinds of matters.[127]

Both an institutional hermeneutic and Christian moral/political reasoning generally need to be adept at operating at both speeds—able to recognize what things are fixed and what things are flexible. In that sense, Christian moral reasoning is more sophisticated than secular moral reasoning, which typically operates only at one speed. Either someone is a

---

*Old Testament Theology: An Exegetical, Canonical, and Thematic Approach*, with Charles Yu (Grand Rapids: Zondervan, 2007), 913.

[126]Robert Benne, *Good and Bad Ways to Think about Religion and Politics* (Grand Rapids: Eerdmans, 2010), 34

[127]The two categories of "principle" and "wisdom" are not hermetically sealed. Implicit theological implications, for instance, I would say, fall onto the side of principle, but sometimes they seem to fall somewhere in between principle and wisdom. The Reformed "regulative principle," in my mind, does exactly this.

moral realist, who treats most things as fixed, or a moral relativist, who treats everything as flexible. Christians make allowances for both. One of the crimes that Jesus charged Israel's leaders with was taking prudential matters and converting them into absolutes, confusing what is fixed and what is flexible: "You leave the commandment of God and hold to the tradition of men. . . . Thus making void the word of God by your tradition" (Mk 7:8, 13).

To be sure, Christians concerned with political engagement should sort out which is which when talking among themselves before turning to the general public. Which things do we hold with a firm grip, and which things do we hold with a loose grip? Which arguments might prove publicly accessible, and which will not? That's not to say Christians should only make publicly accessible arguments. Principle might require us to do otherwise. The point is, it's always good to know which hills are worth dying on before you die on the wrong hill.

## Conclusion

Western Christians are quick to criticize any talk of a church's institutional authority. We are "spiritual, not religious." Institutions, recall, are the application of authority to a relationship, which is exactly what people do not want for their "spiritual" life. Could it be that Western Christians might take a cue from the political scientists and that they need an institutional revival of their own? One can think of three benefits of such a revival.

First, a right understanding of institutional authority aids clarity of identity. After all, commands and covenants define. They confer identity. Until a relationship is defined, it lacks identity, direction and even purpose, as most couples who prolong their dating relationship eventually discover. But clarifying the church's identity through clarifying who its members are serves both those inside and outside the church.

Second, a right understanding of institutional authority aids a Christian understanding of language and truth. Words, after all, are kinds of institutions. A word is a complex of rules and judgments that govern pronunciation, spelling, meaning and usage. Those rules, no doubt, are elastic and forever evolving, but they are rules nonetheless. "This is the truth behind Wittgenstein's dictum," says Charles Taylor, "that agreement in meanings involves agreement in judgments."[128] Postmodernism's work of deconstructing the word, then, is but the culminating act of rejecting all authority and the very idea of rules. Surely this is not the place to pursue the matter in depth, but it is worth at least casting a headlong glance toward the epistemological significance of the keys of the kingdom. If the keys of the kingdom include the authority to define right gospel doctrine, as I shall argue in chapter six, then Jesus was fundamentally defying Kant's noumena/phenomena divide, not just by claiming to speak for heaven himself, but by claiming *to give others* the authority to say who and what represents heaven.

Third, a right understanding of institutional authority might aid in developing Christian spirituality and discipleship.[129] Christianity in the West—its sense of spirituality and its concept of the Christian life—is arguably individualistic, consumeristic and anti-institutional. Many Christians, especially evangelical ones, bear a notable preference for spontaneous prayers over scripted ones, new songs over old ones, creativity over liturgy, humor over reverence. What might it mean to conceive of Christian discipleship "institutionally"? One gets a hint in a Hugh Heclo chapter called "Thinking Institutionally." He points to four attributes of institutional thinking. First, institutional thinking is *not* the modern impulse to critically challenge, question, unmask, expose and demystify everything that's placed in front of us. It is not a hermeneutic of suspicion. Second, institutional thinking instead involves a posture of faithful receiving and not just continual inventing. It aims to preserve and pass on the valuable and true old things, not just write new things. This requires knowing when "to be submissive," Heclo says, since some things are of inestimable value. This brings us to a third characteristic: institutional thinking includes strong moral evaluations of right and wrong or better and worse; and therefore it involves moral obligations and not just decisions of convenience. It presumes that some things are larger than us and more important than what is immediately likable. There is therefore a place for duty and deference. Fourth, institutional

---

[128]Taylor, *Sources of the Self*, 35.
[129]I spend a chapter considering the significance of church polity for Christian discipleship. See "Introduction—Why Polity," in *Baptist Foundations: Church Government for an Anti-Institutional Age*, ed. Mark Dever and Jonathan Leeman (Nashville: B&H Academic, 2015), 1-23.

thinking involves lengthened time horizons. It considers both the lessons of the past and the impact to be made on the future. It values the long-term over the short-term.[130]

I do not think it is very difficult to imagine how these four principles might apply to Christian discipleship. And I would add a fifth principle: institutional thinking presupposes a reshaped and enlarged sense of identity, such that one sometimes values and prioritizes institutional responsibilities over and above immediate personal preferences. Parents make sacrifices for their children because they view themselves as "parents," which is, in some sense, to think institutionally. Spouses do the same because they have learned to think within the constraints of the institution of marriage. The individualism that is implicit in our culture's acceptance of divorce and absentee fathers is one more variety of anti-institutionalism.

Ayn Rand might have advised the world to "redeem your mind from the hockshops of authority,"[131] but I would like to offer a fundamentally different vision. By recovering the ability to think institutionally, hopefully this book, at least in a small way, will help to "aid a process of healing the fragmentation which is so much a feature of our world."[132]

---

[130]Hugh Heclo, "Thinking Institutionally," in *Oxford Handbook of Political Institutions*, 731-42. See also Thomas Sowell, *A Conflict of Visions: Ideological Origins of Political Struggles*, rev. ed. (New York: Basic Books, 2007), 36-101.
[131]Ayn Rand, *Atlas Shrugged*, centennial ed. (New York: Plume, 2005), 1058.
[132]Gunton, *The One, The Three and the Many*, 7.

THREE

# The Politics of Creation

Theologian John Webster has observed, "A doctrine of the church is only as good as the doctrine of God which underlies it."[1] That is to say, a person's beliefs about God are in some sense prior and logically determinative for his or her beliefs about God's people.

The same determinative relationship abides between one's doctrine of salvation and one's doctrine of the church. Webster, again, writes, "It is . . . an especial concern for evangelical ecclesiology to demonstrate not only that the church is a necessary implicate of the gospel but also that gospel and church exist in a strict and irreversible order, one in which the gospel precedes and the church follows."[2] In other words, God's people are whatever they are by virtue of whatever gospel they embrace.

This chapter and the next three try to make good on Webster's theological wisdom. If we wish to contend that the church is a political entity, then it would stand to reason that the gospel, which gives life to the church, must be political. And if the gospel is political, then it would seem that something about God himself is inherently political. Perhaps his good news is political because something about his very character or being requires it? That, in reverse course, is our general path for this chapter and the next three: from God, to the gospel, to the church.

---
[1] John Webster, "The Church and the Perfection of God," in *The Community of the Word: Toward an Evangelical Ecclesiology*, ed. Mark Husbands and Daniel J. Treier (Downers Grove, IL: InterVarsity Press, 2005), 78.
[2] Ibid., 76. Cf. Kevin J. Vanhoozer, "Evangelism and the Church: The Company of the Gospel," in *The Futures of Evangelicalism: Issues and Prospects*, ed. Craig Bartholomew, Robin Parry and Andrew West (Grand Rapids: Kregel, 2003), 70-77.

The previous two chapters have provided some of the tools for this biblical construction project. In chapter one, we both acquired a way for speaking about the political and pointed toward the inadequacies of a strict liberal bifurcation between the political and the spiritual. Politics, we saw, can be described narrowly as those activities that fall within the jurisdiction of those public-wide and coercive institutions responsible for governing a people. Yet there is also a sense in which politics can be described more broadly with reference to the dynamics of power and authority that infiltrate all of life. The conversation might have proceeded directly from the end of chapter one to the place where we now stand, ready to begin building our own political theology. But instead we used chapter two like a trip to the hardware store to acquire a few more tools for the project, specifically the language of institutions, political communities and political membership.

The goal now is to begin building that "fuller political conceptuality," one that "pushes back the horizon of commonplace politics and opens it up to the activity of God."[3] This chapter's constructive argument proceeds as follows: all political reality begins (1) with the fact that God is Three and One, meaning he is social but his sociality possesses a particular (holy and just) order and shape and (2) with the rule that he possesses over every human creature. Political reality then becomes an essential aspect of human existence by virtue of (1) the fact that our relationships should bear the same (holy and just) ordering or shape of the triune God, which leads to (2) our absolute and comprehensive subjection to the institution of God's authorizing, citizen-making law.

If all of this is true, it should not be too difficult to see that all political reality is utterly "spiritual" or "religious" and that all religion, true or idolatrous, is utterly "political." In fact, the so-called religious phenomena of both sinful rebellion and heart-wrought worship are as political as they are religious.

To this end, I will offer an institutional reading of the Old Testament in this chapter and the next two, which means focusing on *who* gives *whom* authority to do *what*. Of course, this institutional reading will not be exhaustive but selective.

---

[3]Oliver O'Donovan, *Desire of the Nations: Rediscovering the Roots of Political Theology* (New York: Cambridge University Press, 1996), 2.

## THE POLITICS OF GOD

Every secular conception of politics restricts its gaze to the relationship between two parties, an earthly ruler and an earthly ruled. But a theological conception of politics openly accounts for an all-defining third party, namely, the one who is the source of all legitimate authority or rule in the universe: God. Any descriptive or normative statements about political activity, authority or obligation between two or more human parties need to be interpreted within the larger framework of God's "politics" and how he both exercises authority and delegates authority to humanity.[4]

Attempting to examine the analogy between divine and earthly authority, no doubt, is an enterprise fraught with difficulty. David Nicholls, commenting on the cultural, economic and political embeddedness of all theological construction, observes, "How Christians think of God's authority . . . will inevitably be affected by their experience of earthly structures of domination."[5] Nicholls's own work then traces a number of different images of God in the last few centuries, and how these images have been reciprocally related to different political movements: the medieval God of unmitigated sovereignty and the absolute state; the covenant-making God of the Puritans and the beginnings of a federal vision for the state; the basic law–establishing God of deism and the night-watchman state of libertarianism; the perfection of God among Romantics and nineteenth-century German nationalism; the benevolent God of liberal Christianity and the welfare state; as well as the crucified God of liberation theology and the perpetual protest against the state.[6] And Nicholls perceives this as a two-way street. A society's cultural and political situation will dramatically impact its conception of God, and simultaneously, "language used about God has habitually been

---

[4]Two secular political theorists put it this way: "The religious traditions ground their political morality in a fuller, more substantive understanding of human good, deriving ultimately from their understanding of human beings' place in the Divine order, whereas the secular traditions begin with the idea that human beings have certain generic interests—interests in liberty, material resources, and so forth—but try to avoid taking a stand on questions of ultimate value." David Miller and Sohail H. Hashmi, introduction to *Boundaries and Justice: Diverse Ethical Perspectives*, ed. David Miller and Sohail H. Hashmi (Princeton, NJ: Princeton University Press, 2001), 13.

[5]David Nicholls, *Deity and Domination: Images of God and the State in the Nineteenth and Twentieth Centuries* (New York: Routledge, 1994), 28; see also his *God and Government in an "Age of Reason"* (New York: Routledge, 1995).

[6]Nicholls, *Deity and Domination*, 15-23.

adopted in political discourse and has in turn influenced the course of events at the institutional level."[7]

Though the danger exists of reading our experiences and preferences of human government into the divine government, it remains the case that many of the biblical images of God have political referents, such as king, lord and judge. Further, chapter one's discussion suggested that it is impossible to separate our political and spiritual thinking. Each shapes the other. The only question is, are people aware of their assumptions about God, and can they articulate how these assumptions impinge on their political views and vice versa? Ironically, to the extent that people articulate this relationship, to that same extent they potentially become less likely to impose their political views on God, precisely because articulation forces a level of transparency and—for Christians—fidelity to Scripture. Individuals who have not done the intellectual work of asking what their politics say about God may be imposing those views upon God as much as anyone, only they don't know it. Articulating these connections opens up a thinker to self-critique and the critique of others, which is generally salubrious. So instead of criticizing *that* someone explicitly draw points of connection between a doctrine of God and politics, I would propose it is better to criticize *how well* one does such work.

From a biblical perspective, the realities of human politics are grounded in truths about God. If "every family in heaven and on earth is named" by virtue of its resemblance to the prototypical heavenly Father (Eph 3:14-15), it would seem that the same is true of every earthly "king" (even if Israel originally received its own king as a kind of concession). It is unfortunate then that "theologians . . . have generally paid scant attention to the significance of the political language used about God."[8]

Fully understanding the relationship between divine and human authority would require nothing less than a complete doctrine of God. But for our more modest purposes here, we will focus on the sovereign rule that God possesses by virtue of his status as Creator. And here I am interested not so much in God's power to rule but in his right to rule. Yet before we turn to such an institutional reading, it is worth setting God's rule in the

---

[7]Ibid., 3.
[8]Ibid., 10.

systematic and canonical context of his triune nature. Just as understanding *who* Christ is helps us understand *what* he did, so understanding the *who* of the Trinity helps us grasp the *what* of God's rule.⁹

**Divine sociality.** To get at a theological conception of politics we begin with the fact that the Christian conception of God is distinctively trinitarian. He exists in three persons who abide in eternal relatedness, and these three persons share one nature and essence. Furthermore, it is critical for our political formulations to emphasize both the threeness and the oneness.

Emphasizing God's threeness reminds us that a social being is at the center of all existence, and the study of politics concerns, among other things, the matter of sociality. Though I would not adopt the whole of Karl Barth's doctrine of the Trinity, I believe his Buber-esque language of the I-Thou relation within God himself is useful here. Within God, says Barth, there is "a genuine but harmonious self-encounter and self-discovery; a free co-existence and co-operation; an open confrontation and reciprocity."[10] God is essentially—by nature—personal, which is to say, interpersonal or social. There are within God self-conscious encounters between the three persons (unlike Barth, I would even say three subjects) of the Godhead. God has the relational resources within himself to affirm and acknowledge another, another who is, somehow, himself. The Father is aware of himself as himself relative to the Son and the Spirit, and vice versa, a reality which is at least implicit in statements such as John 17:5.

Yet just as soon as we emphasize the three persons, we must also emphasize the one nature and essence.[11] Politics is not just about sociality; it is about structured sociality—constrained and commissioned sociality, to use

---

[9]Cf. John Webster: "And because God's identity is enacted in his works, theological reflection upon God's attributes is to proceed on the basis of the given reality of God's making himself known as the Father, the Son and the Spirit, who stands in relation to the world and is at work in the world as its creator, saviour and perfecter." Webster, *Holiness* (Grand Rapids: Eerdmans, 2003), 40.

[10]Karl Barth, *Church Dogmatics*, III/1, *The Doctrine of Creation*, ed. G. W. Bromiley and T. F. Torrance (New York: T&T Clark, 1958), 185.

[11]The importance of giving equiprimacy to both the Three and the One goes back at least to Gregory of Nazianzus, who is quoted by Calvin in *Institutes of the Christian Religion*, trans. Ford Lewis Battles (Philadelphia: Westminster, 1960), 1:141. For contemporary articulations, see Paul D. Molnar, *Divine Freedom and the Doctrine of the Immanent Trinity: In Dialogue with Karl Barth and Contemporary Theology* (New York: T&T Clark, 2002), 232-33; Robert Letham, *The Holy Trinity: In Scripture, History, Theology, and Worship* (Phillipsburg, NJ: P&R, 2004), 463-64.

institutional language from the last chapter. And this is where at least some formulations of the so-called Social Trinity prove inadequate,[12] especially as they define the divine "persons" purely as relations[13] unconstrained by any ontological necessity.[14] God's three persons do not relate to one another in an unconstrained, willy-nilly fashion. They relate by the ontological necessity of their shared nature and essence, which is to say, according to the constraints and purposes of God's love, holiness, wisdom, justice and all the other attributes of God's nature. Each person of the Trinity is not merely aware of himself relative to the others—an undefined sociality of separate individuals. Instead, each bears himself toward the others as governed by a shared nature and essence. So the Father's person careens invariably toward love of the Son: "This is my beloved Son." And the Son bends invariably in holy consecration toward the Father: "I have come . . . not to do my own will but the will of him who sent me."[15] God's attributes must be understood, not as abstract Platonic principles, but as "character trait predicates" or "personal qualities,"[16] which becomes all the more evident when we consider the fact that the Word became flesh (Jn 1:14).

---

[12]Numerous examples of Social Trinitarians might be cited. Two of the more prominent examples include Jürgen Moltmann, *The Trinity and the Kingdom* (Minneapolis: Fortress, 1993), and John Zizioulas, *Being as Communion: Studies in Personhood and the Church* (Crestwood, NY: St. Vladimir's Seminary Press, 1985). Also J. Scott Horell, "Toward a Biblical Model of the Social Trinity: Avoiding Equivocation," *Journal of the Evangelical Theological Society* 47, no. 3 (September 2004): 399-421. For a description, see Stanley J. Grenz, *Rediscovering the Triune God: The Trinity in Contemporary Theology* (Minneapolis: Fortress, 2004), 117-62. For a critique, see Kevin Vanhoozer, *Remythologizing Theology: Divine Action, Passion, and Authorship* (New York: Cambridge University Press, 2010), 139-78.

[13]E.g., Colin E. Gunton, *The Promise of Trinitarian Theology* (Edinburgh: T&T Clark, 1991), 98; see also Gunton, "The Church on Earth: The Roots of Community," in *On Being the Church: Essays on the Christian Community*, ed. Colin E. Gunton and Daniel W. Hardy (Edinburgh: T&T Clark, 1989), 70. Cf. Wesley Hill, "Divine Persons and Their 'Reduction' to Relations: A Plea for Conceptual Clarity," *International Journal of Systematic Theology* 14, no. 2 (April 2012): 148-60.

[14]E.g., Zizioulas, *Being as Communion*, 44, 46. Vanhoozer offers a succinct critique: "The point is that relationality alone does not exhaust what we want to say either about God's being or about God's triune personhood. It is unnecessarily reductionist to collapse God's essence or deity into his interpersonal communion or onto-relationality. . . . While it is true to say that 'one can only be a person in relation to other persons,' it need not follow that persons are nothing but relations." Vanhoozer, *Remythologizing Theology*, 143.

[15]Admittedly, these verses refer to the divine Father's affirmation of the incarnate Son's obedience, but I do not believe it is a stretch to presume that such verses give us a glimpse into the relationship between Father and Son in eternity past (cf. John 17:5). We do not need to affirm Karl Rahner's "the economic is the immanent" in order to say that the economic will certainly not contradict the immanent.

[16]See Webster's helpful discussion in *Holiness*, esp. 39-43.

To put the One and the Three together, we can say, for instance, that God's attribute of love is ontologically inseparable from his triune nature.[17] God is not a divine monad, which by definition cannot love or affirm the existence of another "within" itself but would depend on the presence of another—namely, creation—to love.[18] His love is "a fundamental characterization of his Trinitarian being."[19] God's holiness, likewise, is a *relational* concept."[20] To say that God was holy in eternity past (before the advent of sin) requires us to assume that he was utterly consecrated to something.[21] But consecrated to what? He was and is utterly consecrated to himself, which is to say, the Father is utterly devoted to the Son, the Son to the Father and so forth. In other words, a concept of three persons is essential for understanding the nature of God's holiness. The same sensitivity to the One and the Three must be given to our understanding of God's justice. True justice depends on a rightness that exists within the context of relationships, relationships that possess both the mutually given respect and honor commensurate with "free co-existence and co-operation" (to borrow Barth's language again) and a holy trajectory that singularly aims at the glory of God. Make God a monad or propose that his affections are not holy, however, and it becomes more difficult to claim that God, by nature, is just. There would be no (Barth again) "self-encounter and self-discovery," no "free co-existence and co-operation," no "open confrontation and reciprocity" within God's being by which to predicate justice. In short, God's holy, just and loving nature, to say nothing of his other attributes, are ontologically inseparable from his triune being. We need both the Three and the One—a concept of sociality and a concept of constrained/purposeful sociality.

---

[17] Letham, *Holy Trinity*, 444.
[18] Hence, Vanhoozer observes, "His being love . . . is fully realized in the immanent Trinity before the economic Trinity actualizes it in history." Vanhoozer, *Remythologizing Theology*, 462.
[19] John Frame, *The Doctrine of God* (Phillipsburg, NJ: P&R, 2002), 416.
[20] Webster, *Holiness*, 44 (italics original). My understanding of God's holiness comes close to John Webster's as it is articulated in *Holiness*, 39-52, but there is not space (or need) here to explain the ways in which it differs. For a fuller explanation of my approach, see my *The Church and the Surprising Offense of God's Love: Reintroducing the Doctrines of Church Membership and Discipline* (Wheaton, IL: Crossway, 2010), 99-102.
[21] Peter Gentry, drawing on the work of French evangelical scholar Claude-Bernard Costecalde, argues that the word "holiness" in the biblical literature does not merely mean being "separated from" but also "consecrated to" or "devoted to." Peter J. Gentry, "The Covenant at Sinai," *Southern Baptist Journal of Theology* 12, no. 3 (Fall 2008): 48.

***Human sociality.*** How is God's triune nature relevant to a conversation about theological politics?[22] First, it is important as we consider what it means for humanity to bear the divine image.[23] I do not think we need to adopt Barth's strained exegesis of Genesis 1:27, or reduce our interpretation of image language to pure relationality, as Barth does, in order to affirm with him that being created in God's image surely must entail or at least presuppose "the analogy of free differentiation and relation" within humankind.[24] To put it plainly, God has a social nature and so do human beings. And politics—here is the point of relevance—is the business of organizing and governing groups of social beings according to a certain concept of

---

[22]For a chapter-length overview of twentieth-century discussions of the relationship between Trinity and politics, see Frederick Christian Bauerschmidt, "The Trinity and Politics," in *The Oxford Handbook of the Trinity*, ed. Gilles Emery and Matthew Levering (New York: Oxford University Press, 2011), 531-45. He concludes that it is best *not* to build a foundation or draw lessons for politics from the immanent Trinity, but that we should restrict our consideration to the economic Trinity: "The political relevance of the doctrine of the Trinity remains directly proportional to the faithfulness of the baptized, to their living out of the distinctive way of Christ, the way of friendship with God through the Spirit" (ibid., 541). Whereas I affirm his concerns about the approach to politics taken by Social Trinitarians, and that the theology of Trinity serves the theology of mission, I also believe that God's triune mission, in the words of Scott Swain and Andreas Köstenberger, "also reveal *how* those three distinct persons relate to one another *as persons.*" In short, we cannot not divide God's being and mission: "The economic Trinity *is* the immanent Trinity personally engaged in the act of becoming *our* Father, through the Son, by the Spirit." Köstenberger and Swain, *Father, Son and Spirit: The Trinity in John's Gospel* (Downers Grove, IL: IVP Academic, 2008), 172, 182. A full treatment of the relationship between the Trinity and politics, therefore, would need to consider the relationship between God's being, the church's mission and the relationship between the church's mission and politics. In other words, I believe there is another way of approaching the relationship between Trinity and politics—the one discussed in this chapter—that Bauerschmidt's argument does not consider.

[23]No doubt, trying to trace out the "social analogy" between God's triune being and humanity is fraught with difficulty, as is evident in so many of the recent ecclesiologies that attempt to ground the church in the doctrine of the immanent Trinity. For instance, I believe Cornelius Plantinga Jr. overextends the analogy in "Images of God," in *Christian Faith and Practice in the Modern World: Theology from an Evangelical Point of View*, ed. Mark A. Noll and David F. Wells (Grand Rapids: Eerdmans, 1988), 51-67; also Plantinga, *The Hodgson-Welch Debate and the Social Analogy of the Trinity* (Ann Arbor, MI: UMI Dissertation Services, 1982). Miroslav Volf handles the "limits of the analogy" much more carefully by reminding us that language is analogical and that we should not assume that "person" and "communion" mean the same thing at the human and divine levels. See Volf, *After Our Image: The Church as the Image of the Trinity* (Grand Rapids: Eerdmans, 1998), 198-200, 210-12, including his explicit disagreement with Plantinga, 212n. Volf writes elsewhere, "All attempts at connecting the Trinity with the character of human life that operate with one-to-one correspondences are false.... Human beings are manifestly not God." Volf, "Being as God Is," in *In God's Life in Trinity*, ed. Miroslav Volf and Michael Welker (Minneapolis: Fortress, 2006), 5.

[24]Barth, *Church Dogmatics*, III/1, 185.

righteousness and justice.²⁵ Old Testament scholar Christopher Wright summarizes and draws the connection to politics:

> God, therefore, in the mystery of the Trinity, lives in the harmonious relationship of equal Persons, each of whom possesses his proper function, authority and relatedness to each of the others. Human beings, therefore, made in God's image, were created to live in the harmony of personal equality but with social organization that required functional structures and patterns of relationship. The ordering of social relationships and structures, locally, nationally and globally is of direct concern to our Creator God, then. But such ordering is precisely the stuff of politics.²⁶

We are by nature political beings, at least in part, because we are social beings, as Aristotle famously observed.²⁷ To be human is to live "in free differentiation and relation" (Barth's phrase) with other persons. It is to affirm the separate existence of others while simultaneously recognizing the mutual dependence of our identities: I am not you, but I am who I am at least in part through my relationship with you. But Wright helps us to see beyond Aristotle. We're political beings not just because we are "social beings," vaguely defined. God's three persons live in a "harmonious relationship" in which each person "possesses his proper function, authority and relatedness." That is, these relationships must conform to the requirements of God's nature—his holiness, justice, righteousness and love. God's holiness and love, I said above, require a certain kind of ordering between Father and Son. Their relationship must bear a certain shape. It cannot be, say, unloving or unholy. And that structured ordering between Father and Son on account of God's holiness and love is the very beginning or seed of politics. The seed sprouts and shows its flowers in humanity as we reflect on what it means to be made in God's image. If Father and Son must relate to one another—organize their interpersonal postures toward one another—according to the character-trait predicates or "rules" of holiness and love, then it stands to reason that every relationship for every being made in

---

²⁵See Joseph L. Mangina, *Karl Barth: Theology of Christian Witness* (Louisville, KY: Westminster John Knox, 2004), 96.

²⁶Christopher J. H. Wright, *Old Testament Ethics for the People of God* (Downers Grove, IL: IVP Academic, 2004), 215.

²⁷Aristotle, *Politica*, trans. Benjamin Jowett, in *The Basic Works of Aristotle*, ed. Richard McKeon (New York: Random House, 1941), bk 1, chap. 2, p. 1253.

God's image, likewise, will need to organize itself according to the requirements of God's own love and holiness. Human politics, in other words, is the yield of God's three persons organizing their lives according to the requirements of God's nature. This is what I meant at the beginning of the chapter when I said that if the church and the gospel are political, it would seem to point us back to something about God.

The political significance of God's triune nature among image-bearing human beings can be discerned all the better by setting it against a contrast, namely, the political implications of a nontrinitarian conception of God, say, the God of Islam.[28] Theologian Robert Letham observes, "Islam has no way to explain or even to maintain human personhood. Relationality among human beings cannot be founded on man being the image of God, since God himself is not and cannot be a relational being. Moreover, love cannot exist in God. A monad cannot love."[29] The political implication of this for Islam, says Letham, is an inability to affirm diversity or plurality. Instead, the God of Islam requires a unitary community.[30] Lacking a theological basis for "free differentiation in relation" (Barth's phrase), conformity is pursued through sheer force of will. This is why, Letham suggests, Muslim states are often authoritarian dictatorships, why church and state are equated, why

---

[28]Miroslav Volf argues that Christians should not so quickly dismiss Allah as one and the same with the Christian God since, he observes, Christians "overwhelmingly" affirm that nontrinitarian Jews and trinitarian Christians have the same God. Volf, *Allah: A Christian Response* (San Francisco: HarperOne, 2011), 144. The trouble with Volf's argument is that Jesus explicitly tells his followers, "No one who denies the Son has the Father" (1 John 2:23; cf. John 15:23; 2 John 9). If, then, a Jew rejects Jesus (and by implication the Trinity), a Christian must *not* affirm the Jew's God as his or her own.

[29]Letham, *Holy Trinity*, 444. Contra Volf, who compares Sufi references to self-love within Allah to the interpersonal love within the Trinity as an example of "widespread convergence" between the two faiths, two faiths which—Volf is at pains throughout the book to suggest—worship the same God, in spite of Islam's denial of the Trinity (Volf, *Allah*, 166-67, see also 143). The problem, of course, is that a unipersonal being cannot be in a relationship within himself, which, strangely, Volf simultaneously recognizes (ibid., 169-70).

[30]This is not to say that all Islamic scholars would agree with these statements. There is, for instance, a robust debate among Islamic scholars over whether or not Islam is compatible with democratic values and institutions. See Hamid Enayat, *Modern Islamic Political Thought* (Austin, TX: University of Texas Press, 1982) 77, 125-30; Anthony Black, *The History of Islamic Political Thought: From the Prophet to the Present* (New York: Routledge, 2001), 294, 327, 339-41; John L. Esposito and Dalia Mogahed, *Who Speaks for Islam? What a Billion Muslims Really Think* (New York: Gallup Press, 2007), 35-57; W. Montgomery Watt, *Islamic Political Thought* (Edinburgh: Edinburgh University Press, 1968), 121-22; L. Carl Brown, *Religion and State: The Muslim Approach to Politics* (New York: Columbia University Press, 2000), 49; Olivier Roy, *Globalized Islam: The Search for a New Ummah* (New York: Columbia University Press, 2004), 78-79, 334.

conversion from Islam is often illegal, why women are required to wear veils and so forth.[31]

Colin Gunton helps us see a larger principle here: unitary conceptions of God have tended historically to lend themselves to totalitarian or repressive forms of political order.[32] Interestingly, Gunton also perceives such a strong monist tendency in modern secular individualism, which he calls a "non-relational creed" that teaches, "I do not need my neighbor to be myself." Secular individualism provides a "false universal" that "breeds homogeneity."[33] Gunton's solution is a social doctrine of the Trinity, which, though it may push too far toward the Three and compromise the One, rightly perceives the significance of God's relational nature for society at large. Ultimately, it should not be surprising that, bereft of a triune conception of God, traditional Islam at one end of a theonomist spectrum and secular individualism at the other can both offer a brand of politics that tends to be dehumanizing.

In conclusion, I would propose that our understanding of politics, that constraining and commissioning of relationships across an entire society, must have its origins in the God who is Three and One. To put an even finer point on it, we can find a suitable starting point for our understanding of politics in the divine Father's affirmation of the divine Son and the Son's submission to the Father, an affirmation and submission on display at least in the incarnate Son's submission to the righteousness and love of the Father: "This is my beloved Son, with whom I am well pleased" (Mt 3:17) and "You have loved righteousness and hated wickedness; therefore God, your God, has anointed you with the oil of gladness beyond your companions" (Heb 1:9). Political society, we observed in the last chapter, begins with an asymmetrical relationship of affirmation and submission. We do not need to speculate about the relationship of Father and Son in eternity past in order to maintain that, in the incarnation, the Father and Son enacted a perfect society for the sake of the watching universe, where relationships of affirmation and submission were employed to display the holiness, justice, unity and love of God.

---

[31]Robert Letham, *Holy Trinity*, 444.
[32]Colin E. Gunton, *The One, The Three, and the Many: God, Creation, and the Culture of Modernity* (New York: Cambridge University Press, 1993), 24, 25. See also Nicholls, *Deity and Domination*.
[33]Gunton, *The One, The Three*, 32, 31, 30. See also Charles Taylor, *Hegel and Modern Society* (New York: Cambridge University Press, 1979), 131-33.

And this display was to then be mimicked by God-imagers.[34] We should indeed be careful about overextending the social analogy between the Trinity and human relationships, but the Gospel of John provides several areas of explicit warrant: that rightly oriented God-imagers will obey Christ as Christ has obeyed the Father, and so love obediently as he has loved obediently (Jn 15:10, 12); that they will be one as the Father and Son are one (Jn 17:22); that they will love one another as the Father and Son have loved one another (Jn 17:26; cf. 13:34-35). What then is the lesson to be learned from the relationship of the divine Father and the incarnate Son? Good government works according to principles of righteousness, justice and love; and good government works best when ruler and ruled are perfectly in sync. These lessons might seem obvious, but it is worth observing that the obvious roots itself in the nature and being of the triune God himself, assuming, as I do, that we can draw lessons about the immanent Trinity from the economic Trinity.[35]

### THE POLITICS OF CREATION

If the first aspect of the doctrine of God to be considered for political purposes is his triune nature, the second aspect is the sovereign authority he possesses by virtue of his work of creation. And here we move from systematic to biblical theology and what I am calling an institutional reading: *who* has given *whom* authority to do *what*? Moving from systematic to biblical theology may seem out of order, but my purpose has been to establish the triunity of God as a foundational given, a creedal guardrail for the road. Partly, this is for the sake of counterbalancing any temptation to a monistic and authoritarian concept of authority in what follows, particularly as we consider the authority of the Creator God. It is my sense, for instance, that the tension among Medieval theologians between the *potentia ordinata* and the *potentia absoluta* of God would have been served by a healthier dose of trinitarian thinking.[36] But I have also begun with these systematic assertions

---

[34]Colin Gunton helpfully establishes the social analogy between divine Father and Son and God's eschatological purposes for humanity (how he means humans to ultimately live together) through the obedience of the incarnation. Gunton, *The Triune Creator: A Historical and Systematic Study* (Grand Rapids: Eerdmans, 1998), 24.

[35]See Köstenberger and Swain, *Father, Son and Spirit*, 179-85.

[36]For a quick introduction to the general lines of the discussion, see "*Potentia Dei absoluta*" in Justo L. González, *Essential Theological Terms* (Louisville, KY: Westminster John Knox, 2005), 136; or Jean Bethke Elshtain, *Sovereignty: God, State, and Self* (New York: Basic Books, 2008),

because the relationship between the divine Father and the incarnate Son helps us understand the nature of political authority and citizenship among people. It recasts the relationship between authority and submission, positing them as two sides of the same coin in one individual, but in irrevocable order: first submission, then rule. The incarnate Son submitted entirely to the will of the Father, just as Adam and Israel should have submitted. But that act of submission established Jesus as the true image of God with all lordship or authority (Col 1:15-20). The divinely ruled becomes ruler. Obedience to God becomes biblical freedom. It took the triune God himself to intervene in history, assume the human office of citizen (ruled ruler) and enact what human rule was to be like.

*The Creator is king.* To build on a biblical-theological foundation means beginning in the opening chapters of Genesis and observing that God's rule over humankind—the stuff of which political authority is made—begins with his role as creator.[37] To the secular outlook, political authority is typically gained by military conquest, by tradition or inheritance, or by the consent of the governed.[38] Yet God's authority over the nations of the earth is a consequence or a property of his role as creator. Just as an author has authority over what she writes, so a creator with creation.[39] God made all things, and therefore he has the moral right to rule all things.[40]

---

[34-39]. Richard Muller offers a more thorough discussion at multiple points in *Post-Reformation Reformed Dogmatics: The Rise and Development of Reformed Orthodoxy, ca. 1520 to ca. 1725*, vol. 3, *The Divine Essence and Attributes* (Grand Rapids: Baker Books, 2003), esp. 61-70, 532-40, including some mischaracterization on both sides of the discussion (see 70, also 81-82). For my part, I would affirm O'Donovan's sensitive articulation of God's *potentia ordinata* in *Desire of the Nations*, 32, also 19, 31.

[37]Cf. Richard Bauckham, *God Crucified: Monotheism and Christology in the New Testament* (Grand Rapids: Eerdmans, 1998), 10-12.

[38]Daniel J. Elazar, *Covenant and Polity in Biblical Israel: Biblical Foundations and Jewish Expressions*, Covenant Traditions in Politics 1 (New Brunswick, NJ: Transaction Publishers, 1995), 35.

[39]Indeed, it is precisely at this point one should recall that the Creator is a triune Creator, which helps one's doctrine of sovereign authority from veering toward the medieval nominalist's *potential absoluta*.

[40]For our purposes here, more important than the medieval distinction between *potentia ordinata* and *potentia absoluta* is the distinction the Reformed scholastics made, says Richard Muller, between "the power of God as *potentia* or the power inhering in the divine essence to do as it wills and the power of God as *potestas* or the power of God over things, that is the absolute *jus* and *authoritas* of God to control what is his." The latter, says Muller, is the "right of the creator over the creation." See Muller, *Post-Reformation Reformed Dogmatics*, 537. My primary interest through this discussion is not God's power, per se, but his right to exercise power (within the

This is precisely what we see in the movement from Genesis 1 to Genesis 2, as the Creator God of chapter one becomes the ruling God of chapter two who establishes the social and moral boundaries of Adam and Eve's life. This inseparable and intrinsic connection between creator and ruler is also made in the rest of the Old Testament.[41] The God who formed light and darkness is also the God who, by the same right, raises up individuals and nations and then brings vengeance upon them (Deut 32:39; 1 Sam 2:6-10; Is 45:7; Jer 10:1-16). The God who set the stars in place and gave them each names is the God whose arm rules and brings the warfare of his people to an end (Is 40:2, 10, 12-26; also Is 43:6-7). The God who owns the earth because he founded its seas is the "king" who is strong and mighty in battle (Ps 24:1-2, 8; see also Ps 29:9-10; 74:12-17; 95:3-8; 136:5-18).[42] God also reproaches those who question his rule by invoking his status as creator: "Where were you when I laid the foundation of the earth?" (Job 38:4; also Job 41:11). To heighten the connection between creation and rule, the Bible employs the illustrations of pottery and parenting:

> Woe to him who strives with him who formed him,
>   a pot among earthen pots!
> Does the clay say to him who forms it, "What are you making?"
>   or "Your work has no handles"?
> Woe to him who says to a father, "What are you begetting?"
>   or to a woman, "With what are you in labor?" (Is 45:9-10)

The creature has no *right* to quarrel (a political statement) with the one who *made* him (a creation statement) any more than a pot has a right to quarrel with the potter or a child with his or her parents.

---

boundaries of his own *potentia ordinata*). This is what I have in mind whenever I refer to God's rule, sovereignty, dominion or authority.

[41]Several generations of critical Old Testament scholars have disputed the relationship between Israel's creation accounts and its accounts of subsequent redemptive history, sometimes demoting the significance of its creation accounts, sometimes elevating it. See H. H. Schmid, "Creation, Righteousness, and Salvation: 'Creation Theology' as the Broad Horizon of Biblical Theology," in *Creation in the Old Testament*, ed. Bernhard W. Anderson (Philadelphia: Fortress, 1984), 102-117; Walter Brueggemann, *Theology of the Old Testament* (Minneapolis: Fortress, 1997), 159-164. Most today affirm that the two cannot be bifurcated.

[42]While I have characterized the relationship here between the Creator God and the ruling God, N. T. Wright makes an analogous equation between the Creator God and the covenant God in *Paul: A Fresh Perspective* (Minneapolis: Fortress, 2009), 21-39.

In other words, politics is bound up with the very creation of humanity.[43] To read the Bible's first two chapters is to be confronted with a Creator, a creature, and, betwixt the two, an unchangeable ontological distinction (Creator/creature) and, as a property of that ontological distinction, an eternal distinction of social position and power (ruler/ruled).[44] It is not enough to say that the Creator and the creation dwell together in a "personal relationship." Is the personal relationship a romantic relationship? A professional relationship? A fraternal relationship? The key concept for our purposes is that a creator and an ontologically dependent creature relate authoritatively or politically.[45] Again, the author has authority.

How can we further characterize God's "political" rule?[46] Four qualities stand out in Genesis 1 and 2 as well as in subsequent canonical reflection upon them:

*Absolute.* The Creator's authority or rule is absolute. By this I mean it does not require Adam or anyone's consent. The authority simply *is*. It has intrinsic warrant. God did not need to ground his commands to Adam or his threat of judgment in any other authority, and Adam has no other court of appeal, no bill of rights, no possibility of a representative recall, nothing in himself by which he can legitimately say to God, "What have you done?" (Dan 4:35).

*Legitimate.* Not only is God's authority *intrinsically* legitimate, the point just made; it is intrinsically *legitimate*. It is morally right.[47] God has the (moral) right to bind the world by his law, the right to raise up and topple nations, the right to pronounce life and death, the right to eternally bless or damn, and the right to do all things against a person's will. Within the boundaries of his own law (themselves an expression of his character-trait

---

[43]See Peter Scott, "Creation," in *The Blackwell Companion to Political Theology*, ed. Peter Scott and William T. Cavanaugh (Malden, MA: Blackwell, 2004), 337.

[44]See Richard B. Miller, "Christian Attitudes Toward Boundaries: Metaphysical and Geographical," in *Boundaries and Justice: Diverse Ethical Perspectives*, ed. David Miller and Sohail H. Hashmi (Princeton, NJ: Princeton University Press, 2001), 16.

[45]See also Frame, *Doctrine of God*, 295.

[46]In *Resurrection and Moral Order: An Outline for Evangelical Ethics*, 2nd ed. (Grand Rapids: Eerdmans, 1994), Oliver O'Donovan distinguishes "political authority," by which he means human political authority, from "divine authority" (see 127-37). I do not think what I am saying is incompatible with what he writes there. I am simply drawing the lines a little differently.

[47]See R. S. Downie, "Authority," in *The Oxford Companion to Philosophy*, ed. Ted Honderich (New York: Oxford University Press, 1995), 68-69.

predicates), he has the right to exercise his power whichever way he wills (see Ps 115:3): "Has the potter no right over the clay, to make out of the same lump one vessel for honorable use and another for dishonorable use?" (Rom 9:21). As we observed in chapter one, the concept of legitimacy is what separates the ideas of power and authority.[48]

*Comprehensive.* There is no distinction between "public" and "private" in God's kingdom. Everything belongs to him, and so his rule is comprehensive. To say there is some area of life outside God's jurisdiction would be to say there is some other authority to whom God is beholden, at least in that area. But God is not just a monarch; he is a totalitarian monarch. His claim on humanity is *total*. He commands people to love him with *all* their minds, hearts, souls and strength (Deut 6:5; Lk 10:27). That includes everything from what they eat and do not eat (Gen 1:29; 2:16-17) to a reproductive mandate and the constituting of a vocational and sexual partnership (Gen 1:28; 2:18, 22-25).

*Authorizing.* The last thing worth observing about God's authority is that he uses it to authorize rule in others. Unlike every human totalitarian, God's rule is an authorizing rule, not an exploitive, oppressive, abusive or life-stealing one. It is, by definition, a life-giving rule. God uses his authority to create and then to give the male and female the ability to multiply (re-create) and bring dominion to the earth (Gen 1:28). He "crowns" humankind with rule over every domain of creation—the heavens, the earth and the sea (Ps 8:5-8). He even shares the "glory and honor" of a creator with humankind (Ps 8:5).

It is as we consider the authorizing activity of God's rule that we find that God's trinitarian nature becomes especially significant. It is not difficult to imagine a monistic God with absolute, legitimate and comprehensive authority. Yet God's triune rule is by nature generous.[49] It is an authorizing authority: "All authority in heaven and on earth *has been given* to me," said the man Jesus (Mt 28:18, italics added). Sure enough, a number of examples

---

[48]Here's how theologian John Frame puts it: "The relationship between control and authority is one between might and right. Control means that God has the power to direct the whole course of nature and history as he pleases. Authority means that he has the right to do that." Frame, *Doctrine of God*, 80. Also, see Frame's helpful discussion of whether "might makes right" for God (ibid., 82-83n5).

[49]See Brueggemann, *Theology of the Old Testament*, 240-41.

can quickly be cited throughout Scripture that demonstrate that godly authority creates and promotes life, prosperity, peace, justice and righteousness. The Bible speaks of godly authority as analogous to the sun, which makes grass sprout from the earth (2 Sam 23:4); as defending the cause of the poor and needy and bringing justice (Ps 72:1-4); and as causing the wolf to lie down with the lamb (Is 11:6). Godly authority authors and authorizes. It is not used selfishly and harmfully, as fallen human authority so often is. God is, as it were, the ultimate delegator; and this seems to be a property of his triune nature, as the divine Father was pleased to make the divine Son "the head" and "the firstborn" and "preeminent" by communicating the fullness of himself to the Son (Col 1:18-19).

***The archetypal body politic and citizenship mandate.*** The reality of God's absolute and authorizing rule over humanity is given institutional expression in Genesis 1 and 2's power-conferring rules (Gen 1:28; 2:16; 2:22-25) and Genesis 2's mandatory rule (Gen 2:17). Here we find the world's first political institutions. A political institution, I observed in the last chapter, is any identity- and behavior-shaping rule structure whose purview embraces the entire public and is directly or indirectly backed by the threat of authorized force. Sure enough, these power-conferring and mandatory rules backed by the threat of force establish the purposes and boundaries of human life, respectively. They empower and constrain on a public-wide basis. And they provide structures of meaning and identity. Adam and Eve fundamentally exist as God-imagers, charged with replicating God's fruitfulness and his rule throughout creation.

Christian theologians have enjoyed a long and fruitful discussion of what it means to be created in God's image, but many scholars these days seem to get around to saying, in one way or another, that whatever it means to be created in God's image ontologically, the ontological serves the functional purpose of bringing God's dominion to the ends of the earth: as God's images (noun), Adam and Eve image (verb) God.[50] The form (image)

---

[50]One can turn to countless places to find a discussion of the "image" and "likeness" language in the early chapters of Genesis. A few that have informed my own understanding include Anthony Hoekema, *Created in God's Image* (Grand Rapids: Eerdmans, 1986); Stephen Dempster, *Dominion and Dynasty* (Downers Grove, IL: InterVarsity Press, 2003); Peter Gentry and Stephen Wellum, *Kingdom Through Covenant: A Biblical-Theological Understanding of the Covenants* (Wheaton, IL: Crossway, 2012), 183-204; J. G. McConville, *God and Earthly Power* (New York:

informs the function (rule).[51] The identity informs the office or vocation. Further, the idea of sonship is added to this discussion a couple chapters later when Genesis 5 says, "[Adam] fathered a son in his own likeness, after his image, and named him Seth" (Gen 5:3). Adam, being created in God's image, was a kind of son of God (Lk 3:38).[52] Sons, to put it colloquially, look and act like their dads, and in the ancient Near East they would have followed their fathers vocationally. Adam's father was a king. Adam, too, was to be a kind of king.

That said, God warns these would-be kings that they would forfeit their purpose for existing if they defied his law (Gen 2:17).[53] In fact, Simon Roberts's definition of the state from chapter one is worth recalling here. God confronts Adam and Eve as the "supreme authority, ruling over a defined territory, who is recognized as having power to make decisions in matters of government" and who "possesses the power of life and death over his subjects."[54] At the risk of some anachronism, this description of the state's authority sounds like God's rule over Adam and Eve in the Garden of Eden. In order to rule, these human rulers were to be ruled.

The fact of God's supreme authority brings with it a corporate corollary: a political community. A political community, we saw in the last chapter, is a community of people united by a common governing authority, which is precisely what Adam and Eve share with respect to God. In other words, the rules of Genesis 1 and 2 constitute the society of God, Adam and Eve as the archetypal body politic. They establish a basic institutional framework involving a formal hierarchy between ruler and ruled, as well as a structure for the relationships between ruled and ruled (i.e., between humans). These rules act as a constitution for this society. Adam and Eve, in addition to

---

T&T Clark, 2008), 36; Gordon J. Wenham, *Genesis 1–15*, Word Biblical Commentary 1 (Waco, TX: Word, 1987), 29-32.

[51]Gentry and Wellum, *Kingdom Through Covenant*, 191-203, 616; Gordon J. Wenham, *Genesis 1–15*, 31-32.

[52]See Dempster, *Dominion and Dynasty*, 58-59; Gentry and Wellum, *Kingdom Through Covenant*, 196-98, 615-16.

[53]Stephen Dempster observes that "the language used to describe this penalty, 'You will certainly die,' is often used to state the penalty for capital crimes in the later Siniatic covenant"—twenty-one times, in fact. Dempster, *Dominion and Dynasty*, 65.

[54]Simon Roberts, quoted in Stuart Hall, "The State in Question," in *The Idea of the Modern State*, ed. Gregor McLennan, David Held and Stuart Hall (Philadelphia: Open University Press, 1984), 1.

being united by the one-flesh union of marriage, were politically united as "subjects" of God's rule. They had no hand in writing this constitution, but they stood equally before God's law, threatened with the same penalty for disobedience and entitled to the same protection and other benefits from his law (cf. Gen 2:16). The codification or institutionalization of God's rule meant, among other things, that it was public: the lines of obligation and accountability were clear to every member of said society.

Should we characterize Adam and Eve as "citizens" in the more specialized democratic sense of the term—participants in the political process? In one sense, no—Adam and Eve were subjects in the face of God's absolute authority. The rules of Genesis 1 and 2 were not established by ballot and were not subject to judicial review.

In another sense, however, yes, they were politically participatory citizens both objectively and subjectively. Objectively, God created these paradigmatic humans not only to be ruled but to rule over creation, as we've been considering. Adam's subjecthood was, simultaneously, Adam's authorized and empowered employment (Gen 1:26-28; see the analogy in Mt 8:9-10). God established him in the office of vice-regency. Subjectively, Adam and Eve assented. They united their wills to the will of God, at least in the beginning. And, as we saw in the last chapter, what separates a community of citizens from a community of subjects is the voluntary assent of community members to the community's rule. Of course, Adam and Eve would eventually fail in this assignment, but it is worth at least briefly glancing ahead in the story line to see that the incarnate Christ's eventual submission and rule, as we have already said, was the antitype to which Adam's own type pointed, and is the most vivid portrayal of citizenship in the Bible. Astonishingly, the Bible eventually uses the language of (a redeemed) humanity reigning *with* God (in 2 Tim 2:12; Rev 20:6—literally, "be kings with"). In short, political citizenship, as we defined it in the last chapter, is established with Adam and Eve and is fulfilled in the God-man Jesus Christ.[55]

---

[55]Karl Barth wrote, "As the man Jesus is himself the revealing Word of God, he is the source of our knowledge of the nature of man as created by God." Barth, *Church Dogmatics*, III/2, *The Doctrine of Creation*, ed. and trans. G. W. Bromiley (New York: T&T Clark, 2004), 41. My argument is that Barth's assertion pertains to the political nature of humankind as much as it does every other aspect of human life. If the essence of being human entails the vocation of citizenship, we see that pictured most clearly in the person of Jesus Christ.

More broadly, all human political authority and politics start right here with the corollary concepts of authorization and representation. To represent something, observes Hanna Pitkin, is to *re*-present it or "make it present again." "Representation, taken generally," she says, "means the making present *in some sense* of something which is nevertheless *not* present literally or in fact."[56] We can make use of this definition by saying that people make God's invisible rule visibly present by speaking or acting in an authoritative capacity, questions of misrepresentation aside for the moment. Which brings us to authorization. In order to have the authority to do something, someone must be authorized (except for one with absolute authority).[57] A person must be given permission or, better, a commission to act within a set of boundaries for a particular purpose. To connect the two concepts of representation and authorization, then, we can say that acting in a representative capacity, at least legitimately, requires authorization. People can represent God's rule when and where God authorizes them to do so, and only insofar as God has authorized them to do so.

That means that every conceivable exercise of human authority, including the authority exercised by the state, is an exercise of God's own authority.[58] Earthly rule, whether a dictator's or a deacon's, is a borrowed authority for the purposes of representing God's own authority and revealed will. Human rule—in the home, workplace, church or state—is contained *within* God's rule. It is never endemic to a human. Nicholas Wolterstorff, following Abraham Kuyper, observes, "Authority is something one *has*, not something one *is*."[59] It is always an office that humans step into for the sake of performing

---

[56] Hanna Fenichel Pitkin, *The Concept of Representation* (Berkeley: University of California Press, 1967), 8-9 (italics original).

[57] See W. Richard Scott on authorization in "Unpacking Institutional Arguments," in *The New Institutionalism in Organizational Analysis*, ed. Walter W. Powell and Paul J. DiMaggio (Chicago: University of Chicago Press, 1991), 176. See also O'Donovan, *Resurrection and Moral Order*, esp. 121-24.

[58] Daniel J. Elazar and Stuart A. Cohen write, "The Jewish political tradition does not recognize state sovereignty in the modern sense of absolute independence. No state—a human creation—can be sovereign. Classically, only God is sovereign and He entrusts the exercise of His sovereign powers to people as a whole, mediated through His Torah-as-constitution as provided through His covenant with Israel." Elazar and Cohen, *Jewish Polity: Jewish Political Organization from Biblical Times to the Present* (Bloomington: Indiana University Press, 1985), 5.

[59] Nicholas Wolterstorff, *The Mighty and the Almighty: An Essay in Political Theology* (New York: Cambridge University Press, 2012), 48; cf. Abraham Kuyper, *Lectures on Calvinism* (Grand Rapids: Eerdmans, 1931), 78-109.

a certain action. This means, first of all, that human rule must always operate within the field of being ruled. Every office comes with its own set of rules that the office holder must obey. Humans never have authority to do whatever they want with it. Second, it means that any power of sanction possessed by that office holder must be explicitly authorized and delineated by the office giver.[60]

While God's authority is inherently absolute, every earthly authority's rule is inherently derivative and contingent. While God's authority is inherently legitimate, every act of human rule is legitimate only if it has been expressly authorized by God and expresses his will. While God's authority is inherently comprehensive, human rule is delimited by God's authorization. The only aspect of God's authority that (rightful) human authority mirrors is its work of authorizing life and rule in still others.

Pitkin calls the concept of representation a "modern" one.[61] But Genesis 1 indicates that representation is primordial, even though it moves "downward" from ruler to ruled and not "upward" from ruled to ruler, as in a democratic legislature. God created humanity to be ruled and to do so by representing his rule. He authorized these ruled rulers to make his rule present over land, sea and sky. This, then, is humanity's archetypal political program or mandate. Just as voters send their presidents and parliamentarians into office with a mandate—the authority to pursue a particular course of action—so being human comes with a political mandate: to reflect God's own holiness, justice, unity and love in humanity's corporate life together, a life of multiplying and bringing dominion.[62] The institutionalized political structures of creation did not simply establish the boundaries of the playing field; they established the goal of the game: life in the human *polis*, as it increasingly spread over the surface of the earth, was to look like life in the divine *polis* of Father, Son and Spirit, a society that spreads beyond all time and space.[63]

---

[60]A recent and useful theological meditations on the topic of authority and office in creation is David Koyzis's *We Answer to Another: Authority, Office, and the Image of God* (Eugene, OR: Pickwick, 2014).

[61]Pitkin, *Concept of Representation*, 2.

[62]In chapter four, we will complexify this concept of representation by following Nicholas Wolterstorff's distinction between a delegate model and a deputy model of representation.

[63]On God's intention for Adam and Eve "to widen the boundaries of the Garden in ever increasing circles by extending the order of the garden sanctuary into the inhospitable outer spaces,"

Why call the power-conferring rules in Genesis 1 a political mandate or citizenship mandate and not just a creation mandate? Precisely because, when fully unpacked, these rules pertain to the governance of relationships and the mediated rule of humankind—life in the *polis*. To rule in God's image means ruling in the context of a society where just and loving individuals use their rule to authorize rule in still others, just as God does. I do not mean to limit the creation mandate to these political and institutional elements, but I do mean to highlight these elements as occupying a prominent role.

It is not surprising, then, that Jewish and Reformed theologians alike have long employed the political concept of a covenant to describe the nature of God's relationship with Adam and Eve at creation. "A covenantal society," says Jewish political theorist David Novak, "is based on God's initiation of a political relationship between Himself and a people. Unlike a contract, it is not the coming together of equal parties, nor do the people have any right of initial refusal or subsequent termination of the covenant."[64] Whether or not we use the term *covenant* to characterize life in the Garden,[65] Novak's description of a covenantal relationship is exactly what we find there. God initiated a political relationship with his people in the Garden through establishing a citizenship mandate for their lives (Gen 1:28) and the boundaries within which they were to fulfill this mandate upon pain of death (Gen 2:16-17), a mandate and a boundary that they both chose and had no right to refuse. They were members, subjects and citizens of God's kingdom.

***Two classes of political membership.*** To be painstakingly clear, then, we find two classes of political membership at least implicit in the Garden. First, Adam and Eve were *subjects* of God's rule because God held the power of

---

see G. K. Beale, *The Temple and the Church's Mission: A Biblical Theology of the Dwelling Place of God* (Downers Grove, IL: InterVarsity Press, 2004), 85.

[64]David Novak, "Land and People," in *Law, Politics, and Morality in Judaism*, ed. Michael Walzer (Princeton, NJ: Princeton University Press, 2006), 73.

[65]For recent additions to the debate as to whether or not God made a covenant with Adam in creation, see the argument *against* in Paul R. Williamson, *Sealed with an Oath: Covenant in God's Unfolding Purpose* (Downers Grove, IL: IVP Academic, 2007), 52-58, and the argument *for* in Gentry and Wellum, *Kingdom Through Covenant*, 179-233, 613-30. For examples of the use of covenantal language in Jewish literature, see G. K. Beale, *A New Testament Biblical Theology: The Unfolding of the Old Testament in the New* (Grand Rapids: Baker, 2011), 43n46.

the sword over them whether they liked it or not. Their inclusion in this archetypical body politic did *not* depend on their consent (permission) or their assent to (agreement with) God's rule. God's rule is absolute. It is an irrevocable property of the fact that he is an all-powerful creator.

Yet God just so happens to be an authorizing, rule-distributing creator. He establishes Adam and Eve in the office of vice-regent, which allows for a second category of membership: they could be *citizens*. God created them in his image so that they might represent his rule. They were given the capacity of volition and asked to unite their wills to his. They were asked to assent, to agree, and in so doing, to participate in God's own righteous rule.[66] The difference between subjecthood and citizenship, we saw in chapter two, depends on the exercise of the will and this capacity for assent. Did the requirement to assent to God's will in all things mean Adam and Eve were to put their brains on hold and move about like robots? Not in the biblical perspective. God granted them a broad remit: skies, seas and land. The cosmos was theirs. Further, the boundaries were mere: only one thing was forbidden.

The role of assent and affirmation is central to what a covenant is. "A covenant," says one Old Testament scholar, "is an elected, as opposed to natural, relationship of obligation under oath."[67] And God formally affirmed these citizens and their domain by describing all creation as "very good" at the close of the sixth day (Gen 1:31). What's more, marriage is the best example of how covenants work, say other scholars: "Thus, by a ceremony or (quasi-)legal process, people who are not kin are now bound as tightly as any family relationship."[68] Here in the Garden, then, we have the seeds of all political society between two humans and God as well as between the two humans. Good government works best, I said a moment ago, when ruler and ruled are perfectly in sync, as between the divine Father and Son.

---

[66]Contemporary Western culture has difficulty conceiving of anything like this as freedom, being wholly taken with what Isaiah Berlin calls a "negative freedom" from restraint. But the freedom of rule offered throughout Scripture is the positive freedom of knowing the truth and living by it. See Berlin, "Two Concepts of Liberty," in *Four Essays on Liberty* (Oxford: Oxford University Press, 1969).

[67]Gentry and Wellum, *Kingdom Through Covenant*, 132, quoting Gorden Hugenberger, *Marriage as a Covenant: A Study of Biblical Law and Ethics Governing Marriage Developed from the Perspective of Malachi*, Supplements to Vetus Testamentum 52 (Leiden, Netherlands: Brill, 1994), 11.

[68]Gentry and Wellum, *Kingdom Through Covenant*, 133.

And this state appears to have characterized life in the Garden for at least a brief period.

***Political worship, the priestly mandate and the archetypal sanctuary.*** Four more inferences can be drawn from this vision of God's rule in creation:

1. If God's rule and judgment is comprehensive, it would seem that all of life is in some sense political. Thomas Mann was right to say that "the destiny of man presents its meaning in political terms," even if Mann was saying it for different reasons.[69] There is no "prepolitical" state, as in philosophical liberalism. Politics for the human being begins at conception.

For Adam and Eve to have been created in the divine King's image for the purposes of ruling on his behalf means that everything that a human being does (1) is an act of rule and (2) represents God's own rule. Simply to live, for a creature made in God's image, is to act out a political drama. Indeed, this is where the corollary between freedom and authority becomes evident. To be free to act within some domain means that one has been authorized to act in that domain. It means that one has authority to make decisions or govern there.[70] For instance, being free in the morning to make a decision between one breakfast cereal and another, or between one international peace treaty and another, means that a person has authority over such a decision. The only question is, does this person choose his or her breakfast cereal, this or that treaty, with God's greater rule and reputation in mind? This brings us to a second inference—the intimate connection between politics and worship.

2. Worship is utterly political. Worship is commonly described by Christians as the act of giving honor and praise to God, as in New Testament scholar D. A. Carson's definition: "Worship is the proper response of all moral, sentient beings to God, ascribing all honor and worth to their Creator-God precisely because he is worthy, delightfully so." Further, such worship is said to be comprehensive in a person's life: "It manifests itself in all our living . . . both in adoration and in action, both in the individual

---

[69]Quoted in William Butler Yeats, "Politics," in *Selected Poems and Three Plays of William Butler Yeats*, ed. M. L. Rosenthal, 3rd ed. (New York: Collier Books, 1986), 199.

[70]Again, I am thinking of freedom in terms of Berlin's "positive" conception of freedom (freedom as self-determination) as opposed to a "negative" conception (freedom from external restraint). See Berlin, "Two Concepts of Liberty."

believer and in corporate worship."⁷¹ Carson's definition seems to be a reasonable inference from the apostle Paul's command, "Whether you eat or drink, or whatever you do, do all to the glory of God" (1 Cor 10:31). What is interesting, then, is theologian Bernd Wannenwetsch's observation that it is within this very activity of responding to God in worship that God's people manifest their political character. Where Carson uses the language of "the proper response" of "ascribing all honor and worth" to God, Wannenwetsch uses analogous language of a "human receptivity" to the acting and judging of God and an "assenting to God's judgments."⁷² If God has determined that he deserves glory, honor and praise for the food and drink that he provides, then the activity of worship involves a person in assenting to his judgment and so giving him praise for one's daily bread. Adam and Eve's act of political assent to any given law, the assent that constituted them as citizens of this paradigmatic body politic, was therefore simultaneously an act of worship. It was an agreement with God that he deserves obedience and that he should be "imaged" or reflected because all honor and glory belong to him. Submission, it appears, is praise. Political obedience is worship. Wannenwetsch writes that worship "in the fullest sense" is "a form of life," and that "it is the acting and judging of God experienced in worship which guides believers to a *specific* form of life."⁷³ It is within the context of a corporate gathering of God's people, however, that people learn what it means to assent to God's judgments and how to assume the specific form of life that God desires: "Worship would be political inasmuch as God's activity provides the *initium*, an activity to which people assent in baptism, in praise, in prayer, in the hearing of the Word, in the confession of faith, and in the Lord's Supper."⁷⁴ It is when the congregation of God's people gathers in worship that it forms a "public in its own unique sense: the particular political form of life which is determined by 'the law of the Spirit' (Rom. 8:2)."⁷⁵ Yet what occurs in the ordinances of corporate worship then defines the people's entire political

---

⁷¹D. A. Carson, "Worship Under the Word," in *Worship by the Book*, ed. D. A. Carson (Grand Rapids: Zondervan, 2002), 26.
⁷²Bernd Wannenwetsch, *Political Worship* (New York: Oxford University Press, 2004), 6.
⁷³Ibid., 5, 6 (italics original).
⁷⁴Ibid., 10.
⁷⁵Ibid., 7. Oliver O'Donovan similarly observes, "The community is a political community by virtue of being a worshipping community." O'Donovan, *Desire of the Nations*, 47.

existence: "This judging and acting in accord with God and with other believers is not merely the mark of the felicitous moment when heart, lips, and hands keep time with one another. Rather, it forms a specific, social form of life, a *communio* in which believers find their basic *political existence*."[76] It seems that worship, like politics, admits of both broad and narrow definitions, the former involving an entire life and the latter its institutional and corporate form. Wannenwetsch then draws the same connection between worship and the freedom of God's people: "[Worship] is free in that it accepts the liberating activity of God as its rule."[77] No doubt, we've jumped ahead in the biblical storyline by locating this description in the church and its ordinances, but I do not think it is difficult to see how these same realities characterized the archetypal body politic in the Garden. Adam and Eve's obedience to God's power-conferring and mandatory rules alike was not just their citizenship mandate; it was also their worship. Their activity of bringing God's holy, just and loving rule to the earth was their praise.[78] To put it as simply as possible, the political mandate of humanity is to worship God.

3. It should not be too surprising, then, that Bible exegetes and theologians refer not just to Adam's kingly office but also to his priestly office. The Garden is treated as God's archetypal sanctuary that Adam was to "work" and "keep" since God dwelled there (Gen 2:15), paired activities that would eventually be given to Israel's priest with respect to the temple (Num 3:7-8; 8:26; 18:5-6).[79] Like a priest, Adam was to be utterly consecrated to God (Ex 19:22), which is to say, careful to ensure that God's ways were kept and his judgments accepted. Priests mediate (see Heb 9:15; 12:24), but they also guard and protect. Adam, then, was to guard this holy place where God dwelled and ensure that only worshipers would enter. For Adam, being a king meant being a priest, and being a priest meant

---

[76]Wannenwetsch, *Political Worship*, 6-7.
[77]Ibid., 10.
[78]See O'Donovan, *Desire of the Nations*, 48-49.
[79]Beale, *Temple and the Church's Mission*, 66-87; Gentry and Wellum, *Kingdom Through Covenant*, 213-18; T. Desmond Alexander, *From Eden to the New Jerusalem: An Introduction to Biblical Theology* (Grand Rapids: Kregel, 2008), 13-73, esp. 25; G. J. Wenham, "Sanctuary Symbolism in the Garden of Eden Story," in *Proceedings of the Ninth World Congress of Jewish Studies* (Jerusalem: World Union of Jewish Studies, 1986), 19-25; John H. Walton, "Eden, Garden Of," in *Dictionary of the Old Testament: Pentateuch*, ed. T. Desmond Alexander and David W. Baker (Downers Grove, IL: InterVarsity Press, 2003), 202-7, esp. 205-6.

being a king. Representative rule requires consecration, and consecration leads to representative rule.

Simply to live, for a creature made in God's image, is to act out a religious drama just as much as it is to act out a political drama. Human life is innately religious. Every action and thought is either for or against God. Every action and thought will either be a priestly activity of worship and consecration to God or it will be antiworship. Humanity's political mandate is matched by a priestly mandate: to be consecrated to God and to make his ways known. A priest-king, we might summarize, is an office with a structural aspect as well as inward and outward activities. Structurally, Adam was to represent, or image, God. Inwardly, he was to watch over the Garden since it was where God dwelled, keeping it consecrated to God and free of serpents. Outwardly, he was to work the Garden and push back the borders of Eden.

The simultaneity of worship and politics becomes most explicit in canonical history not with Adam and Eve but with their antitype, the second Adam. What they should have done, Jesus would do. They succumbed to the serpent's temptation. Jesus did not: "And the devil took him up and showed him all the kingdoms of the world in a moment of time, and said to him, 'To you I will give all this authority and their glory, for it has been delivered to me, and I give it to whom I will. If you, then, will worship me, it will all be yours'" (Lk 4:5-7). In other words, the devil asks Jesus to assent to the devil's own judgment of who deserves worship. In return, he promises to authorize Jesus with all rule. Jesus responds by quoting from Deuteronomy and explicitly affirming the simultaneity of worshiping and obeying God, religion and politics: "And Jesus answered him, 'It is written, "You shall worship the Lord your God, and him only shall you serve"'" (Lk 4:8). Christ would assume the offices of king and priest a different way.

4. If God is both creator and comprehensive ruler over all, all justice and righteousness are utterly and irrevocably rooted in his nature and character. There is no neutral standard of righteousness and justice. There are only competitors.

## Absolute Versus Mediate Authority and Conscience

By way of segueing to the next chapter on the fall, there is one more implication to draw out of the fact that only God's authority is absolute and that human authority is always mediated. A tension will inevitably exist in a fallen world between the absolute obligation to obey God and the relative obligation to obey any human authority that he has authorized.

Divinely established authorities—such as parent, pastor or prince—possess the moral licence to generate prima facie moral obligations among subjects within their jurisdictions.[80] And that obligation involves what Nicholas Wolterstorff calls a prima facie "surrender of judgment,"[81] or what I would nuance slightly with the language "surrender of *acting upon* one's judgment." I become morally obligated to do or not do something based not on my judgment over the decision to be made but on the judgment of the one in authority over me. This prima facie surrendering of acting upon my judgment, of course, is a property of the fact that I should be utterly surrendered to God's absolute and comprehensive judgment, and he has judged it necessary for me to obey this human authority figure.

So Luther's celebrated parry against usurpatious princes and priests, "To go against conscience is neither right nor safe," makes for good Protestant sermon fodder, but a theology of authority and submission is a bit more complex. God does in fact authorize various individuals and institutions to place burdens on the conscience. When a parent instructs a child to go to bed, the child should feel conscience bound to obey. So with a prince and subject or an elder and church member in their areas of jurisdiction. Luther's quip must therefore be complemented by its inverse: to go against parent or prince for the sake of conscience just might not be right or safe either. These two claims must be held in tension.

After all, the obligation to obey a divinely established human authority and suspend acting upon one's judgment is always prima facie, never *ultima facie*.[82] Absolute authority belongs to God alone. Authority, we said earlier, is something that a creature made out of clay can *have*, not something it *is*. God delegates it to human beings for the sake of performing certain ends, and authority figures can generate moral obligations only for the sake of those

---

[80]Wolterstorff, *Mighty and the Almighty*, 60-66; also Wolterstorff, "'The Authorities Are God's Servants': Is a Theistic Account of Political Authority Still Viable or Have Humanity Accounts Won the Day?" in *Theology and Public Philosophy: Four Conversations*, ed. Kenneth L. Grasso and Cecilia Rodriguez Castillo (Lanham, MD: Lexington Books, 2012), 52-54.

[81]Wolterstorff, "Authorities Are God's Servants," 55.

[82]Wolterstorff, *Mighty and the Almighty*, 61.

ends and never in contradiction to anything else that God has commanded (leaving aside questions of irreconcilable moral dilemmas). Therefore, whenever a divinely established authority acts unjustly, requires something that is wrong or unjust, or even makes requirements outside his or her jurisdiction (like an elder requiring a certain dental procedure), a subject must recall the authority figure's mediated and relative status. The authority figure has no moral licence (authority) to generate obligations unjustly, to require injustices or to drive outside the lanes of his or her jurisdiction.

All this yields the aforementioned tension between the absolute obligation to obey God and the relative obligation to obey any human authority that he has established. It also yields the dilemmas of conscience that so often characterize life in a fallen world. Suppose a parent, prince or pastor requires something that the conscience claims is contrary to God's Word, bringing us back to Luther's "Here I Stand" speech. The solution might be to disobey, but the solution might also be to instruct the conscience because *it* is wrong.

Really, situations like these present us with an ethical standoff, which often admits of no clean prioritization of duty, much to the chagrin of the fundamentalist who demands black-and-white decision trees and case law for all occasions. But such standoffs are a property of the fall, and the wisdom of fearing the Lord may offer the only solution for such moments. Specifically, an individual might be so convinced that, on the last day, Jesus will vindicate the decision to disobey that he rightly determines to do so. But he also might rightly decide that the obligations of submission to the authority in question outweigh his assessment of the situation at hand, and his submission will be vindicated on the last day. One wishes, for instance, that Arias had humbled himself and chosen the latter course, and that the Nazi officer Eichmann had stood stronger and chosen the former. The point is, it is reductionistic to say that the individual's fallen conscience must be the "final" authority. In a world of mediated authorities, any concept of a final authority is at least somewhat relative, always contingent on the last divine judgment. Acknowledging tensions can sometimes be ethically better than insisting on rationalistic hierarchies. Tensions encourage all parties to pray and to seek the Lord's wisdom rather than to mindlessly rely on rule book answers. This discussion will arise again in chapter six in the question of who is the final authority in the church.

## Conclusion

In conclusion, all political reality begins with (1) God's social nature as it is constrained by his attributes and (2) the rule that God possesses over every human creature. The divine society is a society of holy, just, loving and united persons. Political reality then becomes an essential aspect of human existence by virtue of (1) our constrained sociality and (2) our absolute and comprehensive subjection to the institution of God's authorizing, citizen-making law. We are by creation subjects and citizens. Political obligation is built into the very structure of our existence, which means that all of life is political in a broad sense of the term. It also means that that most religious of acts, worship, is political in its very essence. We are, by creation, worshipers (and by the fall, antiworshipers). To bow the knee in worship is an act of political fealty—an affirmation of God's persons, activities and judgments. Indeed, humanity's political mandate, in a word, is to worship. It is to corporately reflect the Trinity's own holiness, justice, love, unity and glory through the process of bringing God's generously authorizing rule to all creation.

# The Politics of the Fall

ABANDONING A SECULAR CONCEPTION of politics and beginning instead with God's authority radically changes the shape of "politics" or "the political." It is a bit like bringing a king into the room where his mutinous ambassador has been holding court—heads turn and the ambassador goes quiet (this is precisely what happens in Psalm 82). Yet it is the act of mutiny that brings us to the fall, the grand complexifier for any theological account of politics. Adam and Eve did not merely disobey; they launched the archetypal revolution.

Can we translate their act of heeding the serpent's promise to be "like God" (Gen 3:5) into institutional terms? At least four institutional descriptions of their disobedience come to mind, drawing from the discussion of political rebellion in chapter two:

- *Identity.* It was a reconceiving of their identities so as to exclude the moral legitimacy of God's claim upon them (see Ezek 28:1-19).

- *Authority.* It was a rejection of God's authority, an act of self-enthronement and, at the same time, strangely, of obedience to another lord (the serpent) and that lord's system of rules.

- *Justice.* It was a refusal to assent to God's judgments and the justice of his claim on them. It was, in that sense, antiworship, worship being the act of assenting to God's judgments, as we saw at the end of chapter three. Adam and Eve employed an "alternative legitimation"[1] for their desires

---

[1]This phrase and concept taken from Peter L. Berger and Thomas Luckman, *The Social Construction of Reality: A Treatise in the Sociology of Knowledge* (New York: Doubleday, 1966), 92, 157;

and decisions; they set themselves up as judge over God's judgments;[2] and they condemned his law and judgments, as the apostle James would eventually argue (Jas 4:11-12).

- *Community.* It was a rejection of God's ruled people *in their corporate capacity* as God's ruled people. The statement "*I* am not *his!*" brings with it a fraternal twin: "*We* are not his and, therefore, not each other's, at least in that capacity."

Sin, like worship, is an utterly political and institutional act because it is the rejection of one identity for another, one lord for another, one concept of justice for another and one body politic and constitution for another.[3]

Of course, Adam and Eve's rebellion did not succeed. A political rebellion succeeds, we said in chapter two, only when the threat of one sword holder is removed and another one is established in its place. And as Genesis 4 and following show, Adam and Eve do not successfully remove the threat of God's sword, in spite of the serpent's promises that they would ("you will not surely die" [Gen 3:4]). God tells them instead that they would return to the dirt, and he keeps his word: the genealogical tables in Genesis 5 conclude every name with "and he died"—the repetition driving home the point that God indeed holds the sword.

Yet it is both the time lag that occurs between the act of disobedience and the moment of death as well as God's act of removing himself from the presence of humanity that permits the conceptual complexities to enter. God does not execute them posthaste, and they cannot *see* that it is he who still holds the sword. Once they are removed from the

---

cf. O'Donovan, *Resurrection and Moral Order: An Outline for Evangelical Ethics*, 2nd ed. (Grand Rapids: Eerdmans, 1994), 104.
[2]Concerning the tree of the knowledge of good and evil, Greg Beale observes, "Having 'the knowledge of good and evil' refers to making judgments. The tree by that name was the place where Adam was to recognize either concurrence with or transgression of God's law.... Accordingly, as a priest-king, he was to pronounce judgment on anything not conforming to God's righteous statues." G. K. Beale, *A New Testament Biblical Theology: The Unfolding of the Old Testament in the New* (Grand Rapids: Baker, 2011), 360.
[3]Though we cannot explore the idea here, it may be worth considering whether every sin is also an implicit denial of God's triune nature by virtue of the fact that the authorized office of kingdom citizen is a property of God's triune nature, as I advocated in the last chapter. Insofar as sinning involves giving an unjust preference for the one (self) over the many (others), it presents a picture of God as a power-hungry monad who does not generously authorize the Son through the Spirit.

Garden, his rule becomes invisible. This allows human beings to live for a few years pursuing their own agendas and living according to what feels like self-rule.

For our purposes the dilemma becomes, how do we describe such temporary insurrectionists institutionally? On the one hand, Adam and Eve drafted their own constitutions—"I am the master of my fate: / I am the captain of my soul," as a later poet would put it. And the law of self would require them to seek out whatever protection they could find, whether that meant working in collusion ("the man and his wife hid themselves" [Gen 3:8]) or in opposition and betrayal ("the woman whom you gave to be with me, she gave me fruit" [Gen 3:12]). The original body politic was exploded, the rejection of God signifying the rejection of a king and his politically incorporated people. On the other hand, the curse of death would now loom permanently in the background, slowed by a time lag, indeed, but inescapable. God's rule was uninterrupted; the sword was still in hand, even if it became an invisible one.

How then do we map out the political cartography of a whole world of insurrectionists whom we know won't finally succeed? We observed that, before the fall, all of life was political and God was king. Can we still affirm this following the fall? After all, the existence of a political community—which is what I am advocating the local church is—depends in part upon a shared acknowledgment or submission to a common governing authority, a "common acceptance of the rule" (Barber's words).[4] Indeed, many Enlightenment conceptions of authority define the concept to say that rejected authority is no authority; it must be accepted.[5] Must we say that Adam and Eve no longer belong to God's kingdom or political

---

[4]See chap. 2, n. 51.
[5]See Max Weber, *The Theory of Social and Economic Organization*, paperback ed. (New York: Free Press, 1964), 152. Though sociologists like Weber might say that their purposes are merely descriptive, what is unfortunate is when Christian scholars simplistically treat authority, like the sociologists, as fundamentally grounded in the individual's consent. See, for example, Bengt Holmberg, *Paul and Power: The Structure of Authority in the Primitive Church as Reflected in the Pauline Epistles* (Eugene, OR: Wipf & Stock, 1978), 127. A better description of authority, which is not based entirely in consent, can be found in Joseph Raz, *The Authority of Law* (New York: Oxford University Press, 1983), 8; also R. S. Downie, "Authority," in *The Oxford Companion to Philosophy*, ed. Ted Honderich (New York: Oxford University Press, 1995), 69.

community simply because they reject his rule? Or does the fact that their rebellion ultimately fails (they die via the curse) mean they remain subject to his rule?

Subsequent canonical reflection on the imbroglio of Genesis 3 politics seems to offer material for both sides of the argument, namely, that Adam and Eve and their fallen children both do and don't belong to God's rule or kingdom. Exegetical tensions over the nature of God's rule are embedded in biblical time and space. In biblical time, some passages affirm that God is king over all the earth: "The LORD has established his throne in the heavens, and his kingdom rules over all" (Ps 103:19; see also 2 Kings 19:15; Ps 29:10; 47:8; 99:1-4; Is 6:5; Jer 46:18; Dan 4:34-45). Other passages point to a time when he will become king over all: "And the LORD will be king over all the earth. On that day the LORD will be one and his name one" (Zech 14:9; or, famously, Is 9:6). The two kinds of texts lead George Eldon Ladd to say, "While God is the King, he must also become King."[6]

A similar tension is found in biblical space, or rather, over where or among whom God is king. Some texts affirm that Yahweh is king right now of his special people (Num 23:21; Is 9:6; 41:21; 43:15; 44:6; Jer 8:19; Mic 4:6; Zeph 3:15), an idea that corresponds to language about "my people" versus "not my people" (e.g., Hos 1:10, 2:23). Other texts, again, suggest that he is the king of all nations, which would imply that he is king right now even of "not my people" (see Ps 22:28; 47:2, 7; 96:10; Jer 10:7, 10; Zech 14:9, 16-19; Mal 1:14).[7] Jumping ahead to the New Testament, the same two exegetical tensions exist with respect to Christ.[8]

In short, biblical texts say both that God *is* king over all and that he *will be* king over all as if he's not now. They also say that he is king over *all* now

---

[6]George Eldon Ladd, *A Theology of the New Testament*, rev. ed. (Grand Rapids: Eerdmans, 1993), 58.

[7]See Gerhard von Rad, "*Basileus*," in *Theological Dictionary of the New Testament*, ed. Gerhard Kittel, vol. 1 (Grand Rapids: Eerdmans, 1964), 568-69. N. T. Wright has also written much about God becoming king even while affirming the fact that he's already king. See Wright, *Jesus and the Victory of God* (Minneapolis: Fortress, 1996), 615-45; Wright, *The Challenge of Jesus: Rediscovering Who Jesus Was and Is* (Downers Grove, IL: InterVarsity Press, 1999), 99-106; Wright, *Simply Jesus: Who He Was, What He Did, Why It Matters* (New York: HarperOne, 2011), 37-56.

[8]For example, see Mt 6:10; 13:11, 31; 18:1-4; 28:18; Jn 3:18; 1 Cor 15:28; Eph 1:21; 2:2; Col 2:10; 1 Pet 3:22.

and that he is king over *some* now. What then do we make of this, and how does it help us answer our original question, is God king over all humanity in the fallen world or not?

The question of God's rule in a fallen world becomes even more pressing when we pursue the inevitable follow-up questions of whether and how his rule is mediated through human rule and earthly institutions. The history of Christian political theology from Augustine's two cities, to Gelasius's two swords, to Luther's two kingdoms, to Kuyper's one kingdom with separate spheres is, in a sense, a response to such exegetical tensions concerning how God's rule may or may not be mediated through human institutions. Several proposals will be briefly considered in chapter five, but there is one worth highlighting here for the sake of drawing out this book's own view of God's rule. David VanDrunen, a recent advocate of a two-kingdoms doctrine, envisions "God as ruling all human institutions and activities, but as ruling them in two fundamentally different ways," one rooted in his identity as creator and sustainer and one rooted in his identity as redeemer. These different ways of ruling correspond to "two kingdoms [that] have significantly different ends, functions, and modes of operation."[9] All the earth belongs to God's "common kingdom" now and is subject to the institutions of the common kingdom such as the state or family, while some of humanity also belong to his "redemptive kingdom" now and the institutions of the redemptive kingdom such as the church. But one day all the earth will be subject to his redemptive kingdom[10]—either in salvation or judgment.

It is difficult to disagree with the general claim that, in Scripture, God rules "my people" and "not my people" in two different ways, or that his rule now and in the eschaton will look different. Every king rules over

---

[9] David VanDrunen, *Natural Law and Two Kingdoms: A Study in the Development of Reformed Social Thought* (Grand Rapids: Eerdmans, 2010), 1; also VanDrunen, *Living in God's Two Kingdoms: A Biblical Vision for Christianity and Culture* (Wheaton, IL: Crossway, 2010), 15.

[10] VanDrunen explicitly argues that the passages that refer to Jesus' universal kingship now, such as Matthew 28:18 or Ephesians 1:21, refer to his rule "through the Noahic covenant" and "the common kingdom." Yet those passages that refer to Christ's future universal rule, such as Revelation 11:15's promise of a day when "the kingdom of this world has become the kingdom of our Lord and of his Christ," speak of the redemptive kingdom and the covenant of grace which began with the Abrahamic covenant, a kingdom with privileges and blessings that only the church can claim right now. VanDrunen, *Living in God's Two Kingdoms*, 118.

upstanding citizens and treasonous subjects differently. And every king will exercise his rule between one institution and another differently—the royal society of historical artifacts one way, his majesty's royal air force another way. But does that mean every king rules over more than one kingdom?

In Martin Luther's original formulation, the two kingdoms divided a person's life between the inner and outer person. One kingdom was placed over the inner, and the other kingdom was placed over the outer. VanDrunen offers an updated jurisdictional bifurcation by distinguishing between the work of the "common covenants" and the "special covenants." God's common kingdom established through the common covenant given through Noah

- concerns ordinary cultural activities,
- embraces the human race in common,
- ensures the preservation of the natural and social order, and
- is put in place temporarily.[11]

This is not to say that the common kingdom is "a realm of moral neutrality or human autonomy,"[12] but VanDrunen does mean to say that it is not particularly concerned with faith and worship. Instead, the redemptive kingdom, which God established through the Abrahamic covenant,

- is about religious faith and worship rather than cultural activities,
- embraces a holy people rather than the whole human race,
- bestows the benefits of salvation rather than just preservation, and
- will endure forever.[13]

VanDrunen does not draw a line between an inner and outer person, but he distinguishes cultural and political activities from the activities of religion and worship. And God, he says, rules those two different kinds of activities in two different ways.

It is easy to see how VanDrunen's scheme offers one resolution to the biblical tensions. God is king over *all* people now as their creator and provider. And he is king over *some* people now as their redeemer. But one day

---
[11]Ibid., 79-81.
[12]Ibid., 81.
[13]Ibid., 83-85.

the redeemer will assert his kingship over all. Therefore, in answer to our original question, "Is God king over all humanity in the fallen world?" this strategy essentially says yes and no. He is presently king of all in *one way*, but not in *another way*.

What should we make of VanDrunen's proposal? I am very sympathetic to his project, and I perceive myself to share his goals, which include responding to some of the errors to which he's responding. He's a partner, in that sense. And it does seem there must be *some* version of the Two, again assuming God distinguishes how he comports himself with "my people" and "not my people," or between the now and the not yet. But at least two concerns arise for me, one institutional and one phenomenological. Institutionally, what exactly does it mean to speak of a providential (or creator) rule versus a redemptive rule? How exactly does one specify those separate authority structures beyond generic theological labels like "providential" and "redemptive"?

Let's think about this institutionally. A king is one who possesses the sword of imperium. And we saw in the last chapter that God possesses the sword of imperium over all humanity for salvation or judgment by virtue of being creator. The author has authority. There's a linear—from cause to effect—progression. By virtue of being creator (cause), God possesses imperium to save or to judge (effect). To speak of the Creator's rule and a separate Redeemer's rule, strangely, makes the cause and effect simultaneous and places a separate crown over both cause and effect: the Creator is king, and the Redeemer/Judge is a king, as if God is two separate kings. If one says, no, there is only one king, the logical corollary would be to say there is only one kingdom. Furthermore, what is the sword of the Creator/Provider if it's not being exercised for the sake of salvation and judgment? What does this Creator/Provider sword then do? The very purpose of the sword of government, of course, is to exercise judgment. It's to divide right from wrong, upstanding citizens from rebellious subjects. Perhaps, then, a two-kingdoms advocate would say that God holds one kind of sword in judgment and another kind of sword in redemption to correspond with "not my people" and "my people." Yet again, this hardly comports with the work of kings who hold merely one sword for the purposes of redemption and judgment. After all, redemption typically comes *through* judgment. To be sure, God exercises his rule or sword in two different *ways* between my-people and not-my-people, just as he will exercise it differently between the now and the not-yet. But isn't there still only one sword (God's), and one king (God), and one kingdom (God's)? In my mind, a more intuitive institutional explanation for God's different *ways* of ruling is to observe (as I did both above and in the book's introduction) simply that a king gives different kinds of licenses or authorizations, just as a CEO will give one kind of license to his vice president of marketing and another kind to his lawyer, or as a king will give one kind of license to the director of the royal institute for historical artifacts and another kind to his generals. Just because the state possesses the power of the sword and the church possesses the power of the keys (as I will contend in chapter six) doesn't mean they belong to separate kingdoms; it only mean they have different licenses from the same king. And just because God promises to exercise his rule later differently than he does now doesn't mean he will go about acquiring a different sword or become a different king; it just means he's changing strategies or tactics or executing what he's promised, like the CEO who promises to promote some and let go of others if the impending acquisition succeeds. Ultimately, I will arrive at many of the same conclusions as VanDrunen because of our shared concern for some kind of institutional distinction between the Two, but I would contest that his Two needs a more institutionally specified understanding of the One. Of course, this whole institutional critique is dealing in conceptual or logical categories. What should ultimately prove decisive is the biblical discussion, which we'll come to momentarily.

Phenomenologically, VanDrunen correctly roots the institutional foundations of the state and the church in the common and the special covenants, respectively (e.g., Gen 9 and Gen 12). Yet chapter one's discussion on the coterminous nature of our religion and our politics makes me slightly leery of tagging the common covenants with the label "common cultural concerns" (such as politics) and the special covenants with the label "religion" or "worship." Yes, God initiates salvation and therefore the beginning of *true* worship and *true* religion through the special covenants. Yet religion and worship, functionally and constructively understood, are common cultural concerns, as we considered in chapter one. And if worship is "an assent to judgment," as defined in chapter three, our worship determines, is determined by and displays our politics. A common cultural concern like the stock market is for many people a place of worship. And Abraham's worship shaped his political activity for the remainder of his life. All that to say, I understand what VanDrunen is getting at by assigning the separate labels to the separate kinds of covenants, but we need to make sure we don't miss how both kinds involve politics and religion, as I will explain further shortly.

Scripture is not a book of political philosophy, and so it does not define the nature of God's kingship as precisely as we might like.[14] But I do believe we can proceed on the assumption that such matters can be "derived inductively from the biblical discussion of the political history and hopes of the Israelites and from biblical critiques of institutions not fully described."[15]

That brings us to the argument of this chapter, which offers a slightly different resolution of the exegetical tensions than VanDrunen and two-kingdoms doctrine generally, as well as a different construal of the relationship between the Noahic and Abrahamic covenants. Specifically, I will argue (1) that God rules over all humanity after the fall as a king over subjects with the power of the sword, requiring obedience and worship; (2) that he uses covenants to enact and publicize that rule; (3) that he specifically uses the common covenants to command all people to worship him by acting as his image-bearing citizens; and (4) that he specifically uses the special covenants to create a people who will model true

---

[14]Old Testament exegete Gerhard von Rad observes, "In what the kingship of Yahweh consists the majority of passages do not tell us precisely. . . . The description of Yahweh as King impressively depicts His power, greatness and readiness to help, but this thought is so general, and so little related to the specific concept of 'king,' that there is little hesitation in combining it with other lines of thought. Thus Micah intermingles the idea of Yahweh as Shepherd (5:3) and Deutero-Isaiah introduces the parallelism of Creator, Redeemer and King (43:14 f.). The nature of the *malkut* of Yahweh is seldom delineated with any greater precision." Von Rad, "*Basileus*," 569.

[15]To put this quote in context, Daniel J. Elazar helpfully observes, "Less formally articulated than Greek political thought, the biblical political teaching must be discovered in the same manner that all biblical knowledge must observe, by careful examination and analysis of the text. . . . The Bible does not offer us a philosophically systematic presentation of its political theory or of the working of particular political institutions. Rather, the theory must be derived inductively from the biblical discussion of the political history and hopes of the Israelites and from biblical critiques of institutions not fully described." Elazar, *Covenant and Polity in Biblical Israel: Biblical Foundations and Jewish Expressions*, Covenant Traditions in Politics 1 (New Brunswick, NJ: Transaction Publishers, 1995), 12, 13.

citizenship and worship. The key lies in properly relating the common covenants (the covenants with Adam and Noah) and the special covenants (the Abrahamic, Mosaic, Davidic and new covenants).[16] And though there is much more we could say about the relationship between the common and special covenants in matters of continuity and discontinuity, my interest here is with this: what the common covenants *command* the special covenants *give*. Redemptive history serves creation's purposes.[17] And God is king over all of it.

Based on these four conclusions, I will further argue that the movement from present to future rule, as well as the movement from ruling "my people" to ruling "not my people," represents the movement from the *possession* of rule to the *execution* of that rule. Or to put it another way, it represents a movement from the invisibility of God's rule to a visible manifestation of it. When the Bible speaks of God's kingdom "coming" or of someone "entering" it, it does not mean that God gains rule where he didn't have it. It means that his rule is now named and made visible through a mediator in salvation or judgment. It is now executed.[18] That God always possesses rule is demonstrated in the fact that his rule is invisibly mediated through the institutions of the family and the state. He delegates authority to parent and prince. When God turns to executing his rule or making it visible, he doesn't just *delegate*—he *deputizes* people to speak and identify themselves in his name. We'll consider the distinction between delegation and deputization shortly.

Among other things, God's covenantal rule over all of life means all of life is political. The activities of the state are but one piece of God's larger

---

[16]My sense that many of the contemporary theological disputes concerning neo-Calvinistic transformationism or a Lutheran two-kingdoms doctrine have their roots not just in differing eschatologies or in differing conceptions of continuity/discontinuity between the Testaments, as is commonly observed, but in differing ways of relating the common covenants and the special covenants. See Dan Strange, "Not Ashamed! The Sufficiency of Scripture for Public Theology," *Themelios* 36, no. 2 (July 2011): 238-60, http://tgc-documents.s3.amazonaws.com/journal-issues/36.2/Themelios_36.2.pdf#page=61.

[17]J. G. McConville, *God and Earthly Power* (New York: T&T Clark, 2008), 31-34.

[18]Oliver O'Donovan has a similar distinction in mind, it seems, when he describes the international order as unified by "law rather than government." O'Donovan, *Desire of the Nations: Rediscovering the Roots of Political Theology* (New York: Cambridge University Press, 1996), 72. I understand him to mean that God's law is binding upon all, though he has established "no unitary mediator."

covenantal rule. Politics, I will argue in the conclusion of the chapter, is nothing more or less than the mediating of God's own covenantal rule. His covenantal rule, enacted both commonly and specially, is public-wide; it brings unity across all other forms of division while also distinguishing between the treasonous and nontreasonous; it is concerned with justice; and it is always backed by the power of God's sword. Indeed, a covenant bears an intrinsic political dynamic, as Jewish political philosopher Daniel Elazar has observed:

> Politically, a covenant involves a coming together (con-gregation) of basically equal humans who consent with one another through a morally binding pact supported by a transcendent power, establishing with the partners a new framework or setting them on the road to a new task that can only be dissolved by mutual agreement of all the parties to it. . . . They have their beginnings in the need to establish clear and binding relationships between God and humans and among humans, relationships that must be understood as being political far more than theological in character, designed to establish lines of authority, distributions of power, bodies politic, and systems of law.[19]

Insofar as this book is interested in what constitutes a "coming together (con-gregation)" of Christians, it makes sense for us to spend some time examining the device that Scripture uses to "establish lines of authority, distributions of power, bodies politic, and systems of law" among God's people—namely, the covenant. Politics, we said in the last chapter, beginning with the Trinity, is about structured relationships. Elazar says something similar: "A covenant is the constitutionalization of a relationship. As such, it provides the basis for the institutionalization of that relationship."[20] It should hardly be surprising, then, that the covenant must play a defining role in any political or institutional reading of Scripture, which this chapter will continue from the last chapter.

## God's Universal Rule and the Noahic Covenant

After disembarking the ark, Noah builds an altar and offers sacrifices whose aromas please Yahweh. Yahweh then promises to never again

---

[19]Elazar, *Covenant and Polity*, 1, see also 19-33. It is not clear to me what he means by saying that a covenant establishes a relationship that is "political far more than theological in character." Otherwise, I am happy to affirm what he says here.
[20]Ibid., 24.

"strike down every living creature as I have done" (Gen 8:21). The text then rearticulates the institutional framework first expressed in Genesis 1. Genesis 1 reads,

> And God blessed them. And God said to them, "Be fruitful and multiply and fill the earth and subdue it, and have dominion over the fish of the sea and over the birds of the heavens and over every living thing that moves on the earth." (Gen 1:28)

Genesis 9, similarly, reads,

> And God blessed Noah and his sons and said to them, "Be fruitful and multiply and fill the earth. The fear of you and the dread of you shall be upon every beast of the earth and upon every bird of the heavens, upon everything that creeps on the ground and all the fish of the sea. Into your hand they are delivered." (Gen 9:1-2)

Chapter nine also repeats chapter one's affirmation of humanity as created in God's image, and it does so by stepping out of prose and into poetry, also like chapter one. Genesis 1 reads,

> So God created man in his own image,
>   in the image of God he created him;
>   male and female he created them. (Gen 1:27)

Genesis 9 then reads,

> Whoever sheds the blood of man,
>   by man shall his blood be shed,
> for God made man in his own image. (Gen 9:6)

The first pair of texts present God's power-conferring rule: multiply and establish dominion over every sphere of the earth. The second pair of texts establish humans' identity as God-imagers. Taken together, we find humanity's archetypal political and priestly mandates: humanity has been given the office of vice-regent or priest-king for the sake of representing God's own rule throughout creation, which in turn requires being consecrated to him. And the scope of these commands is clearly universal: "Behold, I establish my covenant with you and your offspring after you, and with every living creature that is with you. . . . This is the sign of the covenant that I make between me and you . . . for all future generations" (Gen 9:9-10, 12, see also v. 17). Genesis 9, in short, rearticulates Genesis 1.[21] Noah is the new Adam[22]—a subject called to the office of citizenship.[23]

Of course, Genesis 9 does a bit more than mimic Genesis 1 word for word. It situates these mandates within a post-fall context,[24] as at least four clues in the text show. First, animals will fear humankind, and God gives them all for food. Second, the language of imaging is not placed in the context of the relational realities of male and female, but of murder (Gen 9:5-6). Third, Noah appears to stand in for Adam not just in the office of king but in the office of priest, but now the office involves a sacrifice (see Gen 7:1-3; 8:20-21). Adam as priest did not have to account for sin; Noah did. As such, Noah is "exercising a priestly ministry on behalf of the rest of humankind, just as Israel would later be called to act as a kingdom of priests on behalf of all the nations in the world (cf. Exod 19:6)."[25] He is the righteous sacrifice-offering mediator who both enables God's people to pass over the floods of God's judgment and plays a role in delaying God's final judgment.

Fourth, and most crucial, God promises to delay his punishment (Gen 8:20-21; 9:11), which effectively institutionalizes the aforementioned conceptual complexity: the Noahic covenant affirms that God rules all

---

[21] Gordon J. Wenham observes, "[God's] blessing on the new humanity repeats almost verbatim his blessing on the old pre-flood humanity; cf. 9:1 with 1:28a." Wenham, *Genesis 1-15*, Word Biblical Commentary (Waco: Word Books, 1987), 192. Discussions of the flood story as describing an uncreation and then a new creation can be found in Gentry and Wellum, *Kingdom Through Covenant: A Biblical-Theological Understanding of the Covenants* (Wheaton, IL: Crossway, 2012), 162-63; Bruce K. Waltke with Cathi J. Fredricks, *Genesis: A Commentary* (Grand Rapids: Zondervan, 2001), 128-29. Some argue that the latter three commands in Genesis 1:28 shouldn't be read into 9:1 and subsequent references. But I believe this overlooks the fact that (1) the three realms of dominion are repeated in 9:2; (2) the five commands of 1:28 are tied to the idea of imaging God, and 9:6 affirms that man is created in God's image; (3) multiplying surely necessitates filling and subduing—just ask any parent; and (4) verses 3 to 6 offer the adjustments necessitated by the fall, including the inevitable need for dominion to extend from one human being over another. To be sure, the prospect of murder and other injustice after the fall means God needs to more carefully qualify the dominion mandate. Hence, verses 5 and 6.

[22] Gentry and Wellum, *Kingdom Through Covenant*, 163; G. J. Wenham, "Flood," in *New International Dictionary of Old Testament Theology and Exegesis*, ed. W. A. VanGemeren, vol 4. (Grand Rapids: Zondervan, 1997), 642; cf. Paul R. Williamson, *Sealed with an Oath: Covenant in God's Unfolding Purpose* (Downers Grove, IL: IVP Academic, 2007), 75.

[23] See Gentry and Wellum, *Kingdom Through Covenant*, 156, 163f; also Paul Williamson, *Sealed with an Oath*, 59-76; William Dumbrell, *Covenant and Creation: A Theology of the Old Testament Covenants* (Carlisle, UK: Paternoster, 1984; 1997 ed.), 11-43.

[24] Gentry and Wellum, *Kingdom Through Covenant*, 165. Also Wenham, *Genesis 1-15*, 192-93.

[25] Wenham, "Flood," 642; also T. Desmond Alexander, *From Eden to the New Jerusalem: An Introduction to Biblical Theology* (Grand Rapids: Kregel, 2008), 28n32.

humanity (by virtue of the fact that judgment is his to withhold); but then it maintains the invisibility of that rule, depriving it of direct enforcement—or teeth—at least temporarily. It is "a covenant in which God binds himself,"[26] as if God is saying, "I still have the sword, but I promise not to swing it myself, which would end history." Indeed, the sign of this covenant, a bow, which in Hebrew is the ordinary term for an archer's bow, points to the fact that God has temporarily "laid his weapons down."[27] Effectively, this divine self-binding formalizes in covenantal terms something that had already been implied in the curse of Genesis 3: God would separate in time his declaration of rule from his final execution of rule, his promise of judgment and his enforcement of judgment, like a judge who condemns and sentences the criminal but delays imprisonment for a prolonged period (see esp. Gen 8:21). And it is this element of *time* that makes any political cartography of the Bible much more difficult to visualize than a simple map of nation-states. Political power, after all, is typically tied to space (maps show where one person's rule ends and another's begins), but not time per se. How does one draw time onto a map? This is precisely the complexity that the Noahic covenant presents to us and within which the remainder of Scripture's divine-human covenants operate.[28] Another term for this institutional complexity, of course, is eschatology. Divine judgment is delayed to the end of history. Does eschatology mean that God does not rule? That humans live under someone else's rule, such as their own? From the biblical perspective, it simply means that God is patient, "not wishing that any should perish, but that all should reach repentance" since "the day of the Lord will come like a thief" when "the works that are done . . . will be exposed" and his judgment enacted (2 Pet 3:9-10).

***The justice mechanism and the foundation of government.*** Ultimately, the purpose of this book is to understand the political nature of the church. But doing so, I have said, requires at least some understanding of the larger

---

[26]Gentry and Wellum, *Kingdom Through Covenant*, 170.
[27]Ibid., 171.
[28]As Gentry and Wellum state, "There is no evidence anywhere in the complete canon of Scripture as a whole that this covenant has been annulled or superseded," and, quoting Paul Williamson, that "the Noahic covenant provides the biblical-theological framework within which all subsequent divine-human covenants operate." Ibid., 171, 176; see Williamson, *Sealed with an Oath*, 68.

playing field. For that reason, I believe it is important for us to spend at least a few moments trying to understand government and what I will call the "justice mechanism" that is established in Genesis 9:5-6. A divine authorization to kill as an act of retribution occurred back in Genesis 4, where Cain says to God, "Whoever finds me will kill me," to which the Lord replies, "Not so! If anyone kills Cain, vengeance shall be taken on him sevenfold" (Gen 4:14, 15). Yet this specific authorization is turned into a general authorization in Genesis 9 for a carefully calibrated action against the murderer of any person:

> And for your [plural] lifeblood *I will require* a reckoning: from every beast *I will require* it and from man. From his fellow man *I will require* a reckoning for the life of man.
>
> "Whoever sheds the blood of man,
> > by man shall his blood be shed,
> for God made man in his own image." (Gen 9:5-6, italics added)

The institutional question to ask here is, to whom does God give authority to do what? Let us take each of those interrogatives in turn:

*Who?* Who is given authority in verses 5 and 6? The easy answer is, man is: "From his fellow man I will require" and "by man shall his blood be shed."

But which man? Which men? This is the harder practical question that drives John Locke's response to divine right's theorist Robert Filmer in the first of the two *Two Treatises*, and that drove the seventeenth- and eighteenth-century movement toward consent-based formulations of government and democracy generally. No one doubts *that* there should be governments, said Locke. But how do we know *who* exactly should govern?[29] Charles II? Why him? Genesis 9 offers no explicit instruction on how to choose who should govern, but that doesn't mean it says nothing. Verses 5 and 6 read as indicatives, but the heralding "whoever" of verse 6, combined with its poetic form, seems to give the verse an

---

[29]"The great question which in all ages has disturbed mankind, and brought on them the greatest part of those mischiefs which have ruined cities, depopulated countries, and disordered the peace of the world, has been, not whether there be power in the world, not whence it came, but who should have it." John Locke, "First Treatise," in *Two Treatises of Government and a Letter Concerning Toleration*, ed. Ian Shapiro (New Haven, CT: Yale University Press, 2003), 66 (chap. 9, para. 106).

illocutionary force that imposes a duty upon all humanity. The verses provide, in other words, (1) a divinely imposed obligation and (2) authorization (3) for all people.

Let's unpack each point. (1) These two verses, first of all, *obligate* all human beings, as a matter of obedience to God, to ensure that a reckoning for crimes against humans occurs. Humans in society together must do it because God obligates them to do it. Three times in verse 5 God says, "I will require." This justice mechanism is not an expression of human will. It comes *from above*.

(2) By token of the obligation, these verses also *authorize* a human to stand in God's stead: "by man" shall this "reckoning" be enacted. God gives human beings the authority to wield the sword.

(3) In all this, there is something vaguely democratic about the authorization here. It seems that all humanity is imposed upon to find a solution to injustice. The verses don't go out to a certain subsection of humanity. They are spoken to all descendents of Noah, which means all possess a measure of responsibility, each for his or her part. We are *all* obligated. We are *all* authorized to participate in the solution. John Locke uses language, interestingly, that comes close to making this point, though he introduces the conceptuality of "rights" as a way of acknowledging what we possess by being created in the divine image: "And that all men may be restrained from invading others' rights, and from doing hurt to one another, . . . the execution of the law of nature is . . . put into every man's hands, whereby everyone has a right to punish the transgressors of that law to such a degree as may hinder its violation."[30] I don't know that Locke has these verses specifically in mind, but I am inclined to think that the Noahic obligation and authorization does in fact "put into every man's hands . . . a right to punish . . . to such a degree as may hinder its violation." Imagine, for instance, an eighteenth-century mountain man living in uncharted territory hundreds of miles from civilization. Supposing another mountain man wanders by and steals his horse or kills his wife, I believe the Noahic covenant gives the first man a power

---

[30]John Locke, "Second Treatise," in *Two Treatises of Government and a Letter Concerning Toleration*, ed. Ian Shapiro (New Haven, CT: Yale University Press, 2003), 102-3 (chap. 2, para. 7). Yes, Locke is invoking the law of nature here instead of what the God of the Bible "requires," but for him the law of nature was a way of giving reason-based public accessibility to the truths of Christianity among multiple revelatory denominations and religions. See Greg Forster, *John Locke's Politics of Moral Consensus* (New York: Cambridge University Press, 2005), 30-32, 84-127.

over the second, but not (in Locke's language) an "absolute or arbitrary power . . . but only to retribute to him . . . what is proportionate to his transgression."[31] Perhaps Cain is illustrative here? Cain and Abel, we could say, dwelled in such a government-less state. God directly punished Cain's crime through exile (Gen 4:12), but then he established the obligation for "vengeance" on an individually specified basis (Gen 4:15)—for crimes against Cain's own person. But now Genesis 9:5-6 takes what we see individually with Cain in a government-less state and expands it universally: "*Whoever sheds the blood of man, by man . . .*" In other words, God's rules of justice that bind people universally are of a piece with God's rules of justice in an individual circumstance, yet now "exacting retribution is not a personal matter but a societal obligation."[32] Humanity receives this obligation collectively, whether a society consists of three people or three million.

The inevitable and unavoidable implication of these two verses is that groups of people living in society *must* form or support a government—an orderly set of publicly recognized institutional processes—in order to employ this God-given justice mechanism justly. In most circumstances, only a society-wide institutional solution stands any chance of *employing* the justice mechanism while simultaneously *satisfying* the justice mechanism. To settle for a method less likely to yield a full reckoning (for instance, because those means will provoke retaliatory violence, or because they involve economically or ethnically prejudiced judgments) is to disobey God. Any vigilantism or otherwise unjust acts of retribution committed in the name of the mechanism will simply trigger the mechanism to boomerang back and strike the unjust actor. Therefore, whoever would employ the authority of this justice mechanism must first figure out how to employ it justly, that is, according to the rules of the mechanism itself. The mechanism is, in that sense, self-reinforcing and requires human beings to attend to a host of matters that will help to ensure that "reckoning" occurs in the most "reckoned" way possible. Any lack of due diligence in searching for the processes that yield the most "reckoned" outcomes can therefore be characterized as disobedience to God—again, God says that *he requires it*.

---

[31]Locke, "Second Treatise," 103 (chap. 2, para. 8).
[32]Kenneth Mathews, *Genesis 1–11:26* (Nashville: Broadman & Holman, 1996), 405.

To be clear, I am not saying that God directly establishes governments or a government in Genesis 9:5-6. I am arguing that he gives human beings (1) an *obligation* that will best be fulfilled in society by forming or supporting a government and (2) the *authority* to do this.[33]

In the movement from the rules of justice between two mountain men in uncharted territory to the rules of justice within an entire collective, John Locke moves very subtly but crucially beyond Scripture. And I think highlighting these differences might serve to illumine misplaced assumptions many Western Christians today have concerning government. Locke begins, I believe, where Scripture does: asserting the "executive authority" (Locke's phrase) or "dominion" (the Bible's phrase) of each individual by virtue of the equal dignity God has given every human being. Our grizzly mountain men are equal before God; neither possesses inherent rule over the other; and both have the right of self-preservation.[34] So far, so agreed.

From here, however, paths diverge. For starters, Scripture doesn't say anything explicit or binding about how governments should be formed. By inheritance? Conquest? Popular election? Nowhere does the Bible say. And though Genesis 9 imposes an obligation on every human to support the formation or work of government, that does not quite amount to Locke's claim (which we'll explore in a moment) that the *only* morally legitimate government is government by consent. The Bible does not moralize the manner in which a government should be formed or the earthly foundation of its sovereignty. In this regard, Christian political philosophers have something to learn once again from Jewish counterparts. Daniel Elazar and Stuart Cohen offer an instructive word from their own tradition:

> The Jewish political tradition, like every other political tradition, is concerned with the question of power and justice, but it differs from the political traditions growing out of classic Greek thought in that it begins with a concern for relationships rather than structures. More specifically, it is less concerned for

---

[33] Old Testament scholar Bruce Waltke describes this passage as "the legislation" that "lays the foundation for government by the state" (Waltke, *Genesis*, 145), which seems to point to the matter of authorization. I'm adding to what Waltke is saying the idea of obligation.

[34] Like others before him, Greg Forster has shown quite decisively that Locke ultimately appeals to God's revealed law as the ultimate foundation of all morality and government; see Forster, *John Locke's Politics*, 162-63, 218-19, 225-28, 246-58. See also the works of Ian Shapiro, John Dunn, James Tully, John Marshall and Jeremy Waldron featured in note 28 of the introduction.

the best regime than with the proper relationships between power and justice, the governors and the governed, and God and man.[35]

I would not place the words *relationships* and *structure* into antithesis as they do, but I believe they are correct about Scripture's reticence concerning a "best regime." Scripture does seem to afford some measure of institutional flexibility. Elazar and Cohen accordingly observe that the political journey of Abraham's descendants from Pharaoh's rule, to Moses' rule, to the rule of the judges, to the monarchy, to a divided monarchy, to exile, to vassal state in the Persian Empire demonstrates God's willingness to govern his people first in one polity, then in another: "The rank order of the several arenas of government is deliberately left flexible, allowing the system as a whole to adapt to the changing political circumstances of its environment."[36] Bible scholar N. T. Wright offers similarly, "The Jews didn't, it seems, care very much how rulers became rulers; so much for our modern ideals of 'legitimacy through voting.' They cared very much what the rulers did once they were in power."[37] *That* God's people will in some sense be ruled through human mediators is fixed; *how* they are ruled, surprisingly, is somewhat relative—relative to considerations of wisdom and wisdom's contextually conscious pursuit of justice. And if this is true of God's special people, it stands to reason that it is probably true for nations in general. In many circumstances, some form of government by consent might do. On an island of pirates and brigands, perhaps not. Indeed, if the last several decades of "state building" has taught today's global policy-makers anything, it is that a nation's unique cultural and historical circumstances must be considered when writing a country's constitution from scratch.[38] A liberal democratic constitution cannot simply be plopped down on top of

---

[35] Daniel J. Elazar and Stuart A. Cohen, *The Jewish Polity: Jewish Political Organization from Biblical Times to the Present* (Bloomington: Indiana University Press, 1985), 8. Elazar observes elsewhere, "In a political sense, biblical covenants take the form of constituting acts that establish the parameters of authority and its division without prescribing the constitutional details of regimes." Elazar, *Covenant and Polity*, 68.

[36] Elazar and Cohen, *Jewish Polity*, 15, also 7. O'Donovan makes similar observations in *Desire of the Nations*, 20, 35.

[37] N. T. Wright, *How God Became King: The Forgotten Story of the Gospels* (New York: HarperOne, 2012), 170.

[38] See Lawrence Harrison and Samuel P. Huntington, eds., *Culture Matters: How Values Shape Human Progress* (New York: Basic Books, 2000), on the importance of culture for political development; see also Robert Putnam, *Making Democracy Work: Civic Traditions in Modern Italy*

a former Soviet state, the fallen regime of a Latin American dictator or a deposed Middle Eastern government without considering whether that nation possesses the social norms, civil society and rule of law necessary to sustain democracy.

Where Genesis 9 is very clear is that government authority comes from God. As we have already seen, three times verse 5 says God will require this reckoning. So no matter how a government is formed as a matter of historical accident, it seems pretty clear that the authority of government comes *from above*, not *from below*.

Right here, however, is where Locke subly but crucially angles his theory in another direction. He, too, attempts to establish a theory of government in which authority comes from above, but he also wants to ensure that governing authority comes *from below*. Therefore he turns what Scripture would call a moral *may* into a moral *must*. Governments *must* form by consent. Says Locke:

> Men being . . . by nature all free, equal, and independent, no one can be put out of this estate, and subjected to the political power of another, without his own consent. The only way whereby any one divests himself of his natural liberty, and puts on the bonds of civil society, is by agreeing with other men to join and unite into a community.[39]

Recall, after all, Locke's response to Filmer: Scripture does not specify *who exactly* should rule. This means that any human who simply asserts his or her rule over other humans is asserting what God has not given. He or she is doing an injustice, and that government is not legitimate. It is not a true authority. The only authority that is legitimate in a society of equals, according to Locke, is authority that is voluntarily ceded or consented to. What that means is, government by consent is a moral imperative. Greg Forster summarizes, "Consensual government [for Locke] is therefore morally necessary," "is morally mandatory," "is the only legitimate option."[40] This universal moral claim is pretty clear in Thomas Jefferson too. Pay attention to the words "deriving" and "just" in his famous preamble:

---

(Princeton, NJ: Princeton University Press, 1994), a seminal work on the importance of civil society and culture in democracy.

[39]Locke, "Second Treatise," 141-42 (chap. 8, para. 95).

[40]Forster, *John Locke's Politics*, 250, 219.

"Governments are instituted among Men, *deriving* their *just* powers from the consent of the governed." Any power *not* derived from consent is not just.

In all this Locke failed to recognize the two speeds that chapter two above importuned of theologians—knowing how to distinguish between what's fixed and what's flexible, what's divinely mandated and what's left to wisdom. And by turning the *mays* into *musts* in the realm of universal moral principles, Locke effectively earned Jesus' rebuke, "You nullify the word of God by your tradition" (see Mk 7:13; cf. 7:8). By insisting that something must always be the case that God doesn't, he puts himself in God's throne and makes what's morally right accountable to his own standard. Where God says, "I authorize governments and require you to submit to them," Locke says that every individual "authorizes the society . . . to make laws for him."[41] Where Scripture says that God puts every individual under obligation, Locke's individual puts himself under obligation: "And thus every man, by consenting with others to make one body politic under government, puts himself under an obligation."[42] To summarize, where Genesis 9 establishes government "from above," Locke and the contractarian tradition establish it "from below."

Locke would contest this, of course. He insists on both above *and* below. He excludes athiests from the social contract because he assumes "the social fabric depends on commitments underpinned by the fear of God."[43] He writes, "The true ground of Morality . . . can only be the Will and Law of a God, who sees Men in the dark, has in his Hand Rewards and Punishments, and Power enough to call to account the proudest Offender."[44] His evangelical sympathizers, too, would say that his theory of government from below is compatible with a theory of government from above.[45] And I would agree, so long as we leave government by consent in the realm of wisdom—in the *mays* and not the *musts*—which means acknowledging that a government's legitimacy doesn't come from the people's consent. A government in

---

[41]Locke, "Second Treaties," 138 (chap. 8, para. 89).

[42]Ibid., 142 (chap. 8, para. 97).

[43]Jeremy Waldron, *God, Locke, and Equality: Christian Foundations in Locke's Political Thought* (New York: Cambridge University Press, 2002), 223.

[44]Cited in ibid., 225, from Locke, *An Essay Concerning Human Understanding*, ed. P. H. Nidditch (Oxford: Clarendon Press, 1971), 1.3.6.

[45]E.g., Greg Forster, *The Contested Public Square: The Crisis of Christianity and Politics* (Downers Grove, IL: IVP Academic, 2008), 192.

any given historical moment *may* be, *might* be, *can* be formed through the consent of the governed as a matter of historical process. This happens most clearly (but not exclusively)⁴⁶ through the democratic process. *But its moral legitimacy does not come from the citizens' consent.* Consider: suppose a citizen withdraws her consent. Does God no longer require her to obey said government? Does her obligation "from above" just evaporate? Genesis 9 and Romans 13 give us absolutely no reason to think it does. The person remains obligated to obey in the biblical perspective.⁴⁷ Now, a particular elected office holder might hold office by virtue of my consent, and he or she might lose that office by my withdrawing of that consent. But in both scenarios I remain submitted to that nation's constitution, *because God has required it*. In other words, the obligation to obey is not created by my consent. It's created by God's requirement. Even if I participate in establishing a brand-new government, giving my consent to a new constitution, my obligation to obey that government which I helped to create does not depend upon that consent. It depends on the fact that God requires me to obey what *he* has established, even if he established it through me.⁴⁸ Scripture could

---

⁴⁶See Locke, "Second Treatise," 141-54 (chap. 8); also Forster, *John Locke's Politics*, 249.

⁴⁷Ironically, Locke seems to recognize that a person cannot arbitrarily withdraw his or her consent: "Whosoever therefore out of a state of nature united into a community, must be understood to give up all the power necessary to the ends for which they unite into society, to the majority of the community." Locke, "Second Treatise," 143 (chap. 8, para. 99). Locke either fails to be internally consistent or exposes the fact that something else within his system is doing the real work of creating obligation—namely, the law of God.

⁴⁸Along these lines, one political theorist argues for their compatibility by likening the idea of consent to the "human responsibility" side of the divine sovereignty/human responsibility equation or balance. Joshua Mitchell, "Is Consent a Theological Category," in *Theology and Public Philosophy: Four Conversations* (Lanham, MD: Lexington Books, 2012), 81-85. I think there is something to this, but I'd add another layer. The role of consent in any given historical situation can also be described as *accidental* rather than *necessary*, to use the Aristotelian distinction. I might participate in an election or even in establishing a government, but the obligation to obey still depends upon God since the authorization to rule comes from him. It's his authorization that gives government its essence. My participation in any given moment is a historical accident. What's more, the democratic vote itself should be viewed as a form of obedience to the requirement that God has placed on all humanity to fulfill Genesis 9:5-6, and it should be exercised in accordance with the purposes for which God has established governments. In short, so long as we keep democratic governments in the flexible-wisdom category and not the fixed divine-principle category, matters of accident rather than necessity, I am more than content to say they are compatible with a biblical theory of government *from above*. In fact, I am even willing to say that what I called the "vaguely democratic" imposition of Genesis 9:5-6 upon on all humanity creates a downward push on authority, such that, in a nation of so-called Christians or otherwise moral people, democracy is optimal! But by arguing that governments *derive* their authority from consent, Locke and Jefferson place consent into the

not be clearer on the source of a government's legitimacy and therefore of our obligation to obey:

> For there is no authority except from God, and those that exist have been instituted by God. Therefore whoever resists the authorities resists what God has appointed. . . . He [the one who is in authority] is the servant of God, an avenger who carries out God's wrath on the wrongdoer. . . . The authorities are ministers of God. (Rom 13:1-2, 4, 6)

Philosophically, the authority of government can only come from above or from below. It cannot be both. A man cannot serve two masters, in spite of Locke's philosophical attempt to do exactly that. Which means, Locke's system is inconsistent and not internally coherent.[49]

Furthermore, the critique leveled against the liberal theory of religious freedom in chapter one applies against contractarianism too: a theory of consent effectively removes God from the foundation of government, and it rests upon a view from nowhere. A contract, after all, depends upon agreement. Insofar as an unbeliever does *not* agree or consent to the proposal that God is the source of governmental authority, God is not a part of that contract, objectively speaking, in spite of whatever subjective sense of obligation *from above* a believer might feel. In a consent-based formulation, then, the obligation to obey derives from the obligation to keep one's promises,[50] not from an obligation to obey God. As such, there is an irreconcilable contradiction between a concept of government from below (at least on Locke and Jefferson's absolutist contractarian terms) and from above.[51] Locke's failure to reconcile these two impulses, in that sense, is the same old failure of so much early-Enlightenment piety, which tried to treat faith and reason as separate and equal.

---

necessary essence of what government is. And this absolutization of consent (and, by implication, democracy) bespeaks an overrealized eschatology and an inadequate grasp of the fall. Expedience and the call to justice may, from time to time, recommend some other form of government.

[49]On the mythology of coherence, see Quentin Skinner, "Meaning and Understanding in the History of Ideas," *History and Theory* 8, no. 1 (1969): 16-22.

[50]Nicholas Wolterstorff, *Understanding Liberal Democracy: Essays in Political Philosophy*, ed. Terence Cuneo (New York: Oxford University Press, 2012), 261.

[51]Wolterstorff finds Locke's theory historically untenable and contractarians theories generally insufficient. He does, however, briefly sketch out an alternative theory of government *from below*. See ibid., 245-74.

What then of the right to revolution through the withdrawal of consent, which Jefferson was after? I am not positive there is biblical license for overturning an unjust government, but I think there probably is, and I believe that Genesis 9:5-6 provides that licence. It's not in the withdrawal of consent per se. Rather, we only need observe that no government should presume to be "above" the justice mechanism, but government must always remain "under" it (1) because the authority ultimately derives from God and (2) because every member of society is created in God's image. As such, every government is subject to the demands of the justice mechanism. Rebellion is justified not according to the withdrawal of consent (since consent is not what creates the obligation to obey); rebellion is justified when the government fails to do what God has obligated *it* to do (since God creates the obligation to obey by assigning government with its task).[52]

In other words, the formally designated holder of the sword has no authority to set aside the demands of the justice mechanism in the process of fulfilling its mandate, lest it boomerang back and strike him as it does the vigilante. The mere fact that a particular government is in place by God's secret providence does not mean that all its actions or directives are morally legitimate. God gives authority to government for certain ends only, and its rule is legitimate to the extent it pursues just ends by just means.[53] A characteristically unjust government, by virtue of its injustice, has exceeded its authorization and self-refuted its own mandate, thereby triggering the operations of God's Noahic justice mechanism to strike back.[54] And precisely

---

[52]Insofar as Locke views the injustice of government as grounds for rebellion, as I do, we find a second kind of internal inconsistency within his system (see also n. 47 above). If government is by consent, strictly speaking, a person should be able to rebel simply by withdrawing his or her consent. But anyone who justifies rebellion on the grounds of a government's injustice is implicitly acknowledging that that government's right to rule and to create obligations of obedience comes from whoever or whatever tasked that government with enforcing the rules of justice in the first place. Insofar as Locke therefore grounds rebellion in a breech of God's law and God's justice, he is implicitly acknowledging that the government's right to rule comes from God, not from the people's consent. Jefferson's famous preamble verges on this same inconsistency.

[53]See Nicholas Wolterstorff, "'The Authorities Are God's Servants': Is a Theistic Account of Political Authority Still Viable or Have Humanity Accounts Won the Day?" in *Theology and Public Philosophy: Four Conversations*, ed. Kenneth L. Grasso and Cecilia Rodriguez Castillo (Lanham, MD: Lexington Books, 2012), 65; see also his critique of Calvin's view of the state in *The Mighty and the Almighty* (New York: Cambridge University Press, 2012), 67-82.

[54]In his study of the Hebrew noun for judgment, *mishpat*, biblical scholar Leon Morris writes, "When the righteous 'does judgement' he does not necessarily preserve the established order. On the contrary, if the wicked are in power he disrupts it with considerable vigour. And what

because Scripture does not specify *how* a society must form a government, it just might leave a society with the freedom to topple an unjust ruler and to establish a new one by just means. Bonhoeffer, for instance, might have made such an argument in defense of his support of an assassination attempt on Hitler. Does Genesis 9:6 not apply to Hitler, after all? The fact that Bonhoeffer's coconspirators could not remove Hitler through the ordinary channels of government but had to resort to quiet conspiracy, by my reckoning, was a just response to the unjust structures that Hitler had erected to protect himself from such a removal so that he could perpetrate his injustices. In other words, going outside the channels of the formally recognized government, in the case of Nazi Germany at least, was itself part of a just response to such horrific injustices.

In short, the authority of government does not derive from the consent of the governed or a social contract; it derives from the one who "requires" justice. The "redemptive narrative" of liberalism begins similiarly to the biblical one, but then it diverges at a critical point. Both begin with a kind of Eden where every individual possesses equal dignity and executive authority. Both perceive the need of human government in light of the fall, though without the loss of equal dignity and executive authority. Then comes the divergence. The liberal narrative continues from the individual's perspective and presumes a kind of innocence in the individual, whereby he or she maintains the objectivity necessary for judging where to yield executive authority to the government and where to retain it. At the moment when the social contract is formed, liberalism's individual is to the moral domain what Descartes's thinking self is to the epistemological domain: an objective sovereign able to discriminate between just and unjust, legitimate government and illegitimate government.

Genesis 9, however, emerges from a divine perspective and denies precisely such human objectivity. God establishes governments because no human has proven trustworthy since Genesis 3. What this means is, political

---

in this way he does partially and imperfectly he constantly looks for Yahweh to accomplish fully and perfectly. . . . To take an example at random, when Amos tells Israel that Yahweh says, 'I hate, I despise your feasts . . . let judgement roll down as waters, and righteousness as a mighty stream' (Am. v. 21-24), it is impossible to hold that he is urging the retention of the *status quo*. He is advocating radical reform. Far from denoting an adherence to custom, a retention of the old order, *mishpaṭ* is nothing less than revolutionary dynamite." Morris, *The Biblical Doctrine of Judgment* (1960; repr., Eugene, OR: Wipf & Stock, 2006), 13.

obligation *precedes* the formation of what liberals call political society—a political obligation to God.

*What?* The plainest way to describe the "what" of a government's mandate in verses 5 and 6 is to say that God authorizes governments to pursue a "reckoning" (in the ESV's translation) for crimes against human beings all the way up to capital punishment for murder. Justice, at least as it is represented here, involves parity: a like for like. Presumably, this authorization to reckon a capital crime marks the outer limit of that authority, and we can take it by implication that a government possesses the authority to prosecute lesser crimes (cf. Lev 24:20). It is because of Genesis 9:5-6, then, that I am inclined to agree with the opening sentence of chapter one in Oliver O'Donovan's book on government, "The authority of secular government resides in the practice of judgment."[55]

The immediate context of verses 5 and 6—verses 1 to 7—is instructive as well, with its bookend commands: "Be fruitful and mulitiply" (Gen 9:1, 7). The whole passage is about the creation mandate in this post-fall setting. Verses 5 and 6 (and 4), then, are one component in this larger enterprise.[56] If all of life is political in a broad sense by virtue of the creation mandate, then the institutions of state that we associate with politics in a narrow sense fit inside that broader purpose—like verses 5 and 6 fitting inside verses 1 to 7. Politics narrowly conceived serves politics broadly conceived. It should hardly be surprising, then, that societies often debate how far the hand of government should extend into people's lives. The narrow *protectionist* view of government affirmed in verses 5 and 6, insofar as it serves the larger goals of human flourishing and prosperity, will always feel pulled toward the expansive *perfectionist* views of government, where, as in Aristotle, governments are charged with cultivating virtue and securing the ideal

---

[55]Oliver O'Donovan, *The Ways of Judgment* (Grand Rapids: Eerdmans, 2005), 3. O'Donovan does not mean by this that "the whole operation of government is thinned down . . . to the operations of civil courts of justice," but instead that "political authority in all its forms—lawmaking, warmaking, welfare provision, education—is to be reconceived within this matrix and subject to the discipline of enacting right against wrong" (ibid., 4-5). See also Nicholas Wolterstorff, "The Authorities Are God's Servants," in *Theology and Public Philosophy: Four Conversations*, ed. Kenneth L. Grasso and Cecilia Rodriguez Castillo (Lanham, MD: Lexington Books, 2012), 62. Cf. Leon Morris's critique of equating "biblical judgment" and "rule" in *Biblical Doctrine of Judgment*, 8-11.

[56]Verses 4 and 5 both begin with the same Hebrew adverb for "surely" (*ak*), which suggests they stand in grammatical parallel to one another in how they fit into the larger context.

community.⁵⁷ Push too far toward perfectionism and you have idolatry, but precisely where the Bible lands on the spectrum between a protectionist and a perfectionist view of government, gratefully, is a question that we can assign to the realm of wisdom and leave for another day. At the very least, we can say the government has the power of the sword to ensure sufficient peace and tranquility for citizens to pursue their God-assigned mandate.

Once again, John Locke and the classical liberal tradition provide a helpful contrast here since (I believe) his answer to the "what" question remains a kind of default setting for many Western citizens. Locke argued that governments should concern themselves with "outward things" such as "life, liberty, health, and indolency of body" as well as "money, lands, houses, furniture and the like."⁵⁸ The "what" over which government is authorized to act in classical liberalism is the outer self.

Is this what we see in Genesis 9—that God authorizes governments to acts over bodies but not minds or consciences? The immediate context indeed recognizes the inner and outer self as distinct phenomenological realities, as when God observes "the intention of man's heart is evil from his youth" (Gen 8:21; also 6:5, 11). Further, Genesis 9 indeed employs corporeal, even graphic language: "Whoever sheds the blood of man . . ." And the larger testimony of Scripture surely carves out a space for the individual conscience to respond in obedience and faith to God's call or command.

Still, strictly speaking, Genesis 9 draws a line of jurisdiction not in between the inner self and the outer self, but—I would contest—in between humanity and God.⁵⁹ Recall, once again, that God lays down his bow of war here and promises to not punish humanity presently for their wickedness as he had done in the flood. But to ensure that social chaos does not ensue, he licences humans to protect themselves against harm from one another with the justice mechanism. What he specifically does not do in this same moment is authorize humans to prosecute crime (or sin) against him. There is no authorization to prosecute false worship, idolatry, atheism and so forth, unless of course these "upward" crimes manifest themselves as crimes

---

⁵⁷See Wolterstorff, *Mighty and the Almighty*, 100-102.
⁵⁸John Locke, "A Letter Concerning Toleration," in *Two Treatises of Government and A Letter Concerning Toleration*, ed. Ian Shapiro (New Haven, CT: Yale University Press, 2003), 218.
⁵⁹See Vern S. Poythress, "False Worship in the Modern State," in *The Shadow of Christ in the Law of Moses* (Phillipsburg, NJ: P&R, 1991), 294-95.

against humans: "Whoever sheds the blood *of man*." Crimes against humanity can be measured and parity restablished. But it is difficult to imagine how a government would assess human hearts for crimes against God, calculate the appropriate penalties and recompense God.[60] Do the commandments in Deuteronomy to stone those who pursue other gods contradict this claim (see Deut 13)? Only if one believes the civic elements of the Mosaic covenant are explicitly binding upon nations besides Israel. I do not.

Yet the governing philosophy of Genesis 9 is more complex still. This governmental charter ("Whoever sheds the blood of man, by man shall his blood be shed") is grounded in a theological claim: "*For* God made man in his own image." Right governmental policy, it would seem, has a theological ground. Remove the ground and you remove the foundation of good policies and good constitutions. Or again, remove the ground and watch governmental policy warp from right to wrong, from just to unjust. To the extent that governments deny this theological ground and to the extent that government policy warps toward injustice as a result, that government has earned its own judgment. All human authority, I said in chapter three, is representative, mediated, derivative. It is not absolute.

***Religious tolerance—part one.***[61] This discussion runs us headlong once again into the topic of religious freedom or tolerance. Unlike James Madison, in fact, I prefer the language of *tolerance* instead of *freedom* because there is no such thing as a "view from nowhere," as discussed in chapter one. At most we can *tolerate* one another, each from our own perspective. A politics that begins with the covenanting God of the Bible requires us to consider what a doctrine of religious tolerance might look like that is grounded in a "right order" conception of justice (O'Donovan) rather than an "inherent rights" conception (Wolterstorff), the latter of which is generally adopted by heirs of the liberal tradition. I would like to propose a right-order doctrine of religious tolerance in two parts, the first half now as it pertains to the power of the state and the second half toward the end of chapter six as it pertains to the local church.

A little background may be useful here concerning the difference between right order and inherent rights. Nicholas Wolterstorff has helpfully

---

[60]Poythress, "False Worship," 296.
[61]Part two of this discussion will come in chapter six.

distinguished between these two concepts of justice, with O'Donovan representing justice as right order and Wolterstorff himself as representing justice as inherent rights.[62] O'Donovan, in a reply, concedes Wolterstorff's basic distinction and represents it as the difference of an *s*—between right and rights.

- Justice as right order begins with the law—right order. Justice as inherent rights begins with the idea of personal worth—inherent rights.
- With right order, duties come from the law. First law, then duties. With inherent rights, duties to other people create the law. First duties based on the worth of others, then laws that articulate those duties.
- With right order, individuals are measured in relation to the law: "Am I keeping the law and impartially executing it?" With inherent rights, the fairness of laws are measured in relation to what people are due—their rights.
- With right order, murder is wrong because it breaks God's law. With inherent rights, says Wolterstorff explicitly exegeting Genesis 9:6, "The proscription against murder is grounded not in God's law but in the worth of the human being. All who bear God's image possess, on that account, an inherent right not to be murdered."[63]

The liberal doctrine of religious freedom that is grounded in Madison's "sacred conscience" or Locke's inner person depends upon a concept of justice as inherent rights. Sure enough, Wolterstorff grounds his own definition of religious freedom, among other places, in "the natural right or duty to worship God according to the dictates of his own conscience."[64] This is the formulation of religious freedom that we considered and critiqued in chapter one.

---

[62]O'Donovan, *Desire of the Nations*, 37-41; then see Nicholas Wolterstorff, *Justice: Rights and Wrongs* (Princeton, NJ: Princeton University Press, 2008), 68-75; and then see Oliver O'Donovan, "The Language of Rights and Conceptual History: Focus on Nicholas Wolterstorff," *Journal of Religious Ethics* 37, no. 2 (2009): 193-208.

[63]Wolterstorff, *Justice*, 95. The difficulty with Wolterstorff's view of Genesis 9:6 is that human worth may be the ground for the wrongness of murder, but only derivatively because man is *in God's* image. It is a theological ground, as I have already said, not an anthropological one. The language of *image*, furthermore, necessarily places the human creature and his or her worth in a secondary and derivative position, just as an image in a mirror is derivative of the object the mirror beholds. Most significantly, murder is wrong because God *says* it's wrong in these verses! It violates his law.

[64]Nicholas Wolterstorff, "A Christian Case for Religious Freedom," in *Religious Freedom: Why Now? Defending an Embattled Human Right*, The Witherspoon Institute Task Force on

With this distinction between two conceptions of justice as the backdrop, we can recast chapter one's critique of the liberal formulation of religious liberty as a critique of any conception of justice-as-inherent-rights that does not rest upon a doctrine of justice-as-right. The sacred conscience, by itself, not only does not establish any conception of right; just the opposite, it turns into the tautology of respecting consciences for the sake of respecting consciences. There is no justice-as-inherent-rights without a deeper justice-as-right.[65] What makes rights right?! Or again, there is nothing to make rights right apart from a transcendent right, which the free conscience won't permit. As such, the only thing that actually begins to limit the free conscience in the public square is the preferences of whoever can win the most votes.

Genesis 9, however, offers us the first half of a distinctively Christian doctrine of religious tolerance that is grounded not in the free conscience as such but on God's law or covenantal authority—on justice as right.[66] And the formulation is fairly simple: *God has not authorized human beings to prosecute crimes against himself.* Or to put it slightly differently: nothing authorizes us to prosecute another person's worship or religious activities institutionally defined. Not only that, establishing the limits of this theory of religious tolerance is fairly simple: *any form of worship that leads to harming others should be punished, according to the justice mechanism of Genesis 9:5-6.* None of this denies that the conscience must in some sense be free in order for the individual to respond to God's call to obedience or faith. It is to say, however, that the free conscience need not play a significant role in formulating a doctrine of religious tolerance.

The distinction between the liberal theory of religious freedom and a biblical theory of religious tolerance may look subtle at first, but it is significant for at least three reasons. First, a theory of religious tolerance can dispense with nonsensical talk about religious neutrality in the public

---

International Religious Freedom (Princeton, NJ: Witherspoon Institute, 2012), 40. See also Wolterstorff, *Understanding Liberal Democracy*, 329-52.

[65] Jeremy Waldron essentially comes to this same conclusion regarding the doctrine of equality, namely, that it needs a theological ground. Waldron, *God, Locke, and Equality*, 235-43.

[66] We will consider the second half of a doctrine of religious tolerance in chapter six. I will argue there not just for "free exercise" but against "an establishment of religion." God gives the church, not any other institution, the authority to exercise the keys of the kingdom to organize an establishment of religion.

square and describe it for what it really is: a battleground of gods. What the reigning conception of religious freedom does, ironically, is slant the public square toward secularism. It is like an airport security metal detector that screens out supernatural big-G Gods but lets all the socially constructed and self-manufactured little-g gods through. Believers in recent years have taken to pleading that "we should be able to exercise our religion in all of life." I agree. The trouble is, these believers simultaneously endorse a concept of religious freedom that screens their beliefs out of the public square. Take the issue of same-sex marriage. Believers have insisted that their bakers and cakemakers should be able to live according to their consciences in their vocations—not just at church. Yet the lesbian couple, of course, says that they want to be able to live according to *their* consciences, and, what's more, they feel oppressed by the Christians' discriminatory practices. Who wins the clash of consciences? The one who can appeal to something other than a big-G God since any talk of big-G Gods is not permitted. A theory of religious tolerance allows us to more honestly describe the processes of constitution writing and lawmaking: every party steps into the public square in order to make the best case for the political and ethical mandates handed down from his or her gods. As I argued in chapter one, this happens anyway, like it or not, since there is no such thing as spiritual neutrality. But religious *tolerance* protects people's ability to gather privately with the religious group of their choice, as well as to pursue their policies publicly,[67] so long as their religion causes no manifest hurt to others.

Second, a theory of religious tolerance acknowledges that governments must necessarily address both the inner and the outer person. Scripture frequently points to the inseparability of inward desires and outward activities, even if it distinguishes them (see Gen 6:5, 11)—out of the heart the

---

[67] The trouble with recent talk of restricting "freedom of religion" to "freedom of worship" is that "freedom of worship," which restricts free religious practice to a religious institutional life (i.e., what they do inside the church building on Sunday), adopts the entire liberal paradigm of maintaining a neutral public square. It places the political and spiritual in separate domains, one public and one private. Religious tolerance, as I'm describing it, similarly begins by saying we should tolerate false worship in its institutional manifestation, but then it also releases that false worship into the public square so long as no one can demonstrate manifest harm to human beings. This, I think, is precisely where Genesis 9:5-6 draws the boundaries.

mouth speaks (Lk 6:45).⁶⁸ Neither can governments fully separate them, which is why prosecuting a crime, historically, has required demonstrating that the *actus reus* was accompanied by a *mens rea*—a guilty mind. There is a difference between manslaughter and premeditated murder. More broadly, the larger project of sustaining and protecting human life must view human beings as wholes.⁶⁹

Third, a theory of tolerance requires any Christian theory of civil disobedience or revolution to conform to God's law. A citizen has grounds to disobey when the government asks a citizen to defy God's laws. And a citizenry potentially has grounds for a revolution, as suggested above, when a government systematically defies the justice mechanism and falls under its condemnation. A doctrine of freedom of conscience, no doubt, can also challenge the government independently or corporately for the same biblical reasons; but, strictly speaking, it can choose to defy or overthrow the government for any reason it wishes since the self always remains the true source of authority. One might therefore expect that the more the citizens of a nation perceive the gods of their own consciences as the ground of government, the more that nation will be characterized by widespread disobedience, crime and anarchy. And as the historic virtues of Western nations slowly vanish, are we not seeing exactly this? George Washington and John Adams expected as much.

To be sure, I am not in this book attempting to find language that will persuade a non-Christians of a doctrine of religious tolerance on his or her terms. I am not seeking public accessibility here. I am beginning with the Bible and speaking to those inside my own house in order to ask, what does

---

⁶⁸N. T. Wright offers a helpful distinction between "dualism" (which invokes Zoroastrian, Gnostic or Platonic cosmologies and anthropologies that are unbiblical) and "dualistic" (which indicates "normal features of most if not all biblical theology . . . [that] the great majority of Jews accepted"). Wright, *The New Testament and the People of God* (Minneapolis: Fortress, 1992), 253. That said, Wright places an anthropological distinction between body and soul on the wrong side of the ledger. Based on his brief and vague definition of anthropological dualism, which, again, he suggests is unbiblical, it is not clear to me whether I would agree or disagree with him on this point, even though I think he's right to distinguish dualism and duality generally. See ibid., 252-56.

⁶⁹States have always had an interest in what their populations think and believe, if nothing else for the survival of that state in its present form. This is even true of liberal states. See, for example, Robert Putnam, *Making Democracy Work*, or the works of John Dewey such as *A Common Faith* or *Democracy and Education*.

Scripture mandate and allow for those of us who believe Scripture is authoritative? We must get our own conceptual house in order first by asking that question. The trouble with much Christian political philosophy is that it jumps straight to what should be a second conversation—the conversation with non-Christians. And by attempting to build on publicly accessible terms from the get-go, it risks compromising its own fundamental beliefs.

Genesis 9, no doubt, strikes a complex balancing act. It seems to place these two ideas in tension:

- The God of the Bible gives governments authority to prosecute crimes against human beings, not the authority to prosecute crimes against himself. So long as people remain unharmed, false religion should be tolerated publicly and privately. This is the call to free exercise. At the same time . . .

- Right government authority is grounded in a right concept of God and a right theological anthropology, which would imply that a government has an interest in ascertaining that right doctrine and in some sense submitting itself to it. Christians should therefore work for *Christian* conceptions of justice in the public square.

In short, a Christian's description of the public square depends upon embracing two principles that bear a measure of tension between them: governments must tolerate false religions, and following a false religion will eventually make a government unjust. Injustices occur whenever a government forgets one principle or the other. In the final analysis, the state must not prosecute idolatry or false religion directly, but it must continually be on the lookout for the ill-fruit of false religion that harms human beings and hinders their flourishing, which of course means that it benefits from having some sense of what true religion is. Interestingly, the tension here is somewhat analogous to the tension between the two religious clauses in the First Amendment to the US Constitution. The free exercise clause provides a special protection to religious exercise, while the establishment clause forbids special treatment.[70]

One last question for this discussion: how should Christians respond to impositions on their own religious freedom by non-Christians, if not by

---

[70] Andrew Koppelman, *Defending American Religious Neutrality* (Cambridge, MA: Harvard University Press, 2013), 5.

appealing to conscience? To be clear, that is a practical question. And my answer is fundamentally pragamatic: use whatever arguments work! As stated in chapter one, one might legitimately decide to appeal to the "free conscience" for pragmatic reasons. It's not morally wrong to make this older argument. My only point is, this very language might show up again tomorrow in the demand to give up something else that the Christian does not want to give up—for example, "You must not impose your faith on your child's conscience. Therefore, we are removing them from your house." Furthermore, recent court decisions increasingly indicate that this appeal is *not* working.

I do think there may be other publicly accessible arguments a Christian might develop, exposing the inconsistency of liberal impositions on Christianity or demonstrating the distinct secular good of religion.[71] Furthermore, we might surmise that continually appealing to "rights of conscience" presents a cheapened witness to unbelievers. It's one thing to appeal to "my conscience." It's another thing to appeal to "my God." Unbelievers recognize the first because it's exactly what they do. And so it's easy for unbelievers to construe such appeals as just another brand of individualism because, finally, they are appeals to the self—"don't touch *my* conscience." It feels self-protective. It lacks the audacity of conviction which itself may prove compelling to the unbeliever.

Nicholas Wolterstorff, along these lines, has remarked that we may need fewer Luthers and more Polycarps in the coming years. When asked to deny Christ, Polycarp famously replied, "For eighty and six years have I been his servant, and he has done me no wrong; how can I blaspheme my King, who has saved me?" Wolterstorff has observed that, typically, Christians in the West don't resist governmental incursions as Polycarp did. Instead, our resistance "is in the name of religious freedom. We will not declare that Christ is our king and that loyalty to our king requires that we not concede to the goverenment's demands. No Polycarps among us." But might biblical faithfulness require something else? Wolterstorff thinks so: "Fidelity to Christian scripture requires that Christians join Polycarp in declaring that Christ is our sovereign."[72]

---

[71]See chap. 1, n. 133 above.
[72]Wolterstorff, *Mighty and the Almighty*, 17.

***Seven lessons from the Noahic covenant.*** We can draw seven further lessons from the Noahic covenant as a whole for our purposes. First, the Noahic covenant is where the creator God's rule over all creation is given institutional expression in the post-fall world. This rule is grounded in the fact that he is Creator, as we have seen, but it is reinstitutionalized over all humanity here.[73]

Second, this covenant introduces the element of time as a significant factor for understanding the nature of God's rule in the fallen world. It promises a gap between declaration and execution, between promise and manifestation, between invisible words and visible wrath. That said, it remains a political institution nonetheless—an identity- and behavior-shaping rule structure whose purview embraces the entire public and is directly or indirectly backed by the threat of authorized force.

Third, pre-fall Adam and post-fall Noah inhabit the same divine-human institutional structure. Both are subjects. Both are called to be citizens. Both should consecrate themselves to God by assenting to his judgments in every domain of life. And both should worship God in all of life. In other words, there is one divine King and one grand human political community even after the fall—a community of subjects called to live as ruled rulers, citizens, worshipers. Genesis 9 does not explicitly say it, but we can reasonably surmise that God's future judgment over these subjects depends on whether or not they live as worshipful citizens.

Fourth, governmental authority as we conceive of it today is a mediated or representative authority, depending on God's authorization. As such, there is no such thing as a truly secular politics, even in the post-fall world. Instead, all human politics involves three parties: a human ruled, a human ruler and a divine ruler. Daniel J. Elazar and Stuart Cohen put it like this: "The universe and all its parts is under Divine sovereignty (*malkhut shamayim*) and hence all human institutions possess only delegated authority and powers."[74] The apostle Paul said something similar: "For there is no authority except from God, and those that exist have been instituted by God. Therefore whoever resists the authorities resists what God has appointed" (Rom 13:1-2). The ideas of representation and authorization are

---

[73]See Elazar, *Covenant and Polity*, 110-15.
[74]Elazar and Cohen, *Jewish Polity*, 5.

hard to miss in this New Testament passage. The one in authority is God's "servant" (Rom 13:4). The kings and kingdoms of this world operate *within* God's law and one body politic, almost like state governments in a federal system. "Law, in the sense of the Divine constitutional teaching (the *Torah*), provides the foundation of human polity," say Elazar and Cohen.[75] This means that the "politics" of parties and parliaments, peace treaties and trade tariffs, are nothing other than the mediation of God's covenantal rule. By means of a covenantal authorization, they mediate God's political rule on a public-wide basis, bringing unity across all other forms of social division, for the purposes of justice, with the power of the sword. They carry out one portion of God's comprehensive political rule, like one federal department in a larger government. Elazar and Cohen again: "The basis for political authority is invariably covenantal, and political obligation flows from a covenantal base. Covenanting makes Divine sovereignty concrete and human self-government possible in the world."[76]

Fifth, a state is finally accountable to God, not just an electorate. Its every act must finally be defensible or justifiable before him. No doubt this is deeply contrary to the conventional wisdom of philosophical liberalism. For instance, Jocelyn Maclure and Charles Taylor write,

> The state must be able to justify to everyone the decisions it makes, which it will be unable to do if it favors one particular conception of the world and of the good. The reasons justifying its actions must be "secular" or "public," that is, they must be derived from what could be called a "minimal political morality" potentially acceptable to all citizens.[77]

But this is not quite right. The state must be able to justify its decisions before God since he is the one who authorizes it, even when something is not potentially acceptable to all citizens. That is not to say that Christian shouldn't build liberal institutions for prudential reasons. But Christians must always be willing to depart from societal approval for the sake of what is acceptable to God. Public accessibility cannot be the first goal of a Christian political philosophy. Faithfulness is.

---

[75]Ibid., 4.
[76]Ibid., 5.
[77]Jocelyn Maclure and Charles Taylor, *Secularism and Freedom of Conscience* (Cambridge, MA: Harvard University Press, 2011), 21.

Sixth, the governments of this world do not have the authority to prosecute false worship or other crimes against God.[78] That said, a government driven by false worship is more likely to misjudge what is or is not an ill-fruit according to the standards of the God of the Bible.

Seventh, the governments of this world exist to aid and abet the cause of true worship by providing the platform for the activity of Adamic citizenship. Governments exist to sustain life and preserve a place where the political and priestly drama can unfold. In the book of Acts Paul put it like this: "[God] made from one man every nation of mankind to live on all the face of the earth, having determined allotted periods and the boundaries of their dwelling place, that they should seek God, and perhaps feel their way toward him and find him" (Acts 17:26-27; cf. Rom 2:4). The proximate goal of government may be judgment. But this proximate goal must not be separated from the ultimate goal, which is to help subjects become citizens and worshipers. Guardrails, by analogy, have the proximate goal of keeping cars on the road. But ultimately they serve the larger purposes of the road, which is to help drivers get to their destinations.

When these seven lessons are added together, it makes no sense to say that the Noahic covenant as a whole merely serves "common cultural concerns" and not the cause of worship or religion. Governments invisibly mediate God's rule over matters of temporal judgment for the larger purpose of abetting God's plan of salvation. They exist to implement his judgments, which is why Oliver O'Donovan goes as far as to say that "within every political society there occurs, implicitly, an act of worship of divine rule."[79] When people assent to a government's decisions, they implicitly assent to God and thereby honor him.[80] Indeed, this is the very nature of mediated rule. Also, relatedly, common cultural concerns like politics can never be separated from worship. People's political and cultural convictions always root in their valuations of who or what deserves worship.

---

[78]The only possible biblical exception that I am aware of, at least as pertains to an authority figure outside the Mosaic covenant, is found in Daniel 3:29, which I assume most people would not say is normative.

[79]O'Donovan, *Desire of the Nations*, 49.

[80]This also allows us to understand, O'Donovan continues, how political loyalties can go so wrong: "A worship of divine rule which has failed to recollect or understand the divine purpose can only be an idolatrous worship which sanctions an idolatrous politics." Ibid., 49.

## The Political/Religious Accountability of the Nations

The political and religious accountability of all nations to God is easily seen in the rest of the Old Testament canon. A few chapters after the Noahic covenant, the interchanges between King Abimelech and God demonstrate that Abimelech is accountable to God and that "the basic obligations that lie upon God's created humanity can in principle be met by any people" (e.g., Gen 20:9; also 20:4-7).[81]

In the opening chapters of Exodus, Pharaoh presents a much bleaker example of the nations' accountability to God. Pharaoh, like a good Rawlsian liberal, begins with his own pagan version of secular public reason: "Who is the LORD, that I should obey his voice and let Israel go? I do not know the LORD, and moreover, I will not let Israel go" (Ex 5:2). In essence, Pharaoh reenacts Adam and Eve's original sin, albeit more brazenly and audaciously: he has conceived of his identity so as to exclude the moral legitimacy of God's claim upon him, employed an alternative legitimization for his desires, refused to assent to God's judgments, set himself as judge over God's judgments and rejected God's people *as* God's people.[82] Adam's autonomous individualism and Pharaoh's tyranny are differences of degree, not kind. Yahweh, politically unintimidated by Pharaoh's philosophical posturing, reasserts his planetary supremacy, saying to Pharaoh, "But for this purpose I have raised you up, to show you my power, so that my name may be proclaimed in all the earth" (Ex 9:16). God then judged Pharaoh and simultaneously redeemed his people. Old Testament scholar Walter Brueggemann summarizes the showdown nicely: "In that paradigmatic narrative [of the exodus], YHWH is rendered as the great force and agent who confronts the absolute political power of Pharaoh and, through a series of contests, delegitimates and finally overthrows the imperial power of Egypt that at the outset appeared to be not only intransigent but beyond challenge."[83]

In episodes like these, can we divide politics and religion?

---

[81]McConville, *God and Earthly Power*, 47.
[82]See McConville's excellent description of Pharaoh's rule, describing Pharaoh as an anti-Adam, in *God and Earthly Power*, 52.
[83]Walter Brueggemann, "Scripture: Old Testament," in *The Blackwell Companion to Political Theology*, ed. Peter Scott and William T. Cavanaugh (Maldan, MA: Blackwell, 2004), 10. See also McConville, *God and Earthly Power*, 55.

Jumping ahead in the storyline, the prophets and the Psalms, too, affirm the political and religious accountability of all nations before God. Jeremiah, for instance, affirms God's political supremacy: "There is none like you, O LORD; you are great, and your name is great in might. Who would not fear you, O King of the nations? For this is your due; for among all the wise ones of the nations and in all their kingdoms there is none like you" (Jer 10:6-7). The fear of God ("religious" language) is Yahweh's "due" among the nations ("political" language). Worship is his right. The nations owe it to him. Thus, he will visit all such insurrectionists with judgment, whether they belong to his Abrahamic people or not: "But the LORD is . . . the everlasting King. At his wrath the earth quakes, and the nations cannot endure his indignation" (Jer 10:10).

Perhaps more noteworthy still for our purposes are the series of extended oracles that indict different nations like Egypt, Babylon and others (cf. Is 13-23; Jer 46-51; Ezek 25-32; Amos 1-2; Zeph 2). Brueggemann observes that "the assumption" of these oracles "is that Yahweh has created the nations (see the verb in Ps. 86:9), has given them life, authorized them to be, and placed in their midst the possibility of life and blessing." Yet the oracles are required because "the nations have violated the mandate and command of Yahweh to which they are subject, and so they must be punished or even nullified."[84] The nations may reject God's authority or fail even to be conscious of it. But no matter: "Because of Yahweh's massive, overriding sovereignty, these oracles assert that the nations are subject to a governance, a requirement, and an expectation, no matter how secure and self-sufficient they seem to be or think they are."[85] Hence, it is not without reason that the psalmist declares, "Say among the nations, 'The Lord reigns!'" and "'he will judge the peoples with equity'" (Ps 96:10). God's justice is universally binding. Brueggemann observes of this particular verse in the Psalms, "In a quick liturgical utterance, the dynastic temple establishment [of Israel] subsumes all other worldly powers under their theological governance."[86]

---

[84]Walter Brueggemann, *Theology of the Old Testament: Testimony, Dispute, Advocacy* (Minneapolis: Fortress, 1997), 502.
[85]Ibid., 503.
[86]Ibid., 492-93.

The God of creation is the King of the nations, and the King of the nations is the Redeemer of his people. It is one piece. He alone is God. He alone has rule. Surely he adopts different postures toward different people. Kings always do. But that is not to speak of two different kingdoms. Furthermore, the two-kingdoms division between God's "creation rule" and his "redemptive rule" does not adequately account for God's activity of judgment, and judgment goes to the heart of government and politics, as we observed above. Judgment is the flip side of redemption. And the two often occur in the same act.[87] The judgment of Egypt *is* the redemption of Israel. God's judgment, conducted on the basis of his righteousness and law, articulated in one form or another, is the political reality that incorporates all humanity.[88] Here the categories of "creation rule" and "redemptive rule" dissolve into one another and prove insufficient.

The fact that God rules all things means there is no division, strictly speaking, between some so-called spiritual or religious domain and an alternative political domain. At least from an Old Testament perspective, the liturgical profession "Yahweh is king," observes Oliver O'Donovan, fuses together the categories of the "political" and the "religious."[89] It is a profession that an invisible deity has ultimate political authority over the peoples. And this is precisely what the Bible says: "For kingship belongs to the LORD, and he rules over the nations" (Ps 22:28). The "religious" affirmation is a "political" affirmation.[90] The religious God of salvation is the political king of justice and law: "For the LORD is our judge; the LORD is our lawgiver; the LORD is our king; he will save us" (Is 33:22).[91]

Perhaps the clearest picture of the coterminous nature of religion and politics occurs in 1 Samuel when the people of Israel say to Samuel, "Now

---

[87]See Morris, *Biblical Doctrine of Judgment*, 17.
[88]See O'Donovan, *Desire of the Nations*, 72.
[89]Ibid., 32.
[90]Walter Brueggemann similarly writes, "This theological imagination that affirms YHWH, the God of Israel, as the key political player in Israel, is not a late 'add-on' to an otherwise available historical report. Rather, in the Old Testament and its imaginative presentation of political theology, YHWH stands front and center in the political process and is the defining factor and force around which all other political matters revolve." Also: "In Israel's self-presentation, there is no politics not theologically marked, no theology not politically inclined." Brueggemann, "Scripture: Old Testament," 9.
[91]The opposite perspective, which contrasts the religious and the political, can be found in more traditional historical-critical works; e.g., see Norman Gottwald, *The Politics of Ancient Israel* (Louisville, KY: Westminster John Knox, 2001), 32-33.

appoint for us a king to judge us like all the nations," which God himself then interprets by saying, "They have rejected me from being king over them" (1 Sam 8:5, 7; also 10:18-19; 12:12). The tradeoff for the nation is not characterized as a political existence over a spiritual existence. It is a tradeoff between a human king and a divine King, or between an unspiritual politics and a spiritual politics. God does what a king does, which is why a human king can, in one sense, "replace" him.

To put it another way, politics is always contained *inside* religion. A nation's gods determine its politics. First religion, then politics. The political always involves spiritual realities, and a people's spiritual state plays out in political terms, whether they live in harmony with the divine King's righteousness or in rebellion against him. There is no such thing as political or spiritual neutrality. Everything *is* political, because all of life is lived beneath the rule of God, incurring either his affirmation or his judgment. This perspective was hardly unique to Israel in the ancient Near East. Among others, there was an Egyptian form of religio-politics, which treated Pharaoh as a god, and a Mesopotamian form, which viewed the king as a "great man," who like Pharaoh was "charged with maintaining harmonious relations between human society and the supernatural powers."[92] But in Scripture the political stakes are especially clear: nations and individuals are either for God or against him. This is the Augustinian insight, as we saw in chapter one. The first group Augustine called "citizens above"; the second group he called "citizens of this world," a division that belongs not just to the Old Testament but "extends throughout the whole time of this time or age."[93]

A host of passages characterize political trust as a spiritual or religious matter. Just as God's spiritual activities are political, so placing one's trust in a human king is often connected in the Old Testament's landscape with trusting that king's gods or at least trusting in that king over against God. For instance, God exhorts Israel, "Ah, stubborn children . . . who make an alliance, but not of my Spirit, that they may add sin to sin; who set out to go

---

[92]Henri Frankfort, *Kingship and the Gods: A Study of Ancient Near Eastern Religion as the Integration of Society and Nature* (1948; repr., Chicago: University of Chicago Press, 1978), 6.

[93]Augustine, *The City of God Against the Pagans*, ed. and trans. R. W. Dyson, Cambridge Texts in the History of Political Thought (New York: Cambridge University Press, 1998), bk. XV, chap. 1, pp. 634, 635.

down to Egypt . . . to take refuge in the protection of Pharaoh and to seek shelter in the shadow of Egypt!" (Is 30:1-2). The phrase "make an alliance" translates literally as "pour out a drink offering," not to God here, of course, but to an idol, as part of sealing the political pact with Egypt.[94] Greg Beale summarizes this connection between trust in kings and gods: "Since the political and religious were inextricably linked for all ancient Near Eastern nations, this meant that Israel's pact with Egypt's political authorities also included giving allegiance to Egpyt's idols."[95]

The king of Assyria's field commander likewise challenged the besieged Jerusalem precisely at this point where kings and gods overlap:

> Hear the words of the great king, the king of Assyria! . . . Beware lest Hezekiah mislead you by saying, "The LORD will deliver us." Has any of the gods of the nations delivered his land out of the hand of the king of Assyria? Where are the gods of Hamath and Arpad? Where are the gods of Sepharvaim? Have they delivered Samaria out of my hand? Who among all the gods of these lands have delivered their lands out of my hand, that the LORD should deliver Jerusalem out of my hand? (Is. 36:13, 18-20; see also Jer. 10:11)

The categorical equivalency is impossible to miss: one can trust the human Assyrian king or one can trust a god.[96] It is the same *kind* of trust, whichever object of trust one chooses.[97]

Similar thinking occurs in the book of Daniel, but there political loyalty to Nebuchadnezzar is characterized as a loyalty to or worship of his "gods" (Dan 3:14, 18; see also Is 21:9). Nebuchadnezzar is not a god like Pharaoh but, in good Mesopotamian fashion, the "great man" who maintains good relations with the gods. Therefore, the king offers the three Hebrews a golden image to worship as a test of their submission to him, presenting perhaps the most vivid illustration of the religiousness of politics in the Bible.

---

[94]G. K. Beale, *We Become What We Worship: A Biblical Theology of Idolatry* (Downers Grove, IL: IVP Academic, 2008), 167; also Peter J. Leithart, *Between Babel and Beast: America and Empires in Biblical Perspective* (Eugene, OR: Cascade Books, 2012), 15.
[95]Beale, *We Become What We Worship*, 269.
[96]McConville observes the divine and global pretensions behind the Assyrian challenge. McConville, *God and Earthly Power*, 21-22.
[97]Contemporary political theorists come perilously close to teaching idolatry when they say the state possesses a claim to an "over-riding allegiance" and that "the political order no longer stands on an equal footing with other associations." S. I. Benn and R. S. Peters, *Social Principles and the Democratic State* (London: George Allen & Unwin, 1959), 256, 257.

In both the Assyrian and Babylonian examples, political and religious loyalties are coterminous, like two lenses placed on top of one another. Looking back to an earlier moment in Israel's history, then, it should not surprise us to rediscover that Yahweh judged not only Pharaoh and Egypt but also their gods: "On all the gods of Egypt I will execute judgments: I am the Lord" (Ex 12:12; see also his judgment on Moab and Ammon in Zeph 2:11).

The fact that these texts occur in the Old Testament do not make them any less relevant to us because we are dealing with the nations; and the movement from old covenant to new, which applies particularly to God's special people, does not change the institutional status of the nations before God in a way that is pertinent to this discussion. In fact, what we learn about the merger of idolatry and state power from Egypt, Assyria and Babylon seems to culminate in Revelation's discussion of the beast, seemingly a symbol of state power that is worshiped, turning Adam's original dominion mandate over the beasts of the earth upside down (e.g., Rev 13:1-8; cf. Dan 4; 7).[98] The Rome that the apostle John knew, for instance, required political loyalty through the worship of Caesar, and "such similar idolatrous state powers will come and go until Christ's final return."[99] In fact, governments will often (typically?) fulfill their Romans 13 work as "servants" even while raging and plotting against the Lord and his Anointed One (Ps 2:1-2).

## Modeling God's Universal Rule Through the Special Covenants

How then should we characterize the relationship between God's redeemed and nonredeemed people, between Israel and the nations? This question brings us back to the relationship between the common covenants and special covenants.

A few moments ago we observed that the Noahic covenant plays a preservative function, offering "a firm stage of history where God can work out his plan for rescuing his fallen world."[100] The temptation at this point is to

---

[98] Beale, *We Become What We Worship*, 258. See also H. Schlossberg, *Idols for Destruction: The Conflict of Christian Faith and American Culture* (Wheaton, IL: Crossway, 1990); Leithart, *Between Babel and Beast*, 3-53.

[99] Beale, *We Become What We Worship*, 254.

[100] Gentry and Wellum, *Kingdom Through Covenant*, 175.

view this common covenant separately from the whole series of special covenants that follow—to view preservation separately from redemption, morality separately from worship, and politics separately from religion. The interpretative narrative would go like this: God establishes governments through a covenant with all people for the sake of providing a basic platform of morality and justice for all; but then he provides a series of special covenants for his purposes in redemption with a special people.

This interpretation, which focuses on points of discontinuity between common and special, is true enough. But there is continuity to be accounted for as well. So here is an additional narrative to complement the last one: Through the common covenants given to Adam and Noah, God commands all his *subjects* to act as his *citizens*, his ruled rulers. They do not. So God establishes a series of special covenants to call out a people who will embody this citizenship, modeling what God intended for all humanity.

Notice that with this second narrative, which adds points of continuity, the redemptive storyline that begins with Abraham serves creation's purposes.[101] Specifically, the special covenants serve the purpose of the common covenants by fulfilling them.

The larger lesson here is, creation theology must not be divided from history and salvation. God's activities in creation and redemption are indeed distinct activities, but they are inseparable because the Creator God is the ruling God, and his purposes in creation and redemption are one. Preservation is distinct from redemption, but not separate. Morality is distinct from worship, but not separate. Politics is distinct from religion, but not separate. When we fail to recognize this, we overly separate these things, and eventually we overly spiritualize salvation and the life of the church.

**Abrahamic covenant.** The first and perhaps most important place to see the lines of continuity between the common and special covenants is in the movement from the Noahic covenant to the Abrahamic covenant, which can be described as a movement from creation to a kind of new creation.

---

[101]McConville observes, "Creation is not in one category, while history, politics, and salvation are in another. Rather, salvation is restoration to how things ought to be." McConville, *God and Earthly Power*, 32. I think it's *more* than restoration, but it's at least that. G. K. Beale argues something similar as he sets out to demonstrate in a chapter entitled "The Redemptive-Historical Storyline of the Old Testament" that "Gen. 1-3 lays out the basic themes for the rest of the OT." Beale, *New Testament Biblical Theology*, 29.

Abraham and his family "inherit . . . the role of Adam and Eve."[102] They "constitute another Adam"—a "pilot project" who would "be an example, a light to the world of what it meant to be properly related to God and to treat each other properly according to the dignity of our humanity."[103] After all, God gave "the essence of the commission of Genesis 1:28 to Abraham (Gen. 12:2; 6, 8, 16; 22:18), Isaac (26:3-4, 24), Jacob (28:3-4, 14; 35:11-12; 48:3, 15-16), and to Israel (see Deut. 7:13 and Gen. 47:27; Exod. 1:7; Ps. 107:38; and Is. 51:2)."[104] Paul therefore describes God's promise to Abraham in the language of creation *ex nihilo* (Rom 4:16-17).[105]

What this means is Abraham inherits the Adamic citizenship mandate, a role that combines political and priestly concepts—a vice-regent who is consecrated to God and so rules by being ruled. God's Genesis 12 promises to Abraham, institutionalized as a covenant in Genesis 15 and 17, point us to nothing less than a political institution, an identity- and behavior-shaping rule structure whose purview embraces an entire public and is directly or indirectly backed by the threat of authorized force: "I will bless those who bless you, and him who dishonors you I will curse, and in you all the families of the earth shall be blessed" (Gen 12:3). Abraham and his seed are then to exemplify true citizenship among all of God's subjects, which means abiding together as a just body politic under God's rule. It is among these people that true righteousness and justice should be displayed, since the way of citizenship in Genesis is eventually described as the way of righteousness and justice. J. Gordon McConville nicely summarizes what I hope to demonstrate:

> In Genesis the created order is at the same time political, and contains a mandate grounded in the divine character, for humanity to exhibit righteousness in its corporate life. Yahweh is "the judge of all the earth," committed to ruling in justice and righteousness. Abraham and one line of his descendants bear special responsibility to embody and witness to this righteousness as the proper condition of human relationships. Yet the story of

---

[102]N. T. Wright, *The Climax of the Covenant* (Minneapolis: Fortress, 1992), 22; *New Testament and the People of God*, 262; *Paul in Fresh Perspective*, 23-24, 109. See also William Dumbrell, *The Search for Order: Biblical Eschatology in Focus* (Eugene, OR: Wipf & Stock, 2001), 9-10.
[103]Gentry and Wellum, *Kingdom Through Covenant*, 226, 138.
[104]G. K. Beale, *The Temple and the Church's Mission: A Biblical Theology of the Dwelling Place of God* (Downers Grove, IL: InterVarsity Press, 2004), 95.
[105]Gentry and Wellum, *Kingdom Through Covenant*, 227.

Genesis makes it clear that Yahweh's ultimate interest is in his entire creation, and that the standard of righteousness is demanded equally of all.[106]

I propose to demonstrate these claims in three steps: (1) While all humanity inherits the Adamic/Noahic citizenship mandates, God promises to fulfill these mandates through Abraham and one line of his descendants; (2) while all humanity is called to righteousness, God means to use Abraham and his offspring to demonstrate true righteousness and so bless the nations; and (3) God is interested not merely in righteous people but in *a* righteous *people*.

*Fulfillment through Abraham.* First, all humanity inherits the Adamic/Noahic citizenship mandates, as we have already seen; but God promises to employ Abraham and his descendants through Isaac for the work of modeling such citizenship. The redeemed line of Abraham will fulfill God's creation purposes. The easiest way to see this is through observing how Genesis takes language from 1:28 and applies it specially to Abraham and his descendants through Isaac:[107]

> And God *blessed* them. And God said to them, "*Be fruitful* and *multiply*." (Gen 1:28)
>
> And God *blessed* Noah and his sons and said to them, "*Be fruitful* and *multiply*." (Gen 9:1, see also 7)
>
> [God promises Abraham] And I will make of you a great nation, and I will *bless* you and make your name great, so that you will be a *blessing*. I will *bless* those who *bless* you. (Gen 12:2-3)
>
> That I may make my covenant between me and you, and may *multiply* you greatly.... I will make you exceedingly *fruitful*. (Gen 17:2, 6)
>
> Because you have done this ... I will surely *bless* you, and I will surely *multiply* your offspring as the stars of heaven and as the sand that is on the seashore ... and in your offspring shall all the nations of the earth be *blessed*, because you have obeyed my voice. (Gen 22:16-18)

What is striking about this trajectory of texts is both the shared language and the change from commands to promises.[108] In Genesis 1 and 9, God

---

[106] McConville, *God and Earthly Power*, 48-49. See also Brueggemann, *Genesis*, 105.
[107] The following compilation of texts appears in Wright, *Climax of the Covenant*, 21-22, who is followed by Beale, *New Testament Biblical Theology*, 46-47; Beale, *Temple and the Church's Mission*, 94-95; and Gentry and Wellum, *Kingdom Through Covenant*, 228-29.
[108] Wright, *New Testament and the People of God*, 263. For a fuller discussion of the ways in which Abraham's promises and commissions differ from Adam's, see Beale, *New Testament Biblical Theology*, 52-57.

commands Adam and Noah to be fruitful and multiply. In Genesis 12 and beyond, God promises that *he* will make Abram's name great,[109] *he* will multiply them and *he* will make them exceedingly fruitful. The same pattern can be seen with Isaac and Jacob:

> [The Lord said to Isaac,] "I will be with you and will *bless* you.... I will *multiply* your offspring as the stars of heaven.... And in your offspring all the nations of the earth shall be *blessed*, because Abraham obeyed my voice and kept my charge, my commandments, my statutes, and my laws." (Gen 26:3-5)
>
> "Fear not, for I am with you and will *bless* you and *multiply* your offspring for my servant Abraham's sake." (Gen 26:24)
>
> [Isaac blessed Jacob, saying,] "God Almighty *bless* you and make you *fruitful* and *multiply* you, that you may become a company of peoples." (Gen 28:3)
>
> And God said to [Jacob], "I am God Almighty: *be fruitful* and *multiply*. A nation and a company of nations shall come from you, and kings shall come from your own body. (Gen 35:11)

Augustine famously prayed that God would give what he commands, and the opening chapter of Exodus suggests that he does: "But the people of Israel were *fruitful* and increased greatly; they *multiplied* and grew exceedingly strong, so that the land was filled with them" (Ex 1:7).

In short, God promised to bless Adam and Eve by commissioning them to be fruitful and to multiply, and then he began to fulfill his own mandate through the line of Abraham, from which will come "a nation and a company of nations ... and kings."

By way of transitioning to the second step, it is worth noticing the role that Abraham's obedience plays in the aforementioned passages. To repeat:

> In your offspring shall all the nations of the earth be blessed, *because* you have obeyed my voice, because you have obeyed my voice. (Gen 22:18)
>
> In your offspring all the nations of the earth shall be blessed, *because* Abraham obeyed my voice and kept my charge, my commandments, my statutes, and my laws. (Gen 26:4-5)

And Genesis 35 repeated the command as a command: "Be fruitful and multiply." God could give what he commanded because he was still commanding it.

---

[109]For a discussion of the royal overtones of the language of making Abram's name great, see Bill T. Arnold, *Genesis* (Cambridge: Cambridge University Press, 2009), 132; also Gentry and Wellum, *Kingdom Through Covenant*, 238.

God will fulfill his own citizenship mandate through the line of Abraham, yet Abraham's obedience plays a large role. God's blessing is distinct from Abraham's obedience, but it is also inseparable from it. Abraham, in other words, was acting in the role of a ruled ruler who brings God's dominion to creation—a priestly vice-regent or a prototypical citizen.

*Demonstration of true righteousness.* Second, all humanity is called to righteousness, but God purposed to use Abraham and his offspring to exhibit true righteousness and so bless the nations. McConville, in his remarkable work *God and Earthly Power*, draws from the cycles of judgment in Genesis to present both sides of this equation. He observes that the "political mandate" given to humanity but implemented in God's Abrahamic people is a life of *righteousness and justice*.[110]

Round one: Adam and Eve receive the dominion charge in Gen 1:28, defy God's word and receive God's judgment.

Round two: Noah is called "righteous." Everyone else is called "wicked": "Every intention of the thoughts of [man's] heart was only evil continually" (Gen 6:5). Which means, God's rule extends even to the heart, and he expects righteousness there. The psalmist agrees: "For he comes to judge the earth. He will judge the world in righteousness" (Ps 96:13).

Round three: humanity after Noah proves just as wicked, leading to the judgment at Babel. Back once more to the drawing board. But now, interestingly, a man is drawn from the mass of humanity and called "righteous" because he believes God's promises (Gen 15:6).

Round four: God plans to judge Sodom and Gomorrah, but first he tells Abraham that he will "bless" the nations as Abraham keeps "the way of the LORD by doing righteousness and justice" (Gen 18:17-19). The "blessing" language of Genesis 1:28 collides with the language of righteousness and justice, and three lessons emerge: the way of God is righteousness and justice; all nations are called to live by God's righteousness and justice; and Abraham's citizenship task is to model righteousness and justice, which will bless the nations. These lessons are affirmed when Abraham asks God if he will

---

[110]McConville has also observed that Abraham's obedience is described "in terms reminiscent of Deuteronomy." Specifically, God says, "Abraham obeyed my voice and kept my charge, my commandments, my statutes, and my laws" (Gen 26:5; cf. Deut 4:30; 5:31). God's words here introduce "a connection in Genesis between Abraham's *torah*-obedience and his possessing *tsedaqah* [righteousness], as in Deuteronomy (Deut. 6.24-25)." McConville, *God and Earthly Power*, 43.

"sweep away the righteous with the wicked" (Gen 18:23). After all, "Shall not the Judge of all the earth do what is just?" (Gen 18:25). Sodom and Gomorrah's judgment, observes McConville, presents "a paradigm of the criteria by which nations, set to be blessed through Abraham, will be judged."[111]

The last occurrence of the word *righteous* occurs when the Abrahamic son Judah concedes that the non-Abrahamic Tamar "is more righteous than I" (Gen 38:26). Apparently righteousness, a universal measurement, is hardly an intrinsic property of the Abrahamic people.

In all of these episodes, McConville summarizes, the "political question" at stake is "how the just rule of the one God Yahweh in the world might be implemented in the political life of a people.... Can there be a recipe for mature political life, nurturing the creation intention to bless humanity, the dignity of humanity as such, and the divine will to righteousness in the world?"[112] Abraham and his descendants specially inherit the purpose of modeling a mature political life, but the remainder of the Old Testament demonstrates what the episode with Tamar teaches—that such righteousness is not a natural property of any human people, even God's chosen.

*Corporate righteousness.* Finally, true citizenship or true righteousness in the biblical landscape is not an individualistic concept but a corporate concept. The good citizen is not simply the person who is a little more likely to vote, recycle and attend church on Sunday, but who otherwise lives a private life. Rather, the idea of true citizenship as it develops in the Abrahamic, Mosaic and eventually Davidic storyline is increasingly presented as the life of a community. Greg Beale therefore refers to Israel as the "corporate Adam."[113] The life of one person submitting to God's rule is good. But the lives of two or three submitting together is even better. It yields a social dynamic that fulfills the meaning of true righteousness and justice and proves to be a powerful witness. Together, two or three can exemplify shared giving, loving and justice better than the lone individual, as was suggested in chapter three's discussion of the Trinity. "Righteousness exalts a nation, but sin is a reproach to any people" (Prov 14:34). The true citizen's life is one of social harmony and justice, where

---

[111]Ibid., 44.
[112]Ibid., 171.
[113]Beale, *New Testament Biblical Theology*, esp. 57, 93, 387, 393, 411, 427-28.

people share the same values, ends, judgments and worship. All this is not immediately evident in Genesis, but the idea first begins to grow up here.

Noah is a lone righteous figure. But the covenant with Abraham suggests that when the seed of the Adamic citizenship mandate sprouts, it becomes a corporate idea. The corporate idea is surely implicit in the notion of fruitfulness. But more significantly it sprouts up through the same trajectory of verses we considered above: Abraham's offspring will be a blessing to the nations (Gen 22:18), and from his body will come not just a nation but a company of nations and kings (Gen 35:11; cf. 17:16). Father Abraham, it seems, will produce not only biological children but political children—a multitude of nations.[114] And blessings will come to the nations as Abraham "command[s] his children and his household after him to keep the way of the LORD by doing righteousness and justice" (Gen 18:19). The concepts of righteousness and justice, however we define them, appear to be social. It would seem that God is interested in not only righteous individuals but also a righteous people, not just model citizens but a model body politic.

The idea of a model body politic first shows up most concretely in Genesis 12. There, Peter Gentry observes, God uses the term *gôy* when he promises to make Abraham into a great nation (Gen 12:2). The use of *gôy* in this context is striking, Gentry argues, because (a) the Old Testament typically describes Abraham's descendants, the nation of Israel, with another term suggestive of kinship or family relations, *'am*, and (b) the term *gôy* is typically used for Gentile nations and has a basic meaning of an organized community with a governmental, political and social structure.[115] The other nations in this passage are described with a term meaning clans or families, *mišpāhr. hâ*. Why the exception here? Gentry infers:

> Genesis 12 presents us with a political structure brought into being by the word of God, with God at the center and God as the governmental head and ruler of that community. In other words, we have the Kingdom of God brought into being by covenant (between God and Abram). The author's choice of terms emphasizes that the family of Abram is a real kingdom with

---

[114]See Paul Williamson, "Covenant," in *Dictionary of the Old Testament Pentateuch*, ed. T. Desmond Alexander and David W. Baker (Downers Grove, IL: InterVarsity Press, 2003), 147.
[115]Peter J. Gentry, "The Covenant at Sinai," *The Southern Baptist Journal of Theology* 12 (Fall 2008): 39; Gentry and Wellum, *Kingdom Through Covenant*, 245-46.

eternal power and significance, while the so called kingdoms of this world have no lasting power or significance.[116]

But even more significant than connotations of the word *gôy* in Genesis 12 is the covenant that God gives Abraham in Genesis 15 and 17, which was God's way of institutionalizing or administrating his promises of Genesis 12. God promises three things through this covenant: a land (Gen 15:18; 17:8), many descendants (Gen 17:2, 6) and the status of being God's special possession—"to be God to you and to your offspring after you" (Gen 17:7). The Abrahamic covenant, in short, promises to create a people, a people who will be God's treasured possession and who, by following in the Lord's ways of justice and righteousness, will embody true citizenship and implement a true politics. Through Abraham, the Adamic citizenship mandate was to be put into effect. It was *how* God's purposes for Adam were to be fully realized.

These ideas blossom more fully in the following covenants.

**Mosaic covenant.** I have spent a bit of time on both the Noahic and Abrahamic covenants in order to trace out continuity between the common and special covenants, or between God's purposes in creation and redemption. In order to watch the seed of the Adamic citizenship mandate blossom into its full corporate flower, we could spend just as much if not more time on the Mosaic and Davidic covenants, where Abraham's descendants come to possess statehood under God's specially revealed law. Yet since I believe the basic ideas have already been communicated, I will only offer brief treatments of these two covenants. Fuller treatments of the particular themes I am tracing can be found in Gentry and Wellum, Beale, Wright, Dempster, and especially McConville, who is most explicit concerning the political nature of these themes.[117]

To jump back in, Greg Beale traces the aforementioned language trajectory of Genesis 1:28 into the nation of Israel (Gen 47:27; 48:3-4; Ex 1:7, 12, 20; Lev 26:9; Num 23:10-11; Deut 7:13; 15:4, 6; 28:11-12 [LXX]; 30:16; Ps 107:37-38; Is 51:2-3), the Davidic covenant (2 Sam 7:29 [LXX]), and

---

[116]Gentry, "Covenant at Sinai," 40.

[117]Gentry and Wellum, *Kingdom Through Covenant*, especially chapters four through fifteen, or the summary chapter sixteen; Beale, *New Testament Biblical Theology*, especially chap. 2; Wright, *Climax of the Covenant*, 21-26, and *New Testament and the People of God*, 262-79; Dempster, *Dominion and Dynasty*; McConville, *God and Earthly Power*.

eschatological Israel and its end-time king (Ps 8:5-8; 72:8, 17, 19; Is 54:1-3; Jer 3:16, 18; Jer 23:3; Ezek 36:9-12; Dan 7:13-14; Hos 1:1-10).[118] Thus, God will employ Israel and its Davidic king to fulfill his creation mandate. N. T. Wright observes, "If Abraham and his family are understood as the creator's means of dealing with the sin of Adam, and hence with the evil in the world, Israel herself becomes the true Adamic humanity."[119]

The picture of a distinct body politic first sharpens dramatically in the book of Exodus. Over and over the reader encounters Yahweh's words "my people," led in by the royal promise of Exodus 6, "I will take you to be my people, and I will be your God" (Ex 6:7). This pronouncement is immediately followed by the plagues, in which Yahweh "makes a distinction between Egypt and Israel" (Ex 11:7; also 8:23; 9:4, 26). Exodus as a whole offers a contrast between the "rival [royal] claims of Pharaoh and Yahweh upon the life and allegiance of Israel" and all that comes with these rival claims, such as the contrast between the Edenic "synthesis of constructive work, worship, and rest" and "Pharaoh's degradation and enslavement of humanity."[120] The theme of the tabernacle and sacred space begins to play a more prominent role in the life of Israel, whereby "the holiness-geography of Exodus is in direct opposition to that of Egypt, with the people in a different presence, under a different authority, and in a different spatial organization."[121] The prospect of worshiping in God's presence points to what political reconciliation between God and humanity looks like.

Occupying the center of the institutional stage in Exodus and the remainder of the Pentateuch, of course, is the massive edifice of the Mosaic covenant and its legal administration, which will administer God's Abrahamic promises to the nation as a whole, and through them to the entire world.[122] After reminding the people that he carried them on eagles' wings out of Egypt, God promises, "If you will indeed obey my voice and keep my covenant, you shall be my treasured possession among all peoples, for all the earth is mine; and you shall be to me a kingdom of priests and a holy nation"

---

[118]Beale, *New Testament Biblical Theology*, 48-51.
[119]Wright, *New Testament and the People of God*, 262; also Gentry and Wellum, *Kingdom Through Covenant*, 305, 306; Dumbrell, *Search for Order*, 45.
[120]McConville, *God and Earthly Power*, 55, 54, see also 52-54.
[121]Ibid., 56.
[122]Gentry and Wellum, *Kingdom Through Covenant*, 306, 326.

(Ex 19:5-6). Both the political and priestly mandates bound up in the Adamic commission become fully explicit here. "As a kingdom of priests," observe Gentry and Wellum,

> [Israel] will function to make the ways of God known to the nations and also to bring the nations into a right relationship to God. Israel will display to the rest of the world within its covenant community the kind of relationships first to God and then to one another and to the physical world, that God intended originally for all humanity.[123]

Israel's ability to serve the world would depend on its very distinctiveness from the world. Says Bible scholar William Dumbrell, "Just as a priest is separated from an ancient society in order to serve it and serves it by his distinctiveness, so Israel serves her world by maintaining her distance and her difference from it."[124] Israel's priestly dominion was supposed to redefine authority for a world that had perverted it, as Pharaoh had. Its rule, grounded in submission to God, was intended to create life and hope in the nations by mediating God's character and glory to them.[125] They would do this not as holy individuals but as a holy nation.

In chapter two of this book, I defined a political community or body politic as a community of people united by a common governing authority, and typically it involves their assent to it. This definition applies at least vaguely to Abraham, Isaac and Jacob's family beginning with the Abrahamic covenant. It is then formalized and cast in bright international relief with the giving and receiving of the Mosaic covenant: "Then [Moses] took the Book of the Covenant and read it in the hearing of the people. And they said, 'All that the LORD has spoken we will do, and we will be obedient'" (Ex 24:7). McConville helpfully connects their submission to law and nationhood:

> The giving and accepting of law, therefore, is an essential part of the formation of Israel as Yahweh's people. . . . Here in Israel's experience is what might be called its "initial moment of political faith." By submitting voluntarily to the law of Yahweh, with the implication of responsibility for its implementation (e.g. 23.6-8), Israel accepts a vocation to nationhood.[126]

---

[123]Ibid., 305; cf. 320-29. See also Dempster, *Dominion and Dynasty*, 172.
[124]Dumbrell, *Covenant and Creation*, 90.
[125]See Dempster, *Dominion and Dynasty*, 101-2, quoted in Gentry, "Covenant at Sinai," 47.
[126]McConville, *God and Earthly Power*, 63; cf. Elazar, *Covenant and Polity*, 12.

Tied to accepting the vocation of nationhood is accepting the job of being a contrast society and model body politic. McConville continues:

> The covenantal law, like the arrangements of worship, both marks the uniqueness of Israel and exhibits its exemplary role within the story of creation and humanity. As the provisions for worship created a space for ultimate loyalty aside from loyalty to Pharaoh, so the laws given to Israel are a part of the demonstration of Yahweh's rule in its life in contrast to Pharaoh's.[127]

Several books later, in Deuteronomy, Moses confirms that it is Israel's obedience that will commend this alternative body politic in the sight of the nations: "Keep them and do them, for that will be your wisdom and your understanding in the sight of the peoples, who, when they hear all these statutes, will say, 'Surely this great nation is a wise and understanding people.' . . . And what great nation is there, that has statutes and rules so righteous as all this law that I set before you today?" (Deut 4:6, 8). In short, "God's purpose to bring into being a human society that lives according to justice and righteousness in his creation," McConville observes, was to be "carried forward by means of his chosen people Israel."[128] Obedience would establish them as righteous ruled rulers—model citizens: "And it will be righteousness for us, if we are careful to do all this commandment before the LORD our God, as he has commanded us" (Deut 6:25).

Since God elected Israel to be his model body politic, a priestly kingdom whose citizens were consecrated to him, it is not surprising that God's law is articulated through the Mosaic covenant at a much deeper and broader level than what the nations as a whole receive. Those aspects of the law which some theologians have divided into moral, civil and ceremonial all blended together in the creation of this righteous and just political community put on display for the nations. Nor is it surprising, therefore, that the Mosaic covenant would draw a different jurisdictional line than was drawn by the Noahic covenant, which authorized governments to bring the weight of the sword only for crimes against humans and not for crimes against God. The Mosaic covenant contained provisions for crimes exclusively against God, like idolatry (see Deut 13:1-18; 17:2-7), precisely because this nation was to be set apart as a

---

[127]McConville, *God and Earthly Power*, 63.
[128]Ibid., 71.

nation of God's assenting citizens—his ruled rulers. God's comprehensive rule was to be demonstrated not at the end of history, when it will become manifest over all nations at the final judgment, but in the life of Israel now.

***Deputized in God's name.*** Before proceeding to the Davidic covenant, it's worth specially observing the new emphasis that the Mosaic covenant gives to the name of God and how his name will be tied to these people. They will name his name. Recall that God made his rule invisible following the fall. And in a sense he made his name as ruler and judge "inaudible" with the Noahic covenant by setting down his bow of war. Strikingly, God tells Moses that he appeared to Abraham, Isaac and Jacob, "but," he continues, "by my name the LORD I did not make myself known to them" (Ex 6:3). Instead, he specifically tells Moses his name and instructs him to tell the people of Israel his name (Ex 3:13-14; cf. 33:14; 34:5). Moses also speaks to Pharoah in God's name (Ex 5:23), and God himself tells Pharoah that he raised Pharoah up for defeat so that God's name might be proclaimed in all the earth (Ex 9:16). He subsequently tells the Israelites not to take his name in vain (Ex 20:7) or to mention the names of other gods (Ex 23:13). He establishes multiple laws for the sake of not profaning his name (Lev 18:21; 19:12; 20:3; 21:6; 22:2, 32; also 24:16). In short, God was identifying himself and his rule with these people. His name would "dwell there" (Deut 12:5, 11; 1 Kings 8:16) among the people as it would among no other nation. What is the difference between "my people" and "not my people"? God makes his name institutionally audible among his people.

God's decision to place his name on his people helps us to understand better the idea of "representation" discussed in chapter three. Nicholas Wolterstorff distinguishes between delegated authority and deputized authority. The department head of a company, Wolterstorff illustrates, possesses authority delegated from the CEO to perform a certain function, say, run the marketing department. But no one would regard the department head as a stand-in for the CEO. The CEO has some responsibility for any mistakes the department head makes, to be sure, but the department head isn't said to be acting in the CEO's name. A lawyer, on the other hand, can be deputized to act *on behalf of* the CEO such that the lawyer can sign documents in the CEO's place. So with an ambassador acting in the place of his king.[129]

---

[129]See Wolterstorff, *Mighty and the Almighty*, 50; Wolterstorff, "Authorities Are God's Servants," 63-65.

This distinction between a *delegate model* and a *deputy model* of representation helps us grasp something of the difference between the authorized institutions of the common covenants and the authorized institutions of the special covenants. Those who possess authority under the common covenants (parents, governments) do indeed represent God's authority, but they represent him like a delegate might. God has charged them with fulfilling a certain function, and they will be judged according to whether or not they maintain his standards. But God does not attach his own name to every parent and to every prince in quite the same way as he does with the people of Israel (and, as we will see, with the church). The people and institutions of Israel do very much bear God's name in a special way. This is why God told Abram from the beginning, "I will bless you and make your name great" (Gen 12:2). They would be deputies specially authorized to act in his name, like lawyers or ambassadors. This deputization culminates and is most centrally embodied in the Davidic son.

In the remainder of this book, I will refer to God's named or *deputized* rule through the special covenants as his *visibily* mediated rule and his unnamed or *delegated* rule through the common covenants as his *invisibly* mediated rule.

**Davidic covenant.** "And I will make for you a great name, like the name of the great ones of the earth," says God to David when establishing his covenant with David (2 Sam 7:9). Just as the Mosaic covenant was to administrate the promises of the Abrahamic covenant, so the Davidic covenant (2 Sam 7:11-17; 1 Chron 17:10-15; cf. Ps 89:3-4) assigned the king the task of administrating the people's obedience of the Mosaic covenant.[130] The occupant of David's throne was expected to preeminently embody the values of Sinai, thereby reflecting the kingship of God as God's preeminent citizen, deputy, vice-regent, son (Deut 17:18-20).[131] David was also put to work marking out the borders of the land, so that a permanent residence for God's presence might be built.[132] In all this, the king of Israel bore a special relationship with God such that the "son of David" was the "son of God"

---

[130]Gentry and Wellum, *Kingdom Through Covenant*, 391, 424; Dumbrell, *Covenant and Creation*, 127; Craig Blaising and Darrell L. Bock, *Progressive Dispensationalism* (Grand Rapids: Baker, 2000), 168-69.

[131]Gentry and Wellum, *Kingdom Through Covenant*, 401, 424-25; Dumbrell, *Covenant and Creation*, 150-52.

[132]Dumbrell, *Covenant and Creation*, 151, 162-63.

(Ps 2:7; cf. 45:6; 89:26–28). Not only that, but the king of Israel had a unique role in relation to God's covenant with Israel. He was the covenant mediator, representing God's justice and righteousness as covenant Lord to the people but also representing the people to God, embodying them and their cause before him.[133] David's son Solomon sings, "Blessed be the LORD your God, who has delighted in you and set you on the throne of Israel! Because the LORD loved Israel forever, he has made you king, that you may execute justice and righteousness" (1 Kings 10:9). God also promised David that his offspring would build a house for God's name, which Solomon does (2 Sam 7:13; 1 Kings 8:19-20).

God's work of establishing a kingdom for himself progressed as redemption history moved from the Abrahamic to the Mosaic to the Davidic covenants, each building on the last.[134] Here God would uniquely assert the prerogatives of his rule, make his rule visible through mediators and call those mediators to name his name, even as he blessed them with a great name. The Abrahamic promises of a great nation and a great name that would, in turn, bless other nations were finally to be realized through the Davidic son. The son of David alone could establish God's kingdom through covenant: "In this important sense, the Davidic king becomes the mediator of covenant blessing, tied back to Abraham, ultimately tied back to Adam, as the covenant head of the human race."[135]

### INSTITUTIONAL CHANGE, NAMING NAMES AND VISIBLE RULE

I began this chapter by asking whether the Bible affirms that God remains king over all people even after the fall. The answer, I said, seems to be yes since Genesis 3–5 show that God's hand remains firmly on the sword. Most of this chapter has then been spent considering the universality of God's rule. What this leaves unanswered, however, is the other question posed at the beginning of the chapter, which was, how can we affirm the universality of God's rule in

---

[133] O. Palmer Robertson, *The Christ of the Covenants* (Phillipsburg, NJ: P&R, 1980), 235; Stephen J. Wellum, "Baptism and the Relationship between the Covenants," in *Believer's Baptism: Sign of the New Covenant in Christ*, ed. Thomas R. Schreiner and Shawn D. Wright, NAC Studies in Bible and Theology (Nashville: B&H Academic, 2006), 39.

[134] Blaising and Bock, *Progressive Dispensationalism*, 172-73; Robertson, *Christ of the Covenants*, 185-90, 268.

[135] Wellum, "Baptism and the Relationship," 39.

the face of passages that speak of God's rule in the proverbial future tense, or with the divide "my people" and "not my people" in the present? Plenty of examples of the former, for instance, can be cited from the prophetic literature, as when the prophets speak of God's "coming" or "returning" or simply the fact that he "will" rule (e.g., Is 40:10; 52:7-8; Ezek 34:11; Zech 8:3; 9:10; also 14:9).[136] But such language also occurs earlier, as in a passage we just considered. Preparing his Abrahamic people for the Mosaic covenant, Yahweh promises Moses, "I will take you to be my people, and I will be your God" (Ex 6:7; see also 20:2-3). If God *will* take them to be his people, were they *not yet* his people by virtue of the Abrahamic covenant or even creation? Would they somehow become more his people than they were already? This same idea is repeated again and again in Deuteronomy and later histories, not to mention the Prophets and the Psalms.[137] How then do we account institutionally for this idea of God's rule in the future tense or God's rule in an exclusive sense if in fact he is ruler over all?

**Institutional relativity and change.** In chapter two we observed that an institution is a *"relatively* enduring collection of rules [or] organized practices, embedded in structures of meaning and resources that are *relatively* invariant in the face of turnover of individuals and *relatively* resilient to the idiosyncratic preferences and expectations of individuals and *changing external circumstances."*[138] Institutions are relatively enduring, relatively invariant and relatively resilient. Relative to what? From the canonical perspective, they are relative to how God's overarching purposes work themselves out in the "changing external circumstances" of redemptive history. The structure of a child's education may change from nursery school to elementary school to high school to college, even though the parent's overarching purposes remain the same. McConville, too, perceives this kind of institutional relativism at play:

---

[136]Though I do not agree with all of his conclusions regarding Christ's awareness of his vocation over against his awareness of his divine identity (it strikes me as a false dichotomy), N. T. Wright offers an otherwise helpful discussion of these kinds of texts, particularly in tracing out how Jesus fulfills both the Davidic/messianic texts as well as the texts which promise that God himself will come to rule. See Wright, *Jesus and the Victory of God*, 612-53; Wright, *Simply Jesus*, 37-56; Wright, *Challenge of Jesus*, 96-125.

[137]John Bright, *The Kingdom of God: The Biblical Concept and Its Meaning for the Church* (1953; repr., Nashville: Abingdon, 1981), 27.

[138]James G. March and Johan P. Olsen, "Elaborating the 'New Institutionalism,'" in *The Oxford Handbook of Political Institutions*, ed. R. A. W. Rhodes, Sarah A. Binder and Bert A. Rockman (New York: Oxford University Press, 2006), 3 (italics mine).

> The political vision in the books [of Joshua to Kings] is misread if one tries to force them in advance into apologia for one political agenda or another. Rather, they refrain from promoting any political programme as if it could be effective in itself. In the midst of an ever-changing political landscape, the narrative illustrates Yahweh's patience and grace in his dealings with Israel under all kinds of rule.[139]

Or again: "The story of Israel has borne witness . . . to the provisionality of particular structures of power. . . . As rule by judge-deliverers gave way to rule by kings, so now rule by kings of Israel and Judah passes into history."[140] Agendas, programs and regimes come and go, but God works out his purposes in all of them. Elazar and Cohen argue the same. They spend the entirety of a book, *The Jewish Polity*, chronicling the precise path of institutional change in both the Jewish Bible and post-biblical Jewish commonwealth, while observing the common threads that run through all such changes. They observe that "no single form of political organization is mandated by Jewish law or tradition"; rather, "a Jewish polity is one which embodies a proper set of political relationships rather than any particular structure or regime," and "there is latitude in choosing the forms of government as long as the proper relationships . . . are preserved."[141] God asserts his rule and royal prerogatives *through* the universal structures of the Noahic covenant, the family structures of the Abrahamic covenant, the legal structures of the Mosaic covenant and the royal structures of the Davidic covenant. God even asserts his rule through the imperial structures of Egypt and Babylon because all political authority, as Elazar and Cohen put it, "is invariably covenantal, and political obligation flows from a covenantal base."[142] Pharaoh and Nebuchadnezzar, in addition to being Yahweh's Psalm 2 challengers, are simultaneously Yahweh's covenantally authorized delegates, his Roman's 13 "servants," possessing rule by virtue of the Adamic and Noahic covenants.

What all this amounts to is, the distinction in space between "my people" and "not my people" signifies an institutional difference, even while all

---

[139]McConville, *God and Earthly Power*, 100.
[140]Ibid., 155.
[141]Elazar and Cohen, *Jewish Polity*, 6, 7.
[142]Ibid., 5.

remain utterly subject to God's rule. And the distinction in time between his rule now and his "coming" or "returning" rule signifies an institutional change, even though God rules over both the nations and Israel before and after that change. So there sits Ezekiel "in the land of the Chaldeans" discovering that "the hand of the LORD was upon him there" (Ezek 1:3), not back in Jerusalem as the Jews would have feared. Daniel learns the same while serving under pagan king (Dan 3:28-29; 4; 6:25-28). God rules at all times and places. Nonetheless, both prophets anticipated when God's rule would manifest itself differently, which is to say, institutionalized into a different form.

In short, God's people-specific-rule and God's rule-in-the-future-tense concern institutional difference and institutional change. God is going to switch up the players, change the boundaries of the field and give everyone a slightly different rulebook. But across time and space, God's overarching rule remains constant. At every step he has a purpose, and at every step he possesses ultimate rule: "The LORD is king forever and ever" (Ps 10:16).

*The execution of rule in salvation and judgment.* How then should we describe the nature of the institutional change promised by the prophets? Or, how should we describe the nature of the institutional change bound up in Yahweh's words "I will take you to be my people, and I will be your God" (Ex 6:7). Would they somehow become *more* his people than they were already?

Such institutional changes mean that God is asserting his ruling prerogative in a new way. More often than not, they mark the transition from ownership to execution, from declaration to action, from something invisible to something visible.

Consider a king's rule. First, he makes a threat or a promise, one that he can back up. He can do this because rule *already belongs to him*. He possesses it by right. Supposing his subjects either ignore his threats or pursue his good promises, he can then employ a number of institutions to give his subjects a taste of judgment or a taste of reward. For lawbreakers, he might impose financial penalties, or confiscate land, or send someone to prison—all of these like gradual, preventative steps in the movement toward taking their lives. For the loyalist, he will offer financial rewards, or land, or commissions—all on the way to a noble title. In both directions, a king possesses relative flexibility for deciding which institutional devises to employ for pedagogical purposes on the way to final judgment or noble endowment.

In the same way, redemptive history presents God's subjects with a succession of covenantal regimes and saving-judging acts that, among other things, serve God's pedagogic or, better, proleptic purposes. And these successive regimes typically involve some *type*—to use the word both generically and in its technical hermeneutical sense—of salvation or judgment. They typically make his saving and judging rule more and more visible and audible. And his name is typically named.

It is worth keeping in mind, of course, that Scripture's institutional storyline is a bit more complicated than one institutional administration following another, like the row of boxcars in a train or the succession of presidential administrations in history, each one ending where the next one begins. Rather, Scripture's covenants work sometimes within, sometimes through, sometimes on top of one another, and there may be multiple moments of fulfillment with any one covenant. The advent of one covenant (say, the Mosaic) may serve to administrate a previous covenant (the Abrahamic) even though the first covenant will ultimately outlast the second covenant and eventually be subsumed by another covenant (such as the new covenant). So when I speak of these institutional changes as characterized as the movement from ownership to execution, or from invisible to visible mediation, or from delegation to deputization, we need to keep these complexities in mind. God's possession of rule might be indicated by one (say, the Noahic), partially executed in another (say, the Davidic) and more fully executed in still another (say, the new).

But generally speaking, we can say that salvation and judgment are simply the execution of God's covenantal rule, in which an institutional mediator is often installed or deputized.

- Salvation, institutionally speaking, is God's unilaterally initiated act[143] of affirming a group of people as his citizens—that is, deputized, not just

---

[143] The editors of *The Jewish Political Tradition*, a remarkable multivolume compendium of original sources and contemporary commentary, devote a decent percentage of the volume on membership to election, since, most fundamentally, "election marks off Israel from all the other nations." Michael Walzer, Menachem Lorberbaum, Noam J. Zohar and Ari Ackerman, eds., *The Jewish Political Tradition*, vol. 2, *Membership* (New Haven, CT: Yale University Press, 2003), 11.

delegated, representatives—which entails the whole host of benefits and obligations that come with citizenship. It involves, in other words, not just a restoration to God but a restoration to an office, a vocation, an ethic.

- Judgment, institutionally speaking, is the axe of execution for a failure of citizenship, indeed, for treason and loyalty given to a false lord.

Both activities typically make God's rule in some sense visible. I say "typically" because redemptive history's first institutional shakeup did not make God's rule visible—just the opposite, it made it invisible, as we considered at the beginning of the chapter. Following that, the Bible presents a succession of institutions that variously mediate and symbolize visibility once more.

Indeed, here is where the signs of the covenant occupy an important part of the storyline. In the Noahic covenant, God's rule remains invisible, but he gives the rainbow to remind the nations that they abide within the terms of his peace treaty. In the Abrahamic covenant, he provides another sign, circumcision, which makes visible the familial element of his people. With the Mosaic covenant, the sign of the covenant, the Sabbath, ironically reminds the people that God is creator and therefore that his rule is universal. And so forth.

The judgment of Pharoah, the exodus and the nationalization of Israel represent the execution and "visible-izing" of God's rule in an even more dramatic way. God promised Abraham that his descendants would be a *gôy*, as we considered earlier. The institutional change described in Exodus 6:7 ("I will take you to be my people") points to the execution of that promise in the exodus and in the Mosaic covenant. The exodus, which involved both the judgment of Pharaoh *and* the salvation of Israel, forced all nations to reckon with God's rule. It was an international and public event. That, at least, is Moses' interpretation:

The Lord is a man of war;
    the Lord is his name.
Pharaoh's chariots and his host he cast into the sea,
    and his chosen officers were sunk in the Red Sea. . . .
You have led in your steadfast love the people whom you have redeemed. . . .
The peoples have heard; they tremble;

> pangs have seized the inhabitants of Philistia.
> Now are the chiefs of Edom dismayed;
> > trembling seizes the leaders of Moab;
> > all the inhabitants of Canaan have melted away. (Ex 15:3-4, 13-15)

McConville called the Mosaic covenant Israel's "initial moment of political faith," as we saw a few moments ago. I think it would be slightly more accurate to say that it was the manifestation or visible-izing of their political faith. Nationalization and statehood made God's rule over this model body politic visibly manifest both to themselves and to the world in a way that could be recognized as God's political rule.[144] The covenant asked for their *assent*, an essential element of citizenship we saw in chapter two. A community of citizens are joined by their shared acknowledgment of a common governing authority. Since the world rejected God's rule, it needed something on a field of vision that it would recognize as ultimate rule—as imperium. Israel's statehood therefore gave the world an utterly clear object lesson in the nature of God's rule: it is absolute, legitimate and comprehensive, covering everything from mold and menstrual cycles to the courses of kings, but it also is authorizing and calls for assent. Indeed, this is why Scripture characterizes political trust as a spiritual matter, as we considered a moment ago.

The same connection between the execution of God's rule and the mediated visibility of earthly salvation and judgment is made in the exilic king-in-the-future-tense passages. Words about God's coming rule are tied to words about his rule becoming visible, and all of this is tied to words concerning Israel's salvation.

> *Your eyes will behold* the king in his beauty;
> > they will *see* a land that stretches afar. . . .
> You will *see* no more the insolent people,
> > the people of an obscure speech that you cannot comprehend . . .
> > *Your eyes will see* Jerusalem . . .
> But there the Lord in majesty will be for us . . .
> For the Lord is our judge; the Lord is our lawgiver;
> the Lord is our king; he will save us. (Is 33:17, 19-22)

---

[144]See also Frank S. Frick, *The Formation of the State in Ancient Israel: A Survey of Models and Theories* (Decatur, GA: Almond, 1985).

> Comfort, comfort my people, says your God.
> Speak tenderly to Jerusalem,
> > and cry to her
> that her warfare is ended,
> > that her iniquity is pardoned. . . .
> And the glory of the Lord *shall be revealed*,
> > and all flesh shall *see* it together . . .
> Behold, the Lord God comes with might,
> > and his arm rules for him. (Is 40:1-2, 5, 10; cf. Ex 15:16)

> How beautiful upon the mountains
> > are the feet of him who brings good news,
> who *publishes* peace . . .
> > who *publishes* salvation . . .
> for *eye to eye they see*
> > the return of the Lord to Zion. . . .
> The Lord has bared his holy arm
> > before the *eyes* of all the nations,
> and all the ends of the earth shall *see*
> > the salvation of our God. (Is 52:7, 8, 10; cf. Ex 14:13)

> And I will set my glory among the nations, and all the nations shall *see* my judgment that I have *executed*, and my hand that I have laid on them. (Ezek 39:21; see also Mic 7:16; Zech 9:5; Mal 1:5; 3:18)

People will *see* that God has been their ruler all along when he *executes* his *salvation* and *judgment*.

Finally, it is worth noting that the visibility of God's rule in salvation will be accompanied by the visibility of this model body politic's political maturity, citizenship, righteousness: "The nations shall see your righteousness, and all the kings your glory, and you shall be called by a new name that the mouth of the Lord will give" (Is 62:2).

## Conclusion

Systematic theologians sometimes distinguish between God's "creation rule" and "redemptive rule." There may be convenient lessons that can be drawn from this theological shorthand. Still, we need to make sure that such language does not utterly separate things that, in the biblical text, are not separated. In fact, God's creation activity legitimates all his ruling activity, as we saw in the last chapter. For this reason, I believe it is sufficient, at least for our purposes here, simply to speak of "God's rule" or his "political rule." God's political rule, to define it, is his right to affirm and reward those who acknowledge his rule and pursue righteousness, as well as his right to judge those who reject his rule and pursue unrighteousness (see Rom 2:6-11). It is his *moral prerogative* over the universe he has made—unfallen and fallen.

Since God's rule is grounded in his creation activity, the fact of his rule does not depend on whether humans assent to that rule. He was the universal king who deserved obedience and worship before the fall, and he remained so after. His possession of the sword remained and remains morally legitimate.[145] That is not to say that human assent has no political role to play. The matter of assent divides those who are citizens from those who are merely subjects. A citizen, I said, is a ruled ruler. In God's body politic, a ruled ruler is one who is consecrated to God and who is therefore characterized by God's righteousness.

After the fall, God's rule was given institutional expression through common and special covenants. His rule exists comprehensively by virtue of the fact that he is creator, which means that human life is intrinsically and comprehensively political, but these political realities formally institutionalize through the covenants. The biblical covenants provide the "constitutionalization" and "institutionalization" of human relationships.[146] Daniel Elazar writes,

> The Bible necessarily holds that the covenantal relationship is the only proper basis for political organization—that is, the structured allocating of authority and power among humans—as well. In a political sense, biblical covenants take the form of constituting acts that establish the parameters of authority and its division without prescribing the constituting details of regimes. Thus, the Sinai covenant establishes once for all God's kingship over Israel and the partnership between God and Israel in *tikkun olam* (the repair of the universe). It does not establish any particular political regime.[147]

---

[145]Contra Jason J. Stellman, *Dual Citizens: Worship and Life Between the Already and the Not Yet* (Lake Mary, FL: Reformation Trust, 2009), xx.
[146]Elazar, *Covenant and Polity*, 24.
[147]Ibid., 68.

We can therefore define politics as *the mediating of God's covenantal rule*,[148] a definition that encompasses the concept both narrowly conceived (in reference to a society's governing institutions) and broadly conceived (in reference to all of life).

- *Politics narrowly conceived* implements God's sword-wielding covenantal rule invisibly through the justice mechanism of the Noahic covenant (Gen 9:5-6) and visibly through the oaths and institutions of the special covenants.

- *Politics broadly conceived* is the acknowledgment that all of life exists within the jurisdiction of God's comprehensive rule or judgment (as indicated in the Adamic covenant), yet it awaits the visible performance of that judgment in the eschaton (the larger share of the Noahic covenant: Gen 9:1-3, 7-17).

Also, a righteous politics gives rise to righteous and just political communities. The common covenants call all humankind to the citizen's life of righteousness and justice; the special covenants bear the purpose of putting this just body politic on display as a model to the nations. They make God's rule visible through (1) the covenantal signs, (2) the terms of the covenants and (3) the activities of salvation or judgment that they either enact or anticipate. Salvation and judgment represent the execution of God's rule, or the asserting of his royal prerogatives. What exactly is the relationship between the common and special covenants? There are points of discontinuity, to be sure, but there are also points of continuity. Both are concerned with the human being imaging or representing God in the entirety of one's life in the context of community. The common commands such a life; the special means to give this life and hold it up as exemplary.

It is because of the continuity between the common and special covenants that we can briefly return to chapter two's discussion of Richard Bauckham's political hermeneutic and agree with his statement that the "fundamental New Testament principles for life in the Christian community extend in

---

[148]This definition captures the basic relationship between kingdom and covenant articulated in Peter Gentry and Stephen Wellum's book *Kingdom Through Covenant*—namely, God establishes his kingdom throughout redemptive history through covenants, as the title suggests. Greg Beale, too, writes, "Covenant is the primary means by which God, the suzerain, governs his people, the vassal." Beale, *New Testament Biblical Theology*, 174.

principle to life in human community as such, and therefore have political relevance."[149] That word *relevance* requires institutional specification insofar as New Testament principles are relevant to God's people according to the specifications of the new covenant, and relevant to all humanity according to the specifications of the Adamic covenant. Still, we can say that the New Testament requirement to "turn the other cheek," for instance, binds all humanity *through* Genesis 1's command to image God by taking dominion of the earth, even if Jesus explicitly gave that command to his disciples for the purpose of explaining the ethic of the new covenant community.

Finally, the Bible's covenantal storyline teaches us that political loyalty is invariably religious. Worship and political ethics cannot be divided. One either trusts a human king and his god(s), or one trusts God, who may or may not employ a king for his purposes. There is no such thing as trust in a king that is spiritually neutral or separated from one's trust in God. And there is no such thing as trust in God that is politically neutral. Such worshipful trust is the very beginning of politics. One might object that these lessons are drawn from the Old Testament. But two things are worth observing. First, the religio-political nature of Caesar's rule is no different than Pharaoh's or Nebuchadnezzar's. The spiritual domain didn't suddenly evaporate from Caesar's palace with the coming of Christ. Second, the political domain didn't suddenly evaporate from gatherings of God's people with the coming of Christ, either. Instead, the new covenant pushed that political element deeper in—all the way into their hearts.

---

[149]Richard Bauckham, *The Bible in Politics: How to Read the Bible Politically* (Louisville, KY: Westminster John Knox, 1989), 9. For similar sentiments from Karl Barth, see chap. 5, n. 89.

# FIVE

# The Politics of the New Covenant

"THE SPECIFICALLY POLITICAL QUESTION faced by the primary history," says J. G. McConville about the history narrated in Genesis through Kings, "is how the just rule of the one God Yahweh might be implemented initially in the life of a people."[1] God asks Adam and Eve to represent his just and righteous rule—to act as citizens or ruled rulers. They do not. God therefore grants a series of covenants to establish Israel as his model body politic. But they mimic the nations, worship the Baals and Ashtoreths, neglect God's law and so break his covenant. "While there are moments of sound rule, the political life of Israel never conforms to the pattern anticipated in Deuteronomy." Instead, "Israel . . . progressively takes forms which place it at a distance from the creation mandate, the Abrahamic purpose, and the Mosaic ideal," and the Old Testament concludes with the same political question it had at the beginning: "Can there be righteousness on earth?"[2] As a political program, the nation of Israel and the Mosaic covenant look like a failure.

Why then was the so-called Israel-dimension[3] included in God's political drama in the first place? It feels like a detour. Yes, "the New Testament is substantially dependent on Old Testament categories for the understanding and expression of the events which it records."[4] But the question here is

---

[1] J. G. McConville, *God and Earthly Power* (New York: T&T Clark, 2008), 171.
[2] Ibid., 173.
[3] N. T. Wright, *Justification: God's Plan and Paul's Vision* (Downers Grove, IL: IVP Academic, 2009), 95.
[4] David Baker, *Two Testaments, One Bible* (Downers Grove, IL: InterVarsity Press, 1991), 257.

slightly more philosophical: Why didn't God jump straight from Adam and Eve's disobedience and exile to Jesus Christ, assuming that Jesus was the solution all along? Why the elaborate legal and cultic pageantry of the Mosaic covenant and the broad time-expanse of Israel's ill-fated history?

I would like to propose an answer in two steps. Step one, we must reconsider the original point of conflict in the Bible's plot line—Adam and Eve's act of disobedience—from an institutional perspective. I argued in chapter four that Adam and Eve reconceived of their identity so as to exclude the moral legitimacy of God's claim upon them, allowing them to reject his commands and judgments and enthrone themselves. They sought to be "like God" (Gen 3:5). (The relationship between identity and authority holds for society as well: "In acknowledging political authority, society proves its political identity.")[5] The argument goes something like this: "God might be $x$, but I am also $x$. God might be $y$, but I am also $y$," which culminates in the conclusion, "I am like God. I am his moral equal." Once moral equivalency is established, it is not difficult to see how political autonomy and disobedience follow. The argument that begets a sense of equivalency also begets autonomy. "If I am his moral equivalent, I can make up my own mind about right and wrong."

This argument—the argument that manufactures a new identity, a sense of political equivalency with God and finally autonomy from God—is what I call *self-justification*. It can first be spoken by a serpent, a spouse or the structures of society, but at some point a human actor must believe and adopt the argument before it means anything for that actor. And here we discover *the inseparable existential relationship between self-enthronement and self-justification*. Self-justification is self-enthronement's legitimation, ground, basis. A person enthrones himself or herself over against God only after justifying that action with a reconceived identity of being God's moral equal—being "like God." The person must judge himself or herself as somehow worthy or entitled or justified to rule. One must say, "The person who I am is right and justified to sit in this throne. I deserve it. My rule is legitimate." Even a cartoonish evil villain like Lex Luther who ostensibly laughs off moral convention with a cackle has convinced himself, by some

---

[5]Oliver O'Donovan, *Desire of the Nations: Rediscovering the Roots of Political Theology* (New York: Cambridge University Press, 1996), 47.

tortuous route, that his desire to kill Superman and rule the planet possesses a moral justification. He thinks he *deserves* it, which is to say, he has concocted some calculation of moral desert and of himself that uniquely entitles him to planetary rule. So with the one-year-old in the high chair who angrily screams at her mother when her mother pulls back the spoon. Self-justification and self-enthronement are inseparable correlates. The first is the argument or rationalization for the second. Step one for understanding ethnic Israel's role, then, is to see the ubiquitous connection between self-justification and self-enthronement.

Step two for understanding Israel's role in the Bible's political drama is to see the Mosaic law in light of this primordial political problem of self-justification. In the face of people who feel morally equivalent to God, the Mosaic law offered a showdown, a showdown set on an even larger historical stage than the standoff with Pharaoh. And what was God's challenge to those professing moral equivalency and the equivalency of wisdom and judgment? If you are my equal, you should be able to imitate me precisely. "You shall be holy, for I the Lord your God am holy" (Lev 19:2). One purpose of the law, it is said, is to expose sin, and it exposes sin by forcing us into a comparison with God, whom the law reveals. Through the law, it's as if God says, "If you think that you, like me, are both $x$ and $y$, very well, be $x$ and $y$. Be me. Let us see, then, whether you can sustain your self-justifications." Both the individual Israelite and the nation as a whole had the opportunity to prove it stood righteously with God in a position of moral equivalency by obeying his perfect law: "And it will be righteousness for us, if we are careful to do all this commandment before the Lord our God, as he has commanded us" (Deut 6:25).

This is not to say that God gave the law to Israel as a way to merit salvation, a view that proponents of the New Perspective on Paul sometimes wrongly attribute to those of us with a traditional Protestant understanding of justification.[6] But I do mean to say that the fallen human heart is naturally legalistic and self-righteous, which, again, is as plain as the fact that the fallen human heart is self-enthroned. To admit that the human being is self-enthroned demands that one also admits that that human adopted an

---
[6] E.g., Wright, *Justification*, 129, 135.

argument for that enthronement, which is nothing other than self-justification. The law was then given not to provide humanity with a way to justify itself but to exhaust its fallen appetite for self-justification. To give a self-justifier the law is to give him or her an impossible task. Indeed, this is how the law exposes sin (e.g., Rom 3:20; 7:7). Enough failures of trying to climb the unscalable peaks of the law bring the self-proving, self-explaining, blame shifting, excuse making and rationalizing to an end, as Christian discovered in Bunyan's *Pilgrim's Progress*. At the risk of overstatement, whether or not Second Temple Judaism was a legalistic religion is almost beside the point. The deeply biblical insight of Martin Luther, says traditional Protestantism, is that self-justification and legalism are not distinct to Medieval Rome or the Jews of Jesus' day; they are universal conditions of the fallen human heart requiring exposure.

Hence, Lutheran theologian Oswald Bayer argues that the theme of justification "embraces the totality [of life]. All reality is involved in the justification debate."[7] The battle for justification, Bayer argues, is at the center of our individual lives, as well as at the center of "the histories of great social groups or movements" and "the histories of alliances, nations, and blocs."[8] How can this be? Because, says Bayer, individual and group identities, which is where we began this chapter, are socially constituted:

> As social beings we live by the word given and heard. This word either grants or denies us recognition and justification. . . . The individual [as well as the group] is always socially formed. It is self-consciousness as it has formed itself and continues to be formed in the process of mutual recognition. Striving to find approval in the yes of others, being noticed and not being dismissed as nothing by others, demonstrates that I cannot relate to myself without relating to the world. . . . I constantly vacillate, even to the very end of life, between the judgment others make about me and my own judgment of myself. . . . What I am, I am in my judgment about myself, intertwined with the judgment made of me by others. Person is a "forensic term."[9]

---

[7]Oswald Bayer, *Living by Faith: Justification and Sanctification*, trans. Geoffrey W. Bromiley (Grand Rapids: Eerdmans, 2003), 9.
[8]Ibid., 4. Speaking of world history as a battle for justification, he writes, "These world histories are nothing but the histories of the seeking, enforcing, denying, or lacking of mutual recognition. They are the histories of vindications and of the assigning of guilt. They are one long story of the battle for mutual recognition, a life and death battle" (ibid).
[9]Ibid., 2-4.

That is to say, life is spent having internal and external conversations that serve to form, define, build up or break down, condemn or justify who "I" am or "we" are. And laws, including the Mosaic law, provide the terms and categories in which those conversations transpire: for example, "I kept that law. The person I am must be good/smart/upstanding." Ever since Adam and Eve sought to reconceive their identities as something other than as God's subjects, all people and all nations have had to labor continuously "to legitimate our existence. We have [had] to demonstrate each moment that we deserve to exist, to be noted, addressed, welcomed, and honored, even if it is by contradiction."[10] Adam and Eve's first sin, after all, signified not only the rejection of God's law but the rejection of God's justifying word: "It was very good" (Gen 1:31). We live every moment of every day attempting to justify ourselves because we do not embrace the affirmation and identity that God would give if only we would humble ourselves. The law, then, exposes the problem of self-enthronement and—in the ground underneath it—the root of self-justification, something that characterizes individuals and governments, athletic teams and business corporations, armies and social movements. Furthermore, Israel's failure to keep God's law proves the futility of self-justification. The nation's disobedience and exile demonstrated that no human is God's moral equal, and that all forms of self-justification are a dead end. Ironically, moreover, Martin Luther's Protestantism and its doctrine of *sola fide* is often accused of promoting individualism, when in fact self-justification is the source of all social division, and justification by faith alone is the source of political unity, as I will contend over the next two chapters.

Yet this storyline and argument raises another dilemma. If the law exposes the ubiquitous problem of sin and the futility of self-justification, how then can people actually be justified? How can these rebellious subjects be called upstanding citizens? How can they be justly included and affirmed as citizens in God's body politic, assuming they have broken God's law, rejected his people and harmed their neighbors? How can they be said to possess good standing as "ruled rulers" before both the divine King and other citizens in his model political community? Solving the subjective self-justification and

---

[10]Ibid., 10.

self-enthronement problems, in other words, runs us straight into an objective justice problem that is at the heart of the New Testament doctrine of justification. If the self-justifying argument fails, another argument or legitimation is needed.

Theologians do not always treat the doctrine of justification as a political doctrine, but it indubitably is. "The concept of justice is coextensive with the political,"[11] we heard Iris Marion Young say in chapter two. After all, a just or righteous person, at a bare minimum, stands in a right position with respect to a governing authority and body politic. This means that declaring someone just or righteous is often a political statement, involving vertical and horizontal dimensions. The doctrine of justification does not merely have political *implications*; it is a political doctrine outright. In the New Testament program, Christ the king alone can justify by virtue of his authority. Justification, like Adam's original mandate, is not just a priestly work but a kingly one.

Of course, this argument runs directly against the critics of *sola fide*. The idea that a person can in some sense be considered just "by faith" and not by his or her activity, to a political philosopher, sounds like cheating the system. It sounds like a hollow claim that goes against the very thing that is needed to produce a just society—just actions. Political philosophy is a meritocratic enterprise. It concerns itself with how people live, and it awards the title of "just" to those with the right behavior, however defined. It asks how a citizen should rightly relate to the body politic and how the citizen's individual action contributes to the good of the corporate whole. To speak of justice "by faith," then, seems to gut the word *justice* of the very thing it needs—action or works. This leads some parties to critique *sola fide* outright, while it leads those who embrace *sola fide* to treat the doctrine as nonpolitical.

On the other hand, the Augustinian and medieval instinct to subsume the whole of the Christian life and sanctification under the aegis of justification[12] provides a basis for justification to *mean* something from a political

---

[11]Iris Marion Young, *Justice and the Politics of Difference* (Princeton, NJ: Princeton University Press, 1990), 9.

[12]There is no shortage of dispute over the Augustinian and medieval concepts of justification, and I do not mean to offer the definitive interpretation here since that is well outside my purposes. Instead, I rely here on Alister McGrath's interpretation of them, which I take to be a fairly

philosopher's point of view. Such a concept of justification ensures that a person is declared "just" based on some activity of his or hers, even if that activity is said to be a gift of grace. But does this not reintroduce the self-justification problem (see Lk 18:9-14)?

## A Political People

All this may seem a long-winded way to introduce both this and the next chapter, but I am attempting to draw out in brief compass the lessons of the old covenant and to set up the discussion of the new covenant and the New Testament in these last two chapters. What is remarkable about the new covenant is that it offers solutions to the subjective self-enthronement and self-justification problems as well as the objective justice problem. To have a truly just and righteous society, there must be a group of people who are willing to step off the throne that belongs to God alone—to be dethroned. But the only way rebellious human beings will be willing to step off God's throne is for them first to discover that their self-justifications are futile and foolish, that self-enthronement is illegitimate, that God's condemnation of them is correct, that they are not his moral equal and that they require not a self-justification but a divine justification. A divine justification, however, is possible for rebels only if God does something to satisfy his own requirements of justice—if he can be both just and the justifier (Rom 3:26). What all this points toward is justification by faith alone, or *sola fide*.

Yet before we get to *sola fide*, we need to work through its typological predecessor: the prophets' new covenant promise that God will forgive sins and write his law on the hearts of his people. Which brings us to the complicated relationship between this chapter and the next. Beginning with chapter three, this book has attempted to follow the contours of the biblical canon so that its theological argument rests squarely on the Bible's own covenantal framework. Yet moving from prophetic new covenant promises to New Testament fulfillment is a bit like moving from a job advertisement

---

common one: "For Augustine, justification includes both the beginnings of humanity's righteousness before God and its subsequent perfection, the event and the process, so that what later became the Reformation concept of 'sanctification' is effectively subsumed under the aegis of justification." McGrath then makes precisely the same point concerning medieval views. Alister E. McGrath, *Iustitia Dei: A History of the Christian Doctrine of Justification*, 3rd ed. (New York: Cambridge University Press, 2005), 49, 68-71.

in a newspaper to a photograph of the new hire sitting in his office chair. The Prophets provide the conceptual categories; the Gospels and the Epistles place Jesus and his church into those categories, even while elaborating on the categories. I have chosen to restrict this chapter *mostly* to the Old Testament job descriptions because that will allow for extended meditations on the concepts without getting bogged down in the dizzying New Testament details about Jesus as Son of Man, Son of God and Messiah, the relationship of the church to these things, the keys of the kingdom, Paul's approach to justification and so forth. All that will come in the next chapter. The downside of this approach is that the basic arguments of this chapter will feel somewhat incomplete without their fuller resolution in the next chapter.

The primary argument of this chapter is that the new covenant establishes a model body politic—a nation of righteous citizens—for God by solving the self-enthronement and self-justification problems, as well as the objective justice problem. The new covenant does this through God's regenerating and forgiving work as well as his atoning work.

Making this argument will require us to return to chapter four's discussion of how redemption serves creation's ends, but now redemptive history and creation history divide with the new covenant, producing what New Testament theologians refer to as a doctrine of two ages. Unless we affirm that redemption serves creation's purposes *and* that the new covenant then divides history, we will either fall into hyperspiritualism and quietism on one side of the road or into overrealized eschatology and oppression on the other side. And, amidst all the other arguments, it will be the cumulative argument of this chapter and the next that *sola fide* offers the greatest hope for a truly just body politic. It vanquishes self-justification and, therefore, self-enthronement. Just as self-justification and self-enthronement are correlates, so justification by faith and repentant obedience are correlates.[13] Just as self-justification divides humans from one another and from God, so *sola fide* covenantally and politically unites them. It creates a new body politic. The seeds of that discussion in chapter six can be found in the discussion of new covenant forgiveness in this chapter.

---

[13]Graham Cole offers an analogous observation in *God the Peacemaker: How Atonement Brings Shalom* (Downers Grove, IL: InterVarsity Press, 2009), 115-17.

## The New Covenant

The first task of this chapter is to pick up our institutional reading of the Bible's covenantally structured storyline from where it left off. At the end of chapter four, we concluded that salvation is God's authoritative act of drawing a group of subjects to himself and deputizing them with the office and vocation of citizen, ruled rulers who bear his name and walk in his way individually and corporately. When the people of Israel refused to assent to God's judgments, he removed them from himself and their office, which raises the need for a better political solution.

***Deuteronomy.*** The political promise of a truly just and righteous people first shows up when Yahweh commands the people to circumcise their hearts (Deut 10:16), predicts that they will not (Deut 29) and then promises to give what he has asked for: "God will circumcise your heart and the heart of your offspring, so that you will love the LORD your God with all your heart and with all your soul, that you may live" (Deut 30:6). The Mosaic covenant, as a political program, cannot provide what it asks for because it does not go "deep" enough into the human being. The people cannot change their natures any sooner than a leopard can change its spots (Jer 13:23). "The heart wants what it wants," said Woody Allen, justifying his adultery.[14]

A political program in a fallen world, to be successful, requires more than the right combination of external institutional structures. It needs those, but more importantly it needs new (or renewed) natures. And that is what the new covenant promises.

***Jeremiah.*** The promise of the new covenant occurs in a number of texts that deserve elaboration,[15] but we will examine only three more. First is Jeremiah, through whom God points to a new era of history: "Behold, the

---

[14] Woody Allen, "The Heart Wants What It Wants," interview by Walter Isaacson, *Time*, August 31, 1992.

[15] Peter J. Gentry and Stephen J. Wellum argue that references to the "everlasting covenant," the "covenant of peace," the promise of a new heart and a new spirit, and the "new covenant" all refer to the same thing. Then they list the Old Testament's major occurrences as follows: (1) Everlasting covenant: Jer 32:36-41; 50:2-5; Ezek 37:15-28; Is 55:1-5; 61:8-9. (2) Covenant of peace: Is 54:1-10; Ezek 34:20-31; 37:15-18. (3) Promise of a new heart and a new spirit: Ezek 11:18-21; 18:30-32; 36:24-32. (4) New covenant: Jer 31:31-34. Gentry and Wellum, *Kingdom Through Covenant: A Biblical-Theological Understanding of the Covenants* (Wheaton, IL: Crossway, 2012), 436.

days are coming, declares the LORD, when I will make a new covenant with the house of Israel and the house of Judah" (Jer 31:31).[16]

Is the new covenant a political institution? And does it create a political community? The answer to both questions, I believe, is yes. McConville explicitly describes it as "an answer to the problem of a disintegrated society."[17] In chapter two we saw that a *political institution* is any identity- and behavior-shaping rule structure concerned with social unity and justice whose purview embraces an entire public and is directly or indirectly backed by the threat of authorized force. A *political community* or body politic, we saw, is a community of people united by a common governing authority (with imperium). And *political membership*, by extension, is a relationship in which an individual is subject to and typically acknowledges a governing authority, combined with the governing authority's public affirmation of the individual as belonging to its charge. If these definitions are suitable, then it is not difficult to discern the political nature of the new covenant:

- The covenant makes provisions for the righteousness and obedience of the people: "I will put my law within them."

- It establishes a community of people ruled by one ruler—a body politic—involving an authoritatively asymmetrical relationship of affirmation and submission established at the level of identity: "I will be their God, and they shall be my people."

- Both the asymmetrical relationships between ruler and ruled and the symmetrical relationships between one member and another exist in a proper or right state, since they rest upon the foundation of judicial pardon and political reconciliation: "I will forgive their iniquity."

---

[16]For an excellent discussion on this passage, see ibid., 485-533, 646-54; see also David G. Peterson, *Transformed by God: New Covenant Life and Ministry* (Downers Grove, IL: IVP Academic, 2012), 17-43; Paul R. Williamson, *Sealed with an Oath: Covenant in God's Unfolding Purpose* (Downers Grove, IL: IVP Academic, 2007), 164-66; Petrus J. Gräbe, *New Covenant, New Community: The Significance of Biblical and Patristic Covenant Theology for Contemporary Understanding* (Waynesboro, GA: Paternoster, 2006), 51-57; cf. W. J. Dumbrell, *Covenant and Creation: A Theology of the Old Testament Covenants* (Carlisle, UK: Paternoster, 1984), 172-85.

[17]J. Gordon McConville, "Theology of Jeremiah," in *The New International Dictionary of Old Testament Theology and Exegesis*, vol. 4 (Grand Rapids: Zondervan, 1997), 765.

- And the covenant establishes a basic equality of political access and privilege among every member of the group: "They shall all know me, from the least of them to the greatest."

No mention of the sword or coercive force is made in this immediate passage, but it hardly need be said that Yahweh still bears the sword and imperium: "I will make with them an everlasting covenant. . . . And I will put the fear of me in their hearts, that they may not turn from me" (Jer 32:40; also v. 39).

One chapter later God promises to "cause a righteous Branch to spring up for David" who "shall execute justice and righteousness in the land" (Jer 33:15; see also 23:5-6), reminding us that Adam's political mandate grew into the command for Abraham's offspring to walk in justice and righteousness. This passage begins with the same phraseology as the new covenant passage, suggesting a simultaneous fulfillment: "Behold, the days are coming, declares the Lord, when I will fulfill the promise I made to the house of Israel and the house of Judah" (Jer 33:14). God apparently meant to implement his political plan for creation in this coming age through a Davidic king and a people of the new covenant.[18]

**Ezekiel.** Another commonly cited new covenant passage occurs in Ezekiel 36.[19] This passage repeats Deuteronomy's promise of a "new heart" for the purpose of obedience, but here the role of God's Spirit is more explicit: "I will put my Spirit within you, and cause you to walk in my statutes and be careful to obey my rules" (Ezek 36:27). The passage does not speak of forgiveness but of being cleansed from "uncleannesses," "idols" and "iniquities" (Ezek 36:25, 33), drawing perhaps on Ezekiel's overall orientation to the temple. The reference to idols suggests that all our politics is beholden either to God or to an idol. Again, there is no religious neutrality in the public square. And, strikingly, the entire passage is set within the framework of God's concern for his reputation: "It is not for your sake, O house of Israel, that I am about to act, but for the sake of my holy name, which you have profaned among the nations to which you came" (Ezek 36:22; also vv. 23, 32, 36). God means to implement his rule within the life of a people, so that these people can act as his deputized

---

[18]See also Jer 30:4-11, which sets a Davidic context for the new covenant passage.
[19]See Williamson, *Sealed with an Oath*, 170-72; Gräbe, *New Covenant, New Community*, 55-56; Dumbrell, *Covenant and Creation*, 185-88.

witnesses to the nations, a people who *stand in* for him with a kind of power of attorney.

As in Jeremiah, God's new covenant promise in Ezekiel is followed shortly thereafter by a reiteration of his Davidic promises. And this passage ties together the new covenant promises and the Davidic promises even more explicitly than Jeremiah does.[20]

> Thus says the Lord God: Behold, I will take the people of Israel from the nations among which they have gone. . . . And one king shall be king over them all. . . . But I will save them from all the backslidings in which they have sinned, and will cleanse them. . . . My servant David shall be king over them, and they shall all have one shepherd. They shall walk in my rules and be careful to obey my statutes. . . . I will make a covenant of peace with them. It shall be an everlasting covenant with them. . . . My dwelling place shall be with them, and I will be their God, and they shall be my people. Then the nations will know that I am the Lord who sanctifies Israel, when my sanctuary is in their midst forevermore. (Ezek 37:21-28)

Again, if a political community is defined as a community of people united by a governing authority, it is not difficult to discern the political nature of this new covenant community. The grammatical movement from the third-person Davidic promises to the first-person new covenant promises suggests that the Davidic king is the one who will establish the new covenant kingdom. Instead of reading, "David shall be king. They shall walk in *his* rules," it reads, "David shall be king. . . . They shall walk in *my* rules and be careful to obey *my* statutes." Apparently, a Davidic king will rule over Yahweh's new covenant body politic.

***Isaiah.*** The last occurrence of the new covenant promise worth discussing occurs in Isaiah 54, and it merits consideration largely for what precedes and succeeds it.[21] Here God promises, "My steadfast love shall not depart from you, and my covenant of peace shall not be removed" (Is 54:10). As a result of this covenant, "all your children shall be taught by the Lord,"

---

[20] As observed in n. 16 above, I think it is reasonable to assume that "the covenant of peace" and "everlasting covenant" in Ezekiel 37 are other ways of referring to the new covenant, especially since the author employs the same phraseology as in Ezekiel 36. See also Gentry and Wellum, *Kingdom Through Covenant*, 436, 481-83.

[21] See Gentry and Wellum, *Kingdom Through Covenant*, 435-45.

and "in righteousness you shall be established" (Is 54:13, 14). Isaiah 55 associates these promises together with God's promises to David, as we saw in Jeremiah and Ezekiel: "Incline your ear, and come to me . . . and I will make with you [plural] an everlasting covenant, my steadfast, sure love for David" (Is 55:3). The two covenants build one building.[22]

Interesting for our purposes is what comes before and after. *After* comes the promise of an effectual word of pardon that culminates in a new creation (Is 55:6-13). *Before* is the account of the suffering servant whose atoning work provides forgiveness for the many (Is 52:13-53:12). He is "smitten by God," "pierced for our transgressions" and "crushed for our iniquities." He "makes an offering for guilt," is "numbered with the transgressors," "bear[s] their iniquity," bears "the sin of many" and "makes intercession for the transgressors." As a result of his "chastisement," he brings "us peace," "shall see his offspring," "make[s] many to be accounted righteous" and is given a "portion with the many." The servant, in short, appears to substitute himself in the place of the many for the purpose of acting as their representative. What should be done to them is done to him, while the name of righteous is given to them.

Who are the "offspring" and the "many" in Isaiah 53? They are the children of the barren woman in Isaiah 54, whose tent cannot contain all her children and who is called to rejoice.[23] The work of the suffering servant becomes the foundation of the new covenant and the way to a new creation. Old Testament scholar Alec Motyer concludes that the relationship between Isaiah 53, 54 and 55 "is clear": "In his saving work, the Servant has done everything, removing sin, establishing in righteousness [*sic*], creating a family. The way is therefore open for response, pure and simple: to sing over what someone else has accomplished (54:1), to enjoy a feast for which someone else has paid (55:1)."[24] God himself responds, "As I swore that the waters of Noah should no more go over the earth, so I have sworn that I will not be angry with you,

---

[22]Ibid., 445; John N. Oswalt, *The Book of Isaiah: Chapters 40–66*, New International Commentary on the Old Testament (Grand Rapids: Eerdmans, 1998), 438; J. Alec Motyer, *The Prophecy of Isaiah: An Introduction & Commentary* (Downers Grove, IL: InterVarsity Press, 1993), 454; see also Peter Gentry, "Rethinking the Sure Mercies of David," *Westminster Theological Journal* 69 (2007): 279-304.

[23]Gentry and Wellum, *Kingdom Through Covenant*, 441.

[24]Motyer, *Prophecy of Isaiah*, 444. N. T. Wright too: "The result [of the servant's work] . . . is the new covenant (Is. 54) and the new creation (Is. 55)." Wright, *Simply Jesus: Who He Was, What*

and will not rebuke you" (Is 54:9). Just as the flood satisfied God's justice and Noah's sacrifice provided a pleasing aroma, so this sacrifice satisfies his just anger.

*A mutually affirmed covenant?* Does the effectual and gracious nature of the new covenant diminish the sense in which the salvation promised is political, at least as it is conceived in Christian theology? For instance, Jewish political philosopher Daniel Elazar affirms that "every covenant involves consenting," that "a covenant embodies mutual oathtaking"[25] and that "in politics, covenant denotes the voluntary establishment of a people and body politic."[26] Elazar, in fact, observes that

> it was only later with the rise of Christianity . . . that covenant took on a more strictly religious character for some, in which the political dimension was downplayed, if not downright ignored by Christian theologians. . . . Christianity embraced the covenant idea as one of the foundations, reinterpreting the old biblical covenant establishing a people as a polity as a covenant of grace between God and individual human beings granted or mediated by Jesus.[27]

The question of whether or not the new covenant is really political in light of its unilateral nature is worth asking not just because of one political philosopher's concept of a covenant but because Elazar does seem to have sniffed out the temptation for Christian theologizing to turn the new covenant's doctrine of salvation (1) into something individual and not social, as well as (2) into something requiring no assent to God. Yet God's Abrahamic and new covenant promises—what Christians today regard as God's gracious promise to save—entail restoring individuals to himself, yes, but they also entail establishing people in political office and therefore membership in the body politic of God's people. Salvation, recall, is God's authoritative act of deputizing a group of people as his office-holding, vocation-bearing citizens.

Also, one needs to be careful with the language of "conditional" and "unconditional." Insofar as the "unconditional" label is meant to communicate

---

*He Did, Why It Matters* (New York: HarperOne, 2011), 157; also Gentry and Wellum, *Kingdom Through Covenant*, 440-41; Oswalt, *Book of Isaiah*, 413-15.

[25]Daniel J. Elazar, *Covenant and Polity in Biblical Israel: Biblical Foundations & Jewish Expressions*, vol. 1, *Covenant Traditions in Politics* (New Brunswick, NJ: Transaction Publishers, 1995), 23.

[26]Ibid., 29.

[27]Ibid., 25-26.

the fact that God himself will ensure that a particular covenant is fulfilled, the label is helpful.²⁸ The danger is that it tempts one to remove the role of human assent,²⁹ as if one were to conclude, "Unconditional means it does not matter if I repent or obey." The very purpose of the new covenant is *to bring about the assent*. It aims to produce the heart that says yes to God and follows in his ways. The prophet Hosea makes this explicit in his version of the new covenant: "And I will make for them a covenant on that day. . . . And I will betroth you to me forever . . . in righteousness and in justice. . . . And I will have mercy on No Mercy, and I will say to Not My People, 'You are my people'; and he shall say, 'You are my God'" (Hos 2:18, 19, 23).

Moving from the Mosaic to the new covenant, then, is not about moving from corporate to individual, from obedience-required to no-obedience-required, or from political to spiritual. It is about moving from a political life dependent on their own strength to a political life dependent on God's Spirit: from "Circumcise your heart" so that you obey (Deut 10:16) to "God will circumcise your heart" so that you obey (Deut 30:6).

In short, the new covenant is indeed effectual and gracious, but it remains political and corporate and involves human assent.³⁰ God can indeed "take

---

²⁸However, I am not convinced that Christian scholars gain as much theologically as they think they do by equating conditional law covenants and unconditional promise covenants with ancient Near Eastern suzerain treaties and royal grants, respectively. The royal grant was hardly unconditional insofar as it was given *as a response* to some type of loyal service. For example, one Assyrian grant reads, "I am Aššurbanipal . . . who does good . . . who always responds graciously to all the officials who serve him [and] to the servant who keeps his royal command, whose heart is devoted to his master, served me with trustfulness, acted perfectly in my place, grew up with a good name and kept the charge of my kingship. I took thought of his kindness and I have established his gift." Moshe Weinfeld, who records this example, summarizes, "The gift comes as a reward for the 'good and kindness' shown by the official to his master, the king." Moshe Weinfeld, "The Covenantal Aspect of the Promise of the Land to Israel," in *The Promise of Land: The Inheritance of the Land of Canaan by the Israelites* (Berkeley: University of California Press, 1993), 225-26.

²⁹See Walter Brueggemann, *Theology of the Old Testament: Testimony, Dispute, Advocacy* (Minneapolis: Fortress, 1997), 419-20; Gentry and Wellum, *Kingdom Through Covenant*, 608-11.

³⁰Several contemporary authors have observed a similarly nuanced view of the covenant in Calvin, namely, that he affirms its unilateral elements in some respects and its bilateral elements in other respects; see J. Todd Billings, "John Milbank's Theology of the 'Gift' and Calvin's Theology of Grace: A Critical Comparison," *Modern Theology* 21, no. 1 (January 2005): 92; Richard A. Muller, *The Unaccommodated Calvin: Studies in the Foundation of a Theological Tradition* (New York: Oxford University Press, 2000), 155.

such an initiative [of writing the law on someone's heart] without crushing the will" of a person, says McConville of the new covenant.[31] For whatever differences I may have with Karl Barth's covenantal program, I believe he is right to say that the new covenant is "one which is mutually kept"—and that because "God Himself will make it so."[32]

**Conclusion: the fulfillment of the previous covenants.** The new covenant promises to fulfill the purposes of the previous line of covenants. It presents the society in which the Davidic son will reign. It will implement a just and righteous rule in the life of a people as the Mosaic covenant intended to do, and it will offer a basis for forgiveness of which all the sacrifices were a shadowy type. The new covenant is also promised to Israel, who are the offspring of Abraham. And in all of this, God's purpose is for humanity to represent his righteous rule.

## Politics of the Heart and Spirit

For our purposes it is worth meditating first on the regenerative element and second on the forgiveness element of the new covenant since these turn out to be the solutions to the self-enthronement problem and the self-justification problem, respectively. First, God promises to regenerate the human heart. Jeremiah describes it as the implantation of God's law, while Ezekiel describes it as both a heart-replacement operation and the implantation of God's Spirit. The heart in ancient Hebrew thinking is where the will is located;[33] placing God's law on the heart therefore means that "people will have to obey it."[34] Hence, Ezekiel uses causative language: God will "cause you to walk in [his] statutes and be careful to obey [his] rules" (Ezek 36:27). In short, "there will be a change in the nature of the human heart,"[35] which in turn "resolves the problem of the people's inability to be faithful."[36] They

---

[31] Gordon J. McConville, "berit," in *The New International Dictionary of Old Testament Theology & Exegesis*, ed. Willem A. VanGemeren, vol. 1 (Grand Rapids: Zondervan, 1997), 752.
[32] Karl Barth, *Church Dogmatics*, IV/1, *The Doctrine of Reconciliation*, trans. G. W. Bromiley (New York: T&T Clark, 2004), 23. For an introduction to Barth's approach to the covenants, see Gräbe, *New Covenant, New Community*, 194-95, 201-3.
[33] Peterson, *Transformed by God*, 31.
[34] Jack R. Lundbom, *Jeremiah 21–36*, Anchor Yale Bible Commentaries (New York: Random House, 2004), 469; also in Peterson, *Transformed by God*, 31.
[35] Gräbe, *New Covenant, New Community*, 54.
[36] McConville, "Theology of Jeremiah," 765.

will no longer enthrone themselves, because they will desire God's rule in their lives.

***Totalitarianism and the new covenant.*** In chapter three I described God's comprehensive rule as totalitarian, by which I was referring to his moral claim on the entirety of the human life—heart, mind, soul and strength (see Deut 6:5; Lk 10:27). What we find in the new covenant is that this totalitarian claim is matched by a total empowerment. Does this mean that God belongs to the dark league of twentieth-century totalitarian rulers, fictionalized, for instance, as George Orwell's Big Brother? Big Brother says regarding political dissidents, "We convert him, we capture his inner mind, we reshape him." The goal is to "bring him over to our side, not in appearance, but genuinely, heart and soul. We make him one of ourselves before we kill him."[37] The methods that the Stalinesque party uses for the exclusive end of preserving its power are threats, propaganda, mass starvation, torture and execution. And the party succeeds. Is this not the promise of the new covenant?

Quantitatively, one might say, there is a comparison to be made.[38] At the heart of both programs is the "assent" of the entire person (mind, heart, soul, body) to the judgments of an ultimate authority figure, and this "assent to judgement" shows itself as "a specific form of life," to reuse Bernd Wannenwetsch's description of political worship from chapter three. And what Orwell's picture of a converted inner and outer person captures, even if Orwell did not mean to, is the fact that a complex and holistic anthropology is necessary for producing a truly successful political program, something which liberalism is explicitly set against. Genuine and lasting political success requires more than the imposition of laws. It requires, in Orwell's words, capturing the inner mind and changing sides by heart and soul. Liberalism of just about every kind, hard or soft, never speaks this way (even if it does it).

Does this mean that the God of the new covenant is a tyrant? Surely, that is what the serpent intimated to Adam and Eve (Gen 3:1-6). But there are

---

[37]George Orwell, *Nineteen Eighty-Four*, centennial ed. (New York: Plume Harcourt Brace, 2003), 263.

[38]By speaking of God's rule as totalitarian quantitatively, I am not advocating an ontology or an epistemology that treats being or knowledge univocally or that smothers all difference. See my discussion of these matters in the introduction.

at least three reasons why the answer is certainly no. First, the doctrine of the Trinity, which we discussed in chapter three, teaches that God's new covenant rule and fallen human rule differ in *nature*. By virtue of the Three, we saw that God's rule is an authorizing rule. God is the ultimate delegator, and his rule is nothing if not generous. God's triune rule creates and affirms difference. By virtue of the One, we saw that God's rule is constrained by all the attributes of his character, including his attributes of goodness and love. For God to capture the inner mind of a human being, and to cause him or her to change sides in heart and soul, is to lead the human over to the side of goodness and love, and away from the side of selfishness and hate. God's rule gives life, freedom and authority to the individual; it does not steal these things.

Second, God's new covenant rule and fallen human rule differ in their *ends*. We saw in chapter four that redemption fulfills or enacts God's purposes in creation. God's rule redeems people to what they should have been in the first place.[39] Regeneration involves a radical element of restoration or fulfillment,[40] and therefore it is the path to the true freedom and social harmony intended in the Garden.[41] Not so with Big Brother or fallen rule generally. The terror of Orwell's novel roots in the irreconcilable conflict between its implicit doctrines of creation and redemption. The unspoken assumption that every reader brings to the book is that its characters *exist* or *were created for* something drastically different than the redemptive scheme required by Big Brother. Big Brother wants to change people into something they were not created to be—cogs in a machine, or slaves. The Party meant to exploit and use people for its own selfish purposes, which is the chronic fear that humans bear in a fallen world where authority is abused

---

[39]J. Todd Billings, commenting on Calvin's Aristotelian distinction between the *substance* of human nature, which was created good, and the *accidental* characteristics of sinful human nature, writes, "In regeneration, the *substance* of human nature is led toward fulfillment in Christ through the Spirit. Grace does not destroy this primal human nature, but fulfills it." Billings, "John Milbank's Theology," 95.

[40]I do not mean to assert that regeneration is merely restoration. One might want to say with Augustine that, whereas pre-fall humanity was able to sin or not (*posse peccare*), the glorified human will not be able to sin (*non posse peccare*).

[41]Billings again: "In terms of the will, the original, created orientation of the will is fulfilled in redemption. It is in this context that Calvin claims that human freedom must be contingent upon the work of the Spirit." Billings, "John Milbank's Theology," 95.

regularly. But God's rule aims to restore fallen people to what they were created to be—kings!

Third, the role of God's Spirit shows that God's new covenant rule and fallen human rule differ in their *means*. The precise operations of God's Spirit are mysterious, but this much can be said: he gives to the new covenant community what he commands, and therefore coercive force is unnecessary within the new covenant.[42] He gives the heart new desires and ambitions. To place God's law in the heart while also commanding obedience is like placing on the track a natural-born runner whose body has wasted away by years of indolence and aimlessness, giving her an insatiable hunger for Olympic gold and then telling her that her full-time job is to train and to win a medal. Not only that, God promises to remove every other obstacle and otherwise ensure success. The person must do it—assent is required—but the Spirit provides all the means, including the desire and the talent. So it is with the new covenant version of the old covenant command to imitate God's holiness. Whereas previously God used such commands to produce a showdown, now his Spirit gives the prospect of imitating God's holiness the luster of Olympic gold, the ability to train toward it and the assurance of attaining it: "Therefore, preparing your minds for action, and being sober-minded, set your hope fully on the grace *that will be brought to you* at the revelation of Jesus Christ. . . . As he who called you is holy, you also be holy in all your conduct, since it is written, 'You shall be holy, for I am holy'" (1 Pet 1:13, 15-16). Fallen human rule, of course, can make no such assurances of success because it cannot give what it commands. Instead, it must rely upon coercive force to accomplish its ends. The covenant community itself is a place where "no longer shall each one teach his neighbor and each his brother, saying, 'Know the Lord,' for they shall all know me" (Jer 31:34), which renders the need for coercive force within the community moot.

***Four lessons for a political theology.*** Both the new covenant promise and modernist totalitarianism envision a society with perfect rule and obedience,

---

[42]See Kevin Vanhoozer on employing speech-act theory for understanding effectual calling in *First Theology: God, Scripture and Hermeneutics* (Downers Grove, IL: InterVarsity Press, 2002), 96-124, 159-203; also Michael Horton, *Covenant and Salvation: Union with Christ* (Louisville, KY: Westminster John Knox), 216-42.

but there the similarity ends. We can draw out four lessons for a political theology from this comparison. The first two lessons will be stated both positively and critically in relation to other political theologies.

The quantitative commonalities between the new covenant program and totalitarianism suggest that:

1. *Positively*: New covenant salvation is political, involving the inner and outer person. *Critically*: Any political theology that separates either the inner person from the outer person or the religious domain from the political domain is anthropologically naive and potentially quietistic. New covenant salvation is political because it involves submitting the inseparable inner and outer person to God as the one who possesses imperium. Systems that argue otherwise are anthropologically naive because they fail to recognize that the outer person always acts according to the inner person's values, loves, gods.[43] And such systems are potentially quietistic because, with such strident bifurcations in place, their adherents may fail to act when they should act. They may fail to embody the necessarily political dimensions of their faith. For these reasons, one can be sympathetic with political theologies that have some notion of a "holistic salvation" or a "political gospel" and a strong doctrine of the One—from liberation theologians[44] to an older generation of political theologians[45] to neo-evangelicals[46] to neo-Calvinists.[47]

Luther's doctrine of two kingdoms, for instance, is sometimes viewed as separating mind and body as well as religion and politics, a critique that is combined with a critique of *sola fide*, since the former appears to some to be a corollary of the latter. The standard critique among recent political philosophers[48]

---

[43] See Luther's definition of a "god" in chapter one (see the section "A Broader Religious Conceptuality and a View from Somewhere").

[44] E.g., Gustavo Gutiérrez, *A Theology of Liberation*, 15th anniversary ed. (Maryknoll, NY: Orbis, 1988), 83-105, 126-34.

[45] E.g., see Jürgen Moltmann's development of the theme of the "political church" in *The Church in the Power of the Spirit* (Minneapolis: Fortress, 1993), 15-18.

[46] E.g., Russell Moore, *The Kingdom of Christ: The New Evangelical Perspective* (Wheaton, IL: Crossway, 2004).

[47] E.g., Cornelius Plantinga, *Engaging God's World: A Christian Vision of Faith, Learning, and Living* (Grand Rapids: Eerdmans, 2002); Ryan C. McIlhenny, ed., *Kingdoms Apart: Engaging the Two Kingdoms Perspective* (Phillipsburg, NJ: P&R, 2012).

[48] Alasdair MacIntyre, *A Short History of Ethics: A History of Moral Philosophy from the Homeric Age to the Twentieth Century*, 2nd ed. (Great Britain: Routledge, 1998), 78-83; Jean Bethke Elshtain, *Public Man, Private Woman: Women in Social and Political Thought* (Princeton, NJ: Princeton

and political theologians[49] goes something like this: (1) Luther's doctrine of *sola fide* bifurcates the human person into the inner person of faith and the outer person of works since God is said to free and to justify only the inner person by faith; (2) Luther's doctrine of the two kingdoms then reifies this division by placing the church over one and the state over the other; (3) this anthropological and political bifurcation leaves Christian virtues privatized and therefore peripheralized; and it leaves Christians themselves passive in the face of unjust and tyrannical states since the state cannot touch their "inner person," which is already free. In short, Luther's doctrines of *sola fide* and two kingdoms, says Jürgen Moltmann, has tempted generations of Christians to conclude that faith is world-less and that the world is faith-less, that God is unreal and reality God-less.[50] Perhaps this is why at least several Protestant theologians who do not want to divorce the political and spiritual domains also adopt doctrines of justification that lean in the direction of the New Perspective on Paul, which sets itself in contrast to Luther.[51]

I do have problems with Luther's two-kingdoms doctrine, which I will come to later. But I am not convinced that it is as apolitical as his critics suggest,[52] because it operates in conjunction with his doctrines of the Spirit, regeneration and faith. Any strident dualism created by the former is tempered by the latter.[53] Faith for Luther gives birth to deeds, and the inner

---

University Press, 1981), 81-83; Elshtain, *Sovereignty: God, State, and Self* (New York: Basic Books, 2008), 78-87; Michael Kirwan (on Hannah Arendt as making the same point as Elshtain), *Political Theology: An Introduction* (Minneapolis: Fortress, 2009), 36, see also 73-78. See Mouw's rebuttal of MacIntyre in Richard Mouw, "Alasdair MacIntyre on Reformation Ethics," *Journal of Religious Ethics* 13, no. 2 (Fall 1985): 253-56; and Bernd Wannenwetsch's critique of Elshtain in *Political Worship* (New York: Oxford University Press, 2004), 179-81.

[49]Jacques Maritain, *Three Reformers: Luther, Descartes, Rousseau* (New York: Thomas V. Crowell, 1970), 35. In Jürgen Moltmann, *On Human Dignity: Political Theology and Ethics*, trans. M. Douglas Meeks (Philadelphia: Fortress, 1984), 71-76.

[50]Moltmann, *On Human Dignity*, 75; also Robert Benne, *Good and Bad Ways to Think About Religion and Politics* (Grand Rapids: Eerdmans, 2010), 22.

[51]John Howard Yoder, *The Politics of Jesus*, 2nd ed. (Grand Rapids: Eerdmans, 1994), 212-27; Stanley Hauerwas, *The Peaceable Kingdom: A Primer in Christian Ethics* (Notre Dame, IN: University of Notre Dame Press, 1983), 93-94. Cf. Nicholas Wolterstorff, *Justice in Love* (Grand Rapids: Eerdmans, 2011), 260-66, 271-76.

[52]Mark C. Mattes also points to an increasing number of scholars who do not equate Luther's not establishing the kingdom through the sword to quietism. Mattes, *The Role of Justification in Contemporary Theology*, Lutheran Quarterly Books (Grand Rapids: Eerdmans, 2004), 90, 90n20.

[53]See Luther, *Christian Liberty*, trans. W. A. Lambert and Harold J. Grimm (Philadelphia: Fortress, 1957), 22, 24. Luther's inner and outer person are distinct but inseparable, *acting in accordance with a single new nature* (on this point, see Oswald Bayer, *Martin Luther's Theology: A*

person governs the outer.⁵⁴ That said, the division truly becomes strict when Luther's two-governments scheme is divorced from these other doctrines and assumes a bastardized form in the liberalism of Locke or Jefferson.

The classical liberalism of Locke and Jefferson does present a strong division of inner and outer persons. And the deontological liberalism of John Rawls, in an analogous move, divides private reason (which would include religious reason) from public reason, as we saw in chapter one. And these basic political divisions (the church governs the inner; the state governs the outer)⁵⁵ work so long as there is, in Rawls's term, an "overlapping consensus" concerning which beliefs are broadly acceptable. So disagreements between eighteenth-, nineteenth- and even twentieth-century Protestants, Catholics and Jews often occurred *within* the boundaries of a broadly shared ethic and worldview. But neither the Lockean nor Rawlsian divisions work so well—their inadequacy is revealed—when the consensus begins to break down. Two individuals can agree to set aside their religious differences in the public square only as long as their religions don't make demands on their political views that conflict with one another—which means that these individuals never really set aside their religious differences at all.

In the meantime, Christians should not be fooled by what N. T. Wright insightfully calls the Enlightenment's "rival eschatology,"⁵⁶ or what William Cavanaugh refers to as the "jealous god" of Hobbesian and Lockean "state

---

*Contemporary Interpretation*, trans. Thomas H. Trapp [Tübingen: J. C. B. Mohr, 2003; repr., Grand Rapids: Eerdmans, 2008], 311-12). Hence, the former "drives" or "compels" the latter by the gift of justification and the Holy Spirit (Luther, *Christian Liberty*, 30). The fact that a person has faith signifies that the Spirit has given him or her a new nature. Good works *will* follow. For a view of Luther different than my own, see W. D. J. Cargill Thompson, "The 'Two Kingdoms' and the 'Two Regiments,' Some Problems of Luther's *Zwei-Reiche-Lehre*," *Journal of Theological Studies* 20, no. 1 (April 1969): 169 (article 164-85); for a sympathetic perspective, see William Lazareth, *Christians in Society: Luther, the Bible, and Social Ethics* (Minneapolis: Fortress, 2001), 110.

⁵⁴As such, his treatise *On Secular Authority* argues that the purpose of the spiritual government is to "fashion true Christians and just persons"; that Christians have no need of the secular government, making the best citizens; and that Christians, too, make the best princes. Martin Luther, *On Secular Authority*, in *Luther and Calvin on Secular Authority*, trans. Harro Höpfl, Cambridge Texts in the History of Political Thought (New York: Cambridge University Press, 1991), 11.

⁵⁵See John Locke's "Letter," in *Two Treatises of Government and A Letter Concerning Toleration* (New Haven, CT: Yale University Press, 2003); see also Locke, "On the Difference Between Civil and Ecclesiastical Power," in *The Life and Letters of John Locke*, comp. Lord Peter King (London: Henry G. Bohn, 1858), 300-306.

⁵⁶N. T. Wright, *The Challenge of Jesus: Rediscovering Who Jesus Was and Is* (Downers Grove, IL: InterVarsity Press, 1999), 21-22; Wright, *How God Became King: The Forgotten Story of the Gospels*

soteriology," a god which brooks no rivals.[57] When people lose sight of the fact that God rules over all, it is not just that his domain shrinks, quarantined as it were to the afterlife. He shrinks, and people increasingly look to the state "to absorb the risk involved in living a moral human life," "to defer the consequences of our actions to some undefined future," "to help us cheat death."[58]

Further, the new covenant member should recognize that the rule of God always enters into the public square or workplace with him or her precisely because the Spirit reigns "inside." The Spirit and the law-implanted heart cannot *not* enter the ballot box, the jury stand, the legislative chamber, the newspaper editorial office, the protest line or the workplace. The "totalitarian" God and Davidic Son of the new covenant transform the heart, mind and soul of its members and then call them to defile the liberal's sacred public square with spiritually profane acts of voting, column writing and legislation crafting.

At the same time, the differences between the new covenant program and totalitarianism, especially the difference of means, suggest:

2. *Positively:* God's new covenant rule, renewal and righteousness are limited to the new covenant community. *Critically:* Any system that applies or imposes God's new covenant rule to any person or part of creation that has not been regenerated or renewed by God's Spirit is theologically naive and potentially tyrannical. The righteousness of the new covenant depends on the special activity of God's Spirit, and it depends, as we have seen, on his work to change a heart. If the heart has not been changed, the actor remains self-justifying and self-enthroned, even if he or she outwardly mimics the righteous deed. Any system that speaks of new covenant transformation or renewal beyond the new covenant community is theologically naive because it fails to recognize that God must work in a regenerating way before true and lasting healing, peace, justice or righteousness is possible. Further, it is potentially tyrannical because it risks asking for what has not been given,

---

(New York: HarperOne, 2012), 163-64. See also William T. Cavanaugh, *Migrations of the Holy: God, State, and the Political Meaning of the Church* (Grand Rapids: Eerdmans, 2011).

[57]William T. Cavanaugh, "The City: Beyond Secular Parodies," in *Radical Orthodoxy: A New Theology*, ed. John Milbank, Catherine Pickstock and Graham Ward (London: Routledge, 1999), 191. But see my cautions in the introduction, n. 90.

[58]Cavanaugh, *Migrations of the Holy*, 3.

like Pharaoh asking for more bricks but providing no straw. For this reason, one can be sympathetic with the political theologies that have a strong doctrine of the Two, whether Luther or his contemporary sympathizers, the pacifist Anabaptist tradition, or aspects of liberalism.

The classic example of a system commonly critiqued on these grounds is Christendom.[59] Medieval Europe was intended to be a Christian community, governed by kings and emperors together with bishops and popes. The former were said to possess the sword of *regnum* over temporal affairs, while the latter were said to possess the sword of *sacerdotium* over spiritual matters, a doctrine first articulated by Pope Gelasius I in 494. The two swords or powers were not welded together per se; but their jurisdictions were essentially coterminous, and the bearers of each sword continually invented ways to wield the other's.[60] The most important thing to recognize for our purposes is that the two swords belonged to one "Christian" body politic. By conflating national citizenship and church membership, Christendom formally affirmed people as Christians in whom the Spirit had not moved (to say nothing of Charlemagne's paladins, who, swords in hand, enforced Christian "conversion" on pagan Europe).[61] The element of tyranny occurred, at the very least, whenever the sword of state was exercised to reinforce the decisions of the new covenant community, the church.

A subtler, more recent version of a system that succumbs to these errors is the liberation theology of Gustavo Gutiérrez. Gutiérrez replaces a "quantitative and extensive" understanding of salvation that attends to "the problem of the number of persons saved" in binary fashion with a "qualitative and intensive" understanding in which people can, in increasing measure, open themselves up to the gracious activity of God by doing the justice-seeking work of God—"even if they are not clearly aware that they

---

[59] However, O'Donovan's nuanced and sympathetic interpretation of Christendom is instructive, particularly his argument that Christendom's historical record of persecutions "can be distinguished from the authentic stock of the Christendom idea," as well as his notion of mutual service with clear limits between the two authorities. O'Donovan, *Desire of the Nations*, 217-18, 221, also 199-226.

[60] Elshtain, *Sovereignty*, 11-13, 51-52, 123; Robert Jackson, *Sovereignty: Evolution of an Idea* (Malden, MA: Polity Press, 2007), 24-38; David VanDrunen, *Natural Law and the Two Kingdoms: A Study in the Development of Reformed Social Thought* (Grand Rapids: Eerdmans, 2010), 32-36; Alexander Passerin d'Entrèves, *The Notion of the State: An Introduction to Political Theory* (London: Clarendon Press, 1967), 133-35.

[61] No doubt, a doctrine of infant baptism in which the child is regenerated could solve this problem.

The Politics of the New Covenant 263

are doing so."⁶² Unlike Hosea's and Barth's explanations of the new covenant given above, where the human will is employed in an act of assent, here assent to God as God, strictly speaking, is not necessary. The larger picture is that Gutiérrez adopts a Hegelian and Marxist view of history whereby creation history and redemptive history meld together dialectically as humankind, through the grace of God, gradually gains self-mastery and freedom through the selfless labor of ordering creation for the good of others:

> Consequently, when we assert that humanity fulfills itself by continuing the work of creation by means of its labor, we are saying that it places itself, by this very fact, within an all-embracing salvific process. To work, to transform this world, is to become a man and to build the human community; it is also to save. Likewise, to struggle against misery and exploitation and to build a just society is already to be part of the saving action, which is moving towards its complete fulfillment. All this means that building the temporal city . . . is to become part of a saving process which embraces the whole of humanity and all human history.⁶³

To work is to save. Creation and redemption meld together. They are one.⁶⁴ In this deeply Hegelian passage redolent with the kind of historicism that sent chills down the spines of the Karl Poppers and Isaiah Berlins, the role of assent is again diminished if not altogether dismissed. God might say, "You are my people," but there is no requirement for the people to say, "You are our God." The many instead dissolve into the one. Insofar as assent is absent, Gutiérrez's flag of liberation, ironically, bears a faint tinge of tyranny,⁶⁵ like that of his nineteenth-century teachers.⁶⁶

---

⁶²Gutiérrez, *Theology of Liberation*, 83-84.
⁶³Ibid., 91, see also 19-22; see also Christian Smith, *The Emergence of Liberation Theology: Radical Religion and Social Movement Theory* (Chicago: University of Chicago, 1991), 28-31.
⁶⁴Gutiérrez, *Theology of Liberation*, 86-97; Smith, *Emergence of Liberation Theology*, 39-43.
⁶⁵My implicit assumption here, which the reader may or may not like, is that soteriological universalism bears that tinge of tyranny insofar as it diminishes the significance of personal decisions in the plan of salvation and reconciling a person to God. Even if a person resists God all the way to the grave, universalism overturns that resistance. It does not give a person what they consciously want and deliberately choose.
⁶⁶Stanley Hauerwas ties Gutiérrez not to Hegel but to Kant and argues that Gutiérrez's system slips not toward tyranny but toward individualism. In fact, I believe his critique equally applies. People who do God's work "even if they are not clearly aware that they are doing so" (Gutiérrez's words) can both be described objectively as dissolving into God (my

Now, my own discussion of the relationship between history and creation in chapter four affirmed, as in Gutiérrez's discussion of the Old Testament, that God as creator and God as redeemer are inseparable because the creator God is the ruling God, and his purposes in creation and redemption are one.[67] At the same time, we must recognize the institutional division that occurs in redemptive history through the special covenants. Those who belong to God's special covenants—contra Gutiérrez—are expected to say yes to God, unlike the rest of humanity.[68] The yeses no doubt should pursue and serve the nos, but yes is not no.[69] The special line was to be distinct from the common line. The two were not one. Salvation is holistic because God will fulfill his purposes in creation through redemption, but history is not holistic.

Hegel's holism was not merely anthropological; it was historical.[70] And a historical holism has little room for hard lines between the yeses and the nos. The very purpose of the new covenant, however, was to turn a purse-lipped "no" to God into a gladsome "yes," the yes of willing identification and obedience: "You are my God" (Hos 2:23). After all, self-enthronement ends only when the heart says yes to the Almighty. Without the yes, there is no true righteousness or justice.

The same erasing of new covenant distinctions can occur when writers speak of a "holistic gospel" or a "holistic salvation." To see this we need to borrow from the New Testament theologian's conception of inaugurated eschatology or a doctrine of two ages. It may be true that "God isn't content to save souls; God wants to save bodies too," and that "God wants to save economic systems and social structures too."[71] But Jesus' inauguration of the

---

critique) and subjectively as promoting the independent Enlightenment new man who bows only to his own reason (Hauerwas's critique). Hauerwas, *After Christendom? How the Church Is to Behave If Freedom, Justice, and a Christian Nation Are Bad Ideas* (Nashville: Abingdon, 1991), 50-56.

[67]See esp. Gutiérrez, *Theology of Liberation*, 86-89.

[68]This statement needs to be qualified for infant members of the old covenant, of course. The point here is that members of God's special covenants, old and new, were expected to obey and so display God.

[69]Hauerwas: "Christian ethics is not written for everyone, but for those who have been formed by the God of Abraham, Isaac, Jacob, and Jesus." Hauerwas, *Peaceable Kingdom*, 97.

[70]See Georg Wilhelm Friedrich Hegel, *Lectures on the Philosophy of World History: Introduction* (New York: Cambridge University Press, 1975).

[71]Plantinga, *Engaging God's World*, 96-97, see also 110-11.

new covenant portrayed in the Gospels does not lift the curse from creation (Rom 8:19-24), other than in his miracles and his resurrected body. The complete removal awaits the consummation of the eschaton. As such, saying that God is not content to save only souls but wants bodies too implies a symmetry between the two that is eschatologically insensitive. The new covenant, in this present era of redemptive history, is very much concerned *with what a person does with soul and body*—the "new self's" purposes and actions. But it does not remove the curse from the "old self" or from humanity's rule of this present world. People die. Buildings collapse. Just laws are overturned. The futility of Ecclesiastes remains in full effect.

Consider, for instance, the illustration of a member of the new covenant participating in the Olympics. That individual might, by the power of the new covenant, run for the glory of God and the good of others. But an asymmetry remains between the Olympian's "new self" and "old self." The "old self" belongs to a cursed creation, as muscle cramps and even corroding gold medals will eventually indicate. The same distinctions must be made were we to compare a Christian's and a non-Christian's architectural drawings or mathematics lectures or legislative resolutions. The Christian's "new self" can participate in the power and freedom of the new creation while pursuing such activities, whereas the non-Christian cannot. But the drawings and lectures and resolutions of both will remain subject to futility, error and all the effects of the curse because they belong to the age of creation.

How far does the new covenant's work extend in this present era of redemptive history? Does it extend to our bodies? Or health care management systems? I think the quick answer has to be that the new covenant has not extended to any place where death, futility and sin still reign. If the beautiful buildings and just constitutions and enlightening classroom lectures created by Christians, like the ones built by non-Christians, are still subject to decay and destruction, one should be very careful in speaking of a "holistic" salvation or gospel. Abraham Kuyper may have been correct to assert, "Our supreme calling must be to impress the stamp of *one-ness* upon *all* human life, because God upholds and preserves it, just as He created it all,"[72] but

---

[72]Abraham Kuyper, *Lectures on Calvinism* (Grand Rapids: Eerdmans, 1931), 54 (italics original).

there is a *twoness* to be preserved as well, a twoness that separates the inside and the outside of the new covenant's rule.

The broader lesson is that a political theology that fails to draw lines between assenting and nonassenting individuals, as well those aspects of creation that do or do not remain under the curse, has imposed the new covenant in places where the Spirit has not yet done his work. To speak vaguely of "transforming culture," for instance, or the "kingdom work" of a non-governmental organization that builds houses for the poor, completely apart from the question of personal assent to Jesus' rule, risks blurring the lines between where the Spirit has or has not worked according to the promises of the new covenant.[73] It risks, in other words, calling something the righteousness and justice of God when it is not, as well as misidentifying the name of God since he intends his name to be worn by his covenantal community.[74] Politicians who swear to speak for Jesus, and pastors who lend their pulpit to a partisan cause not explicitly mandated in Scripture or deduced "by good and necessary consequence" (Westminster Confession), risk doing the same. Central to God's purposes for the new covenant was to ensure the world could properly identify *him* through the righteous actions of his people:

> And I will vindicate the holiness of *my great name*. . . . The nations will know that *I am the* LORD. . . . And I will put my Spirit within you, and cause you to walk in my statutes and be careful to obey my rules. . . . Then the nations that are left all around you shall know that *I am the* LORD. (Ezek 36:23, 27, 36)

Right identification is essential to the new covenant, and it belongs exclusively to those who have assented to the Almighty. Jesus observes, "Unless one is born again he cannot see the kingdom of God" (Jn 3:3). Or in Oliver O'Donovan's words: "The kingship of Jesus is such as can be recognized only by those who recognize it on their own account; it lacks accessibility to public opinion."[75]

---

[73] E.g., Plantinga, *Engaging God's World*, 109-13.

[74] The problem of misidentification not only occurs when those outside the covenant community are said to be inside, but when those inside do not act according to God's righteousness. Hauerwas again: "For the church is known by the character of people who constitute it, and if we lack that character, the world rightly draws the conclusion that the God we worship is in fact a false God." Hauerwas, *Peaceable Kingdom*, 109.

[75] O'Donovan, *Desire of the Nations*, 140; but see also 145-46.

Another word to describe the error being criticized in the second lesson is *utopianism*.⁷⁶ The inability of the Mosaic covenant and Israel's geopolitical kingdom to deliver a righteous and just political commmunity should have ended visions of heaven on earth by such means. Not even heavenly inscribed laws, divinely handpicked kings or God's own temple presence could make a difference. Human nature itself needed changing. How strange then that Christians still approach the promise of new constitutions and presidential campaigns with utopian dreams!⁷⁷ Christians should rest their hopes for true justice and righteousness not upon the state but upon the son of David and the political community that he is forming: "My servant David shall be king over them, and they shall all have one shepherd. They shall walk in my rules and be careful to obey my statutes" (Ezek 37:24).⁷⁸

Does new covenant anti-utopianism then lead to pacifism or the quietism decried in point one above? Surely it forbids acting politically with ends-oriented expectations that our actions will usher in the eschaton. It does not, however, forbid acting politically for the principles-oriented sake of love and justice. Just because you cannot permanently heal a dying man does not mean you should not do everything possible to extend life and give comfort for love's sake. In the same way, love for neighbor should impel Christians into public service for the sake of seeking some measure of justice, even if it will remain imperfect. Hauerwas is mistaken, I believe, to argue that "Christians cannot seek justice from the barrel of a gun."⁷⁹ The fact that humanity has employed the power of the state perversely does not mean its power is not divinely authorized (Gen 9:5-6; Rom 13:1-6). Karl Barth observes better: "The State is not a product of sin but one of the constants of the divine Providence and government of the world in its action against human sin: it

---

⁷⁶Gutiérrez in fact offers an explicit defense of utopianism. Gutiérrez, *Theology of Liberation*, 135-40.

⁷⁷Stanley Hauerwas even applies a kind of anti-utopianism to earthly conceptions of justice. See Hauerwas, *After Christendom?*, 68.

⁷⁸The gospel, says Hauerwas, is not just "an apolitical account of individual salvation," but "the goods news of the creation of a new community of peace and justice formed by a hope that God's kingdom has and will prevail." Hauerwas, *Peaceable Kingdom*, 105. See also his *A Community of Character: Toward a Constructive Christian Social Ethic* (Notre Dame, IN: Notre Dame University Press, 1981), 9-12.

⁷⁹Hauerwas, *Peaceable Kingdom*, 104.

is therefore an instrument of divine grace."[80] Governments may be unable to implement God's justice perfectly, but the pursuit of justice (within the bounds articulated in chapter four) remains their commission.

More broadly, what should the Christian's posture toward the state be? There are, to be sure, conflicting impulses for a Christian. On the one hand, the Christian's "yes" to God's rule and revelation could arguably impel him or her toward an active role in government. That seems to be literary theorist and legal scholar Stanley Fish's hunch, which is why he criticizes those Christian writers who adopt some form of liberalism:

> To put the matter baldly, a person of religious conviction should not want to enter the marketplace of ideas but to shut it down, at least insofar as it presumes to determine matters that he believes have been determined by God and faith. The religious person should not seek an accommodation with liberalism; he should seek to rout it from the field, to extirpate it, root and branch.[81]

And there is a thread of truth in Fish's comments. The Christian entering the public square has no other standard of justice and righteousness than a biblical one. He or she believes that God will judge "the kings of the earth and the great ones and the generals and the rich and the powerful, and everyone, slave and free" by his own standards and none other (Rev 6:15). Certain matters, say, stealing, are not up for debate. Jesus may have said to render to Caesar what is Caesar's and to God what is God's after looking at Caesar's image on a coin (Mt 22:20-21), but he well knew that Caesar himself was created in God's image and belonged to God,[82] which is why he could

---

[80]This from the man who endured the days of Hitler. Karl Barth, "The Christian Community and the Civil Community," in *Against the Stream: Shorter Post-War Writings 1946-52* (New York: Philosophical Library, 1954), 21.

[81]Stanley Fish, "Why We Can't All Just Get Along," *First Things*, February 1996, www.firstthings.com/article/1996/02/001-why-we-cant-all-just-get-along.

[82]D. A. Carson writes, "When Jesus asks the question, 'Whose image is this? And whose inscription?' biblically informed people will remember that *all* human beings have been made in the image and likeness of God (Genesis 1:26). Moreover, his people have the 'inscription' of God's law written on them (cf. Exodus 13:9; Proverbs 7:3; Isaiah 44:5; Jeremiah 31:33). If we give back to God what has *his* image on it, we must all give ourselves to him. Far from privatizing God's claim, that is the claim of religion, Jesus' famous utterance means that God always trumps Caesar. We may be obligated to pay taxes to Caesar, but we owe everything, our very being, to God." Carson then continues by quoting Alan H. Cadwallander: "'Whatever civil obligations Jesus' followers might have, they must be understood within the context of their responsibilities to God, for their duty to God claims their whole selves.'" D. A. Carson, *Christ and Culture*

also say to Caesar's emissary, Pilate, "You would have no authority over me at all unless it had been given you from above," referring to God and not Caesar (Jn 19:11). The state is accountable to God and God's standards of righteousness and justice, as we saw in chapter four (e.g., Ps 96:10), whether or not it will ever live up to them. Nothing changes for "the nations" between the Old Testament and New from this vantage point. Pilate and Caesar are no less accountable to God than are Pharaoh or Nebuchadnezzar.

On the other hand, Fish's comments overlook the new covenant's anti-utopian posture. A new covenant perspective will recognize "the limits of politics," at least the politics of the state.[83] It will not try to transform the world by sword, ballot or even academic argument. True transformation comes through the Spirit and the devices of the church, but God has not placed these tools into the state's hands.

Ultimately, the Bible offers members of the new covenant no one theory of human government, and we can expect, observes Hauerwas, that "different circumstances and social contexts bring different needs and strategies. For example, the church's stance in the context of totalitarian governments is obviously different than its stance in liberal democratic regimes."[84] But that does not mean we cannot say anything about philosophies of government: "It may be suggested that even if there is no one theory of government intrinsic to the church's self-understanding, surely there are some values, which may have diverse institutional forms, that the church has a stake in promoting. For example, Edna McDonagh speaks of 'kingdom values,' such as freedom, inviolability of the person, and equality as necessary correlatives of the Christian commitment."[85] For my part, I believe the Scriptures

---

*Revisited* (Grand Rapids: Eerdmans, 2008), 57. N. T. Wright offers the same interpretation as Carson in *How God Became King*, 147-50.

[83]Jean Bethke Elshtain, relating Augustine's view, wisely observes that "sin should usher into a rueful recognition of limits, not a will to dominion that requires others for one to conquer." Elshtain, *Augustine and the Limits of Politics* (Notre Dame, IN: Notre Dame University Press, 1998), 94.

[84]Hauerwas, *Peaceable Kingdom*, 111.

[85]Ibid., 111-12. Karl Barth also has helpful reflections in this regard. Like Hauerwas, he affirms that "the Christian community has no exclusive theory of its own to advocate in the face of the various forms and realities of political life. . . . The Christian community participates . . . in the human search for the best form, for the most fitting system of political organization; but it is also aware of the limits of all the political forms and systems which man can discover . . . and it will beware of playing off one political concept—even the 'democratic' concept—as *the* Christian concept, against all others" (Karl Barth, "Christian Community," 25). What's especially interesting,

recommend a mixed anthropology not dissimilar from that of James Madison and Alexander Hamilton in the *Federalist Papers*.[86] In many circumstances, this may well call for some kind of check on power, which is why a new covenant perspective has historically found common cause with democratic institutions.

3. The tensions between lessons one and two above make institutional specificity all-important for a political theology. Institutionally ambiguous language about "religious freedom," "the naked public square" or even the "lordship of Christ" needs to be supplemented with a more concrete discussion of institutional authority. Lesson two in fact suggests that the new covenant presents a certain kind of jurisdictional line: Christ's kingship, though universal in its extent and legitimacy, will *not* be acknowledged, or will be acknowledge only falsely, wherever the Spirit is not active in a new covenant capacity—"no one can say 'Jesus is Lord' except in the Holy Spirit" (1 Cor 12:3).[87]

The same institutional vagueness afflicts the New Testament department's discussion over whether Jesus and Paul sought to "subvert" Caesar and imperialist Rome.[88] Some writers are more careful than others to distinguish

---

though, is the criteria that he gives to the Christian community for whatever influence it does have toward the civic community: "In the decisions of the State the Church will always support the side which clarifies rather than obscures the Lordship of Jesus Christ over the whole, which includes the political sphere outside the Church. . . . Its desire is not that human politics should cross the politics of God, but that they should proceed, however distantly, on parallel lines" (ibid., 34). If indeed redemption fulfills creation's purposes, and God's special people are to model the political mandate to which all humanity is called, as I argued in chapter four, then Barth was onto something. He then offers (by my count) twelve places where a correlation exists between the two communities such that the Christian community might have an interest in advocating for whichever side clarifies the lordship of Christ (see ibid., 34-42).

[86]In Federalist 55 they wrote, "As there is a degree of depravity in mankind which requires a certain degree of circumspection and distrust: So there are other qualities in human nature, which justify a certain portion of esteem and confidence." Alexander Hamilton, James Madison and John Jay, *The Federalist Papers*, ed. Gary Wills (New York: Bantam Books, 1982), 284.

[87]For that reason, whether or not Constantine was really a Christian does not strike me as material to the question of whether the idea of a Christian nation or empire has a legitimate basis (even though, with Luther, I think Christians make the best princes). See Peter Leithart, *Defending Constantine: The Twilight of an Empire and the Dawn of Christendom* (Downers Grove, IL: IVP Academic, 2010).

[88]Different forms of the anti-imperial readings themselves can be found in N. T. Wright, *Paul: In Fresh Perspective* (Minneapolis: Fortress, 2009), and Wright, "Paul and Caesar: A New Reading of Romans," in *A Royal Priesthood? The Use of the Bible Ethically and Politically; A Dialogue with Oliver O'Donovan*, ed. Craig Bartholomew et al. (Grand Rapids: Zondervan, 2002), 173-95 (which includes a rebuttal from O'Donovan); also the edited volumes of Richard A. Horsley,

opposition to empire qua empire and opposition to Caesar's claim of divine status.[89] The latter reading is certainly less problematic—it is easier to believe that Jesus and Paul would have Caesar's claim to divinity in their crosshairs than they would a particular kind of constitution. The trouble with any language of "subverting" imperialist Rome, however, is that it tempts the Bible reader to think either that Jesus was an anarchist, determined to do away with human government altogether or that he was pursuing partisan, maybe constitutional, causes.[90] But surely this is difficult to maintain from the biblical data. On the one hand, it may be true that Christians can be "fundamentally disruptive" to false worship and that "such disruption unfolds economically and politically," as C. Kavin Rowe observes in Acts 19, which pits Jesus against the market economy of Artemis.[91] On the other hand, it is also the case, Rowe continues, that Festus, the Roman governor, determined that Paul committed no political crime worthy of death (Acts 25-26), suggesting that Festus, at least, did not view "the early Christian movement [as] a direct attack on Roman political systems, a kind of religiously-based bid for insurrection or imperial power."[92]

What a political theology needs is a clear account of the lines of authority, jurisdiction and competence for each of Scripture's institutions. What authority do they have and how far does it extend? For instance, the main point of separation between church and state is not whether the president believes in God and governs accordingly. The primary point of institutional

---

*Paul and Empire: Religion and Power in Roman Imperial Society* (1997); *Paul and Politics: Ekklesia, Israel, Imperium, Interpretation: Essays in Honor of Krister Stendahl* (2000); *Paul and the Roman Imperial Order* (2004), all published in Harrisburg, PA, by Trinity Press International. In general, my take on the anti-imperial or anti-Caesar readings of the New Testament accords with John M. G. Barclay's chapter "Why the Roman Empire Was Insignificant to Paul," in *Pauline Churches and Diaspora Jews* (Tübingen: Mohr Siebeck, 2011), 362-87. See also Seyoon Kim, *Christ and Caesar: The Gospel and the Roman Empire in the Writings of Paul and Luke* (Grand Rapids: Eerdmans, 2008).

[89]N. T. Wright, "Paul's Gospel and Caesar's Empire," in Horsley, *Paul and Politics*, 164.
[90]John M. G. Barclay helpfully responds to the entire anti-imperial conversation by writing, "Reading Paul's letters with responsible attention to their own dynamics, we find that his theology concerns the subversive and redemptive power of divine grace in Christ which creates and empowers new communities of social (and therefore broadly political) significance.... In fact, Paul's most subversive act, vis-à-vis the Roman empire, was not to oppose or upstage it, but to relegate it to the rank of a dependent and derivative entity, denied a distinguishable name or significant role in the story of the world." Barclay, *Pauline Churches and Diaspora Jews*, 383-84.
[91]C. Kavin Rowe, "The Ecclesiology of Acts," *Interpretation* 66, no. 3 (July 2012): 263.
[92]Ibid., 264.

separation, as I briefly observed in chapter one, is in their membership and therefore their jurisdiction. Membership in a nation must be regarded as distinct from membership in a church, which is why the greatest error of Christendom, I suggested a moment ago, was in the manner in which it blurred the line between the two by automatically inducting citizens of a nation into membership in the church. We will discuss the relationship between the new covenant and the church in chapter six, but to jump ahead, if membership in the new covenant requires both the activity of the Spirit and the assent of the individual to God, as I have been arguing, then membership in God's new covenant people—the church—should likewise be restricted to those who give their assent. To place infants born into a "Christian" nation onto church rolls misidentifies God's presence, reputation, righteousness and justice, as discussed above. It institutionalizes human hypocrisy and a divine misrepresentation. The state's jurisdiction, however, extends to all its members so far as the Noahic authorization permits, an authorization given further clarity by Paul in Romans 13. Indeed, the state possesses authority over members of a church in this regard. But the state possesses no authority over church members *as* church members. It was the error of Magisterial Reformers and Colonial Puritans, therefore, to leverage the power of the sword to conduct some of the church's own disciplinary business, as immemorially fictionalized in *The Scarlet Letter*, where an adulterous Hester Prynne is placed in the village stocks and then *geographically* excommunicated from the village, much like an unclean Jew would have been removed from the camp in theonomic Israel.

A church's jurisdiction is more complicated than the state's. First, a church possesses one kind of jurisdiction over its assenting members, which we will consider in chapter six. Second, it possesses a God-assigned commission (shall we call this a second ring of jurisdiction?) to act with ambassadorial or embassy-like authority over everyone who is not a member but who is within geographic proximity of the church's voice. A church must proclaim that Jesus possesses all rule *now*, and that he will soon come to judge every person and prince who—in the present—departs from his standard of justice and righteousness. Yet a church must also keep these two kinds of jurisdiction or responsibility distinct. On the one hand, it must tell nonmembers that *its* Lord is *their* Lord (see Ps 2). Whether or not they assent to his lordship does not affect their status as his subjects. They are subjects who will be judged, which means that the jurisdiction of a church, in this secondary sense, is public-wide like the state's. Churches have an authorized claim upon the nations. On the other hand, a church must deny these nonassenting *subjects* the recognition of *citizen-in-good-standing*, at least until they repent and are baptized.

Does this mean that a nation becomes "Christian" when its leaders become Christians? Not at all. The public identity of "Christian" should belong only to those who have been made disciples by the church through their assent and their baptism, as we will discuss in chapter six. The fact that a governor confesses Christ hardly means that the Spirit has acted upon every citizen of the nation and produced a genuine profession of assent to Christ's rule. What's more, the Bible points to nothing like a covenantal or federal relationship between a governor and his or her citizens as pertains to Christ's kingdom such that the standing of the former represents the latter, like David representing Israel or Christ his church. There is one meditator—Christ. A Christian governor knows that Christ is king over his or her activities, but he or she must still refrain from taking up the sword *for new covenant purposes*.

Finally, institutional specificity is crucial for getting our doctrine of religious tolerance correct. The problematical, possibly self-contradictory liberal formulation of religious freedom discussed in chapters one and four confuses phenomenological realities for institutional ones. It builds the institutional church/state divide on a make-believe phenomenological religion/politics divide. A more institutionally sensitive approach has no trouble acknowledging that religion infiltrates and saturates the public square and that politics is always spiritual, but it asks more precise questions about who has been authorized to do what. It presents religious freedom as a property of the fact that God has not authorized prosecuting false worship. And it locates religious freedom in the field of formal religious institutional affiliation—that is, membership—not in lawmaking, which is impossible. It also seeks to ensure that legal space exists for churches, so that members of every nation might be drawn into the kingdom of God (see 1 Tim 2:1-2).[93]

---

[93]O'Donovan, *Desire of the Nations*, 146.

In short, Christians should consider the competencies and jurisdictional boundaries of Scripture's institutional authorities—what are the state and the church, how do we define the membership of each and what authority does each possess? From there, it is over to wisdom for determining how to best pursue justice in this or that context (see 1 Kings 3:28), and which particular issues fall into the ambit of one or the other or both.

4. The Spirit-given power of the new covenant requires a doctrine of two ages. A doctrine of two ages or inaugurated eschatology is a popular way among New Testament theologians for characterizing how creation history and redemptive history bifurcated when Christ's kingdom was inaugurated but not consummated through the giving of the new covenant. The history of new creation began even while the history of the old creation continued. Oliver O'Donovan helpfully transplants this New Testament conversation into the domain of political theology: "The passing age of principalities and powers has overlapped with the coming age of God's kingdom."[94] In fact, if I were to choose a title for my own political theology, following O'Donovan (sort of) I would call it a "two ages" view.[95]

A doctrine of two ages is diachronic and derives from the Bible's covenantal framework, unlike Luther's two kingdoms, which is synchronic and is built on a logical formulation. The latter begins, biblically enough, with Augustine's two communities, which are divided between those who submit to God and those who do not.[96] But then it places two governments over those two communities, one being the state, the other being the Word and to some measure the church.[97] The formulation is logically tidy, and it has much explanatory power, but it forces a parallel conceptuality that does not

---

[94] Ibid., 211.
[95] O'Donovan places his own views under the broader rubric of the "doctrine of the two," but it appears to me that this essentially culminates in a doctrine of two ages.
[96] Martin Luther writes, "Here we must divide Adam's children, all mankind into two parts: the first belong to the kingdom of God, the second to the kingdom of the world. All those who truly believe in Christ belong to God's kingdom, for Christ is king and lord in God's kingdom," while the rest of humankind belong to the kingdom of this world. Luther, *On Secular Authority*, 8. Luther's term for kingdom (*Reich*) includes the ideas of "ruling" and "what is ruled over." Harro Höpfl, "Glossary," in *Luther and Calvin on Secular Authority*, xxxv-xxxvi. Though see W. D. J. Cargill Thompson's discussion on this point in "'Two Kingdoms,'" 165-67.
[97] Luther: "Every kingdom must have its own laws and . . . no kingdom or government can survive without law." Luther, *On Secular Authority*, 23. That is, a *Reich* needs a *Regiment* (Luther's main term for government). "And so God has ordained the two governments, the spiritual [government] which fashions true Christians and just persons through the Holy Spirit under Christ,

his lordship does not affect their status as his subjects. They are subjects who will be judged, which means that the jurisdiction of a church, in this secondary sense, is public-wide like the state's. Churches have an authorized claim upon the nations. On the other hand, a church must deny these non-assenting *subjects* the recognition of *citizen-in-good-standing*, at least until they repent and are baptized.

Does this mean that a nation becomes "Christian" when its leaders become Christians? Not at all. The public identity of "Christian" should belong only to those who have been made disciples by the church through their assent and their baptism, as we will discuss in chapter six. The fact that a governor confesses Christ hardly means that the Spirit has acted upon every citizen of the nation and produced a genuine profession of assent to Christ's rule. What's more, the Bible points to nothing like a covenantal or federal relationship between a governor and his or her citizens as pertains to Christ's kingdom such that the standing of the former represents the latter, like David representing Israel or Christ his church. There is one mediator—Christ. A Christian governor knows that Christ is king over his or her activities, but he or she must still refrain from taking up the sword *for new covenant purposes.*

Finally, institutional specificity is crucial for getting our doctrine of religious tolerance correct. The problematical, possibly self-contradictory liberal formulation of religious freedom discussed in chapters one and four confuses phenomenological realities for institutional ones. It builds the institutional church/state divide on a make-believe phenomenological religion/politics divide. A more institutionally sensitive approach has no trouble acknowledging that religion infiltrates and saturates the public square and that politics is always spiritual, but it asks more precise questions about who has been authorized to do what. It presents religious freedom as a property of the fact that God has not authorized prosecuting false worship. And it locates religious freedom in the field of formal religious institutional affiliation—that is, membership—not in lawmaking, which is impossible. It also seeks to ensure that legal space exists for churches, so that members of every nation might be drawn into the kingdom of God (see 1 Tim 2:1-2).[93]

---

[93] O'Donovan, *Desire of the Nations*, 146.

In short, Christians should consider the competencies and jurisdictional boundaries of Scripture's institutional authorities—what are the state and the church, how do we define the membership of each and what authority does each possess? From there, it is over to wisdom for determining how to best pursue justice in this or that context (see 1 Kings 3:28), and which particular issues fall into the ambit of one or the other or both.

4. The Spirit-given power of the new covenant requires a doctrine of two ages. A doctrine of two ages or inaugurated eschatology is a popular way among New Testament theologians for characterizing how creation history and redemptive history bifurcated when Christ's kingdom was inaugurated but not consummated through the giving of the new covenant. The history of new creation began even while the history of the old creation continued. Oliver O'Donovan helpfully transplants this New Testament conversation into the domain of political theology: "The passing age of principalities and powers has overlapped with the coming age of God's kingdom."[94] In fact, if I were to choose a title for my own political theology, following O'Donovan (sort of) I would call it a "two ages" view.[95]

A doctrine of two ages is diachronic and derives from the Bible's covenantal framework, unlike Luther's two kingdoms, which is synchronic and is built on a logical formulation. The latter begins, biblically enough, with Augustine's two communities, which are divided between those who submit to God and those who do not.[96] But then it places two governments over those two communities, one being the state, the other being the Word and to some measure the church.[97] The formulation is logically tidy, and it has much explanatory power, but it forces a parallel conceptuality that does not

---

[94] Ibid., 211.

[95] O'Donovan places his own views under the broader rubric of the "doctrine of the two," but it appears to me that this essentially culminates in a doctrine of two ages.

[96] Martin Luther writes, "Here we must divide Adam's children, all mankind into two parts: the first belong to the kingdom of God, the second to the kingdom of the world. All those who truly believe in Christ belong to God's kingdom, for Christ is king and lord in God's kingdom," while the rest of humankind belong to the kingdom of this world. Luther, *On Secular Authority*, 8. Luther's term for kingdom (*Reich*) includes the ideas of "ruling" and "what is ruled over." Harro Höpfl, "Glossary," in *Luther and Calvin on Secular Authority*, xxxv-xxxvi. Though see W. D. J. Cargill Thompson's discussion on this point in "'Two Kingdoms,'" 165-67.

[97] Luther: "Every kingdom must have its own laws and . . . no kingdom or government can survive without law." Luther, *On Secular Authority*, 23. That is, a *Reich* needs a *Regiment* (Luther's main term for government). "And so God has ordained the two governments, the spiritual [government] which fashions true Christians and just persons through the Holy Spirit under Christ,

quite fit with Scripture's institutions. The Bible does not exactly parallel God's-people/not-God's-people with church/state or even Word/state. The Bible and church have words for not-God's-people. And the state rules over God's people.

A doctrine of two ages, on the other hand, does not start with a contrast of two governments and the division of a person's life between different domains (spiritual/political, inner/outer); it starts with a contrast between two whole stories or ages, which effectively divides two *kinds* of life right where the Bible divides them—life in the flesh versus life in the Spirit. The key anthropological division, then, is not between the inseparable inner and outer person but between the Pauline "old self" and "new self." And the term to be contrasted with secular is not sacred or spiritual but eternal.[98] One age and its rulers are passing; the other is not. The existential line between the two ages, in fact, is death. Everything to which new covenant renewal has come will pass into eternal life. Everything else, still under the curse, will either pass into death or must be transformed.

Both ages possess a representative head—two individuals who emerge from the Bible's covenantal structure and who typologically correspond to Paul's "old self" and "new self," namely, Adam and Christ. One brings condemnation and death; the other brings justification and life (Rom 5:12-19). Both ages are animated by different powers. One is animated by the Spirit. The other by the world, the flesh and the devil (Eph 2:1-3). And both ages possess their own institutional authorities. The creation age possesses marriage, the family and the state. The eschatological age possesses the church and ordained elders. The institutions of both ages rely on biblically authorized means to accomplish their respective mandates: the state, for instance, relies on the coercive powers of metal and money, while the church relies on Word and the keys of the kingdom.

What's important to recognize, then, is that a doctrine of two ages layers the new creation on top of the old creation so that they are simultaneous. It presents a picture of the whole person (mind and body) living within the

---

and the secular [*weltlich*] government which holds the Unchristian and wicked in check and forces them to keep the peace outwardly and be still, like it or not" (ibid., 10-11).

[98] O'Donovan points to the Latin root of "secular" (*saeculum*) as a reminder that the term refers to an "age," which is to say, something which is passing and not eternal. O'Donovan, *Desire of the Nations*, 211.

legitimate but fallen institutional structures of creation (family, state, etc.), and it simultaneously presents a picture of the whole person, once regenerated, living by the power of the Spirit within the institutional structures of the new creation (church, ordained elders). Indeed, it is because these two ages move simultaneously in the present that the Christian struggle between the old self and the new is so well captured by Luther's formulation *simul justus et peccator*. Christians are capable of acting both according to the flesh and according to the Spirit. This means, further, that activities of the flesh and Spirit will inform the activities of both creation institutions and new creation institutions. Hence, churches remain capable of sinful error, while Christian members of governments will be capable of making Spirit-informed decisions about the course of righteousness and justice. And vice versa.

These institutions of family and state may occupy a different age than the church and its elders. But the present simultaneity of the ages means that God often employs the institutions of one age to serve the institutions of the other, whether in direct or typological fashion. The state exists to provide a platform for the church's work of redemption, while the righteousness and justice of the church serves as a prophetic witness for the state. The love and faithfulness of a Christian husband and wife serve as a symbol of Christ's love for the church, and the elders of a church should present an example of patient instruction for parents. More broadly, we can say that new covenant members still belong to creation and the present age. And so they should submit to the institutions of the present age and employ, when occasion permits, the divinely authorized institutional mechanisms of this present age, like the sword or childbearing, for the purposes specifically given to those institutions.[99]

At the same time, new covenant members anticipate that, upon the consummation of the present age and the full coming of the final age, the institutions of the present age will pass, or at least radically change form.

---

[99] For this reason, I believe an analogy can be drawn between political pacifism and celibacy insofar as both positions trade on the tension between the present age and the eschatological age. There is freedom for the new covenant member to live within the present age by picking up the sword or getting married, or to forsake those entitlements for the sake of the values and ends of the eschatological age. To deny this freedom is to succumb to a kind of Gnosticism and legalism.

Marriage, says Jesus, will not continue beyond the resurrection, as the shadow gives way to the substance (Mt 22:30). And presumably some sort of governance will continue in the final age as the saints share in the rule of Christ (see chapter six), but the rule of the tax-collecting and judgment-imposing goverments of Genesis 9:5-6 and Romans 13 will come to an end, or at least be transformed beyond imagination (see Mt 17:24-27).[100]

At this point, we can reintegrate chapter four's description of how the relationship between the common covenants and the special covenants works. There I argued that God did not employ the common covenants for the purposes of one area of life (culture, politics, morality) and the special covenants for another area of life (religion, worship). Rather, the special covenants served the purpose of setting in motion and modeling what the common covenants required. God's special covenant community was to model the kind of citizenship that God requires of all his subjects within the common covenants. Insofar as O'Donovan's theopolitical construct of the two ages contrasts two whole ages and two whole kinds of lives, the construct rightly maps over this relationship between the common and special covenants. The "new self" models for the "old self" what he or she should be. And the institutions and communities of the eschatological age model true justice and righteousness for the institutions and communities of the passing age. It is for this reason that we can affirm the increasing number of writers who employ the Augustinian method of "juxtaposition" by referring to the church as a "sign," "witness," "outpost" or "contrast society" for the world.[101] The new covenant gives what God asks for in the creation covenant as filled out and illustrated in the Mosaic and Davidic covenants. Furthermore, we can say that the church possesses authority not over "religion" or "the inner/private person" but over the new self as it can be discerned in the whole person. And the state possesses authority not over "politics" or "the outer/public person" but over the old self, again, as it can be discerned in the whole person.

The governments of this world, meanwhile, are thrust into a peripheral role, authorized to keep the peace by rendering judgment against

---

[100]Matthew 17:24-27 concerns the temple tax, but Jesus applies the lesson to the "kings of the earth." See O'Donovan's excellent discussion of this passage in *Desire of the Nations*, 92-93.

[101]See Robert F. Evans, *One and Holy: The Church in Latin Patristic Thought* (London: SPCK, 1972), 118.

transgressors. Caesar must be rendered honor, not because he can accomplish salvation but because he uses the sword of judgment to serve God's greater purposes of providing a space for the gospel to go forth.[102]

**Conclusion.** The new covenant uniquely presents the Spirit's own political program that penetrates the inner person and implants a "yes" to God and the Davidic Son among every member. The result is a body politic that images the Trinity's righteous and just inner life. God's own Spirit presents the solution to the self-enthronement problem exposed by the history of Old Testament Israel. In their best moments, the kingdoms of this world reach for justice and sometimes even offer a glimmer of it. In the new covenant community alone will true righteousness and justice be found.

## POLITICS OF FORGIVENESS

Yet self-enthronement ultimately roots in self-justification, we argued earlier. The latter is the former's legitimation, ground or basis. Not surprisingly, the new covenant not only addresses the self-enthronement problem through the promise of law-inscribed hearts; it also addresses the self-justification problem through the promise of forgiveness and suggests that the latter is the ground of the former. The passage in Jeremiah concludes, "*For* I will forgive their iniquity, and I will remember their sin no more" (Jer 31:34), as if to say God will write his law on their hearts and make them his people *because* he will forgive them.[103]

Forgiveness and self-justification, after all, are mutually exclusive. To justify oneself is to profess that one is just, righteous or acceptable on one's own terms, and that any debts owed or harms rendered are somehow excusable or justified and do not jeopardize one's social or institutional standing.[104] Essentially, the self-enthroned self-justifier adjudges himself

---

[102]O'Donovan, *Desire of the Nations*, 146-57.
[103]This is how Peterson appears to view the passage: "Radical forgiveness is the basis for the promised spiritual and moral transformation of the people." Peterson, *Transformed by God*, 35.
[104]On the distinction between an excuse and a justification, see Jeffrie G. Murphy, *Getting Even: Forgiveness and Its Limits* (New York: Oxford University Press, 2003), 13. Also Kathleen Dean Moore, *Pardons: Justice, Mercy, and the Public Interest* (New York: Oxford University Press, 1989), 11, 142-65. In brief, an excuse acknowledges that an action was wrong but that it can be overlooked due to some further consideration, as with an insanity defense; a justification acknowledges that an action might have been wrong under some circumstances but not under the present circumstances, as with the plea of self-defense.

or herself above reproach, whether the case is personal, religious or legal. To ask for forgiveness, however, is to concede that all such arguments are at an end.

A genuine request for forgiveness is an admission that certain elements of the debt cannot be paid back, or harm cannot be undone, and that one has been unjust toward the injured party.[105] It is a confession that both the injury and the injustice are real and significant. No excuse or justification for the conduct can finally be offered. It is not an "I'm sorry, but" but an "I'm sorry, period." It is, furthermore, an admission that one's guilt has put one at the mercy of either the injured party or a publicly recognized authority for offering a solution to the injury and injustice. To put this concisely, to ask for forgiveness is (1) to admit that retribution is warranted, whether that means punishment, paying reparations or some other way to right the moral imbalance; as well as (2) to express hope for forbearance and a restoration to the status quo ante *based on something external to oneself*, be it the affection and mercy of the judge, the intercession of another party, or some other solution.

To be very clear, then, the request for forgiveness occurs when a person recognizes that he or she has no argument or evidence to bring into the dock to be leveraged for repairing the relationship or balancing the scales of justice. The arguments are over, and something from outside the dock must intercede to sustain the hope for a canceled debt, a reaffirmed relationship or favored standing.[106] One requires—as strange as it sounds to say—an alien justification.[107]

---

[105] I say "certain elements" because in many occasions of harm rendered, reparations can accompany the request for forgiveness. If I have stolen from you, I might be able to pay it back, but that would not negate the need for an apology and forgiveness. Why not? Because there has been a breach of trust that is irreparable apart from an act of forgiveness.

[106] I am using the legal metaphor of a dock loosely, since, of course, a court of law is capable only of a binary rendering: guilty or not guilty. When we transfer the question of reconciliation into the relational or political sphere, more levels of reconciliation become possible. Charles L. Griswold lays out four: resigned acceptance, agreement to end hostilities, affirmation and the agreement to rebuild, or joyful endorsement. Griswold, *Forgiveness: A Philosophical Exploration* (New York: Cambridge University Press, 2007), xxiv-xxv.

[107] I am referring here not to a justification of the conduct, as when we say a certain action was "justified" because it was done in self-defense, but to a justifying of the person in spite of the unjustifiable conduct. See Murphy, *Getting Even*, 13. Though separating the person from the conduct and saying that the person can be "justified" in spite of unjustified conduct might sound like a confusion of categories, I will argue that this is the radical nature of forgiveness that the Bible offers.

It will serve our larger purposes in this chapter and book to spend a few more minutes attempting to understand the concept of forgiveness institutionally. Not only does the new covenant promise God's forgiveness, but Jesus grants his disciples the authority to forgive (Jn 20:23). We therefore need to get a good grasp of what forgiveness means, at least forgiveness for those occasions where a breech of God's law and matters of justice are at stake. Perhaps there are situations within interpersonal relationship where a breech has occurred and forgiveness is called for but no questions of justice are at stake. But our concern here is with forgiveness from a judicial-institutional perspective where God's law is at stake. Institutional thinking, as we saw in chapter two, centers on questions of authority and authorization. So several questions arise here. Who has the authority to forgive? What is the basis of this authority in light of the demands of retributive justice? And what does forgiveness mean in political terms?

***Who has the authority to forgive?*** The first problem to solve is the authority problem: Who has the authority to forgive? The quick answer one finds in much of the philosophical literature is that the injured party, or whomever the injured party authorizes in his or her stead, has the authority to forgive. The injured party has the authority to forgive because the debt of justice belongs to him or her. He or she holds the note on the defaulted loan, so to speak. And the injured party's representative can forgive insofar as the representative has been commissioned to do so, but only within the bounds of the explicit mandate. Should a bank owner commission a bank manager to forgive one particular debt, or one kind of debt, that is how far the manager's authority extends and no farther. So with a president and an ambassador, or a god and his priest.

From a theological perspective, we might say that God is always at least one of the "injured" parties, because it is God's law that is broken. It is his authority that has been challenged. More broadly, we can say that more than one party can be injured with any given act of lawbreaking, say, both the lawmaker and the victim of the crime.

***What is the basis of this authority in light of retributive justice?*** By saying that only the injured party or his or her representative has the authority to forgive, we are making one kind of a claim about justice. We are saying it is just for the injured party to forgive, and it is unjust for an unauthorized third party to forgive a crime, sending the criminal happily on his or her way. But the question of *who* is not the only question of justice at stake. There is also the justice-related question of *how*—specifically, how can the injured party forgive an act of injustice without thereby compromising the principles of retributive justice, where both injured and injurer receive what is due?[108] So even though the injured party alone has the right to forgive, that does not mean it is right for him or her to forgive, especially if doing so risks compromising justice. For instance, suppose we determine that God has the right to forgive one person's crime against another person because all sin is against God. Though God's act of forgiveness is just in the first sense (who), that does not mean we have resolved the question of whether it is just in the second sense (how)—namely, how does God's act of forgiveness not compromise his own standards of justice?

Forgiveness and retributive justice do seem to stand in tension: "Where justice requires the receipt of what is due, forgiveness releases what is due."[109] As the paradigmatic retributionist, Kant, famously put it, "The law concerning punishment is a categorical imperative, and woe to him who rummages around in the winding paths of a theory of happiness looking for some advantage to be gained by releasing the criminal from punishment or by reducing the amount of it."[110] Kant, not surprisingly, generally denounced the practice of political pardons.[111] Though the authority problem, too, depends on a matter of justice, we might refer to this "how" problem as the justice problem of forgiveness.

Of course, not all theorists see justice and forgiveness standing in tension, particularly among those of a postmodern bent. Some reject a retributivist conception of justice.[112] Others speak of forgiveness as transcending

---

[108]For a brief narrative on the loss and recovery of retributivism as a theory of punishment, see Moore, *Pardons*, 47-86.
[109]P. E. Digeser, *Political Forgiveness* (Ithaca, NY: Cornell University Press, 2001), 36.
[110]Immanuel Kant, *The Metaphysical Elements of Justice* (New York: Bobbs-Merrill, 1965), 100. Quoted in Moore, *Pardons*, 29.
[111]Moore, *Pardons*, 28-34.
[112]E.g., Linda Ross Meyer, *The Justice of Mercy* (Ann Arbor, MI: University of Michigan, 2010), argues against Kantian retributivism in order to give mercy priority over such ideas about justice.

retribution. Paul Ricoeur, for instance, argues that "pardon does not belong to the juridical order" but "outruns the law" since it "stems from an economy of the gift." Pardon, he says, "is not just a suprajudicial but a supra-ethical value," meaning it "must first have run into the unpardonable, that is the infinite debt, the irreparable wrong," but then overlooked or gone beyond it.[113] The tit-for-tat logic of retribution, it appears, is simply transcended in Ricoeur's thinking. The bigger picture for Ricoeur is that the gift of God in Christ calls people out of "the logic of equivalence, which is the logic of punishment," and into grace, which is "a logic of surplus and excess" and "an economy of superabundance."[114] Grace transcends or explodes the old economy of law, such that a pardon now "accompan[ies] justice in its effort to eradicate on the symbolic plane the sacred element of justice . . . in virtue of which blood calls for blood."[115] God's grace refuses to answer *lex talionis* on its own terms, as it were, but goes beyond it, and true justice envisions all of this. Similar appeals to the economy of gift as interrupting the economy of law have shown up in a number of writers.[116] I do not intend to pursue this line of thought other than to make two comments, one critical and one appreciative. Critically, it is unclear to me how the notion of desert can be transcended. A person deserves something or not. One can ignore that fact and decide to use gift language or transcendence language. But the question of desert still hangs in the air, demanding an answer, even if Ricoeur himself is unable to imagine how punishment can do anything other than perpetuate the "violence in an infinite chain of crimes" and thus how it can ever be considered just.[117] It is not clear to me that the Bible ever transcends or

---

[113]Paul Ricoeur, "Sanction, Rehabilitation, Pardon," in *The Just*, trans. David Pellauer (Chicago: University of Chicago Press, 2000), 144.

[114]Paul Ricoeur, "Freedom in the Light of Hope," in *The Conflict of Interpretations* (London: Continuum, 2004), 405; see also Ricoeur, "Interpretation of the Myth of Punishment," in *Conflict of Interpretations*, 351-73. Kevin J. Vanhoozer offers a very helpful introduction to these aspects of Ricoeur in "The Atonement in Postmodernity: Guilt, Goats, and Gifts," in *The Glory of the Atonement: Biblical, Historical and Practical Perspectives*, ed. Charles E. Hill and Frank A. James III (Downers Grove, IL: InterVarsity Press, 2004), 376-77, 378, 395-96.

[115]Ricoeur, "Pardon," 145.

[116]See Vanhoozer, "Atonement in Postmodernity," 367-404.

[117]Ricoeur, "Interpretation of the Myth," 360; also Vanhoozer, "Atonement in Postmodernity," 377. Ricoeur's argument, resting as it does on a Hegelian conception of right, lacks the resources for an adequate theory of punishment, a theory that, I believe, can find resources in something analogous to Anselmian conceptions of honor—namely, Edwardsian conceptions of the weightiness of God's glory.

goes beyond the cause-effect relationship of retributive justice, illustrated of course in both the Noahic government charter and in *lex talionis*. Rather, the Bible's perspective on forgiveness does not stand in tension with retributive justice but is grounded in it, as I will argue in just a moment.

Appreciatively, the idea of a gift does capture something right about the spirit of forgiveness. As I said a moment ago, something must come from *outside* the dock to interrupt justice's gavel-pounding verdict. "Intercession" must be made for the transgressors. And of course forgiveness is a gift that produces singing over what someone else has accomplished—as we saw in the relationship between Isaiah 53, 54 and 55.

To stay in Isaiah for a second, why did God's anger have to be removed (Is 54:9)? Why was it "the will of the LORD to crush him" (Is 53:10)? Forgiveness must play by justice's rules.[118] It cannot simply dismiss the judge with a wave of the hand but must give the judge a satisfactory answer.[119] In other words, forgiveness may interrupt the courtroom scene and offer the defendant something that, strictly speaking, she does not deserve, but it must also satisfy the judge's "anger." As such, if there is such a thing as a just act of forgiveness, it will need to act in one respect toward the judge and every injured party and in another respect toward the guilty party. Toward the judge and injured party, a just act of forgiveness must pay the necessary due. Toward the perpetrator, the just act of forgiveness will grant an undeserved gift.[120] How can this possibly be done?

The human courtroom analogy breaks down to some measure when applied to guilty human beings before God because a human judge sits under the law and is distinct from the victim. Yet in the biblical framework God is

---

[118]To say that forgiveness must play by justice's rules is not to say that justice is more fundamental than God's other attributes. Assuming that forgiveness is a property of love, I'm not saying that justice is prior to love in God. I'm just saying that his love is always conditioned by his justice, even as his justice is conditioned by his love. In short, the statement that forgiveness must play by justice's rules should not be understood apart from the doctrine of God's simplicity.

[119]See Moore, *Pardons*, 11, 131-78.

[120]C. S. Lewis: "The essential act of mercy was to pardon; and pardon in its very essence involves the recognition of guilt and ill-desert in the recipient." Lewis, "The Humanitarian Theory of Punishment," in *Essay Collection and Other Short Pieces* (London: HarperCollins, 2000), 698-705, on 704. Also Miroslav Volf: "To forgive is to name the wrongdoing and to condemn it." Volf, *Free of Charge: Giving and Forgiving in a Culture Stripped of Grace* (Grand Rapids: Zondervan, 2005), 129.

judge, victim and law. Typically, criticisms of the doctrine of penal substitutionary atonement miss this point and treat the relationship between the two courtrooms as univocal—e.g., "How can it be just to punish an innocent third party?" But the moral calculation changes when the One who is simultaneously the judge, the victim and the law covenantally identifies with the defendant as his federal representative (also a disanalogy with a human courtroom), which is what a proper doctrine of penal substitution proposes. No doubt, a full understanding of these things backs us into the mystery of both the Trinity and the incarnation[121] and what it means, in Karl Barth's words, for the crucifixion to become "the Judge judged in our place"[122] or what John Stott calls "the self-substitution of God."[123]

**What does forgiveness mean in political terms?** A different kind of complexity shows up when we transpose the matter of forgiveness into a political conceptuality. Since many contemporary theorists more or less tie politics to the public arena and institutions of state, they adopt a concept of forgiveness that mimics the public/private and inner-person/outer-person bifurcations that are part and parcel of both the liberal worldview and a spirituality-of-the-church worldview. A popular philosophical definition of forgiveness, for instance, is the forswearing of resentment, or at least the commitment to forswear resentment.[124] Notice, this definition employs a strict inner/outer anthropology. Forgiveness is treated as an "attitude"[125] or as a "matter of the heart, the inner self, [involving] a change in inner feeling more than a change in external action."[126] Contemporary theorists like this definition because it seems to solve the justice problem. It locates forgiveness in the realm of private or interpersonal relationships and moral sentiments:

---

[121]Though I am uncertain about Bruce McCormack's solution, this is exactly the question he is understandably grappling with in "The Ontological Presuppositions of Barth's Doctrine of the Atonement," in *Glory of the Atonement*, 346-66, see esp. 363-65.

[122]Barth, *Church Dogmatics*, IV/1, 273. On the strengths and weaknesses of Karl Barth's doctrine of the atonement, which Robert Letham calls "a vigorous and ingenious exposition of the penal substitutionary view of the atonement," see Letham, *The Work of Christ* (Downers Grove, IL: InterVarsity Press, 1993), 171-72.

[123]John R. W. Stott, *The Cross of Christ* (Downers Grove, IL: InterVarsity Press, 1986), 133-63; see also Graham Cole, *God the Peacemaker: How Atonement Brings Shalom* (Downers Grove, IL: InterVarsity Press, 2009), 132-41.

[124]Griswold, *Forgiveness*, 42; Murphy, *Getting Even*, 12-16; Martha Minow, *Between Vengeance and Forgiveness: Facing History After Genocide and Mass Violence* (Boston: Beacon Press, 1998), 15.

[125]Moore, *Pardons*, 184.

[126]Murphy, *Getting Even*, 13.

"Forgiveness is primarily about the moral relations and sentiments between X and Y, rather than about the administration of justice. On this view . . . there is no inconsistency between a retributive or consequentialist theory of punishment and interpersonal forgiveness."[127] This seems satisfying to both philosophical liberals and (I would assume) proponents of the church's spirituality because it allows one to forgive and still require justice—to believe that "there is no inconsistency in fully forgiving a person for wrongdoing but still advocating that the person suffer the legal consequence of criminal punishment."[128]

The first problem with this definition is that it relies too much on the inner/outer distinction. It is difficult to envision how one can separate the sentiments of forgiveness from the requisite actions. As one contemporary political thinker observes, "Unless the words are accompanied by the appropriate behavior we shall say that A has not really forgiven B."[129] In other words, it is not at all clear that we can quarantine forgiveness to one side of the inner/outer divide, because, as we have observed several times now, the inner and outer person, though phenomenologically distinguishable, is existentially inseparable. It is true that one citizen might forgive another citizen for an injury done, and yet still allow the state to prosecute the injustice. But that is because the injured citizen and the state stand in different moral and institutional positions relative to the guilty party. They bear different authorities and responsibilities. That I forgive you for burning down my house does not mean that the state can relinquish its grievance with you. In a scenario like this, the state does not forgive at all. It prosecutes. But this simply brings us back to the original question of what forgiveness is, as well as how it can be given justly. Dividing the inner and outer person and placing forgiveness on the inside does not solve the justice problem; it just pushes the lump under the carpet to another place in the room.

A second kind of definition for forgiveness among contemporary political thinkers emphasizes not private sentiment but public action. Admittedly, the language here often changes from forgiveness to "pardon,"[130] but others

---

[127] Griswold, *Forgiveness*, 39.
[128] Murphy, *Getting Even*, 14; also Griswold, *Forgiveness*, 39; Moore, *Pardons*, 187.
[129] R. S. Downie, "Forgiveness," *The Philosophical Quarterly* 15, no. 59 (April 1965): 131.
[130] Moore, *Pardons*, 181-96; see also Downie, "Forgiveness," 131-32. The distinction between forgiveness and pardon only works if you accept the public/private divide in the first place, which

(I think helpfully) refer to a broader category of "political forgiveness."[131] The basic idea is that authorized public entities have the ability to issue a performative or illocutionary word—say, of pardon—a word that is public and efficacious. As it is spoken, the pardon is accomplished.[132] Such an act of "political forgiveness" is "not about clearing the victim's heart of resentment" or making any change in the inner person. Instead, it is "an action that forgives a debt, reconciles the past, and invites the restoration of civil and moral equality of transgressors and their victims or the restoration of a relationship between creditors and debtors to the status quo ante." Indeed, this kind of action can be performed while still harboring bitterness—in the same way that "virtues such as self-control, civility, manners, self-possession, unflappability, and imperturbability, as well as vices such as hypocrisy, two-facedness, insincerity, and phoniness all postulate a capacity to feel one way and act another.... Resentful feelings need not issue in action."[133] Furthermore, distinguishing forgiveness of the heart and a formal act of pardon or public forgiveness, from the state's standpoint, seems anthropologically appropriate since "the soulcraft requirements of a sentiment-based politics rest on a contestable moral psychology that is deeply intrusive and potentially tyrannical."[134]

In spite of its problems, which I will address in a moment, I believe this second definition offers a fuller account of what forgiveness means politically, namely, the restoration of civil and moral equality of transgressors and their victims to the status quo ante. And it helps us think in institutional terms. To restore a transgressor to the status quo ante means, specifically, *reauthorizing the transgressor*. Forgiveness is not simply a removal of debt; it is, by token of the debt removal, a reauthorization. One might think analogously of a prisoner who, upon release from prison, is once more

---

I do not, as discussed above. See also Digeser's critique of the distinction in *Political Forgiveness*, 121-25.

[131] Where Moore distinguishes "forgiveness" and "pardon," P. G. Digeser legitimately critiques this distinction but then turns and adopts a similar distinction by dividing "political forgiveness" from "ordinary forgiveness." Digeser, *Political Forgiveness*, 18-30, 121-125.

[132] As in: "Now therefore I, Gerald R. Ford, President of the United States, pursuant to the pardon power conferred upon me by Article II, Section 2, of the Constitution, have granted and by these presents do grant a full, free, and absolute pardon unto Richard Nixon." Moore, *Pardons*, 193.

[133] Digeser, *Political Forgiveness*, 25.

[134] Ibid., 18, also 25.

granted the ability to vote. This is not to deny that sometimes the process of forgiveness is gradual, and that a "forgiven" person may only be restored to positions of authority little by little. Nor is it to deny that forgiveness is almost always institutionally multifaceted. Gerald Ford may have pardoned Richard Nixon for crimes committed while acting as president. But Ford's pardon reauthorized Nixon only in the capacity of US citizen and not in the capacity of president. This is hard to discern, perhaps, because one wants to say that a pardon is a pardon is a pardon. But when two institutional roles overlap (e.g., citizen, president), it becomes necessary to specify the terms of the pardon institutionally, as in, "such and such word of pardon restores the individual to the office of citizen, but not to the office of president."[135] Such institutional distinctions are typically left unstated. People do not say, "I forgive you in *this* but not *that* institutional capacity." But it remains important to recognize such distinctions for any conceptualization of forgiveness. Once these institutional complexities are accounted for, we can see that debt removal and reauthorization are two sides of the same coin. If a person has not been fully reauthorized, that person's debt has not been fully removed. He or she has not been fully forgiven, at least in the relevant institutional capacity.

It is when we perceive the role that reauthorization plays in forgiveness that we can begin to treat different institutional domains with greater descriptive sensitivity. We might compare, for instance, what forgiveness means within the covenantal institution of marriage and within the contractual institution of a lender/borrower relationship. An act of forgiveness within both kinds of institutions means some of the same things, such as the removal of penalties for transgressions committed. But there are also differences that can be appreciated only when we view the authority framework of each institution specifically. When a financial creditor like a

---

[135]One could multiply examples like this. For instance, a pastor who is removed from office for sexual sin might be forgiven in his capacity as "church member" but not as "pastor." That is to say, a congregation might genuinely "forgive" their errant pastor, such that he remains a member of the church, while simultaneously refusing to accept him as a pastor once more. How is this possible? It is possible because the man had occupied two institutional roles: church member and pastor. The office of church member is grounded in forgiveness/grace/*sola fide*, while the office of pastor is meritocratic and is grounded in exemplary character (e.g., 1 Tim 3:1-7). Hence, the congregation's word of forgiveness can legitimately be applied to the first office while being withheld from the second.

bank forgives a borrower's debt, the act restores lender and borrower to a state of neutrality and, formally, no institutional entanglements. It restores them to a precontract state where they are free to engage in further activity or not. Within the institutional context of marriage, on the other hand, forgiveness restores husband and wife to a state of positive affirmation and institutional entitlement. That is, it restores the marriage covenant and all the responsibilities and rights of that covenant, such as the authority that husband and wife possess over one another's body (see 1 Cor 7:4). Our descriptions of marital forgiveness and marital reconciliation must adapt to one set of institutional specifications, and our descriptions of a bank's forgiveness must adapt to another set. The larger picture here is that our description of forgiveness must adapt to the institutional structures and conceptuality of whatever domain the conversation is placed within. And the key question here is, what authority structures belong to the status quo ante? What must be reauthorized?

Every child in Sunday school knows that being forgiven of sins means not having those sins count against you. It means the debt for transgression is cleared. But this explanation, for our purposes, does not say enough. If the new covenant transpires in the political domain, as I have argued it does, it seems we need to conceptualize the act of forgiveness within the institutional framework of citizenship. Two lessons here are important for our purposes.

1. Political forgiveness restores both the promise of protection (ruled . . . ) and the grant of office ( . . . ruler). Forgiving or restoring a citizen to the status quo ante involves restoring a person to all the protections and benefits of subjecthood *as well as* all the responsibilities and authorities of office. The person is placed under the umbrella of protection that comes with being an upstanding subject, and the person gets a voter's card placed into his or her hand once more, so to speak. No doubt this will prove significant for how we understand forgiveness in redemptive history. If God's people are called to be citizens of his rule, it will be insufficient to simply say that forgiveness involves removing a debt. It will also involve a reauthorization, which aligns with chapter four's definition of salvation: God's authoritative act of affirming a group of people as his citizens—restoring them to himself, to one another and to office.

2. Political forgiveness always involves a vertical and horizontal dimension. If the institutional contexts of marriage and banking yield different outcomes, what can we say about the nature of forgiveness within the institutional context of a political community? In short, the lawmaker's act of forgiveness places the forgiven citizen into a right standing with the lawmaker as well as a right standing with everyone else in that community. Vertical reconciliation brings horizontal reconciliation with it. It is always triangular, involving two bottom points and one top point: the individual, others in the group and the lawmaker. If, then, the new covenant produces a political community, as argued above, then new covenant forgiveness has both vertical and horizontal dimensions. The status quo ante is a covenantally united body of people and its king.

The problem with the second description of forgiveness as it is defined in the political and philosophical literature, like the first description, is that it still bifurcates the inner and outer person; and by granting institutions of state the ability to forgive with the outer person only, it risks making the act of forgiveness either tyrannical or hypocritical. Digeser might be correct to argue that the soulcraft requirements of a sentiment-based politics are potentially tyrannical. But the fact remains that his effectively liberal solution rests the pardon or "political forgiveness" on a possible act of hypocrisy—hardly a stable foundation for living together, as any parent who has *required* his or her child to apologize to a sibling knows only too well.[136] See how long such a forced peace lasts between toddlers! Yet it is no different between states or subgroups within a state.

Ideally, what a body politic needs is both approaches to forgiveness—an inner forswearing of resentment and an outer performative word that removes a debt and restores (or, better, reauthorizes) the parties to the status quo ante. In order to abide in true peace and reconciliation, a body politic needs both the subjective and the objective. The trouble is, combining the two is essentially impossible for the kingdoms of this world. They are incapable of producing true forgiveness on the inside, yet enacting it on the

---

[136]A better definition combining both internal and external anthropological elements is offered by Donald W. Shriver Jr., who writes, "Forgiveness in a political context . . . is an act that joins moral truth, forbearance, empathy, and commitment to repair a fractured human relation." Shriver, *An Ethic for Enemies: Forgiveness in Politics* (New York: Oxford University Press, 1995), 9.

outside through an officially performative word yields a division between what an offended populace wants and what it gets. Parliaments and parties might win a day of favor in the press for their peace treaties and acts of amnesty, but such Band-Aids only provide a temporary solution to the deeper resentments that endure for centuries.

In the context of a fallen world, Jeremiah's, Ezekiel's and Isaiah's promises of a new covenant offer a nonutopian political program that addresses both the inner and outer person. It resolves the objective justice problem since it is grounded in the suffering servant's substitutionary and representative death; it resolves the self-justification problem through an act of forgiveness; and it presents this act as the ground of resolving the self-enthronement problem. All sin is fundamentally against God, meaning it is his role to forgive. Moreover, his promise of forgiveness begins with his inner person: "I will remember their sin no more." And it is enacted with a performative word: "I will forgive their iniquity." Furthermore, his forgiveness is not just a debt clearing; it is a reauthorizing, which is why it is critical that the promise of forgiveness is tied to the regenerative promise of a people who will obey. It is only those who are ruled who can rule.

## Reinvoking Creation's Citizenship Mandate

Read in context, therefore, we find that these new covenant promises come with a reinvocation of Adam and Eve's citizenship mandate, albeit in Abrahamic terms whereby God promises to give what he commanded Adam and Eve to do:

> And he will make you more prosperous and numerous than your fathers. . . . The LORD your God will make you abundantly prosperous in all the work of your hand, in the fruit of your womb and in the fruit of your cattle and in the fruit of your ground. For the LORD will again take delight in prospering you. (Deut 30:5, 9)
>
> I will bring them back to the land that I gave to their fathers, and they shall take possession of it. . . . Again I will build you, and you shall be built. . . . Again you shall plant vineyards . . . the planters shall plant and shall enjoy the fruit. . . . So I will watch over them to build and to plant, declares the LORD. (Jer 30:3; 31:4-5, 28)

> The cities shall be inhabited and the waste places rebuilt. And I will multiply on you man and beast, and they shall multiply and be fruitful. . . . And the land that was desolate shall be tilled. . . . And they will say, "This land that was desolate has become like the garden of Eden." (Ezek 36:10-11, 34-35)

These forgiven citizens, whose renewed hearts are in turn capable of forgiving one another, are called to build, plant and multiply once more, knowing that God himself will fulfill these promises. Adam's citizenship mandate and Abraham's promise will be fulfilled. An even more explicit enunciation of these things occurs in Daniel 7:

> But the saints of the Most High shall receive the kingdom and possess the kingdom forever, forever and ever. . . . The Ancient of Days came, and judgment was given for the saints of the Most High, and the time came when the saints possessed the kingdom. . . .
>
> And the kingdom and the dominion
> and the greatness of the kingdoms under the whole heaven
> shall be given to the people of the saints of the Most High;
> his kingdom shall be an everlasting kingdom,
> and all dominions shall serve and obey him. (Dan 7:18, 22, 27)[137]

No doubt we will need to take care when turning to consider *how* the New Testament says God will fulfill all such promises, particularly if one holds to some form of inaugurated eschatology, whereby God inaugurates but does not consummate the fulfillment of his promises with the first coming of Christ. This is especially a matter of institutional relevance. For instance, do the promises of restored dominion mean the saints possess the power of the sword over the ungodly? And what about the land promises? For our purposes here, the simple point can be made that restoration to God means restoration to being ruled and to ruling. It is part and parcel of being created in God's image, as we saw in chapter three. Under the God of the Bible, the obedient action *is* an authoritative action, which means that restoring a people to obedience *means* restoring them to office. It is only natural then that the prophets would locate the vision of restored rule, which follows a new obedience, within an Edenic-Abrahamic-Davidic framework of land, crops and descendants.

---

[137]Thanks to Jason Hood for drawing my attention to these verses.

## Conclusion

With all this in mind, we can return briefly to the self-enthronement and self-justification conversation. In the text of Jeremiah, group membership within the new covenant begins with an act of forgiveness, and this act of forgiveness is explicitly tied to the end of self-rule. God's law will now be placed in the heart.

What that means is, group membership for God's people in the new covenant can only begin once a person stops making the argument for self-justification. "I," a citizen of the new covenant, belong to the group, not because I am intrinsically righteous or just, but because I own the fact that I am not and that I have been given the gift of forgiveness. Assuming that I forget this fact, and that I begin to think that my standing within the new covenant group depends upon some property within me, the old process will repeat itself: I once more assert my equality with God and my ability to determine right from wrong; I once more begin to rule on my own behalf rather than on his; and in the process I will contradict the grounds of my standing within the group. Forgiveness and obedience within the new covenant society are correlates, just as self-justification and self-enthronement are correlates. Amazingly, every true member of the new covenant society has a new inner person that (1) recognizes its need for forgiveness and (2) desires to obey. We can call the new covenant correlates "two graces," as Calvin had it, or we can refer to them as the two distinct but inseparable sides of one gift of grace.

In short, building a truly just and righteous society in the context of a fallen world either requires the pursuit of immediate justice and perfection now (which is what Christendom in its worst forms sought), or it begins and continually depends upon the genuine sentiment and practice of forgiveness.

What can be said of those within this society who act rightly and for whom there is nothing to forgive in some righteous action? For such an action to be truly righteous, it would need to keep self-justification at bay. Which is to say, a good deed by a new covenant citizen can never take credit for itself (truly a loathsome idea to a self-justifying mindset). Such deeds are always an act of worship whereby glory goes to God, like the moon hearing songs of praise for its light but then redirecting all praise to the sun from whom its light comes.

Once the self-justification and self-enthronement problems are addressed among these citizens of the new covenant, it is not difficult to see how their life together should be characterized by peace, justice and everything else that comes from a right use of authority. To belong is to recognize from the heart, so to speak, that I as the paradigmatic office holder do not deserve to belong or possess office. Yet I also recognize that neither does anyone else belong because of some action or property within them. They belong based on the same act of forgiveness that I have received. Therefore, when other office holders sin against me (assuming a nonperfected state), I must not immediately dismiss or judge them based on a standard that has not been applied to me. Rather, I will recognize that I should apply the same standard to them that has been applied to me. Within one set of institutional restraints, this might call for retributive justice, if God pleases. Within another set, it might call for showing mercy. Institutional specificity becomes dramatically important here, but wisdom is also necessary.

Within this framework, we can begin to see how enemies can begin loving one another. Jesus' command to "love your enemies" will be possible only for a person who is genuinely "poor in spirit" (Mt 5:44, 3). It is also why Jesus, in his parable, revoked the membership of the unforgiving servant who, after being forgiven ten thousand talents by his master, refused to forgive his fellow servant the comparatively tiny one hundred denarii (Mt 18:21-35). The unforgiving servant's actions demonstrated that he still fundamentally operated according to the principles of self-enthronement and self-justification, even if he was only too happy to receive his master's grant of forgiveness (see also Lk 18:14). But this brings us to chapter six.

# The Politics of the Kingdom

THE ARGUMENT OF THIS book, in several sentences, is that the local church and its members constitute a political community that exists according to Jesus' explicit authorization in Matthew 16, 18 and 28. In fact, since it is this authorization that gives the local church existence, we have to say that an essential element of the local church is its political structure, without which there is no local church.[1] The purpose of this political community, then, is to publicly represent King Jesus, display the justice and righteousness of the triune God, and pronounce that all the world belongs to this King. His claim is universal.

Hopefully everything written in chapters one to five has prepared the way for making the central argument of this book in this final chapter, particularly its last section. The term "political" is not just being used analogously, as when one refers to "church politics" or "team politics." Rather, this work has attempted to meet Oliver O'Donovan's challenge by developing a "fuller political conceptuality," one that "pushes back the horizon of commonplace politics and opens it up to the activity of God."[2] Unlike O'Donovan, I have attempted to build that conceptuality upon the Bible's covenantal framework and through the use of institutional language

---

[1] Or we might tweak the phraseology of the Protestant Reformers: where does the local church exist? Answer: wherever Christ's political authority is exercised through preaching and the keys of the kingdom in the public affirmation and declaration of his righteous body politic.

[2] Oliver O'Donovan, *Desire of the Nations: Rediscovering the Roots of Political Theology* (New York: Cambridge University Press, 1996), 2.

provided by recent work in political science. Like O'Donovan, my political theology depends upon a doctrine of two ages.

Making the argument here requires two broad steps that pertain to the theological relationship between the universal and the local church. Step one is demonstrating that the heavenly and eschatological assembly that is called the universal church is a political assembly, an assembly united by the new covenant, by the Spirit, by faith and by the lordship of Christ. Step two is demonstrating that this political assembly is manifested or made visible on planet earth through the exercise of the keys of the kingdom. The local church publicly administers the new covenant. Just as the state is a political institution because it has been authorized by a King to borrow and wield his own sword in the "age of creation" upon rebellious subjects, so the local church is a political institution because it has been authorized by a King to borrow and wield his own office keys for declaring who is and who is not a citizen in the "age of new covenant." The keys become visible in baptism and the Lord's Supper, through which a church enacts a covenant-ratification ceremony for the new covenant. It's how the church "does" the kind of ratification we observe for the Abrahamic covenant in Genesis 15 and 17 or the Mosaic covenant in Exodus 24. This relationship between the universal and local church is not only analogous to the relationship between a Christian's positional and existential righteousness; it is one piece of it. Local church membership, like good works, is the mark, proof, badge or, to use citizenship language, "passport" of a true Christian.

Overall, approaching the doctrine of the church from this perspective will relieve some of the tension between the communal and institutional perspectives highlighted in chapter two. The church's faith and order are not unrelated and separable (see Col 2:5). Rather, "Church order is the social shape of the converting power and activity of Christ, which is present as Spirit."[3]

---

[3] John Webster, "The Self-Organizing Power of the Gospel: Episcopacy and Community Formation," in *Community Formation: In the Early Church and in the Church Today*, ed. Richard N. Longenecker (Peabody, MA: Hendrickson, 2002), 183; cf. Markus Bockmuehl, "Is There a New Testament Doctrine of the Church?" in *Scripture's Doctrine and Theology's Bible: How the New Testament Shapes Christian Dogmatics*, ed. Markus Bockmuehl and Alan J. Torrance (Grand Rapids: Baker Academic, 2008), 43.

To put all this in terms of the New Testament "kingdom" language, I am arguing that Christ's kingdom is presented or made visible in the local church through its use of the keys of the kingdom. The church is not the kingdom; it is an embassy of that kingdom. What is an embassy? It is an institution that represents one nation inside of another nation. It declares its *home nation*'s interests to the *host nation*, and it protects the citizens of the home nation living in the host nation. Embassies do not make people citizens of a home nation, but they do formally affirm who is and who is not a citizen of the home nation, as the US embassy in Brussels did for me when I was living in Belgium and my passport expired. The embassy did not *make me* a US citizen the afternoon I visited it, but it did officially *affirm* my citizenship in a manner that I as an individual citizen do not have the authority to independently affirm. The embassy's affirmation, however, gave me the ability to continue living in a foreign city protected by all the rights and benefits of my citizenship. The local church, likewise, is where Christ's kingdom has a little bit of human "space" (by which I mean members) carved out for it on a host planet, Earth. It is not an embassy representing another nation from across geographic space. It represents another nation from across time—from the future. The local church is an eschatological embassy, institutionally speaking. Christians, who are made citizens by "the converting power and activity of Christ, which is present as Spirit," are formally affirmed as citizens by the local church (given a passport); further, they become church members who possess the joint authority requisite for binding and loosing. That joint authority to bind and loose, which is implicit in the reauthorization of God's performative act of justification and which is made explicit in the keys, is how God's New Testament people reassume Adam's lost mandate to guard God's human "space" against serpentine intruders. Faith and order are distinct but inseparably linked.

## The Politics of Jesus and His People

In this first section and the next two (on Matthew and Paul), I will argue that Jesus Christ came as the new Adam to execute God's kingdom rule through the new covenant in the salvation of God's people, thereby establishing them individually as God's citizens and corporately as his model body politic before the nations. To unpack this statement with the concepts and distinctions of the last few chapters, we can borrow the title of N. T. Wright's book *How God Became King* and elongate it. A more institutionally precise (and far less marketable) version would be, "How God Executed His Kingship by Becoming the Perfect Human King." God has always been king by right of creation. At no point in human history did God "become" King per se; he always was and is King, and human rebellion has never changed this, as we discussed at length in chapter four. The God of the Bible did, however, withdraw many of the visible signs of his rule after Adam and Eve's first sin. The story of biblical history, then, is the story of God gradually making his rule visible once more through the Bible's covenantal program, beginning with the colorful bow of war aimed heavenward. Each major covenant represents not the complete revelation or execution of God's rule but a partial revelation and execution of it. The divine King will move his arm and then ensure that the right people see it moving. With the coming of Christ he showed the world what the perfect human king looks like.[4] God's arm moved with Christ's first coming more to save than to judge (a slight oversimplification). Jesus Christ, as the new Adam, manifested God's rule through the prophetically promised new covenant by saving God's people, the church. Specifically, he fulfills these prophetic promises by

- declaring that the nations belong to him,
- forgiving once-rebellious subjects by offering a new covenant in his blood,
- installing them as citizens within his regime,
- tasking them with displaying the heavenly Father's righteousness and justice in their political life together before the onlooking nations, and
- granting them his Spirit to these ends.

Especially in the section on Paul I hope to demonstrate how the New Testament's concept of forgiveness actually entails the second, third and

---

[4]Jason Hood writes, "What is new about God's kingdom when Jesus is enthroned is not that God is on the throne in a new way, but that *a human is finally enthroned with him*. . . . Even if God was not always recognized or honored as King over all, he retained his sovereignty. Through Jesus, however, a human is now enthroned over all according to God's original plan for his world." Hood, *Imitating God in Christ: Recapturing a Biblical Pattern* (Downers Grove, IL: InterVarsity Press, forthcoming), chap. 5 (italics original). See also Dan G. McCartney, "*Ecce Homo*: The Coming of the Kingdom as the Restoration of Human Vicegerency," *Westminster Theological Journal* 56 (1994): 1-21.

fourth bullet points. That is, it follows both chapter five, which defined political forgiveness as forswearing resentment and restoring a person to the status quo ante, a disposition and an act which involves removing a debt, reauthorizing the office, and reconciling the person to the body politic in triangular fashion (using the three points of individual, king and others); and chapter four, which defined salvation as God's authoritative action of affirming a group of people as his citizens—a people restored to him and to an office, a vocation and an ethic. Here, however, the Pauline concept of justification by faith alone comes into blossom as the flower of forgiveness that solves the self-justification and self-enthronement problems, thereby yielding a united and loving body politic. Ethnicity does not divide humans, nor do riches, strength, beauty, good works or anything else. Self-justification is the divider. The self-justifying person employs ethnicity, riches, strength, beauty, good words and other such worldly categories in order to put him- or herself above others and even above God (see Jer 9:23-24).

*Jesus.* We start with Jesus. The New Testament declares Jesus to be the new Adam, the offspring of Abraham, the true Israel and the son of David who will rule over Yahweh's new covenant body politic. He is installed not as head over a voluntary organization like a bowling league or a book club. Instead, he is established as a king over a kingdom, a New Testament term which specifies those places where God's universal political rule is becoming visible both in salvation and judgment.[5]

This activity is set within the covenantal storyline that began in the Garden and moves through Noah, Abraham, Moses and David and then culminates in the new covenant. Israel, we recall from chapter four, was to be a corporate Adam and son of God tasked with fulfilling Adam's mandate. The king of Israel, then, was supposed to embody and represent Israel in himself and in that sense fulfill Adam's mandate on behalf of a whole people.

---

[5]See discussion of kingdom in chapter four and of two ages in chapter five. Also, Richard Bauckham transposes chapter five's discussion of the two ages into the framework of the Gospels when he writes, "The kingdom of God in Jesus' teaching is both present and future." The coming eschatological age when God's rule will be universally visible has broken into the present and been put on display now in Jesus' "works of divine power, overcoming evil, sickness and death, and in his acts of divine grace, forgiving sins and welcoming the outcasts into God's presence." Richard Bauckham, "Kingdom and Church According to Jesus and Paul," *Horizons in Biblical Theology* 18 (1996): 7. To Bauckham's list of where God's rule is displayed I would add the righteousness of Christ's people.

But now, in Jesus, the fulfillment of all these promises and types comes. Jesus is "the son of David, the son of Abraham" (Mt 1:1). He is the true Israel (Mt 2:15) and the king of Israel (Mt 27:42; Jn 12:13), whom great David called "my Lord" (Ps 110:1; Mt 22:44; Acts 2:34; Heb 1:13; etc.). "To put it simply," says N. T. Wright, "the role traditionally assigned to Israel had devolved on to Jesus Christ. Paul now regarded him, not Israel, as God's true humanity."[6]

It is not difficult to see the theologically rich typological connection between Adam and Jesus on the pages of the New Testament. Luke's genealogy of Jesus begins with Jesus' name; it includes "son of David," "son of Jacob [Israel]" and "son of Abraham," and it concludes with "the son of Adam, the son of God" (Lk 3:23-38). In the very next passage, this son of David and son of God obeys God perfectly by resisting the Edenic serpent in the Sinai-like wilderness for forty days (Lk 4:1-13). In so doing, he recapitulates both Adamic creation history and Mosaic redemptive history. Paul explicitly names Jesus as "the last Adam" (1 Cor 15:45) and places Adam at the head of one federal administration and Jesus at the head of another (Rom 5:12-19).

What is important to observe for our purposes is that the New Testament's typological connection between Adam and Christ involves more than Christ's perfect obedience to the law in the face of satanic temptation. It also involves Christ's positive fulfillment of Adam's citizenship mandate (Gen 1:28), a point that should not be divorced too far from the elaboration of Adam's mandate that occurs through the covenants with Abraham, Moses and David. But to pull them apart temporarily, one might borrow the legal theorist's language to say Jesus not only kept God's *mandatory* Mosaic rules but also fulfilled God's *power-conferring* Adamic rules. And this helps us to perceive an even deeper lesson: for as much as Christians want to emphasize the fact that Jesus' rule represents God's rule in the Gospels, his occupancy and fulfillment of the Old Testament covenantal offices also draws our eyes to his humanity. His rule is the perfect Adamic rule and therefore a truly human rule. Gregory Beale has captured this theme especially well. "Christ came," he writes, "to subdue and rule, to multiply and create and to fill, and to rest in the way that God originally designed that humanity should have

---

[6]N. T. Wright, *Climax of the Covenant* (Minneapolis: Fortress, 1992), 26. Cf. Seyoon Kim's critique of Wright on this point in *Paul and the New Perspective: Second Thoughts on the Origin of Paul's Gospel* (Grand Rapids: Eerdmans, 2002), 192-94.

done in the first place."⁷ In other words, Jesus is the God-man, and it is hard to talk long about one nature without talking about the other.

How did Jesus fulfill the Adamic citizenship mandate? The short answer is, by his life, death and resurrection. In his life, he anticipated a complete dominion over creation in everything from taming wild animals (Mk 1:13; cf. Ps 91:11-13; Is 11:1-9) to binding the satanic strong man (Mk 3:27) to walking in perfect submission to the heavenly Father (Jn 5:30; 5:19; 8:28; 12:49; 14:10)—all activities that Adam should have performed in the Garden in the face of serpentine intrusions.⁸ In his death, he produced not children of the flesh but "offspring" of the promise (Is 53:10; Rom 4:16; 9:7-8; Gal 3:29; cf. Mt 3:9), who themselves, through his one righteous act, will "reign in life" (Rom 5:17). In his resurrection, he became the "firstfruits," anticipating the day when he "delivers the kingdom to God the Father after destroying every rule and every authority and power" and "will also be subjected to him who put all things in subjection under him, that God may be all in all" (1 Cor 15:23-28).⁹

Jesus is the Adamic ruled ruler par excellence, whose kingdom brings heaven and earth into congruence (see Mt 6:10).¹⁰ The God-man came to rule as God *and* as man.¹¹ Paul therefore affirms that Jesus is the perfect image of God and ties this directly to his rule: Christ is "the image of the

---

⁷Gregory K. Beale, *A New Testament Biblical Theology: The Unfolding of the Old Testament in the New* (Grand Rapids: Baker Academic, 2011), 386, also 479; see also Beale, *The Temple and the Church's Mission: A Biblical Theology of the Dwelling Place of God* (Downers Grove, IL: InterVarsity Press, 2004), 171-76; Graham A. Cole, *God the Peacemaker: How Atonement Brings Shalom* (Downers Grove, IL: InterVarsity Press, 2009), 103-18, esp. 118-19. Cf. Jonathan Pennington, *Heaven and Earth in the Gospel of Matthew* (Grand Rapids: Baker Academic, 2009), 211-16.

⁸I confess that it becomes difficult to distinguish which of Jesus' acts are meant to point us to his human nature and which point to his divine nature. I have chosen several examples that seem to emphasize the human, but what should we do with his calming of storms, raising of the dead and so forth? These strike me as pointing to the divine. In short, a balanced Christology must maintain both human and divine natures, and it seems reasonable to think that the Gospel writers mean for us to keep our eyes on both, sometimes with one emphasis, sometimes with the other.

⁹Beale, *New Testament Biblical Theology*, 261-62, 438-41, 479.

¹⁰Beale says, "The kingdom in the Synoptics is linked conceptually with the original kingly purpose of Adam, who would reflect God and his rule on earth as a faithful vice-regent" (ibid., 427).

¹¹N. T. Wright gets at the same point in a roundabout way by emphasizing Jesus' self-awareness of his *vocation* to usher in the rule of Yahweh: "[Jesus] believed himself called, by Israel's god, to *evoke* . . . to *enact* . . . and thereby to *embody* YHWH's return." Wright, *Jesus and the Victory of God* (Minneapolis: Fortress, 1996), 651. I do think Wright might press Christ's lack of divine self-awareness too far (see ibid., 653).

invisible God" (Col 1:15; cf. 2 Cor 4:4; Heb 1:3). All things were created by him, including "thrones or dominions or rulers or authorities," but it is as the incarnate new Adam that he becomes "the beginning, the firstborn from the dead" and "preeminent" (Col 1:16-18).[12] Jesus ushered in a new creation, and the very idea of a new creation, like the old creation, comes bearing the promise and mandate of Adamic rule. And the new creation kingdom Jesus came to establish is a nation filled with such heavenly citizens.

**Church.** What then is the church universal? The many metaphors for the church in the New Testament provide a rich source of identification and description: temple, vineyard, bride, assembly, body, household, sheep, family—the list is long.[13] Moreover, certain metaphors will come in vogue for a time, only to be replaced by another a decade or two later. Veli-Matti Kärkkäinen characterizes the Roman Catholic Church, for instance, as having moved back and forth between *people of God* and *body of Christ*, each one bringing with it a host of polity implications and potential misuses.[14] It has been popular among systematic theologians in the last few decades to argue that a doctrine of the church must have trinitarian foundations, by which they often have in mind the immanent Trinity.[15] I, too, could affirm this idea, depending on what one means. I argued in chapter three that all political society should reflect the community of the triune Godhead.

The project here, however, is to build a political doctrine of the church *through* biblical theology, which is to say, through Scripture's covenantally structured storyline as it centers on the person and work of

---

[12]Beale, *New Testament Biblical Theology*, 443-49.

[13]For a fairly exhaustive list of images for the church, see Paul S. Minear, *Images of the New Testament Church* (Philadelphia: Westminster, 1960).

[14]Veli-Matti Kärkkäinen, *An Introduction to Ecclesiology: Ecumenical, Historical and Global Perspectives* (Downers Grove, IL: InterVarsity Press, 2002), 26-38.

[15]Miroslav Volf writes, "Today, the thesis that ecclesial communion should correspond to trinitarian communion enjoys the status of an almost self-evident proposition." Volf, *After Our Image: The Church as the Image of the Trinity* (Grand Rapids: Eerdmans, 1998), 191. A classic statement can be found in the Vatican II document *Lumen Gentium*, which describes the church (quoting from Cyprian) as "a people made one with the unity of the Father, the Son and the Holy Spirit." *Vatican Council II*, ed. Austin Flannery, vol. 1, *The Conciliar and Post Conciliar Documents*, new rev. ed. (Northport, NY: Costello, 1996), 352 (chap. 1, para. 4). Many other sources could be cited, from John Zizioulas's *Being as Communion* to the works of Colin Gunton, where it surfaces again and again; see esp. "The Church on Earth: The Roots of Community," in *On Being the Church: Essays on the Christian Community*, ed. Colin E. Gunton and Daniel W. Hardy (Edinburgh: T&T Clark, 1989), 48-80. Kevin Giles provides a helpful summary of the landscape in *What on Earth Is the Church?* (London: SPCK, 1995), 212-29.

Jesus Christ. Jesus came to fulfill the previous covenants and make God's kingdom's visible among a people, all of which he did by offering a new covenant in his blood. A doctrine of the church that is sensitive to the redemptive storyline might therefore want to begin with Jesus' covenant and Jesus' kingdom.[16] The church may be baptized into the names of the Trinity, but, indeed, it must be *baptized*—Christologically identified—into those names.

After declaring God's kingdom, Christ did something a little more personal. The king went to his death as a representative substitute for sinners. He offered a new covenant and sealed it with his blood. With this act, he joined a people to himself as fellow heirs and vice-regents. Exactly how does this covenant unite a people to Christ?[17] There are many things we could say about the church's union with Christ, beginning with the idea of federal headship whereby "all he has done for me representatively," observes Sinclair Ferguson, "becomes mine actually."[18]

***Recommissioned in Adam's office.*** For our purposes here, we are interested in the fact that the church identifies with Christ in his Adamic office, and that the church is deputized as possessing a renewed Adamic commission. Just as Adam played the role of Everyman and federal head, meaning that all humanity received the commission given to him, so Christ plays the role of second Everyman and second federal head for a new humanity (see Rom 5:12-19). If, then, Adam's office transmits to Christ, it would seem that the same office likewise transmits to Christ's people. Greg Beale observes,

---

[16] E.g., Everett Ferguson's *The Church of Christ: A Biblical Ecclesiology* (Grand Rapids: Eerdmans, 1996); Gregg R. Allison, *Sojourners and Strangers: The Doctrine of the Church* (Wheaton, IL: Crossway, 2012).

[17] On union with Christ generally, see Robert Letham, *Union with Christ: In Scripture, History and Theology* (Phillipsburg, NJ: P&R, 2011), esp. 57-83; J. Todd Billings, *Union with Christ: Reformation Theology and Ministry for the Church* (Grand Rapids: Baker Academic, 2011), 107-9; Anthony A. Hoekema, *Saved by Grace* (Grand Rapids: Eerdmans, 1989), 54-67; John Murray, *Redemption Accomplished and Applied* (Grand Rapids: Eerdmans, 1955), 161-73. Cf. Mark Seifrid, "In Christ," in *Dictionary of Paul and His Letters*, ed. Gerald. F. Hawthorne, Ralph P. Martin and Daniel G. Reid (Downers Grove, IL: InterVarsity Press, 1993), 433-36.

[18] Sinclair B. Ferguson, *The Holy Spirit*, Contours of Christian Theology, ed. Gerald Bray (Downers Grove, IL: InterVarsity Press, 1996), 109; see also Robert Letham, *The Work of Christ*, Contours in Christian Theology, ed. Gerald Bray (Downers Grove, IL: InterVarsity Press, 1993), 75-87; Seifrid, "In Christ," 433-36.

It is important to recall that Jesus's titles "Son of Man" and "Son of God" reflect respectively both the OT figures of Adam and Israel. This is because . . . Adam and Israel are two sides of one coin. Israel and its patriarchs were given the same commission as was Adam in Gen. 1:26-28. . . . The church is also identified with what it means to be the true Adam, especially in its identification with Jesus, the true Israel and last Adam.[19]

Just as the church receives Christ's righteousness, so the church receives Christ's perfect Adamic sonship. All Christians are declared and named "sons" of God and the new humanity (e.g., 2 Cor 5:17; Gal 3:26, 4:6; cf. 6:16). This is our *identity* by virtue of the new covenant and new birth. And just as the church "puts on" Christ's righteousness, so the church "puts on" Adam's political and priestly vocation. This is our *authority* and *work*, again, by virtue of the new covenant and new birth. This combination of identity, work and authority is nothing other than an office, and it is an office for every Christian. Scripture, by referring to Christians as "sons" and "born again" and "new creations," commission every saint to occupy the office of priest-king with Christ.[20]

In chapter three we observed that Adam's office of priest-king had a structural aspect as well as inward and outward activities. Structurally, Adam was to represent or image God. Inwardly, he was to watch over the Garden since it was where God dwelled, keeping it consecrated to God and free of serpents. Outwardly, he was to work the Garden and push back the borders of Eden. The office occupied by every Christian can be construed in the same way. There is a structural aspect of imaging or representing Christ. There is an outward activity of witnessing, expanding or cultivating Christ's kingdom. And there is the inward activity of guarding, protecting or consecrating that kingdom life. Christians witness or cultivate the kingdom life through evangelism, pursuing good deeds and working as unto Christ in everything. And they guard or protect the kingdom life by seeking holiness in their own lives and in the lives of their fellow saints (in the church, we will see). In short,

---

[19]Beale, *New Testament Biblical Theology*, 652, 653.
[20]Yet Malcolm Yarnell's caution here is worth noting: "The Christian priesthood is not a participation in the unique priesthood of Christ, for that entails the offering of propitiatory sacrifice, a sacrifice effective for the removal of sin. . . . We do not share in his priesthood; he makes us a priesthood." Yarnell, "The Priesthood of Believers," in *Restoring Integrity in Baptist Churches*, ed. Thomas White, Jason B. Duesing and Malcolm G. Yarnell III (Grand Rapids: Kregel, 2008), 241.

Christians should push back the boundaries of the garden while keeping serpents out. Beale therefore calls Genesis 1:26-28 the first "Great Commission," and he refers to Matthew 28:18-20 as a "renewal of the Gen. 1:26-28 commission to Adam,"[21] a point we will consider further below.

Christians typically recognize that they will one day reign: Christ "made them a kingdom and priests to our God, and they shall reign on the earth" (Rev 5:10; 1:6; cf. 1 Cor 6:1; 2 Tim 2:12; Rev 22:5; cf. Mt 19:28; Rev 20:6). What all this will look like in the eschaton institutionally and jurisdictionally may be left to the imagination. The present institutional arrangements of Christ's kingdom, after all, *do not look like* a kingdom. Rather, "the political character of the church, its essential nature as a governed society, is hidden, to be discerned by faith as the ascended Christ who governs it is to be discerned by faith." When the church "asserts from its midst a ruling entity to act on Christ's behalf, matching the claims of secular rulers with counterclaims," it compromises itself.[22]

Still, ruling and mediating in the office of priest-king begins among Christ's kingdom citizens now. Hence, Paul tells one church that their "citizenship [*politeuma*] is in heaven" (Phil 3:20; cf. 3:9).[23] And this, he told them earlier in the letter, means they should "live as citizens [*politeuesthe*] worthy of the gospel" (Phil 1:27, my translation).[24] As Oliver O'Donovan observes, "the future age now has a social and political presence."[25] It is a renewal of the vocation that all humanity has had since the beginning: to image or represent God by obeying him. Godly obedience reveals the law of God, and therefore the character of God, and therefore God. Godly obedience is divine mimicry, and it reveals the one being mimicked. In other words, Christian obedience now *is* an exercise of the dominion that God intended for Adam at the very beginning *and* a manifestation and foretaste of the consummated dominion that Christ and his people will enjoy at the end of history. O'Donovan captures the authority/subject principle at play:

---

[21]Beale, *New Testament Biblical Theology*, 57, 390-91, 423.
[22]O'Donovan, *Desire of the Nations*, 166.
[23]See Gordon D. Fee, *Paul's Letter to the Philippians*, New International Commentary on the New Testament (Grand Rapids: Eerdmans, 1995), 378-80.
[24]See Walter Bauer, F. W. Danker, W. F. Arndt and F. W. Gingrich, *A Greek-English Lexicon of the New Testament and other Early Christian Literature*, 3rd ed. (Chicago: University of Chicago Press, 2000), 846; also Fee, *Paul's Letter to the Philippians*, 161-63.
[25]O'Donovan, *Desire of the Nations*, 158.

To be *in* authority you have to be *under* it, and if you are under it you are in it. To be subject to authority is to be *authorised*. In that Jesus exercises the powers of God's Kingdom, he shows himself subject to that kingdom. So God's Kingdom is made known by a true subject of that Kingdom, wholly under God's authority, wholly authorised to act in God's name.[26]

Just as Christ's subjection to God's rule demonstrates something of his authority, so does the subjection of Christ's people. The church, as members of the new covenant through their union with Christ, is placed into Adam's original office of priestly king. This is what it means to be citizens of Christ's kingdom.

In conclusion, the church is the people of the new covenant and the people of the kingdom. "The rule of God [the kingdom] comes to persons when Jesus forgives their sins."[27] He covenantally unites people to himself by his Spirit so that they too would inherit the earth like Adam, bear a great name and be a blessing like Abraham, enter God's rest like Israel, and rule together with Christ like David. He makes all priest-kings.

### Matthew (Part 1): A Heavenly Citizenship

Since we will zero in on Matthew's ecclesial passages later in the chapter, it is worth examining this Adamic theme of covenant fulfillment at closer range in Matthew, particularly as it overlaps with four other themes, namely, the heaven and earth dynamic, regime change, the new covenant and righteousness.

***Covenantal fulfillment.*** Matthew begins with a genealogy that places an overt focus on Jesus as fulfilling the promises given to Abraham and David—"The book of the genealogy of Jesus Christ, the son of David, the son of Abraham" (Mt 1:1). Yet Matthew's Jewish readers might have been able to discern one more covenant head who is at least implicit in this opening passage—Adam. Matthew's words "The book of the genealogy" (*biblos geneseōs*) echo the Greek translation of Genesis 2:4 and 5:1-2,[28] the latter of which refers back to Genesis 1:26-28. Here then in the first verse of the New

---

[26]Ibid., 90.
[27]Ferguson, *Church of Christ*, 36.
[28]See Dale Allison, "Matthew's First Two Words," in *Studies in Matthew* (Grand Rapids: Baker, 2005), 157-62.

Testament, at least implicitly, is the fulfillment of the old Adam's story, as well as the beginning of a new Adam's story, one from whom true dominion and image-bearing children would come.[29] More explicit are the Adamic elaborations—the reader knows Jesus is the new Adam *because* he is Abraham's seed and David's son.

One chapter later, wise men from the nations come asking for the "king of the Jews," perhaps an allusion to the international reach of the Abrahamic blessing (Mt 2:1-2). This episode is followed by the Hosean prophecy, "Out of Egypt I called my son" (Mt 2:15; Hos 11:1), which invokes Israel's sonship (Ex 4:22-23) and, behind it, Adam's (Gen 5:1-3). In general, the term "son of God" in the Synoptic Gospels bears a number of resonances that point in the direction of a higher Christology, but the term also roots in "the OT and Jewish background of Adam and Israel being conceived to be God's son."[30] The Messiah was to be a Davidic son, and the Davidic son, who represented Israel, was a kind of son of God (Ps 2:2; also Lk 3:23-38).[31]

Jesus also claims to fulfill the Law and the Prophets (Mt 5:17), a claim that includes more than the Mosaic covenant but not less. No doubt discussion of this topic is complicated, requiring nothing less than a "scribe who has been trained for the kingdom of heaven" and "who brings out of his treasure what is new and what is old" (Mt 13:52). Gratefully, Jesus himself undertakes this task by drawing out points of continuity and discontinuity (Mt 5:21-48).[32] The gist is that "Jesus 'fulfilled' the 'Law' and 'the Prophets' by fulfilling in his actions and words the OT's direct verbal prophecies, foreshadowing events (e.g., the Passover Lamb) and institutions (e.g., sacrifices and temple), the ultimate meaning of the law, and the true and enduring authority of the

---

[29]D. A. Carson, "Matthew," in *Matthew and Mark*, ed. Tremper Longman III and David E. Garland, rev. ed., Expositor's Bible Commentary 9 (Grand Rapids: Zondervan, 2010), 86; Beale, *New Testament Biblical Theology*, 388-90; see also W. D. Davies and Dale C. Allison, *The Gospel According to Saint Matthew*, vol. 1, *Matthew 1–7* (Edinburgh: T&T Clark, 1988), 150; R. T. France, *The Gospel of Matthew*, New International Commentary of the New Testament (Grand Rapids: Eerdmans, 2007), 28; Pennington, *Heaven and Earth*, 212-15; N. T. Wright, *The New Testament and the People of God* (Minneapolis: Fortress, 1992), 385.

[30]Beale, *New Testament Biblical Theology*, 403.

[31]Thomas R. Schreiner, *New Testament Theology: Magnifying God in Christ* (Grand Rapids: Baker, 2008), 234-40.

[32]On the need for both continuity and discontinuity, see Carson, "Matthew," 174-77; Schreiner, *New Testament Theology*, 625-28.

OT."[33] He is the Lord of the Sabbath (Mt 12:8) and, we might say, the Lord of the covenant.

One last significant Matthean moment of covenantal fulfillment is worth observing. After Peter confesses that Jesus is the "Christ," which is to say, the son of David, this son of David promises to build his church and says that the "gates of hell [or Hades]" will not prevail against it (Mt 16:18). Jesus may have had a number of references in mind with the phrase "gates of Hades,"[34] but it seems possible that he also had the Abrahamic promise in mind: "I will surely bless you, and . . . multiply your offspring. . . . And your offspring shall possess *the gate of his enemies*, and in your offspring shall all the nations of the earth be blessed" (Gen 22:17-18). We saw in chapter four that this Abrahamic promise was in turn built upon the original citizenship mandate of Genesis 1:28. If these links are legitimate,[35] it would seem that Matthew 16, this archetypal charter for the church, offers a fairly explicit connection between the son of David and the blessed dominion of Abraham and Adam.

***Heaven and earth.*** Amidst all these words of covenantal fulfillment in Matthew another theme emerges: the dynamic between heaven and earth, or the kingdom of heaven and the kingdoms of this world.[36] The word "heaven" and the phrase "kingdom of heaven" in Matthew's Gospel do not represent the place people go when they die or a reverential Jewish circumlocution; respectively, they represent God's domain and the domain of his rule.[37] Genesis 1:1, of course, represents heaven and earth existing in harmony under God's rule, but Matthew places them in tension:[38]

---

[33] Beale, *New Testament Biblical Theology*, 805; for a full explanation, see Carson, "Matthew," 172-79.

[34] For a good discussion of this phrase, see Davies and Allison, *Gospel According to Saint Matthew*, 630-34; Ulrich Luz, *Matthew 8-20*, trans. James E. Crouch, Hermeneia (Minneapolis: Fortress, 2001), 363-64.

[35] Admittedly, I have not read anyone else who has made this connection. (Perhaps Carson? See "Matthew," 420.) Hence, I present it merely as a possibility.

[36] Jonathan Pennington has helpfully identified this as a major theme in Matthew. The word occurs eighty-two times in Matthew, eighteen in Mark, thirty-five in Luke, eighteen in John, twenty-one in the Pauline epistles and fifty-two in Revelation. Pennington, *Heaven and Earth*, 125.

[37] Pennington, *Heaven and Earth*, 13-37, 193-216, 279-330. A brief version of Pennington's argument can be found in Pennington, "The Kingdom of Heaven in the Gospel of Matthew," *Southern Baptist Journal of Theology* 12 (Spring 2008): 44-51.

[38] Pennington, *Heaven and Earth*, 7, 84, 199-202.

- Jesus and his disciples must pray that God's will would be done on earth as it is in heaven (Mt 6:10).
- He tells them not to store up their treasures on earth, where moth and rust destroy, but to store up their treasure in heaven, where moth and rust don't (Mt 6:19-20).
- He tells the region of Capernaum that they would not be exalted to heaven but brought down to Hades (Mt 11:23).
- And he tells his listeners not to call any person on earth "father," since they have one Father who is in heaven (Mt 23:9).

Yet the tension will not last forever. The domains of God and man will be reconciled in the eschatological age since God remains king over all (see Mt 11:25; 24:35; also 5:18).[39] Hence,

- Jesus claims that the kingdom of heaven is at hand in his ministry (Mt 3:2; 4:17).
- He professes to know who will both receive the kingdom of heaven and inherit the earth (Mt 5:3, 5).

Furthermore, Jesus, this son of David and Abraham, represents heaven on earth from the beginning of his earthly ministry to the end of it:

- His ministry begins when "a voice from heaven [says], 'This is my beloved Son, with whom I am well pleased'" (Mt 3:17; cf. 17:5), which is immediately confirmed when the tempter offers Jesus "all the kingdoms of the world and their glory," but Jesus resists (Mt 4:8, 10).
- His ministry ends with the heavenly Father giving him all authority for what he has accomplished: "All authority in heaven and on earth has been given to me" (Mt 28:18),[40] words that echo the Septuagint's version of Daniel 7, where it is said of the son of man, "Authority was given to him, and all the nations of the earth . . . [were] serving him."[41] The Danielic son

---

[39]Ibid., 209-11.
[40]Pennington argues that Matthew builds an *inclusio* between Genesis 1:1 and Matthew 28:16-20, with Matthew 1:1 offering a strong pointer that this is Matthew's intention. Pennington, *Heaven and Earth*, 215-16.
[41]Beale, *New Testament Biblical Theology*, 390; Pennington, *Heaven and Earth*, 292; France, *Gospel of Matthew*, 1112-13. In addition to the Danielic son of man theme, France sees the messianic and Davidic theme at work in the final verses of Matthew. He writes, "Here at the end of the

of man possessed authority as Adam should have, as demonstrated by his rule over the sea beasts in Daniel 7, pointing back to the promise to Abraham (Gen 22:17-18) and, finally, to Adam's rule over sky, land and sea.[42]

Yet not only does Jesus represent the Father in heaven; he calls out a people who are to do the same:

- Immediately after proclaiming that the kingdom of heaven was at hand in his ministry, he begins to form a community around himself by calling his first disciples and giving them a vocation—to be fishers of men (Mt 4:17, 19).

- He observes, "All things have been handed over to me by my Father, and no one knows the Son except the Father, and no one knows the Father except the Son and anyone to whom the Son chooses to reveal him" (Mt 11:27).[43]

- He tells his disciples that the secrets of the kingdom of heaven have been given to them (Mt 13:11).

- And he gives the apostles and the local church the authority to bind on earth what will be bound in heaven and loose on earth what will be loosed in heaven (Mt 16:19; 18:18-19).

In short, Matthew's Gospel is preoccupied with the question of who on earth has the authority to represent heaven. Who holds this office? Jesus, the new Adam and Lord of the covenant, does. And his followers do.

***Regime change.*** This brings us directly to a third theme worth observing, a dramatic once-in-history change of regime, a change indicating not so

---

gospel, then, we find the culmination of the theme of kingship which was introduced by the Davidic royal genealogy (1:1-17), developed in the magi's search for the 'king of the Jews' and the political threat to Herod in ch. 2, adumbrated in the developing language of Messiahship." France, *Gospel of Matthew*, 1113.

[42]Daniel 7:13-14, Beale observes, "is among a number of other reiterations ultimately of the Adamic commission, though most directly an allusion to the Gen. 22:17-18 prophecy of an end-time king in Abraham's line, which is also one of the Adamic reiterations" (Beale, *New Testament Biblical Theology*, 400; also 51, 83-84, 394-400). Throughout the Synoptic Gospels, says Beale, the "application of the Dan. 7 'Son of Man' to Jesus . . . carries with it echoes of the Adamic eschatological rule" (ibid., 400). Cf. Wright, *New Testament and the People of God*, 291-97. On "son of man" generally, see Schreiner, *New Testament Theology*, 213-31; George Eldon Ladd, *A Theology of the New Testament*, rev. ed. (Grand Rapids: Eerdmans, 1993), 143-57; Carson, "Reflections: 'The Son of Man' as a Christological Title," in "Matthew," 247-52.

[43]See also "son" language in Mt 5:9, 16, 45, 48; 6:1, 8-9, 26, 32; 7:11; 10:29.

much replacement as fulfillment.[44] Under the old covenant, ethnic Israel spoke for heaven. They held this particular office, which is why ethnic Jews thought of themselves as "sons of the kingdom" (Mt 8:12). Sonship language in the biblical worldview, I said in chapter three, points to the unique relationship between son and father, whereby the son assumes his father's vocation and imitates his father's character. Sons are to a familial conceptuality what citizens are to a political conceptuality, at least somewhat, which is why "sons" and "kingdom" work well together.[45] But now Jesus promises, "Many will come from east and west and recline at table with Abraham, Isaac, and Jacob in the kingdom of heaven, while the sons of the kingdom will be thrown into the outer darkness" (Mt 8:11-12). Many foreign born will be joined to the Abrahamic promises, while many of the natural born will have their passports revoked![46] Then Jesus calls out a new twelve to be the new heads of a new nation and promises that they would sit on twelve thrones and judge Israel (Mt 10:1-4; 19:20). National, cultic and ethnic boundary markers would no longer set off the family of God. Rather, "whoever does the will of my Father in heaven is my brother and sister and mother" (Mt 12:50). After all, God can raise up children for Abraham from the stones (Mt 3:7-9). What is more, Jesus fastens the phrase "sons of the kingdom" onto his followers and says that one day they will "shine like the sun in the kingdom of their Father" (Mt 13:38, 43). He also promises that the Son of Man will usher in a "new genesis" (*palingenesia*) where he and his followers will partake in the political activity of judgment as the new Israel (Mt 19:28). The old office holders were to pack the contents of their desks in boxes and make their way quickly out the capitol building doors.

---

[44]Beale, *New Testament Biblical Theology*, 680-83; see also Bockmuehl, "Is There a New Testament," 43. By speaking of "regime change," I can still affirm that "those who come by this way are not a *new* Israel, as though suddenly created from nothing," in Wright's words. I am happy to agree with him that "they are the true descendants of Abraham, Isaac, and Jacob." Wright, *New Testament and the People of God*, 388.

[45]James Hamilton (in personal correspondence) has also observed that David refers to King Saul as "father" (1 Sam 24:11). See also Sandra L. Richter on the concept of "fictive kinship," in *The Epic of Eden: A Christian Entry into the Old Testament* (Downers Grove, IL: IVP Academic, 2008), 70-72.

[46]Graham N. Stanton refers to Matthew's Gospel as a "foundation document" for clusters of Christian communities probably in Syria. He writes, "The gospel contains a whole series of 'legitimating answers' for 'the new people.' . . . [It] legitimates the recent painful separation of Matthean communities from Judaism by providing divine sanction for the parting of ways. . . . *God himself* initiated the rupture and transferred the kingdom to 'the new people' (21.43; 8.12; cf. also 15.13-14)." Stanton, *A Gospel for a New People: Studies in Matthew* (Louisville, KY: Westminster John Knox, 1993), 378.

Why are ethnic Israel and its leaders being rejected? For one, its leaders "shut the kingdom of heaven in people's faces" (Mt 23:13). But more to the point, these vineyard tenants of Israel reject the Son who represents the heavenly Father (Mt 21:33-41). They even tell Pilate, "His blood be on us and on our children" (Mt 27:25), a politically ironic statement in light of the ethnic basis of their kingdom. After Jesus predicts their rejection of him, he promises, "The kingdom of God will be taken away from you and given to a people producing its fruits" (Mt 21:43).

That said, true Israel itself has not been rejected. It is arriving in the person of Christ, as we saw above.

**New covenant.** How is the kingdom given? It is given through the new covenant, a fourth theme to observe. At the Last Supper, Jesus offers the disciples wine as a sign of his "blood of the covenant, which is poured out for many for the forgiveness of sins," and then promises them that he would drink it with them again in the "Father's kingdom" (Mt 26:27-29). Though emphases vary, commentators appear to agree uniformly that Jesus' words recall (1) Moses' act of sealing the old covenant by splashing blood on both the altar and the people, which established Israel as God's body politic (Ex 24:8); (2) the suffering servant's sacrificial death for the forgiveness of sin (Is 53:11-12); and (3) Jeremiah's promise of a new covenant for the forgiveness of sin (Jer 31:31-34).[47] R. T. France sums up, "Here then is the essential theological basis for that new community of the restored people of God."[48] A new covenant is established which secures the promises of the prophets—the forgiveness of sins—and this provides the grounds for the giving of the Spirit and obedience. The new covenant community will consist of those who receive the benefits of Christ's atonement, forgiveness and the kingdom.[49]

---

[47]France, *Gospel of Matthew*, 994; Carson, "Matthew," 602-3; Robert Stein, "Last Supper," in *Dictionary of Jesus and the Gospels*, ed. Joel B. Green, Scot McKnight and I. Howard Marshall (Downers Grove, IL: InterVarsity Press, 1992), 448; John Nolland, *The Gospel of Matthew*, New International Greek Testament Commentary (Grand Rapids: Eerdmans, 2005), 1079-82; Grant Osborne, *Matthew*, Exegetical Commentary on the New Testament (Grand Rapids: Zondervan, 2010), 968; cf. David C. Turner, *Matthew*, Baker Exegetical Commentary on the New Testament (Grand Rapids: Baker, 2008), 625.

[48]France, *Gospel of Matthew*, 995.

[49]Jonathan T. Pennington helpfully draws out the community-forming element of the Last Supper and the giving of the new covenant: "Thus, our main point to make here is that there is not only a crucially vertical (God-humanity covenant) and eschatological (a new exodus) aspect to the

***Righteous office, righteous community.*** If the new covenant's work of forgiveness is the basis on which Christ's disciples receive the kingdom, why does Matthew also say that it is the "righteous" who will enter the kingdom? The relationship between forgiveness and righteousness in Matthew requires a little sorting out, in part because his treatment of the latter topic bears both polemical and constructive aspects,[50] and in part because his statements on righteousness offer an unexpected "conjunction of radical grace and radical demand."[51] Jesus tells his disciples that their righteousness must surpass the Pharisees and the teachers of the law in order to enter the kingdom of heaven (Mt 5:20); but then he tells the chief priests and elders that the tax collectors and prostitutes go into the kingdom of God before them (Mt 21:31). He categorically states that the lawbreakers and wicked will go into eternal punishment, and the righteous into eternal life (Mt 13:42-43; 25:46). But then he observes that the healthy have no need of a physician, but rather the sick, and that he came "not to call the righteous, but sinners" (Mt 9:12-13). However, as perplexing as it may look at first glance to set the radical-grace and radical-demand statements side by side, here we find the picture of a new covenant politics—a true and lasting politics.

Matthew's picture of a righteous politics begins with two visions of prophetic longing that are accompanied by two calls to repentance in the face of the kingdom of heaven's presentation. First is the picture of Yahweh coming to end Israel's warfare and to pardon her iniquity (Is 40:1-2; Mt 3:1-3); second is the picture of the Messiah coming to establish a just and righteous kingdom that lasts (Is 9:1-7; Mt 4:14-17). Surely we must let Matthew speak for Matthew instead of letting Paul speak for him, as exegetes and theologians are tempted to do at this point.[52] Still, with that

---

enacted parable of the Last Supper, but there is equally a horizontal, new covenant community aspect." Pennington, "The Lord's Last Supper in the Fourfold Witness of the Gospels," *The Lord's Supper: Remembering and Proclaiming Christ Until He Comes*, ed. Thomas R. Schreiner and Matthew R. Crawford (Nashville: B&H, 2010), 55, also 53-56.

[50]Stephen C. Barton, "The Gospel According to Matthew," in *The Cambridge Companion to the Gospels*, ed. Stephen C. Barton (New York: Cambridge University Press, 2006), 128.

[51]Bauckham, "Kingdom and Church According to Jesus and Paul," 10; see also the discussion in Nolland, *Gospel of Matthew*, 1083-84.

[52]One might err in this way, for instance, by imposing a concept of imputed righteousness or "righteousness as the free gift of God" onto Matthew, as in Horst Seebass, "Righteousness," in *New International Dictionary of New Testament Theology*, ed. Colin Brown, vol. 3 (Grand Rapids: Zondervan, 1977), 360; also Gottlob Schrenk, "*dikaiosynē*," in *Theological Dictionary of the New*

warning ringing in our ears, we must also place Matthew's Jesus into a covenantal context. He is the Lord of the covenant who has come to establish heaven's righteous rule on earth, which involves both pardoning iniquity and authoritatively proclaiming God's rule and righteousness. Throughout Matthew, sure enough, true righteousness follows true repentance and true forgiveness. First Jesus explains that the poor in spirit, the mournful, the meek and the ones hungering and thirsting for righteousness will possess the kingdom of heaven (Mt 5:3-6)—here is radical grace. Then he explains that the merciful, the pure in heart, the peacemakers and those persecuted for righteousness will also receive it (Mt 5:7-10)—here is radical demand. He teaches his disciples first to pray, "Forgive us our debts" (Mt 6:12; also 9:12), and then to pray, "And lead us not into temptation" (Mt 6:13). First confession, then obedience.

In short, the political office of representing the righteousness of heaven is established on the platform of forgiveness, which radically changes both the office and the community. It creates a new political world. How? Matthew does not explicitly speak this way, but forgiveness provides an utterly different kind of ground, basis, justification, legitimation or authorization for political office.[53] The office's authority is no longer grounded in self-justification. Instead, it is grounded, justified, authorized in an act of *forgiveness*, which in turn brings a different purpose, scope and ethic to the office. The office is not treated as an entitlement, as it is with political candidates who point to their many virtues that make them worthy of a nation's trust ("I'm great. Vote for me!"). Also, the office does not exist for the purpose of selfish gain, and the office holder does not presume to be able to use others. Rather, the office is treated as a gift, which is to be used to bless

---

*Testament*, ed. Gerhard Kittell, trans. Geoffrey W. Bromiley, vol. 2 (Grand Rapids: Eerdmans, 1964), 198-99. That option would be attractive, concedes D. A. Carson, were it not for the fact that "*dikaiosynē* ('righteousness' . . . ) in Matthew does not have that sense anywhere." Carson, "Matthew," 164. Scot McKnight makes a point similar to Carson's, albeit from a different angle, and argues that righteousness in Matthew has to do with conformity to the Old Testament law in a few instances (e.g., Mt 3:15; 21:32) and conformity to Jesus' teaching and God's law generally. McKnight, "Justice, Righteousness," in *Dictionary of Jesus and the Gospels*, 414.

[53]Stanley Hauerwas offers a complementary perspective to this one, namely, that the different nature of this society depends on the fact that death no longer holds a threat for Christians since they are united to the resurrected Savior, a point Peter obviously did not understand when he rebuked Jesus (Mt 16:21-23). Hauerwas, *A Community of Character: Toward a Constructive Christian Social Ethic* (Notre Dame, IN: Notre Dame University Press, 1981), 49-51.

just as one has been blessed—to authorize rule just as one has been (re)authorized. A counter-example of this occurs with the parable of the unforgiving servant, which begins as so many parables do, "The kingdom of heaven may be compared to . . ." Here the servant of a king—that is, an office holder under the king—is forgiven a vast debt. When the servant refuses to likewise forgive his own debtor a much smaller amount, the king hands him over to the jailers (Mt 18:23-35). He is deprived of office because he has operated by a self-aggrandizing ethic and used his authority to exploit another to his own advantage. Which is to say, he failed to recognize the very grounds of his office—an act of forgiveness. Had he understood and embraced the grounds of his office, he would have forgiven his debtor and reauthorized that servant to continue in his service.

How does grounding political office in forgiveness change the political community? Righteous office holders do not hate, discriminate or murder, but rather seek reconciliation (Mt 5:21-25); they do not exploit or use others (Mt 5:27-30); they honor God's common covenant ordinances (Mt 5:31-32); they speak truthfully on all occasions (Mt 5:33-37); they employ their property to protect and equip others (Mt 5:38-42); they even love their enemies—"so that you may be sons of your Father who is in heaven" (Mt 5:44-45).[54]

To summarize the discussion in two sentences, Matthew's concept of righteousness—or a right use of the political office of representing heaven as a son of the kingdom—begins with confession, is grounded in new covenant forgiveness and produces fruit in keeping with repentance (Mt 3:7-10; 7:15-20; 12:33-37), which in turn consists of acknowledging Christ before others (Mt 10:32) and conforming oneself to the will of the Father in heaven (Mt 7:21). And all this put together creates a righteous and just body politic (e.g., Mt 5:21-45; 25:34-45).

Matthew's concept of righteousness is in the final analysis a totalitarian concept, as we discussed in chapter five. Such a claim needs to be treated within the trinitarian framework of a doctrine of the two ages, also discussed

---

[54]Though I do not draw the lines between the civil kingdom and the spiritual kingdom quite like he does, David VanDrunen's "Bearing Sword in the State, Turning Cheek in the Church: A Reformed Interpretation of Matthew 5:38-42" has much to commend it. In *Themelios* 34, no. 3 (2009): 322-34.

there; and though Matthew does not say nearly as much about the Spirit's work in the life of the believer as Paul does, he says a little (Mt 3:11; 10:20 28:19; cf. 1:18; 3:16; 4:1; 12:28). Still, the point to be observed here is that the broken and forgiven person in Matthew becomes a righteous person on the inside and outside and in every domain of life (Mt 5:17-48). Four times Matthew presents Jesus using the image of a tree that bears good fruit, bad fruit or no fruit (see Mt 3:10; 7:17-19; 13:23; 21:18-22). The basic lesson: things act according to their natures. Matthew's foil, which confirms the point, is the Pharisees and the teachers of the law who "outwardly appear beautiful" and "outwardly appear righteous," but are filled with "hypocrisy and lawlessness" (Mt 23:27-28). The righteous person, however, is actually becoming righteous. Good trees bear good fruit, and bad trees bad.

One last passage is worth viewing in order to conclude this section. Jesus, the Adamic citizen and Davidic king par excellence, seeks to establish a society of people who exercise citizenship authority in the same manner that he does. Responding to a mother's request to place her sons at Jesus' right and left hand in his kingdom, he tells his disciples,

> You know that the rulers of the Gentiles lord it over them, and their great ones exercise authority [NRSV: "are tyrants"][55] over them. It shall not be so among you. But whoever would be great among you must be your servant, and whoever would be first among you must be your slave, even as the Son of Man came not to be served but to serve, and to give his life as a ransom for many. (Mt 20:25-28; also Mk 10:42-45)

There are four things to observe in this text for our present purposes. First, the contrast is not between those who rule and those who do not; it is a contrast between two kinds of rule, which is evident in the counterpoints "rulers of the Gentiles" and "Son of Man," that Danielic figure with supreme authority. One kind of rule "lords it over"; the other kind serves, gives, even sacrifices, which offers further insight into the difference between Trinity-like rule and fallen human rule, as discussed in chapter five's comparison between the new covenant and totalitarianism. Second, Jesus calls his disciples to follow the pattern of his rule. Their citizenship or ruled ruling

---

[55]See the discussion of this text and why the NRSV's translation is preferable here in David Koyzis, *We Answer to Another: Authority, Office, and the Image of God* (Eugene, OR: Pickwick, 2014), 143.

should look like his. In both cases godly rule would begin with dismounting a throne for the sake of serving others (see also Phil 2:1-11), a point evidently missed by the two disciples' mother. Third, Jesus says the nature of his rule will be demonstrated through sacrificing his own life, pointing ahead to his passion. Peter, of course, has already demonstrated that he does not understand the connection, having confessed Jesus as the Messiah and rebuked him for speaking of his suffering and death (Mt 16:21-23). Fourth, it would be wrong to extrapolate from this text that God's rule in Christ never employs violence or coercive force.[56] Jesus always uses his rule to serve, true, but he uses it to serve heaven's causes, which in the case of ransoming sinners calls for self-sacrifice. In the case of judgment it may call for the sword. It would be better to say that *within the new covenant society* force will be unnecessary.[57]

## Paul and Justification

At this point in the argument, it might be easiest to proceed directly from this thematic overview of Matthew into a discussion of the keys of the kingdom in Matthew 16, 18 and 28, where Jesus institutionally establishes the church. But for the sake of clarifying this book's political conceptualization of the church, we will take a brief detour into Paul's doctrine of justification both present and future. A political community, recall, depends upon a shared conception of justice. And so it is with the church.

Understanding the doctrine of justification will help us understand what holds the church together as a political society. Yes, the church is a political society, first, by virtue of the fact that Christ is its king. But nations and kingdoms are held together by laws and, behind those laws, the ability to enforce them through the power of the sword. Understanding what holds the body politic of the church together, once more, requires a doctrine of two

---

[56] As does, e.g., Stanley Hauerwas, *The Peaceable Kingdom: A Primer in Christian Ethics* (Notre Dame, IN: University of Notre Dame Press, 1983), 85.

[57] It should be clear, therefore, that I do not think the Bible teaches Stanley Hauerwas's pacifism. See also Miroslav Volf, *A Public Faith: How Followers of Christ Should Serve the Common Good* (Grand Rapids: Brazos Press, 2011), 17-21, 37-54. That said, this Hauerwas statement pertaining to life within the new covenant society itself is exactly right: "The hallmark of such a community, unlike the power of the nation-states, is its refusal to resort to violence to secure its own existence or to insure internal obedience. For as a community convinced of the truth, we refuse to trust any other power to compel than the truth itself." Hauerwas, *Community of Character*, 85.

ages. Wherever God has acted through the end-time powers of the new covenant, the power of the Spirit and the law of Christ's justifying word hold the body politic of the church together. How radically different from the kingdoms of this world! However, there is also a sense in which the sword—Christ's sword—holds the church together. We live in the time that New Testament theologians call the "already/not yet," which means, among other things, that the Christian's salvation is not yet complete and that there are many who profess to be Christians but who are not. Therefore, the New Testament is filled with warnings of a final justification according to works, many of which were written for those who profess to be Christians. The church's use of the keys, which we will come to in a moment, requires it to be mindful of both a present justification by faith alone, since that is its source of its political life and unity, and the end-time justification in accordance with works, since that is what it must continually fear and discern (1 Cor 5:5, 12; 11:29; Phil 2:12).

***Present justification and covenantal inclusion.*** Like Matthew, Paul teaches that grounding political office in forgiveness or justification by faith alone changes the scope, boundaries and ends of that office, as well as the nature of the entire body politic. For instance, after reminding the Philippian church that he (and they) possess "the righteousness from [*ek*] God that depends on [*epi*] faith," Paul tells them that their "citizenship [*politeuma*] is in heaven" (Phil 3:9, 20).[58] And this, he told them earlier in the letter, means they should "live as citizens [*politeuesthe*] worthy of the gospel" (Phil 1:27, my translation). What is a citizenship worthy of the gospel? It is a life of unity among church members, which shows itself in sacrificing oneself for others just as Christ did (see Phil 1:27; 2:2, 3, 5-7). The end of self-justification means the end of selfish self-rule.

The larger matters at stake in Paul's doctrine of justification arise in letters like Romans and Galatians. There is no way this chapter can delve deeply into the complexities of these books or the recent debates (much less centuries of debate) surrounding the topic. Nonetheless, the political and institutional reading of redemptive history charted by this book does raise the matter of the connection between justification and covenantal inclusion,

---

[58]See Fee, *Paul's Letter to the Philippians*, 378-80.

which has been a contested topic in recent scholarly discussions. N. T. Wright has famously proposed that Paul's doctrine of justification refers to

> the declaration (a) that someone is in the right (his or her sins having been forgiven through the death of Jesus) and (b) that this person is a member of the true covenant family, the family that God originally promised to Abraham and has now created through Christ and the Spirit—the single family that consists equally of believing Jews and believing Gentiles.[59]

No small amount of controversy has occurred over the second part of his formulation concerning inclusion in the covenant family. Though I do not finally adopt this definition or the imprecise manner in which Wright connects justification and the covenant,[60] he helpfully draws our gaze to the question of how Scripture's covenantal storyline interacts with justification, and he rightly insists that justification should be viewed in covenantal terms. Occassional Wright critic Simon Gathercole seems to agree: "I am entirely in favor of understanding righteousness in covenantal terms; there is no chance to return to a previous generation's attempt to generalize the Jewish and Pauline understandings of righteousness as generic good deeds, and the polemic of Wright and others against this line is important."[61]

---

[59] N. T. Wright, "New Perspectives on Paul," in *Justification in Perspective: Historical Developments and Contemporary Challenges*, ed. Bruce L. McCormack (Grand Rapids: Baker Academic, 2006), 258. For a fuller description of how the category of covenant impinges on Wright's definition of justification, see N. T. Wright, *Justification: God's Plan and Paul's Vision* (Downers Grove, IL: IVP Academic, 2009), 94-100, 133-36. Most significantly, it does not appear to separate justification from conversion in the way his earlier writings on the topic did (e.g., *Paul in Fresh Perspective*, 111-13; "New Perspectives on Paul," 260-61). Moo also notes this shift in Douglas J. Moo, "Justification in Galatians," in *Understanding the Times: New Testament Studies in the 21st Century*, ed. Andreas J. Köstenberger and Richard W. Yarbrough (Wheaton, IL: Crossway, 2011), 175n32.

[60] Criticisms of Wright's views on justification as covenantal inclusion can be found in Stephen Westerholm, *Perspectives Old and New on Paul: The "Lutheran" Paul and His Critics* (Grand Rapids: Eerdmans, 2004), 286-96; Simon Gatherole, "The Doctrine of Justification in Paul and Beyond," in *Justification in Perspective*, 228-32, 236-40; Moo, "Justification in Galatians," 171-78; Brian Vickers, *Jesus' Blood and Righteousness: Paul's Theology of Imputation* (Wheaton, IL: Crossway, 2006), 80-88; John Piper, *The Future of Justification: A Response to N. T. Wright* (Wheaton, IL: Crossway, 2007), 39-55; William B. Barclay with Ligon Duncan, *Gospel Clarity: Challenging the New Perspective on Paul* (Carlisle, PA: EP Books, 2010), 121-30. See also D. A. Carson on the relationship between union with Christ, imputation and justification in "The Vindication of Imputation: On Fields of Discourse and Semantic Fields," in *What's at Stake in the Current Justification Debates*, ed. Mark Husbands and Daniel J. Treier (Downers Grove, IL: InterVarsity Press, 2004), 77. Also Mark A. Garcia, "Imputation and the Christology of Union with Christ: Calvin, Osiander and the Contemporary Quest for a Reformed Model," *Westminster Theological Journal* 68 (2006): 219-51.

[61] Gathercole, "Doctrine of Justification," 236-37.

After all, it has been my assumption throughout this book that all commands and commissions, threats and promises, whether divine or human, partake of some institutional framework; and to this list we might add all acts of forgiveness or justification. To forgive or to justify someone is to do so *according to certain terms*, and these terms provide what we might call the "institutional framework" or "context" of an act of forgiveness or act of justification. For instance, we considered in chapter five the difference between forgiving a spouse and forgiving a loan. The institutional context dramatically affects forgiveness's effects, implications or work—what the forgiveness *does*. (By analogy, lemon juice is still lemon juice whether squeezed into a cup of tea or a diet soda, but the different contexts produce different effects.) To ask about the institutional framework or context of justification, then, is to ask which previous commands, obligations or promises God's justifying word fulfills and what exactly is entailed in the act. It is like rooting through the file drawer to find a signed contract in order to reread all the terms and conditions. God does not legislate, adjudicate or justify arbitrarily; he always respects the legal terms previously set. Even when he changes the rules, he follows his old rules' rules for making new rules, since God's word cannot be broken (Jn 10:35). To say that justification produces a "right standing with God" is true, but it remains institutionally underspecified. Right standing by what institutional terms? God has a consistent canonical track record of always expressing his character in some covenant, some law, some articulated codification, especially when legal realities are at play as is the case with justification. Does he justify sinners according to the standards of the US government? An imam? Moses? A personal pact between a sinner and God? God as he has expressed himself how?

Consider how institutional contexts control what an act of justification *does*. Imagine that two individuals in London, a German tourist and a British citizen, are charged by Neville Chamberlain's government the day after Britain declares war on Germany with working in collusion to spy on the British government. But then suppose both individuals are exonerated and justified. The word "justified" *means* the same thing in both cases—declared to be in the right. But the British citizen is restored to all the privileges and responsibilities of British citizenship, such as voting and paying taxes, while the German citizen, too, is cleared of charges, but he is not restored to the status of British citizen. In fact, he now bears no formal relationship with the British government or its people. The same declaratory word *does* different things in light of their different institutional positions.

Of more relevance, consider the witness of Galatians 2 through 4. Paul says that Peter's actions of forcing the Gentiles to live like Jews by separating himself in the meals was "not in step" with the truth of the gospel, which is why Paul turns to drawing a contrast between justification by faith and justification by works of the law (Gal 2:14, 16). Wright comments, "Reading Paul strictly in his own context . . . we *are forced* to conclude, at least in a preliminary way, that 'to be justified' here . . . [means] 'to be reckoned by God to be a member of his family, and hence with the right to share table fellowship.'"[62] Here Wright correctly observes the inseparable connection between justification and covenantal inclusion, but he fails to carefully examine those connections. He conflates the two—one apparently means the other. Douglas Moo therefore rightly responds, "There is no good contextual reason *to insist* that 'justify' in 2:16 must be redefined to mean, or to include, the notion of membership in God's people."[63] He insists instead that it makes perfect sense of Galatians 2:16 to interpret *dikaioō* as "declare righteous," even while we affirm that Peter's action of removing himself from Gentile fellowship "called into question" his understanding of his justification.[64] That is, "membership in God's people and justification are closely related; but they are not identical."[65] And I believe that Moo is correct, as far as he goes.

That said, one might push Moo for a little more institutional specificity as well: "declare righteous" by what institutional norm? Can we open the file drawer and find the contract that specifies the terms and conditions?

To read Galatians 3 is to find the file folder and read the fine print. Here Paul continues his argument for justification by faith precisely by pointing to its covenantal benefits, implications or consequences.[66]

---

[62] Wright, *Justification*, 116 (italics mine).
[63] Moo, "Justification in Galatians," 174 (italics mine).
[64] Ibid.
[65] Ibid., 175.
[66] Four readings of this section of Galatians worth comparing include Wright's (*Justification*, 113-36), Moo's ("Justification in Galatians," 164-69, 173-78), Mark A. Seifrid's (*Christ, Our Righteousness: Paul's Theology of Justification* [Downers Grove, IL: InterVarsity Press, 2000],

- First, he points to the gift of the Spirit. "Did you receive the Spirit by works of the law or by hearing with faith?" (Gal 3:2, also 3, 5, 14). Their justification by faith resulted in the new covenant gift of the Spirit.
- Second, he points to their inclusion in the family of Abraham: "Know then that it is those of faith who are the sons of Abraham" (Gal 3:7). Their justification by faith resulted in becoming sons of Abraham. Verses 10 to 14 appear to repeat the point by invoking the Abrahamic, Mosaic and new covenants. The Mosaic covenant promises a curse to everyone who does not do everything written in the Book of the Law, which leads to the conclusion that no one can be justified by the law (Gal 3:10-11). Christ therefore redeemed a people from the curse by becoming a curse, so that the blessings covenantally promised to Abraham and the new covenant promise of the Spirit might be given through (justification by) faith (Gal 3:12-14).[67]
- Third, now that (justification by) faith has come, Paul says, they are "sons of God" (Gal 3:26).
- And fourth, to be identified with Christ in his death and resurrection through baptism, he observes, indicates that they have already been made "one in Christ" with each other—Jew and Gentile, slave and free, male and female (Gal 3:28).

In short, Galatians 3 essentially alludes to the covenantal history of God's people, from Adam as the first son of God, to Abraham and the covenantal promise of blessing, to the Mosaic guardianship which taught that righteousness would not come through the law (Gal 3:21, 24), to the promise of the Spirit in the new covenant. Then it effectively crowns Christ as the covenantal head who has fulfilled both Abrahamic promises and Mosaic curses in order to grant everyone with faith a covenantal identification with him and a covenantal identification with one another: Christ is the one "offspring" to whom Abraham's covenantal promises were made (Gal 3:16), but "if you are Christ's, then you are Abraham's offspring, heirs according to the

---

80-81, 106-8) and Michael Bird's (*The Saving Righteousness of God: Studies on Paul, Justification, and the New Perspective* [Milton Keynes, UK: Paternoster, 2007], 136-40).

[67]See Michael F. Bird, "What Is There Between Minneapolis and St. Andrews? A Third Way in the Piper-Wright Debate," *Journal of the Evangelical Theological Society* 54, no. 2 (June 2011): 302.

promise" (Gal 3:29). And it is this inheritance, the beginning of chapter four states, that the Galatians were turning their back on by "turning to a different gospel" (Gal 1:6) and relying on works of the law (Gal 3:10) instead of the justification they had received through faith (Gal 4:1-20). The rest of Galatians 4 explicitly ties the conflict between faith and deeds to two covenants, the Abrahamic and Mosaic, in case someone wants to plead the word *covenant* is not actually present in Galatians 3.

What is the institutional context of justification in Galations 2 through 4? Open up the file, read the signed contract and you do not find the words, "You are justified by faith, not works, so stop trying to prove yourself. Case closed." Instead, Paul says, "You are justified by faith, not works, which is how you received the Spirit, and are a child of Abraham, and are not cursed by the law, and are sons of God." He walks the reader directly through the Bible's covenantal storyline.

In short, Wright might wrongly import *the institutional context* of justification into the *definition* of justification by defining it *as* covenantal inclusion; and perhaps some of his critics fail to recognize the significance of the institutional context. Or, to portray both sides positively, Wright rightly calls attention to the significance of the covenant, while his critics rightly guard the definition of justification. With Wright's critics, I believe we should define *justified* as "declared righteous" or "reckoned as righteous." (The lemon juice is still lemon juice whether in the tea or diet soda.) What the critics may underappreciate, however, is the political significance of the covenantal context of justification and how this affects what justification does.[68]

A Christian's "extraordinary righteousness"[69] is not a British or Muslim or even Jewish righteousness; it is a covenantal righteousness, meaning it is measured by the standards of the Bible's entire covenantal storyline. What then is justification? It is being declared in the right according to the terms

---

[68]Simon Gathercole makes a helpful distinction between the "content" and the "scope" of justification, with Gentile inclusion belonging to the latter. I understand Gathercole to mean that inclusion is something that justification *does* but is not what the term *means*. Gathercole, "Justified by Fath, Justified by his Blood: The Evidence of Romans 3:21-4:25," in *Justification and Variegated Nomism*, ed. D. A. Carson et al., vol. 2, *The Paradoxes of Paul* (Grand Rapids: Baker Academic, 2004), 156.

[69]This is Stephen Westerholm's term for the gift of righteousness that Christians receive in justification. See Westerholm, *Perspectives Old and New on Paul*, 273-84.

of the covenant. Michael Horton helpfully calls justification a "covenant verdict."[70] Moo also, while still institutionally imprecise, is pushing in the right direction when he says, "Both justification and inclusion within the people of God are important and, we would argue, overlapping if not referentially equivalent concepts."[71] Justification is grounded in God's covenant faithfulness. It transpires according to the terms of the (new) covenant. And it secures covenantal inclusion.

*The forensic is political.* Why is all this significant for our political inquiries? Quite simply, the covenantal context of justification means that justification has two effects: it politically unites people together and installs them into office. Justification constitutes people as *citizens together*—office holders in a shared body politic.

Justification is forensic. But what is important to recognize is that the new forensic relationship that abides between an individual and God also abides—as a result of the same atoning act and justifying word—between God's people and is the basis of their peace and unity together. The age-old debate between legal/forensic and moral/transformative accounts of justification locates the discussion in the relationship between the individual and God: is the individual made righteous or declared righteous before God?[72] The "forensic" side of the debate (which is where I place myself) then ties the topic of justification to the domain of the court and conceives of the transaction as a two-way drama between defendant and judge in which the judge renders judgment based on the merits of the case. But courts act on behalf of an entire body politic. Judges don't speak for themselves but speak for entire legal systems, and the legal cannot be divorced from the political. Courts do not put detached individuals on trial; they try subjects and citizens. They seek to apply the conclusions of law, a law that structures the public life of a nation. The work of the court is forensic in that it occurs "of or before the forum," as the Latin term would have it (*forēnsis*), or, one might say, of and before the entire public or nation. Forensic is a relational concept that is both judicial and political, bilateral and multilateral. When an indi-

---

[70]Michael Horton, *Covenant and Salvation: Union with Christ* (Louisville, KY: Westminster John Knox, 2007), 121.
[71]Moo, "Justification in Galatians," 171.
[72]For a history of this debate, see Alister E. McGrath, *Iustitia Dei*.

vidual is declared "not guilty," the judgment defines his or her relationship not just with the judge but with the entire body politic. One is acquitted before the judge, the bailiff, the janitor who sweeps the courtroom, the mayor's office, the newspaper editorial staff and every other citizen and institution in the country. The changed status is corporate and nationwide. Not only that, the formerly indicted defendant now has the full office of citizen restored with all the authorities and responsibilities of that office. For instance, he or she can vote.

Hence, defendants of the traditional position correctly defend the individual aspects of justification.[73] And the declaration of righteousness before God's throne is primary and definitional since, unlike a human court, God is both judge *and* law. But we must also recognize that the individual's justification occurs within a covenantal body politic, which means it has a corporate consequence. A horizontal dimension derives from the vertical.[74]

To put it another way, a covenantal head necessitates the existence of a covenantal people (Rom 5:12-21). Christian conversion always involves a corporate element because God is covenantally united to his people—to be converted is to become an "ecclesial person"[75] or citizen of the kingdom. Peter illustrates this with two parallel statements: "Once you were not a people, but now you are God's people; once you had not received mercy, but now you have received mercy" (1 Pet 2:10). Jeremiah had explained it years before: "And I will be their God, and they shall be my people. . . . For I will forgive their iniquity" (Jer 31:33, 34). And Paul's picture of unity between Jew and Gentile in Ephesians 2 is not explicitly about justification or righteousness, but he observes that Christ has *already* "made [Jewish and Gentile converts] both one and has broken down in his flesh the dividing wall of

---

[73]E.g., Andrew Hassler, "Ethnocentric Legalism and the Justification of the Individual: Rethinking Some New Perspective Assumptions," *Journal of the Evangelical Theological Society* 54, no. 2 (June 2011): 311-27.

[74]See Bird, *Saving Righteousness of God*, 100-103, 110, 113-54 (esp. 152-54); Francis Watson, *Paul, Judaism, and the Gentiles: Beyond the New Perspective* (Grand Rapids: Eerdmans, 2007), 6.

[75]Miroslav Volf writes, "Communion with this [triune] God is at once also communion with those others who have entrusted themselves in faith to the same God. Hence one and the same act of faith places a person into a new relationship both with God and with all others who stand in communion with God. The others 'are discovered *equiprimally* with the new communion with God as one's neighbors, as those who belong to the same communion.'" Hence, "to experience faith means to become an ecclesial being." Volf, *After Our Likeness: The Church as the Image of the Trinity* (Grand Rapids: Eerdmans, 1998), 173, 174.

hostility by abolishing the law of commandments expressed in ordinances" (Eph 2:14-15), and he has *already* "reconcile[d] . . . both to God in one body through the cross" (Eph 2:16). Should we assume there is a legal and political backdrop to this? Apparently. Verse 15 says the law has been abolished, and in the next breath Paul says that Christ has *already* made strangers and aliens "fellow citizens" (Eph 2:19).[76]

It is not surprising, therefore, that Galatians 5 and 6 proceed directly from Galatians 2 through 4. These latter chapters present what a church's life together should look like through the freedom they have in the Spirit and their faith-mediated justification (Gal 5:4-5). Churches should deny the self-seeking "desires of the flesh," which lead, as it were, to civil unrest (Gal 5:17-21), but instead pursue Spirit-given, others-centered virtues (Gal 5:22-24), bear one another's burdens and so "fulfill the law of Christ" (Gal 6:2). Justification, in other words, gives birth to a different kind of politics. The forensic unity the Galatians shared with one another in the gospel of justification by faith alone imposed a clear ethic on this body politic.

Christ's performative and forensic word of justification—his covenant verdict—establishes people as citizens of a new body politic. It gives them a new status before God and one another, and it gives them a new job (citizen of heaven) and a set of guidelines for doing that job.

***By faith alone—the unexpected basis for political unity.*** What role does faith play in all of this? As I observed at the beginning of chapter five, the idea that a person can in some sense be considered just "by faith" and not by his or her activity, to a political philosopher, sounds like cheating the system. It seems to gut the word *justice* of the very thing it needs—action or works. This has led many to critique *sola fide* outright, or at least to treat the doctrine as nonpolitical. I believe the opposite is the case. *Sola fide* is history's unexpected ground of political unity. It robs political actors of the incentives to warfare and domination by giving them that which all people, nations and armies primally seek—justification, standing, the recognition of existence, as Oswald Bayer argued in the first pages of chapter five. Ever

---

[76]Peter O'Brien has observed, "The justification of which we have been speaking has dealt with *both* the radical, vertical problem of a relationship with God *and* the horizontal problem of Jew-Gentiles relationships." O'Brien, "Was Paul a Covenantal Nomist," in *Justification and Variegated Nomism*, 2:291.

since God was dismissed as our source of standing, we have had to find it in ourselves, which leads to one-upmanship, boasting, war. But the person justified by faith must no longer prove or justify himself or herself by any earthly measurement: race ("I'm Aryan"), ethnicity ("I'm Serbian"), gender ("I'm male"), class ("I'm aristocracy"), nationality ("I'm Prussian"), wisdom ("I'm Progressive") and all those things that lead to war and political oppression (see Jas 4:1-2).

The presence of faith, first of all, presumes that the self has run out of resources and therefore has no choice but to forsake its self-justifying arguments. Faith means "dying both to justifying thinking and justifying action," and "both thinking and acting are renewed."[77] Being free from self-justification, faith is free—indeed, can afford—to think and work entirely for the sake of the other, not for the sake of validating or vindicating oneself.[78]

Second, faith involves the end of self-enthronement. At the heart of faith is the idea of submitting to the authority of another. The antifaith Ayn Rand, in the form of one of her characters, put this well in an antifaith exhortation, "Redeem your mind from the hockshops of authority. . . . An error made on your own is safer than ten truths accepted on faith, because the first leaves you the means to correct it, but the second destroys your capacity to distinguish truth from error."[79] To take something "on faith" is to take it "on the authority" of another, whether the topic is medical counsel, investment advice or the way of righteousness and salvation. It is to submit to someone else's expertise. To have faith in God is to submit to God,[80] and having faith in Jesus' person and work is, among other things, a political act involving

---

[77]Oswald Bayer, *Living by Faith: Justification and Sanctification*, trans. Geoffrey W. Bromiley (Grand Rapids: Eerdmans, 2003), 25.

[78]Bayer, *Living by Faith*, 21-22.

[79]Ayn Rand, *Atlas Shrugged*, centennial ed. (New York: Plume, 2005), 1058.

[80]This is why as stalwart a Protestant as James Buchanan could refer to faith as "an act of obedience." He writes, "Protestant divines have generally held, that faith itself is a spiritual grace, and that every act of faith is an act of obedience; since it is one of the fruits of the Spirit, which can only be implanted along with a spiritual apprehension of the truth, and a cordial approbation of it, while every exercise of faith is in conformity with the requirements of God's revealed will; and yet they have denied that its being such is at variance with the doctrine of a free justification by the vicarious satisfaction and righteousness of Christ, simply because they exclude FAITH ITSELF, as well as all its fruits . . . from forming any part of the ground of our acceptance with God" (emphasis original). James Buchanan, *The Doctrine of Justification* (1867; repr., Carlisle, PA: Banner of Truth Trust, 1961), 375.

submission to his kingdom.[81] In this light it is worth considering once more the distinction between *justification by faith* and *justification by works*. What makes the former the polar opposite of the latter is not that one involves submission or obedience and one doesn't. What makes these two things antipodally opposed is the *object* of one's faith or trust. One involves trusting oneself, whereas the other involves trusting in God for one's justification.

Indeed, this brings us to the heart of the dispute between the two kinds of justification. Paul explicitly pits the language of justification by faith against justification by works (e.g., Gal 2:16), but, to think theologically, what is actually being compared is justification by one kind of faith and justification by another kind of faith. When Paul says "justification by faith," we can effectively interpret him to mean "justification by faith in God." When he says "justification by works," we can effectively interpret him to mean "justification by faith in oneself." The first, by definition, is the act of submitting to Christ alone as Lord. The second, by definition, is the act of submitting to self alone as Lord, because it means putting confidence in oneself and one's imperious self-verdict in the decision of whether or not one is just. These two faiths are as opposed to one another as God and the devil, heaven and hell, righteousness and sin. Isaiah Berlin might have divided all political philosophy between the purveyors of positive and negative liberty. But history's true political divide occurs between the purveyors of "justification by faith in oneself" (the philosophies of this world) and the purveyor's of "justification by faith in God" (the gospel).

How then is justification by faith alone history's unexpected source of political unity? First, it unites people around not just *a* lord but *the* Lord—the only good, just and all-loving Lord. Second, it brings self-vindication to an end and grants a vicarious and alien righteousness, which means that people lack the incentives to war and domination and one-upmanship. The most politically powerful phrase in the Bible just might be "Where, then, is boasting?" (Rom 3:27 NIV). Boasting is the root of all domination and coercion. We quarrel, fight and murder because we desire and do not have,

---

[81]O'Donovan, *Desire of the Nations*, 117.

covet and cannot obtain (Jas 4:1-2).[82] But now the need to say "I follow Paul" or "I follow Apollos" or "I am a Communist" or "I am a Democrat" or "I am Hutu" or "I am a Tutsi" is extinguished because no one should "boast in men. For all things are yours, whether Paul or Apollos or Cephas or the world or life or death or the present or the future—all are yours, and you are Christ's, and Christ is God's" (1 Cor 3:21-23). In an assembly or gathering of those justified by faith, there is neither slave nor free, Jew nor Gentile, male nor female (Gal 3:28; Col 3:11). Those political categories that divide the world are erased.

***Future justification according to works.*** One last brief comment concerning a final justification or judgment according to works (which I am distinguishing from the "present justification by works" just discussed) is necessary. There are a number of passages that point to this promise, even in the vicinity of affirmations of justification by faith. Here are a few:

> For it is not the hearers of the law who are righteous before God, but the doers of the law who will be justified. (Rom 2:13; also, 2:6-7; 8:1, 13; 14:10)
>
> For we must all appear before the judgment seat of Christ, so that each one may receive what is due for what he has done in the body, whether good or evil. (2 Cor 5:10; also 1 Cor 4:4-5)
>
> I warn you, as I warned you before, that those who do such things will not inherit the kingdom of God. (Gal 5:21)
>
> For the one who sows to his own flesh will from the flesh reap corruption, but the one who sows to the Spirit will from the Spirit reap eternal life. (Gal 6:8)

Many other examples from both Paul and the rest of the New Testament could be cited.

It would take too long to treat the nuances in each of these passages. But Gregory Beale usefully relates a present-time justification by faith and an end-time justification according to works with what he calls his "mundane

---

[82]Charles Taylor observes, "In our day . . . many young people are driven to political extremism, sometimes by truly terrible conditions, but also by a need to give meaning to their lives. And since meaninglessness is frequently accompanied by a sense of guilt, they sometimes respond to a strong ideology of polarization, in which one recovers a sense of direction as well as a sense of purity by lining up in implacable opposition to the forces of darkness. The more implacable, even violent the opposition, the more the polarity is represented as absolute, and the greater the sense of separation from evil and hence purity." Taylor, *Sources of the Self: The Making of the Modern Identity* (Cambridge, MA: Harvard University Press, 1989), 516-17.

illustration": present-day justification is like someone paying for your membership at a discount shopper's club; future justification is like walking into the store and showing your photo ID. The membership cost you nothing, but when the time of reckoning came, you needed something to prove your membership.[83]

The first variety Beale calls causal/initial justification, and the second manifestive/consummative justification,[84] or what I would describe as *performative* and *revelatory*. The present justification by faith alone occurs through God's performative declaration. The future justification occurs through the revelation of one's works, which indicate whether or not faith was genuine. A genuine Spirit-given faith produces Spirit-given good works: "We see that such people will be judged not on whether their deeds have been perfect but rather on whether they have borne the fruit of good works in keeping with and as a result of their resurrection existence and union with Christ's resurrected person."[85] (Beale interprets all of the verses cited above, and others like them, as instances of a consummative or revelatory justification.[86]) A saint's final justification or vindication will occur when God (1) raises him or her from the dead, (2) publicly demonstrates the saint's good works and (3) announces this demonstration to the entire cosmos.[87] Beale's summary of the issue may adequately serve as my own:[88]

> Good works are the badge that vindicates the saints in the sense of declarative proof that they have been truly already justified by Christ. The good works demonstrate not only the prior true justified status of a person but probably also the injustice of the world's verdict in rejecting such works as a witness to Christ, often resulting in political persecution. On the one hand, good works

---

[83]John Piper effectively offers the same distinction, though he arrives here with a slightly different exegesis than Beale of Romans 2. Piper, *Future of Justification*, 110, 116.
[84]Beale, *New Testament Biblical Theology*, 506-7.
[85]Ibid., 509.
[86]Ibid., 507-23.
[87]Ibid., 523.
[88]Michael Bird's comments are helpful here as well: "But Paul's centre of gravity for his conception of how believers are acquitted before the final judgment is found elsewhere [i.e., not in Spirit-empowered good works]. For Paul the final judgment has already been executed in the sacrificial death of Jesus.... What is more, Jesus is raised by God so that believers can participate in the verdict of justification that is enacted in his resurrection.... Whatever role faithfulness and obedience play in the life of the Christian (and they are not to be discounted) the final grounds for acquittal and vindication remains in the death and resurrection of Christ." Bird, *Saving Righteousness of God*, 174; also Bird, "What Is There," 308.

are absolutely necessary at the last eschatological judgment in order to demonstrate and thus vindicate that someone has truly believed in Christ and been justified, with the result that this person is allowed entrance into the eternal kingdom of the new creation. On the other hand, such works do not in and of themselves cause one to gain entrance into the eternal kingdom, but such entrance is granted because these good works are seen as the inevitable external badge of those who have internal justifying faith.[89]

**Conclusion.** Contrary to those who decry *sola fide* as promoting individualism, justification by faith alone, working through the power of the Spirit, is the very thing that produces a truly just and righteous political society, a point no doubt to be connected with chapter five's assertion that it is Jeremiah's and Ezekiel's promises of a new covenant that produces the just and righteous society.

To put the matter in subjective terms, *sola fide* is diametrically opposed to self-justification. It requires an individual "to reach the end" of himself or herself. It requires a change in one's identity on the level of a Copernican revolution. It presupposes that the countless arguments manufactured over the years to prop up a self-identity that insists on its "right" to self-enthronement have finally dissolved, exhausted and spent. The creature, it turns out, is not the Creator. And in place of those old arguments comes a new Spirit-given conviction that the years of self-rule were in fact one grand act of divine usurpation (sin), an act and posture that in turn gave birth to many rebellious actions (sins). "To have excluded the sun from the solar system," says the voice of conviction, "means you have left the planets around you shrouded in darkness, because you are not the sun." This broken and regretful self described so well in Matthew's beatitudes then takes three new steps: (1) it asks for a debt-clearing and reauthorizing word of forgiveness (Matthew) or free gift of righteousness (Paul); (2) it yields the throne once more to God; and (3) it embraces those who were once enemies but are now fellow citizens. The end of self-justification, in other words, leads to the end of self-enthronement. To say

---

[89]Beale, *New Testament Biblical Theology*, 524. Beale says that N. T. Wright's view on the relationship between present and future justification "possibly could be consistent" with the position he has articulated, but that Wright is ultimately "ambiguous" and "unclear." I came to the same conclusion when reading the source that Beale cites: N. T. Wright, *Paul: In Fresh Perspective* (Minneapolis: Fortress, 2009), 111-14; see also Wright, *Justification*, 182-93.

with faith "forgive me" is, politically speaking, to stop playing God. The gift of Martin Luther to the church was putting all this together: the first and continuous thing a sinner must do to keep the first commandment—"You shall have no other gods before me"—is to have faith in God alone for justifying grace.[90]

To think in objective terms, the performative word of justification establishes an individual before God (as government) and God's people (as nation) in the position of upstanding citizen, a ruled ruler who possesses all the protections, benefits and responsibilities of office in the divine kingdom. This new forensic relationship is matched by the new covenant activity of the Spirit for the purposes of vitalizing and effecting the new legal and political bonds, like the marital vow that is matched by a fiery marital affection (see Mt 3:11). *Sola fide* does not divide Christians; it unites them, and it yields an ethic of walking by the Spirit in obedient freedom. Matthew made the same point in his treatment of forgiveness: political office grounded in forgiveness produces a whole new political dynamic.

Yet this entire enterprise takes place while the powers and authorities of the present age continue. "For many deceivers have gone out into the world, those who do not confess the coming of Jesus Christ in the flesh. Such a one is the deceiver and the antichrist" (2 Jn 7). This requires the people of God never to let the future justification in accordance with works stray too far from their field of vision: "Examine yourselves, to see whether you are in the faith. Test yourselves" (2 Cor 13:5). Those who have been truly justified and made citizens by the free gift of grace will demonstrate the good works of a citizen. The false professors will not. For now, says Jesus, "You will recognize them by their fruits" (Mt 7:16). And Paul: "For what have I to do with judging outsiders? Is it not those inside the church whom you are to judge?" (1 Cor 5:12). Political love, like marital love, must sometimes judge—must discern and separate faithfulness from unfaithfulness—not to kill life, but to give it (1 Cor 5:5).

---

[90]Martin Luther, commentary on the first commandment in "The Large Catechism," in *The Book of Concord: The Confessions of the Evangelical Lutheran Church*, ed. Robert Kolb and Timothy J. Wengert, trans. Charles P. Arand (Minneapolis: Fortress, 2000), 386-89; also Luther, *A Treatise on Good Works* (Rockville, MD: Serenity, 2009), 28.

## Matthew (Part 2): Keys of the Kingdom

If salvation, justification and the creation of a just body politic comes through the new covenant, why is anything more needed for establishing outposts of Christ's kingdom on earth? After all, a distinctively Protestant concept of the church begins with the unilateral work of God in giving faith and obedience to the hearts of believers. God doesn't bring people into the new covenant or the invisible and universal church through the authoritative action of some institutional body. It is through the Spirit's work, which accompanies God's preached word.[91] People hear the word of God, repent, trust and so become the church (see, e.g., Rom 10:17; 1 Thess 1:5; 1 Pet 1:23). Theologian Christoph Schwöbel observes, "As the creature of the divine Word the Church is constituted by divine action."[92] God's word creates God's people.[93] As such, you can have the universal church—meaning Christians—alive and well on planet earth even though no ecclesial authority recognizes it as such. What's more, a believer *is* at this moment a new creation, born again, a son, a priest-king. Why is anything more needed?

***Still needed: Public recognition, assurance, reauthorization and authoritative interpretation.*** The short answer is, the members of Christ's body politic still need to be publicly recognized and affirmed as a body politic; they need the assurance of their belonging; they need to be authorized in the work of the body politic or kingdom; and they need to agree upon an authoritative interpretation of the gospel and Scripture—a *status confessionis*, a phrase the early Lutherans used for which beliefs were central to who Christians are and over which the faith is at stake.

Every body politic needs some kind of "visible" glue to hold it together. Yes, it's the shared laws, lawmakers and judges that effectively hold a nation

---

[91]The combination of the new covenant promise in Ezekiel 36 and the demonstration of preaching's power in Ezekiel 37 illustrates this connection between preaching and new covenant life wonderfully (compare especially Ezek 36:27 and 37:14 and their contexts).

[92]Christoph Schwöbel, "The Creature of the Word: Recovering the Ecclesiology of the Reformers," in *On Being the Church: Essays on the Christian Community*, ed. Colin E. Gunton and Daniel W. Hardy (Edinburgh: T&T Clark, 1989), 122.

[93]See my *Reverberation: How God's Word Brings Light, Freedom, and Action to His People* (Chicago: Moody, 2011), esp. chaps. 1–4; Timothy Ward, *Words of Life: Scripture as the Living and Active Word of God* (Downers Grove, IL: InterVarsity Press, 2009); Michael Horton, *People and Place: A Covenantal Ecclesiology* (Louisville, KY: Westminster John Knox, 2008), 37-71.

together. But all that needs to be made articulate, visible, public. A nation still needs birth certificates, passports, flags, oaths, pledges, immigration procedures, customs offices, police departments, executive orders and all the things that publicly and visibly make a nation a nation or a kingdom a kingdom. A nation needs some way of helping to form the "I" and "we" of membership for insiders and a "they" for outsiders.

The promises given in the Old Testament new covenant passages are not enough for establishing God's kingdom on earth precisely *because it is Spirit-given and invisible.* This is the work of God through the preached word, as Schwöbel says. But something more is needed to make the community of the new covenant visible. People need to be deputized and named as citizens of God's kingdom.

The people of the old covenant had circumcision, Sabbath keeping, the law and eventually a land to identify themselves, to say nothing of their familial and ethnic ties. But the people of the new covenant have not been placed in a land, and they don't identify through the ethnic identity marker of circumcision. How then do you exercise border patrol in a kingdom with no borders and no land? For the church to be visible on earth, there needs to be a mechanism for identifying its individual members, its corporate embodiment in its gatherings and its rule of law.

All that to say, theologian John Webster is correct when he remarks that a group of people coming to faith is not the "only constitutive moment for ecclesiology."[94] The bricks might have been made, but they still need mortar to call them a wall. A person is included in the universal church through salvation. Yet at this point the church remains an abstract idea without a palpable and public presence. A second constitutive moment is needed in order for "the church" to show up on planet earth. For that to happen, a group of Christians must gather and organize themselves (or be organized) as a congregation and affirm one another as believers.

This brings us finally to Matthew's ecclesial texts (Mt 16:13-20; 18:15-20; 28:18-20). They provide the second constitutive moment for organizing the church on earth, the local or particular church. They provide an

---

[94]John Webster, "The 'Self-Organizing' Power of the Gospel: Episcopacy and Community Formation," in *Community Formation: In the Early Church and in the Church Today*, ed. Richard N. Longenecker (Peabody, MA: Hendrickson, 2002), 183.

institutional structure for deputizing the citizens of Christ's kingdom.[95] They show us how the new covenant is made visible, how the new covenant people are reauthorized in the work of being the priest-kings who present the way of God's righteousness and justice before the earth. Matthew's doctrine of forgiveness and Paul's doctrine of *sola fide* make a people just, binding them together in one sense. But the keys of the kingdom described in these texts provide the public or legal glue that transforms them into a justice-proclaiming body politic visibly identifiable on the landscape of the nations. And the ceremony of baptism functions like an inauguration ceremony for these reinstalled priest-kings. Finally, it's worth noting that, insofar as the work of priest-king is democratized, Matthew 16, 18 and 28 connect the church's function with its structure, its faith with its order. When a church affirms an individual's profession of faith, thereby recognizing him or her as one of Christ's citizens, or ruled rulers, or priest-kings, it gives him or her a share in the authority of the kingdom on earth.

***Matthew 16 and the keys of the kingdom.*** Matthew 16 opens with Jesus condemning the Pharisees and Sadducees and then warning his disciples against their teaching (Mt 16:1-12). A regime change is coming.[96] Jesus then asks his disciples to consider the dispute over who he is. Some had identified him as the prince of demons, a glutton and a drunkard (Mt 9:33; 11:18). Others had thought he was John the Baptist, Elijah or one of the prophets (Mt 16:14). Jesus presses the disciples a second time, to which Peter, perhaps representing all of them,[97] answers, "You are the Christ, the Son of the living God" (Mt 16:16). Jesus responds by speaking with the heaven-on-earth authority that God had once intended for humanity. First, he pronounces the word of blessing, which in Matthew's Gospel is reserved exclusively for

---

[95]O'Donovan points to Pentecost as the authorization of the church in *Desire of the Nations*, 161-62, see also 174-75. I prefer to tie the language of authorization to what Jesus does in giving the keys in Matthew 16, 18 and (implicitly) 28. At Pentecost we observe instead the empowerment of the church where, indeed, "the church comes to participate in the authority of the ascended Christ" (ibid., 162).

[96]Craig Blomberg, "Matthew," in *Commentary on the New Testament Use of the Old Testament*, ed. G. K. Beale and D. A. Carson (Grand Rapids: Baker, 2007), 35; W. D. Davies and Dale C. Allison Jr., *Matthew*, ed. J. A. Emerton et al., vol. 2, International Critical Commentary (Edinburgh: T&T Clark, 1991), 603.

[97]For helpful discussions on Peter as "typical" versus Peter as "unique," see Carson, "Matthew," 364; Luz, *Matthew 8-20*, 366-68.

moments of eschatological promise: "Blessed are you, Simon Bar-Jonah!" (Mt 16:17a; cf. 5:3-11; 11:6; 13:16; 24:6). Second, Jesus, standing there as a man on earth, professes to know what heaven has done in Peter's life: "For flesh and blood has not revealed this to you, but my Father who is in heaven" (Mt 16:17b; cf. 11:27). Jesus formally affirms, in other words, that Peter had not learned what he learned about Jesus' identity from a philosopher or poet, the glories of nature, or the inner recesses of his own soul. Instead, Peter had learned these things from heaven.[98]

Yet Jesus does not stop there. He wants more people to know who he is, so he continues: "You are Peter, and on this rock I will build my church, and the gates of hell shall not prevail against it" (Mt 16:18). His grammar parallels Peter's: "You are the Christ" and "You are Peter." Peter had just defined Jesus' identity and role in redemptive history as the Messiah. Now Jesus does the same for Peter, defining his identity and role in redemptive history, in this case as the rock or foundation on which the church will be built; hence, there is a play on words between *Petros* (Peter) and *petra* (rock). Both Jesus and Peter would have a role to play in establishing this assembly—the Messiah to build and the Rock to be foundation (though it is not clear to me that Peter needs to be viewed in distinction from the rest of the apostles here).[99]

Of course, Protestant commentators and theologians have sometimes objected to the idea that Peter is the rock for fear of legitimating the Roman Catholic institution of the papacy.[100] Today many acknowledge that viewing Peter as the rock is the plainest way to read the text.[101] The larger point in

---

[98] Davies and Allison argue that "revealed" should be given its "full eschatological content." God has "unveiled an eschatological secret." Davies and Allison, *Matthew*, 623.

[99] (1) Jesus asked all the disciples the question; (2) Peter probably answered on behalf of all of them; (3) Jesus tells all of them to keep quiet about Peter's answer; (4) both Paul and John later refer to all twelve as the foundation (Eph 2:20; Rev 21:14). As Clowney points out, "Peter is not the rock in contrast to the eleven, but in contrast to those who claim to carry the key of knowledge (Lk. 11:52), to sit in Moses' seat (Mt. 23:1-2), and to be Abraham's seed (Jn. 8:33)." Edmund Clowney, *The Church*, Contours of Christian Theology (Downers Grove, IL: InterVarsity Press, 1995), 40.

[100] Davies and Allison list seven different ways interpreters have construed "the rock," from Peter's faith or confession (Ambrose, Chrysostom, Calvin, Zwingli, Locke), to Peter's preaching office (Melanchthon), to Jesus (Origen, Augustine, Luther) and so forth. Davies and Allison, *Matthew*, 627.

[101] D. A. Carson writes, "If it were not for Protestant reactions against extremes of Roman Catholic interpretation, it is doubtful whether many would have taken 'rock' to be anything or anyone

context, I think, is that Jesus builds the church on both Peter and his confession. As commentator Craig Keener says, "Jesus does not simply assign this role arbitrarily to Peter, however; Peter is the 'rock' *because* he is the one who confessed Jesus as the Christ in this context."[102] Theologian Edmund Clowney puts it this way: "The confession cannot be separated from Peter, neither can Peter be separated from his confession."[103] An ambassador does not travel without a king's edict, and edicts do not travel without an ambassador. Essentially, there are two basic questions at stake in Jesus' line of questioning: what is the right answer to Jesus' question, and who knows it? There is both a "what" and a "who": *what* is a right confession, and *who* is a right confessor?

With Peter's job description effectively named, Jesus sets about giving him the tools for it:[104] "I will give you the keys of the kingdom of heaven, and whatever you bind on earth shall be bound in heaven, and whatever you loose on earth shall be loosed in heaven" (Mt 16:19). The connection between verses 18 and 19 suggests that "the church is the agency of kingdom authority on earth."[105] In some fashion, the church, remarkably, will exercise the authority of Christ and his kingdom. A key is often a symbol of authority in the Scriptures (Is 22:15, 22; Lk 11:52; Rev 3:7; cf. Rev 1:18; 9:1; 20:1), though commentators differ on how or whether any of these scriptural texts influence this particular passage.[106] If an institution is an identity- and

---

other than Peter." Carson, "Matthew," 368. See also Craig Blomberg, *Matthew*, New American Commentary (Nashville: Broadman, 1992), 251-53; Leon Morris, *The Gospel According to Matthew* (Grand Rapids: Eerdmans, 1992), 422-24; Donald A. Hagner, *Matthew 14–28*, Word Biblical Commentary 33b (Dallas: Word, 1995), 470; Craig S. Keener, *A Commentary on the Gospel of Matthew* (Grand Rapids: Eerdmans, 1999), 427; France, *Gospel of Matthew*, 620-23; David L. Turner, *Matthew*, Baker Exegetical Commentary on the New Testament (Grand Rapids: Baker, 2008), 404-5, 406-7.

[102]Keener, *Commentary on the Gospel of Matthew*, 427 (italics original). Similar suggestions are made in Morris, *Gospel According to Matthew*, 423; and Nolland, *Gospel of Matthew*, 669.

[103]Clowney, *The Church*, 40; see also Kevin Giles, *What on Earth Is the Church? An Exploration in New Testament Theology* (1995; repr., Eugene, OR: Wipf & Stock, 2005), 54.

[104]Commentator Ulrich Luz concisely connects verses 18 and 19, saying, "What v. 18a expressed 'architectonically,' v. 19 says functionally. Now Peter's function as a rock is stated"; i.e., this is what Peter *does* as the foundation. Luz, *Matthew 8–20*, 364.

[105]Turner, *Matthew*, 405.

[106]I am inclined *not* to build my exegesis on one of these other passages insofar as the only explicit textual connection is the word *key*, and the keys in these passages are used to do slightly different things, such as opening and shutting. Further, there is no reason to think that every time the word *key* occurs in the Bible in a symbolic fashion, the authors must be saying the same thing.

behavior-shaping rule structure, it does seem something institutional is going on here, in spite of affirmations to the contrary.[107]

There is no reason in the text to think that the authority of the keys is anything other than the authority to bind and loose.[108] The first two tough questions to consider are, what does it mean to bind and loose, and what—or who—gets bound and loosed? The questions are as difficult as they are important. One hundred twenty divines at the Westminster Assembly spent several days debating what the keys were and who had the power to use them. One participant, Thomas Goodwin, referred to them as "the substratum of all church government."[109] A quick glance through classic Protestant confessions of faith and writers shows that the keys were treated as (or doing the work of) "preaching the gospel,"[110] "preaching of the holy gospel and of Christian discipline or excommunication,"[111] "the power to retain and remit sins . . . by the Word and censures . . . and by absolution from censures,"[112] discipline and restoration,[113] the "Ordinances . . . to be administered . . . as the preaching of the Word . . . the Seals and censures,"[114] "receiving in and shutting out of the Congregation,"[115] the "power of government"[116] and so on. Among commentators in the last century multiple explanations can be found as well.[117] The present day *Catechism of the*

---

[107] E.g., Ladd, *Theology of the New Testament*, 107-8.

[108] E.g., Davies and Allison write, "In our estimation, it is most natural to think of v. 19a as being explicated by what follows: to have the keys is to have the power to bind and loose." Davies and Allison, *Matthew*, 635. See also Luz, *Matthew 8-20*, 364. Nolland, however, believes the power to bind and loose is a subset of the keys, and he distinguishes them by suggesting that the keys are about entrance, while binding and loosing concern the regulation of behavior. Nolland, *Gospel of Matthew*, 681.

[109] See Hunter Powell, *The Dissenting Brethren and the Power of the Keys, 1640-1644* (PhD diss., University of Cambridge, 2011).

[110] Second Helvetic Confession (1566), XIV.

[111] Heidelberg Catechism (1563), Q 83.

[112] Westminster Confession of Faith (1647), XXX.2.

[113] Johannes Wollebius, "The Outward Administration of the Church" (1650), in *Paradigms in Polity: Classic Readings in Reformed and Presbyterian Church Government*, ed. Peter W. Hall and Joseph H. Hall (Grand Rapids: Eerdmans, 1994), 164.

[114] John Cotton, *The Keyes of the Kingdom of Heaven, and Power Therefore, According to the Word of God* (London: Tho. Goodwin and Philip Nye, 1644; repr., Boston: S. K. Whipple, 1852), 20.

[115] Benjamin Keach, "The Glory of a True Church, and Its Discipline Display'd" (1697), in *Polity: Biblical Arguments on How to Conduct Church Life*, ed. Mark Dever (Washington, DC: Center for Church Reform, 2001), 71.

[116] Which included choosing officers, exercising discipline and administering the Word and ordinances. Charleston Association, "A Summary of Church Discipline" (1774), in Dever, *Polity*, 119.

[117] Davies and Allison present thirteen possibilities in *Matthew*, 630-32.

*Catholic Church* defines binding and loosing this way: "Whomever you exclude from your communion, will be excluded from communion with God; whomever you receive anew into your communion, God will welcome back into his. *Reconciliation with the Church is inseparable from reconciliation with God.*"[118]

What is hermeneutically important here, I believe, is letting each of the admittedly mixed metaphors stand up and have their say, even while allowing the surrounding metaphors to condition one another. It will not do, for instance, to smother the metaphor of binding and loosing with the metaphor of the keys, which is what commentators do when they draw from another biblical text (like Is 22:22 or Rev 3:7) to describe the keys as "opening and shutting" the kingdom of God to people through preaching the gospel.[119] The trouble with this explanation is that "binding" something, if it means anything, means tying, fastening, restraining or imposing something on it, whether one is speaking of constellations of stars (Job 38:31), donkeys (Mt 21:2), people (Mt 12:29) or laws (cf. Mt 5:19). Loosing, of course, is just the opposite.[120] Binding and loosing are constraining activities; opening and shutting are not.

One nontextual and three more textual clues help us interpret what the keys do: (1) the possible background of the phrase in protorabbinic first-century Judaism, (2) the occurrence of the phrase in Matthew 18, (3) the word *whatever* and (4) the oppositional relationship of binding and loosing.

---

[118]*Catechism of the Catholic Church* (New York: Doubleday, 1995), 403 (italics original).

[119]Reformation-era writers across denominations commonly treated the keys as "opening and shutting" instead of binding and loosing. John Cotton, one of the foremost defenders of Congregationalism of the day, recognized that binding and loosing "are not the proper acts of materiall keys; for their acts be opening and shutting, which argueth the keys here spoken of be not material keys, but metaphoricall; and yet being keys they have a power also of opening and shutting." John Cotton, *The Keyes of the Kingdom*, 21.

[120]The Greek root words for "binding" and "loosing" (*deō* and *lyō*) are often used in the New Testament to refer to people. Matthew uses the word for *binding* to refer to people in 12:29, 14:3, 22:13 and 27:2. He doesn't use the word for *loosing* in this context, but in 21:2 he uses binding and loosing together to refer to tying or untying a donkey. The root word for "loose" is often used in the New Testament to refer to laws or commandments (e.g., Mt 5:19), but the root word for "bind," which is used forty times, is in fact *only* used to refer to animals or people (apart from our verses in question), with one exception. The one exception is in the context of marriage and has fairly direct application to a person: "A married woman is bound by law to her husband while he lives" (Rom 7:2).

The Politics of the Kingdom 339

- Many contemporary scholars believe Jesus took the phrase "binding and loosing" from the protorabbinic activity of interpreting Jewish law (*halakha*). That could involve interpreting the law in abstraction (e.g., "Moses' words on divorce must have meant *this*, not *that*."). Or it could involve judging the law's relevance to a particular situation (e.g., "Do Moses' words on divorce apply *to them*?").[121]

- Matthew 18:18, which we will consider further shortly, puts the keys to actual use for the purpose of church discipline (assuming that Jesus is referring to the keys when he speaks of binding and loosing).[122] They are used, to be clear, to remove a *person* (a "who") from the church for living contrary—and unrepentantly—to his or her *confession of faith* (a "what"). That would seem to rule out any interpretation that viewed binding and loosing *exclusively* as the "rabbinic" activity of interpreting law in the abstract (a "what"),[123] as is found in the Good News Bible's translation of Matthew 16:19: "What you prohibit on earth will be prohibited in heaven, and what you permit on earth will be permitted in heaven." Surely, Matthew 18 envisions people being bound and loosed.[124] At the same time, this kind of work of interpreting doctrine (a "what") must surely precede the work of personal application (a "who"). That is, there must be a standard (a "what") by which to measure people (a "who").[125]

---

[121]Discussions of this can be found in most commentaries or in standard Greek theological dictionaries such as Gerhard Kittel's *Theological Dictionary of the New Testament* or Colin Brown's *Dictionary of New Testament Theology* under the entries for *deō* and *lyō*. See also *deō* in Bauer et al., *Greek-English Lexicon*, 222.

[122]Carson helpfully describes Matthew 18:18 as a "special application" of the authority of the keys in 16:19. Carson, "Matthew," 374.

[123]The argument here is that Jesus has just told the disciples to beware of the teaching of the Pharisees, and now he is declaring Peter a kind of new chief rabbi because he confessed rightly. This is the view taken by Davies and Allison, *Matthew*, 638-39; also France, *Gospel of Matthew*, 625-26. To commend this view, one could also point to Matthew 5:19's use of the word "loosed" (*lyō*), which is variously translated as "relaxes," "breaks" or "annuls" ("whoever relaxes one of the least of these commandments") and which is clearly referring to a commandment, not a person.

[124]E.g., Carson, "Matthew," 372; Blomberg, *Matthew*, 254; Keener, *Commentary on the Gospel of Matthew*, 430; Turner, *Matthew*, 408.

[125]Ulrich Luz helpfully captures both the "what" and the "who": "One may conclude from the text that it is Peter's task to open the kingdom of heaven for *people*, and to do it by means of his binding interpretation of the *law*." Luz, *Matthew 8-20*, 365 (italics mine).

- Jesus did not use the masculine "whomever" ("whomever is bound on earth is bound in heaven"); he used the neuter "whatever,"[126] a word that makes room for both the "who" and the "what."[127]
- The oppositional relationship between binding and loosing suggests that use of the keys involves both a thing and its opposite. Doors can be open *and* shut. Donkeys can be bound *and* loosed. This would seem to rule out any interpretation that viewed binding and loosing *exclusively* as church discipline, or at least church discipline and preaching, an interpretation that shows up in both historical and contemporary Protestant writings from time to time.[128] Besides, this could be construed as smothering Matthew 16 with Matthew 18, and the context of 16:19 is not a discussion of removing members but of building the church upon right confessors, like Peter. Instead, the oppositional nature of binding and loosing would suggest, at least by implication, that if the keys could be used to *remove* members, they could also be used to receive or add members. Certainly this implication would make sense of Matthew 16's usage. (Furthermore, the power to remove presupposes the power to receive, at least logically speaking.)

In light of these clues, I believe it makes the most sense to say that Jesus gave Peter and the apostles both the authority to interpret the law, in a teacher-like fashion, and the authority to interpret its claim upon actual people, in a judge-like fashion.[129] They were to ensure that the right people belong to the church according to a right confession. The keys are the authority to judge a "what" (doctrines, confessions, practices) as well as a "who" (the people who speak those confessions). Jesus' "whatever" includes both people and doctrine, or at least any doctrine or statement that is adopted as a requirement for people to enter the fellowship of a church.

---

[126] John Cotton wrote in 1644, "But this word *whatsoever* is here put in the Neuter Gender, (not in the Masculine *whomsoever*) to imply both things and persons; Things, as sins; Persons, as those that commit them." Cotton, *Keyes of the Kingdom*, 22.

[127] Insofar as the action involves both people and a law, it works similarly to a marriage vow, as when Paul speaks of people being bound in or loosed from marriage (e.g., 1 Cor 7:27, 39).

[128] E.g., see question eighty-three in the Heidelberg Catechism or the notes on Matthew 16:19 in the *ESV Study Bible* (Wheaton, IL: Crossway, 2008).

[129] E.g., Luz, *Matthew 8–20*, 365; Nolland, *Gospel of Matthew*, 677–82.

To exercise the keys, in a couple of words, is to render an interpretive judgment over statements of faith and church members. That is, the keys were/are exercised

- whenever the apostles determined once and for all a doctrinal matter that would bind the churches for all ages;
- whenever postapostolic bishops, elders or congregations formally adopt a statement of faith or some ethical statement (e.g., a church covenant, standards for divorce) that binds every member and is treated as necessary for membership;
- whenever a person is brought into membership by confession, removed from membership as an act of discipline or restored to membership following discipline.

To put it another way, the keys represent the power of deputization. They name things on behalf of God. They are like a power of attorney.

The apostolic decision in Acts 15 constituted an exercise of the keys. The decisions of the Council of Nicaea, insofar as they were conceived as binding on what churches had to believe, were an exercise of the keys. The Council of Trent's "anathemas" were an act of the keys. John Smyth's decision that his baptism was not legitimate was an act of the keys. A local church's joint decision to change its statement of faith is an exercise of the keys. And all of these descriptive examples (some legitimate, some not, in my view) are acts of the keys because they effectively determine who can and cannot become a member of Christ's church, and the keys are employed most supremely in the formal affirming or dismissing of members.

What then shall we make of the somewhat common claim that "declaring the gospel" is one way to exercise the keys? It depends on what one means by "declaring." I would say that the act of *teaching* the gospel is not the same thing as exercising the keys, but the act of *affirming* the gospel as the gospel is. In other words, exercising the keys is more like what a judge does than what a law professor does. A law professor teaches the law. But a judge does more than that. He must render a judgment on how to best understand the law as he renders judgment on a particular case. First he must say, "*This*, not *that*, is how we should understand this law." And then he must apply it to an actual case: "According to *this* understanding of the law, *that* person is guilty."

As such, I would say that "declaring the gospel" is an exercise of the keys, but I mean that in the qualified sense of the church making a formal and official declaration of what it believes the gospel is, or of any other matter that belongs to its statement of faith (as part of its *status confessionis*). Now, whenever a church does this, it *also* declares that gospel in the more generic sense of teaching. But the point here is that exercising the keys means making a binding interpretation on the *what* of Scripture, which must then apply to every *who* in the church. As in, "When we speak of 'Jesus,' we're not referring to the Arian Jesus, or the Mormon Jesus, or the Jehovah's Witness Jesus, or the Muslim Jesus. We mean the one who is begotten, not made, being of one substance with the Father, by whom all things were made. Is that the Jesus you believe in too?"

Ultimately, the holder of the keys is being called upon to assess a person's life and profession of faith and then to make a heavenly sanctioned and public pronouncement affirming or denying the person's citizenship in the kingdom and inclusion in the church. The supreme example of this, of course, is Jesus' interchange with Peter: Jesus asked; Peter confessed; Jesus affirmed both the confession and Peter ("flesh and blood has not revealed *this* to you . . . *you* are Peter, and on this rock . . .").

Language in both John and Paul confirms this interpretation of Matthew. In John, the postresurrection Jesus grants the apostles the authority to make a performative pronouncement concerning an individual's inclusion in the gospel: "If you forgive the sins of any, they are forgiven them; if you withhold forgiveness from any, it is withheld" (Jn 20:23). No doubt, such a pronouncement amounts to an act of judgment. Paul, in fact, actually uses the language of judgment in the context of church discipline (see 1 Cor 5:4-5, 9-13).

There is some debate among commentaries on Matthew over whether the keys of the kingdom are used only in ushering people into the new community of the church, or for maintaining the life of the community.[130] In light of the fact that the keys are exercised in the context of discipline, I believe that the answer is both. To brush in broad strokes, Matthew 16 suggests that one must believe the right things to "get in"; Matthew 18 suggests that one

---

[130]Compare, e.g., Luz, *Matthew 8–20*, 364, and France, *Gospel of Matthew*, 625, with Nolland, *Gospel of Matthew*, 676, 681.

must keep believing the right things but also living the right way to "stay in." Theologically, this makes sense insofar as the church is built and the kingdom is extended through repentance and faith (Mk 1:15; Acts 19:4). Without repentance and faith, there is no church because there is no kingdom rule.

Ultimately, New Testament scholar Leon Morris offers a helpful summary of the authority of the keys: by use of the keys, "Jesus meant that the new community would exercise divinely given authority both in regulating its internal affairs and in deciding who would be admitted to and who excluded from its membership."[131] John Calvin sounded similar, though his emphasis was on restoration rather than admission: "But the church binds him whom it excommunicates—not that it casts him into everlasting ruin and despair, but because it condemns his life and morals, and already warns him of his condemnation unless he should repent. It looses him when it receives him into communion, for it makes him a sharer of the unity which is in Christ Jesus."[132] Baptists historically have emphasized less the teacher-like assessment of doctrine and more the judge-like assessment of the person. In 1697 Benjamin Keach wrote, "The Power of the Keys, or to receive in and shut out of the Congregation, is committed unto the Church."[133] Benjamin Griffith in 1743 similarly wrote, "The keys are the power of Christ, which he hath given to every particular congregation, to open and shut itself by. . . . By virtue of the charter and the power aforesaid . . . they are enabled to receive members in, and to exclude unworthy members as occasion may require."[134]

How then should we understand the relationship between the apostolic church's binding and loosing on earth and what transpires in heaven? Interpreters tend to focus on whether the verbal phrases in Matthew 16:19 and 18:18 should be translated in the simple future ("shall be bound/shall be

---

[131] Morris, *Gospel According to Matthew*, 427. Craig Keener says something similar: "In both functions—evaluating entrants and those already within the church—God's people must evaluate on the authority of the heavenly court. . . . Peter must thus accept in the church only those who share Peter's confession of Jesus' true identity" (Keener, *Commentary on the Gospel of Matthew*, 430); cf. Jn 20:22-23. See also Turner, *Matthew*, 408.

[132] John Calvin, *Institutes of the Christian Religion*, ed. John T. McNeill, trans. Ford Lewis Battles, 2 vols., Library of Christian Classics 20-21 (Philadelphia: Westminster, 1960), 2:1214.

[133] Keach, "Glory of a True Church," 71.

[134] Benjamin Griffith, "A Short Treatise Concerning a True and Orderly Gospel Church," in Dever, *Polity*, 99.

loosed," KJV, NIV, NRSV, ESV) or in the future perfect ("shall have been bound/ shall have been loosed," NASB), as if one version or the other will lead to drastically different theological conclusions about the relationship between the church and salvation. Both translations may be technically legitimate,[135] but Protestants have feared that a simple future translation suggests that the church can confer salvation.

Yet as suggested earlier, the concept of "heaven" throughout Matthew, especially as it is used in relation to the kingdom, is not so much a spatial concept referring to where a person goes when they die, as it is a political and eschatological concept. Politically, it refers to the domain of God's rule, particularly in contrast to fallen earthly rule. Eschatologically, it is treated as a rule that both has come and is coming (cf. Mt 4:17; 6:10; 12:28). To bind on earth what *will be* bound in heaven, therefore, is to make an *anticipatory* declaration. It is to say that heaven's end-time rule is visibly displayed in this person, here, now. It is not, in other words, a halfhearted word: "We, the holders of the keys, believe that this person might represent Jesus' end-time rule." It is much more audacious: "Jesus has placed his name and reputation on this person, and you can expect this person as a citizen of heaven to embody Jesus' end-time rule." In other words, the verse does not require a future perfect translation to avoid the idea that the church can simply grant salvation. In fact, the simple future better captures the forensic nature of what is happening on earth now through the church: Christ's citizens are being formally recognized for all the world to witness.

What if the church decides that it was wrong about its judgment and declaration because an individual stops bearing fruit in keeping with repentance? The church excommunicates the individual, which is the matter directly discussed in Matthew 18:15-20.

***Matthew 18 and the local church.*** Matthew 18:15-20 is the only other place where Jesus uses the word *church* and mentions the keys-related activity of binding and loosing, only this time his charge is to a plural "you" when saying "whatever you bind/loose." Since we have already considered

---

[135]But see, for example, Stanley Porter, who argues that the perfect tense conveys a stative meaning, which suggests that the verbal aspect does not have to do with time (as in a past act with ongoing consequences) but with state of being, which may render the debate moot. The participle *estai dedemenon* would not have the sense "have been bound" but simply "[in the state] bound." See Porter, *Idioms of the Greek New Testament*, 2nd ed. (Sheffield, UK: Sheffield Academic Press, 1992), 21-22, 39-40.

the question of what the keys do, we can limit the question here to who is authorized to hold them.

First, the context: Jesus speaks about confronting a Christian brother when he "sins against you" in order to gain him back (Mt 18:15). If the offender doesn't listen, the offended should take one or two others along (Mt 18:16). If the offender still doesn't listen, the offended should "tell it to the church," and if he still doesn't listen to the church, he should be treated as an outsider (Mt 18:17).

Jesus then gives the legitimating grounds of the disciplinary action by repeating Matthew 16's words about the keys: "Truly, I say to you, whatever you bind on earth shall be bound in heaven, and whatever you loose on earth shall be loosed in heaven" (Mt 18:18). In case anyone wonders whether Jesus would really give such authority, he repeats himself: "Again I say to you, if two of you agree on earth about anything they ask, it will be done for them by my Father in heaven" (Mt 18:19). The term for "anything" (*pragma*) frequently refers to judicial matters.[136] The point here seems to be that "behind the binding and loosing of v. 18 stands the praying of v. 19."[137]

Verse 20 then provides the "theological basis" for verse 19:[138] "For where two or three are gathered in my name, there am I among them" (Mt 18:20). Two or three can gather in Jesus' name to bind and loose and to pray, expecting the Father will hear them, *because* Christ is present and has given them his authority. Christ's presence here isn't so much a mystical fog that's hovering in the room where Christians are gathered. Rather, the language of his presence is acting in parallel to the deputized language of verses 18 and 19: "will be bound in heaven," "will be loosed in heaven," "it will be done for them by my Father in heaven." This is what Christ's presence signifies—that the assembled individuals are acting with the authority of heaven, that heaven hears and that the nations should take notice.

Why exactly "two" and then "two or three"? "Two" is the right number to use in verse 19 because binding and loosing—using the keys—takes a minimum of two people agreeing with one another, whether they are

---

[136] Carson, "Matthew," 457; Blomberg, *Matthew*, 281; Osborne, *Matthew*, 688.
[137] Nolland, *Gospel of Matthew*, 749.
[138] Osborne, *Matthew*, 688; also Nolland, *Gospel of Matthew*, 750.

excommunicating a third (in a three-person church) or the two of them are forming a church between themselves for the first time (a missionary and his first convert). Two is the bare minimum required to bind and loose.

"Two or three" is the crucial phrase in verse 20 for the same reason, but also because it invokes the deuteronomic law mentioned in verse 16 requiring two or three witnesses in order for a judicial verdict to be pronounced (see Deut 17:6; 19:15). Yet it doesn't seem to be the action of church discipline that verse 20 has in mind so much as what a church is and how a church is able to make the kind of judicial verdicts that are needed in church discipline. A local church *is* a gathering of two or three (or three thousand) in Christ's name.[139]

Consider again what I said earlier: a body politic needs some sort of *public* glue to hold it together as a body politic and make it identifiable on the landscape of the nations. It should hardly be surprising, therefore, that Jesus would grab hold of the ancient Jewish law for valid judicial testimonies and verdicts in order to describe what glues or binds a church together: the testimonies of "two or three" witnesses are needed. These two or three are gathered *in Christ's name* to act as testifying witnesses to Christ. And they are *gathered* in Christ's name to act as testifying witnesses to one another. The principle enunciated in verse 16 (the testimony of the two or three) is the same principle that holds a church together as a church. It is the binding glue. When two or three come together with this glue, says Jesus, "You are a church (v. 17), speaking on behalf of heaven (v. 18), knowing the Father hears you (v. 19), and all of this is true because, being gathered together with the proper number of witnesses, my name, authority and Spirit are present with you (v. 20)." Verse 20, I believe, can be read like this: "For where two or three witnesses gather to testify to my name and to their shared union under my rule through exercising the keys together, that is, in any such church, my presence and authority is with

---

[139]Miroslav Volf points to Ignatius, Tertullian, Cyprian and then the free-church tradition beginning with John Smyth as all affirming Matthew 18:20 as the key text for locating the existence of the local church on earth. Then he writes, "I will join this long tradition by taking Matt. 18:20 as the foundation not only for determining what the church is, but also for how it manifests itself externally as a church. *Where two or three are gathered in Christ's name, not only is Christ present among them, but a Chrsitian church is there as well.*" Volf, *After Our Likeness*, 136, see also 135-37.

them such that this church speaks on my behalf." Both Matthew 28:20 and 1 Corinthians 5:4, I believe, confirm this reading.

What of the suggestion made by some that the "two or three" can refer to any subgroup within the church, such as a community group? If indeed verses 18 to 20 provide the theological ground for performing something as significant as verse 17's activity of church discipline, granting any group of two or three people in the church this deputized authority is a recipe for tearing a church asunder. One community group can pit itself against another, each claiming to have the presence or deputized authority of Christ with them. It is a Protestantism run amok that makes the basic unit of kingdom authority something smaller than the gathered congregation. Again, the gathering of two or three in Christ's name is a church, and this is the basic unit of kingdom authority: "There am I among them," like Yahweh in the temple.

Does that mean that a church is not a church when it's not gathered? A church is a group of witnesses united by a shared testimony, and the sharedness of their testimony is transacted, in part, through gathering together. The physical gathering is one constituent part of sharing a witness and therefore of making the necessary judicial declaration. But the declaration, once made, continues in time and space even when the church scatters, just like a judge's ruling of a person's innocence continues in time and space beyond the courtroom. There is in fact a sense in which we are more a church together than when apart: "When you come together *as a church*," Paul says to the Corinthian church (1 Cor 11:18). The church is *a people*, but part of what constitutes them as a people is their congregating regularly in the same *place*. A football team is still a team even when it scatters, but if a team never gathers, it is no team.[140]

It is not accidental that Matthew 18 presents an illustration of the keys put to work in excommunication, which has been a historically common and reliable interpretation of Jesus' command to treat an unrepenting individual

---

[140]Volf writes, "The life of the church is not exhausted in the act of assembly. Even if the church is not assembled, it does live on as a church in the mutual service its members render to one another and in its common mission to the world. The church is not simply an act of assembling; rather it assembles at a specific place (see 1 Cor. 14:23). It is the *people* who in a specific way assemble at a specific place. In its most concentrated form, however, the church does manifest itself concretely in the act of assembling for worship, and this is constitutive for its ecclesiality." Ibid., 137.

as a foreigner (*ethnikos*) and sinner.¹⁴¹ The power to remove an individual from the fellowship of the church, like the state's power to end a life, represents the highest authority within the church. Whoever possesses the power of excommunication has, in a sense, the power to do everything else, just as the holder of the sword, within the context of a nation, has the power to do everything else—levy taxes, assemble an army and so forth. Jesus' use of excommunication to illustrate the power of the keys in Matthew 18 does not mean that use of the keys is limited to excommunication; it is simply a poignant and concrete affirmation of what we have already seen in Matthew 16, namely, that whoever possesses the keys can determine *who* does and does not belong to the church according to the *what* of their confession. Placing the keys' use in the context of excommunication additionally demonstrates the significance of a confessor's life, which brings us back to chapter five's discussion of the correlation between self-justification and self-enthronement, or faith and obedience. A person's confession of repentance to Jesus as Lord must be matched by their obedience to Jesus as Lord in order to remain in the church. A true faith evidences itself in action. Otherwise, the confession rings hollow and is not credible.

**Who holds the keys: congregations or elders?** Whom then in Matthew 18 does Jesus authorize to assess a person's life and profession of faith and then make a heavenly sanctioned pronouncement? That is, who holds the keys in a postapostolic era? I believe that everything I've said about what the keys do could be affirmed by Baptists, Presbyterians and Anglicans alike, including what I said about Matthew 18:20 above so long as you read it with something like James Bannerman's concept of ascending church power (described below). The differences between these traditions emerge when we turn to the question of who holds the keys. Is it the whole congregation? The session? The presbytery? Or the bishop? The classic Reformed creeds affirm that it belongs to "ministers,"¹⁴² "officers,"¹⁴³ "the whole Presbytery,"¹⁴⁴ the "minister and the

---

¹⁴¹It is true that in other passages of Matthew Jesus is specifically noted for eating with sinners and affirming foreigners (e.g., Mt 8:10-13; 9:10-11; 11:19). Yet it is not all sinners that Jesus eats with in Matthew, but a particular subset of sinners, namely, the repentant ones, as we considered in our earlier discussion of forgiveness in Matthew.

¹⁴²Second Helvetic Confession (1566), XIV.5.

¹⁴³Westminster Confession of Faith, XXX.2.

¹⁴⁴Johannes Wollebius, "The Outward Administration of the Church" (1650), in *Paradigms in Polity*, 164.

eldership"[145] or "governors ecclesiastical" ("presbyteries and synods; or assemblies congregational, classical and synodical").[146] Older Baptist writers argue that the keys belong to the "Church . . . [though] the Concurrence of the Presbytery is needful"[147] and "every particular congregation."[148] Congregationalist John Cotton believed they simultaneously belonged to the apostles, the elders and the congregation as a whole, albeit in different ways.[149]

I would prefer for the larger political-theological purposes of this book, frankly, not to wade into matters that divide one denominational tradition from another. That said, we have traced the covenantal storyline of the Bible for several chapters and discovered that membership in the new covenant (and universal church) means being reinstated as a new creation priest-king. Where the old covenant separated the offices of priest and king, the new covenant democratizes them once more. And the conclusion of this covenantal storyline, in my understanding, occurs in the Matthew 18 and 28, where Jesus formally inducts every member of the new covenant into the office of citizen or priest-king by placing the keys of the kingdom into their hands through baptism into church membership. And I believe congregationalism best represents this covenantal trajectory, to say nothing of the New Testament texts themselves. Congregationalism tasks every member of the church with the priestly and kingly work of guarding the *who* and the *what* of the gospel with the keys of the kingdom. It is a tool for discipleship, requiring the elders to equip the saints to undertake the three elements of the priest-king office described above: (1) representing Christ (2) through the inward work of watching over the holy temple of the church where God dwells and (3) the outward work of pushing back the borders of the "Eden" or "temple" through evangelistic witness and good deeds.

Perhaps, then, the noncongregationalist reader would be willing to forbear with me for just one subsection's worth of my sectarianism, and let me try to persuade you with ten quick bullet points of why I believe Jesus places the keys into the hands of the whole church. But then I will try to find some common ground by demonstrating places of overlap from church

---

[145] Andrew Melville, "The Second Book of Discipline" (1578), in *Paradigms in Polity*, 235 (I.14, 16), 239 (IV.11).
[146] "Westminster Assembly Directory for Church Government" (1645), in *Paradigms in Polity*, 263.
[147] Keach, "Glory of a True Church," 71.
[148] Griffith, "Short Treatise," 99.
[149] Cotton, *Keyes of the Kingdom*, 23-25.

history. If all this seems deeply obnoxious, my noncongregationalist friends can feel free to skip this subsection and go to the next. I believe the larger argument concerning the keys more or less holds, even if you want to lay off your tenderhearted members from their offices!

Without further adieu, here then are ten largely exegetical reasons for why I believe the keys belong jointly to the entire congregation:[150]

- First, the final court of appeal in Matthew 18 is "the church" (Mt 18:17). The whole church must address the unrepentant sinner ("if he refuses to listen even to the church"), and then the whole church must assent to any act of excommunication in order for it to work.

- Second, there is no mention of bishops or elders in Matthew 18. Some have argued that the elders can represent or stand in for the "church." But (1) verse 17 says *ekklēsia*. (2) Verses 15 to 17 present a clear numeric trajectory: from one, to two or three, to assembly. Inserting an elder here interrupts that trajectory and any pastoral reasons beind it. (3) Commentators are quick to explain the background of the words "tax collector" and "Gentile" in these verses by appealing to the first hearers. What then would the first hearers have thought when they heard *ekklēsia*? Elders? It seems unlikely.

- Third, nowhere does the New Testament explicitly connect the keys of the kingdom to pastors/bishops/elders.

- Fourth, verses 19 and 20 appear to define a church as a gathering of two or three believers. Christ grants his authoritative presence to them. Following on this point:

- Fifth, the New Testament presents evidence that gatherings of believers without elders were called "churches" (Acts 14:21-23; Tit 1:5), even if one wants to describe such churches as disorderly, as I would following the language of Titus 1:5. Still, these gatherings could exercise the keys through baptism and the Lord's Supper.

- Sixth, Paul invokes the language of gathering in Jesus' name from Matthew 18:20 to charge not the leaders of the Corinthian church but

---

[150] For an academic apologetic for congregationalism, see my *Don't Fire Your Church Members: The Case for Congregationalism* (Nashville: B&H Academic, 2016); for a popular-level treatment of the topic, see my *Understanding the Congregation's Authority* (Nashville: B&H, 2016).

the whole congregation to "deliver this man to Satan" (1 Cor 5:5). Notice the setting in which judgment occurs; it's not behind closed session doors: "When you are assembled in the name of the Lord Jesus and my spirit is present, with the power of our Lord Jesus, you are to deliver this man to Satan" (1 Cor 5:4-5). Jesus' power and Paul's apostolic spirit are there with the whole assembly, not just the elders. Verse 12 verifies the fact that he is calling the whole assembly to make this judgment (which, incidentally, attests to my reading of the keys as providing the power of judgment): "Is it not those inside the church whom you are to judge?" (1 Cor 5:12).

- Seventh, Paul appeals to the churches of Galatia, not their leaders, when some began to preach a false gospel. He even suggests that a church listening to a false gospel possesses the right to trump an apostle or angel from heaven (Gal 1:6-9).

- Eighth, lexically, this explanation has the advantage of corresponding more closely with the Greek conception of an *ekklēsia*, which involved an assembly of citizens who shared rule together and each had one vote, not an assembly of subjects.

- Ninth, this explanation has the advantage of corresponding more closely with what I called in chapter four the "vaguely democratic" nature of Genesis 9:5-6 and the latent "downward push" of those verses. If God's special-covenant new humanity should model true citizenship to his common-covenant humanity, it should not be surprising that we can discern democratic tendencies in the government charters for each. I was unwilling to biblically absolutize democracy, the reader may recall, because the Bible doesn't and because it would insufficiently account for the nature of sin. But if the church's very job is to act as an embassy for the eschaton, as I will argue in a moment, we might expect these democratic tendencies to harden into something more principial.

- Tenth, as I said above, it best represents the reauthorization granted to every priest-king.

Now, different traditions will not assign as much authority to the congregation as I do, but with the exception perhaps of medieval Catholicism, congregational authority has long been an undercurrent in most traditions.[151] Clement of Rome around AD 96 referred to pastors being appointed "with the consent of the church."[152] Several decades later, the Didache instructed its readers to "elect for yourselves bishops and deacons."[153] And it showed little interest in who conducted baptisms or the Eucharist,[154] unlike, say, Ignatius, who said that neither practice was permitted "without authorization from the bishop."[155] Hippolytus, in *The Apostolic Tradition* (c. 215), instructed, "Let the bishop be ordained being in all things without fault chosen by the people."[156] Cyprian was elected bishop by the laity in 247, and in turn called for congregational participation and consent in choosing bishops, in readmitting lapsed Christians who were penitent[157] and in removing unfaithful clergy.[158]

Skipping the song track forward to the Protestant Reformation, we hear these same congregational notes. Martin Luther, in his fight against the pope, argued that "it is plain enough that the keys were not given to Peter alone, but to the whole community."[159] Behind this statement was Luther's strong

---

[151] A useful introduction to congregationalism in the early church is Everett Ferguson, "The 'Congregationalism' of the Early Church," in *The Free Church and the Early Church*, ed. D. H. Williams (Grand Rapids: Eerdmans, 2002), 129-40.

[152] St. Clement of Rome, "Epistle to the Corinthians," in *The Epistles of St. Clement of Rome and St. Ignatius of Antioch*, trans. James A. Kleist, Ancient Christian Writers (New York: Paulist Press, 1946), sec. 44, p. 36.

[153] "Didache," in *Ancient Christian Writers*, trans. James A. Kleist (New York: The Newman Press, 1948), 24, 15.

[154] "Didache," in ibid., 19, 7. See Everett Ferguson, *Baptism in the Early Church: History, Theology, and Liturgy in the First Five Centuries* (Grand Rapids: Eerdmans), 202, 209. As late as 306, the Council of Elvira granted laity the ability to baptize when a person was near death and a bishop was absent (canon 38).

[155] Ignatius, "To the Smyrnaeans," in *Epistles of St. Clement of Rome and St. Ignatius of Antioch*, sec. 8, p. 93.

[156] Quoted in Everett Ferguson, "'Congregationalism' of the Early Church," 134.

[157] To the laity, Cyprian writes of a group of penitents, "each one will be examined in your presence with you judging." Letter 17.1, in *The Fathers of the Church: St. Cyprian Letters 1-81*, trans. Sister Rose Bernard Donna, C.S.J. (Washington, DC: Catholic University Press, 1964), 51. (This is epistle 11 in the *Ante-Nicene Fathers* edition.) He repeats later that the penitents would only be received "with your decision" (17.3.2 [p. 51]). See also 16.4.2 (p. 49) and 19.2.2 (p. 53) in the same version. Also J. Patout Burns Jr., *Cyprian the Bishop* (London: Routledge, 2002), 70.

[158] Paul J. Fitzgerald, S.J., "A Model for Dialogue: Cyprian of Carthage on Ecclesial Discernment," *Theological Studies* 59 (1998): 238, 239.

[159] Martin Luther, "An Open Letter to the Christian Nobility of the German Nation," in *Works of Martin Luther*, The Philadelphia Edition, vol. 2 (repr., Grand Rapids: Baker, 1982), 75. Luther said elsewhere, "Peter received the keys not as Peter, but in the stead of the Church, as Matthew xviii. and John xx. clearly say, and not as Peter alone, as Matthew xvi. seems to say." Luther, "The Papacy at Rome," in *Works of Martin Luther*, The Philadelphia Edition, vol. 1 (repr., Grand

belief in the priesthood of all believers. Luther wrote, "Through baptism all of us are consecrated to the priesthood, as St. Peter says in I Peter ii, 'Ye are a royal priesthood.'"[160] Based on this conviction Luther believed members should be involved in affirming their leaders, church discipline, baptism if necessary and scriptural interpretation.[161]

Congregational inflections resound in John Calvin as well. Specifically, he believes the congregation possesses the right to elect its own bishops, a position he ascribes to both himself and Cyprian.[162] Calvin also denied that the power of the keys uniquely rested with Peter or his fellow apostles.[163] Instead, he distinguishes between the key of Matthew 16:18-19 and John 20:23, which he says is the authority given to ministers to preach the gospel since the gospel opens the doorway to heaven, and the key of Matthew 18:17-18, which he says is the authority given to the whole church to excommunicate.[164] The former key is the authority to preach the gospel as well as "to lay down articles of faith, and authority to explain them." The latter key is employed "by vote of the believers,"[165] he says in one context, while in another place he says it should occur in "the tribunal of the church, that is, the assembly of the elders."[166] (It's unclear to me how these two statements are reconciled.)

A fairly common view of church power among Presbyterians is represented by nineteenth-century Presbyterian James Bannerman. In his classic work *The Church of Christ*, Bannerman attempts to find a middle ground between the high-church "papists," high-church Anglicans and an older tradition of Presbyterians, who place all authority in the officers, and the Independents, whom he says place all authority in the congregation, obliterating the distinction between members and officers. Bannerman recognizes that Scripture clearly gives oversight to the elders (e.g., Acts 20:28; 1 Pet 5:1-5; Heb 13:17), yet he also recognizes that churches don't absolutely require

---

Rapids: Baker, 1982), 376. Also, Luther believed the "power of the keys extends only to the Sacrament of Penance, to bind and loose the sins" (ibid., 376-77, see also 377-78).
[160]Luther, "Open Letter," 66.
[161]Luther, "Open Letter," 67, 74, 76-77.
[162]Calvin, *Institutes of the Christian Religion*, ed. John T. McNeill, trans. Ford Lewis Battles, Library of Christian Classics 21 (Philadelphia: Westminster Press, 1960), 4.3.15 and 4.5.2.
[163]Ibid., 4.6.1-5, pp. 1102-7.
[164]Ibid., 4.11.1-2, pp. 1211-14.
[165]Ibid., 4.11.2, p. 1214.
[166]Ibid., 4.12.2, p. 1231.

elders or bishops to be churches. And church authority must ultimately root in every believer's union with Christ: "The primary grant from Christ of Church power is virtually, if not expressly and formally, made to believers in that grant which makes all things, whether pertaining to the present or the future, to be theirs in Christ Jesus."[167] To make a point he uses the illustration of a church on a desert island, where all the elders die. No doubt such a church "must have within themselves all power competent to carry on the necessary functions and offices of a Church."[168] How then does Bannerman put the two sides together? He explains that, whereas congregations possess the *essence* of church power, the officers possess the right to *exercise* or *administer* church power. The congregation exercises that power insofar as they elect their elders.

Bannerman's distinction between *possession* and *exercise* placed him in a long line of Presbyterians who employed this same division. For instance, the seventeenth-century Scottish Presbyterian George Gillespie said that there is a difference "betwixt the power it self [sic], and the execution of it." Referring to the keys of the kingdom in Matthew 18:18, Gillespie observed, "The power of binding and loosing, pertaineth to every particular Church collectively taken. But the execution and judiciall exercising of this power, pertaineth to that company and assembly of Elders in every Church."[169] For Gillespie, this same congregational authority extended to ordination: Christ "hath also delivered unto the whole Church, power to call & ordaine Ministers for using the keyes . . . because the Ministers which shee now hath, may faile." In the elders or presbytery, then, "the Church consisteth representative."[170] A nineteenth-century Presbyterian, Thomas Peck, agreed with this basic way of characterizing the two roles: "The power resides in the body as to its *being*; in the officers as to its *exercise*."[171] And today, the

---

[167] James Bannerman, *The Church of Christ*, vol. 2 (Carlisle, PA: Banner of Truth, 1974), 272. See the discussion of virtual versus formal power in Samuel Rutherford, in Hunter Powell, *The Crisis of British Protestantism: Church Power in the Puritan Revolution, 1638–44* (New York: Manchester University Press, 2015), 157-59.

[168] Bannerman, *Church of Christ*, 273.

[169] Quoted in Powell, *Crisis of British Protestantism*, 38.

[170] Ibid., 39. But see the critiques of Gillespie by fellow Presbyterians John Ball and Samuel Rutherford (ibid., 41-45, 48-53).

[171] Thomas E. Peck, *Notes on Ecclesiology*, 2nd ed. (Richmond, VA: Presbyterian Committee of Publication, 1892; repr., Greenville, SC: Presbyterian Press, 2005), 85. Quoted in Guy Prentiss Waters, *How Jesus Runs the Church* (Phillipsburg, NJ: P&R, 2011), 60.

Presbyterian Church of America's *Book of Church Order* affirms (1) that Christ vests all church power "in the whole body, the rulers and those ruled" (3.1), (2) that "this power, as exercised by the people, extends to the choice of those officers whom He has appointed in His church" (3.1), but (3) that, once elected, the "officers exercise" that power (3.2) such that it has a "divine sanction" (3.6).[172] Other Presbyterian and Reformed denominations have similar language.

But Presbyterians are not the only ones to hold this view. At least some low-church, evangelical Anglicans affirm the priesthood of all believers and therefore the necessity of involving the church in "discerning and ratifying" who the leaders are.[173] They use slightly different arguments, such as the claim that an ordained minister is not of the church's *esse* (essence) but only its *bene esse* (benefit).[174] As such, the minister is "an instrument and a steward" of church authority.[175] "The ordained ministry subserves the ministry of all the people," and to "distance this ministry in any way from the local people would harm the local community."[176] So much do evangelical Anglicans push against high-church Anglo-Catholicism that some seem to be one or two clicks closer to congregationalism than Presbyterians. In the words of the Anglican Gerald Bray, "The Anglican structure is basically a form of Congregationalism held together in an Episcopal framework."[177]

Since Vatican II moved Roman Catholicism in a generally inclusivist direction, the previously rock-hard connection between the authority of church officers and salvation (or a living church) has, of logical necessity,

---

[172] For an excellent discussion of this position both in the Book of Church Order and in presbyterianism generally, see Waters's excellent *How Jesus Runs the Church*, 58-63, a section entitled "The Delegation and Vesting of Church Power."

[173] Tim Bradshaw, *The Olive Branch: An Evangelical Doctrine of the Church* (Carlisle, UK: Paternoster Press, 1992), 161.

[174] Ibid., 144, 175; see also Colin Buchanan, *Is the Church of England Biblical? An Anglican Ecclesiology* (London: Dartman, Longman, and Todd, 1998), 261; Paul Zahl, "The Bishop-Led Church," in *Perspectives on Church Government: Five Views of Church Polity*, ed. Chad Owen Brand and R. Stanton Norman (Nashville: B&H, 2004), 213-16; Peter Toon, "Episcopalianism," in *Who Runs the Church? Four Views on Church Government*, ed. Paul E. Engle and Steve B. Cowan (Grand Rapids: Zondervan, 2004), 36-38.

[175] Bradshaw, *Olive Branch*, 160, and 143-47, 158-69.

[176] Ibid., 158-59.

[177] Gerald L. Bray, "Why I Am an Evangelical and an Anglican," in *Why We Belong: Evangelical Unity and Denominational Diversity*, ed. Anthony Chute, Christopher W. Morgan and Robert A. Peterson (Wheaton, IL: Crossway, 2013).

softened. Hence, even here is a subtle movement toward recognizing a power that inheres in all believers. Dissident Catholic theologian Hans Küng, claiming to build on Vatican II, affirms the doctrine of the priesthood of all believers as giving every Christian the power to teach, baptize, distribute the Lord's Supper and forgive sins. But then, sounding not altogether dissimilar to Bannerman, he observes that "this fundamental right and duty to take an active part in baptism, the Lord's Supper and the forgiving of sins is not of course the same thing as determining who can and may be responsible for administering these sacraments in and for the community."[178] In other words, Küng builds on this same distinction between possession and ordinary exercise.

Even Eastern Orthodox churches possess congregational instincts. A bishop will not lay hands on anyone to ordain them until they have, in the service, stood in the middle of the congregation and had the congregation unanimously affirm them.[179]

I believe the distinction between possession and exercise is problematic, of course. It's not clear to me what it means to possess authority that you cannot exercise. If the congregation can no longer exercise authority after electing the leaders, they don't really possess it. And that means that the members can no longer do the work of a priest-king by protecting the gospel or maintaining the line between holy and unholy. Even if they show up at the office one day, they'll find the locks changed and their keys no good. They might know an elder is a wolf in sheep's clothing, or that some deacon is a snake. Now their only choice is to leave.

Still, my purpose for plowing through these examples is to point to some measure of overlap in these various traditions. Historic evangelical Christianity, if I may call it that, has long recognized that the priesthood of

---

[178]Hans Küng, *The Church* (New York: Sheed and Ward, 1967), 380. Küng points to Vatican II as supporting the point that every member possesses this power in the matter of the sacraments. It reads, "Mother Church earnestly desires that all the faithful should be led to that full, conscious, and active participation in liturgical celebrations which is demanded by the very nature of the liturgy, and to which the Christian people, 'a chosen race, a royal priesthood, a holy nation, a redeemed people' (1 Pet 2:9, 4-5) have a right and obligation by reason of their baptism." *The Constitution on the Sacred Liturgy*, in *Vatican Council II*, vol. 1, *The Conciliar and Post Conciliar Documents*, new rev. ed., ed. Austin Flannery, OP (Northport, NY: Costello, 1975), 14, pp. 7-8. Whether Vatican II is saying what Küng thinks it is saying, I leave for others.
[179]See Nicolas Zernov, *The Church of the Eastern Christians* (London: SPCK, 1942), 47-48.

believers—or what I would prefer to call the priestly rule of believers—has implications for church polity and structure. Every Christian is a priest-king, which means that the congregation as a whole must possess *some* authority in saying what the gospel is (see esp. Jer 31:34). The church's polity grows out of the church's faith, organically, as it were. It's not an artificial superstructure, wholly detachable from and replaceable between one context and another. Both congregational and noncongregational readers, I expect, can adopt my larger argument that the church as a whole consists of kingdom citizens or priest-kings who are responsible for displaying the justice and righteousness of God in their life together. Both kinds of readers can affirm what the keys do. It may only be the congregationalist readers who are willing to take the last step by fully affirming that every member of the church has been formally authorized with the keys of the kingdom to guard the *who* and the *what* of the gospel, thereby keeping the line between the inside and outside of the temple clear. But it may also be that a few noncongregationalist readers would be willing to say that the congregation holds the keys, even if the officers exercise them much of the time. If so, hopefully these historic examples demonstrate for the noncongregationalists that they, too, have material to draw upon as they think through how much authority the whole church possesses. And I will leave it to them to institutionally specify the answer.

Now, just a few more words on how a congregationalist like me views the authority of elders: Are members and elders therefore indistinguishable in the congregationalist conception, as Bannerman accuses?[180] Not at all. Members and elders gathered together possess the office of "keyholder," but elders hold the office of overseer. They are different offices, both direct gifts from God (see Acts 20:28; Eph 4:11), much like lieutenant and colonel are different offices. And members are called to "submit" to their elders (Heb 13:17).

Elder authority, I propose, is backed by a *heavenly and end-time sanction*. Disobey your elders within the arena of their authority, and you will have to deal with Jesus' displeasure *on the last day*. Congregational authority, on the other hand, possesses an *earthly and present sanction*—the ability to bind and loose something *on earth now*. As such, we see Paul authorizing churches to discipline people from membership in a way he never authorizes

---

[180] A classic argument against congregationalism is that it merely gives lip service to the authority of elders/bishops/pastors. E.g., Bannerman, *Church of Christ*, 2:239-40.

elders to do (1 Cor 5:5, 12).[181] Instead, the fact that the elders' sanction must await the eschaton affects the nature or manner of their rule.[182] They can place biblical burdens on the conscience of their hearers by virtue of their office, but they cannot enforce, force or demand something. Instead, they must teach, persuade, exhort, warn, encourage, even woo, with great patience and tenderness. Of course, if they burden the conscience of their hearers with something unbiblical or unwise, Jesus will have words for *them* on the last day.

Instead of distinguishing between *possession* and *exercise*, which I would argue encourages complacency, passivity and nominalism among the priest-kings, I would distinguish between *possession* and *leading in the use*. The whole congregation, elders and members together, possess the keys. But the elders have the task of training, equipping and leading the congregation to use the keys in a right manner. The congregation possesses *and* exercises, and the elders show them how.

Ephesians 4 captures this dynamic. Christ has given pastors and teachers to churches "to equip the saints for the work of ministry, for building up the body of Christ, until we all attain to the unity of the faith and of the knowledge of the Son of God, to mature manhood, to the measure of the stature of the fullness of Christ" (Eph 4:11-13). Notice that church members themselves are responsible for building up the body of Christ to unity and maturity. And they need pastors and teachers to train them for this work. As Paul says a moment later, the body builds itself up in love as each part does its work (Eph 4:15-16).

Other than in extraordinary circumstances, the elders use their authority of teaching and oversight to lead the church in its use of the keys. The congregation cannot wisely adjudicate the *what* and the *who* of the gospel—they

---

[181]The apostles do seem to possess (what Presbyterians call) jurisdictional authority, e.g., Acts 8:21; 1 Tim 1:20.

[182]Oliver O'Donovan's distinction between an authority of counsel and an authority of command is worth considering here. See O'Donovan, *Resurrection and Moral Order: An Outline for Evangelical Ethics*, 2nd ed. (Grand Rapids: Eerdmans, 1994), 170-71. The authority of counsel, which is similar to what I would argue elders have, recognizes that "there is an area of direct address, in which the demand confronts the individual without the reinforcement of social constraint" (ibid., 171). An elder or bishop must lead the congregation to employ the keys to enact that social constraint whenever it is necessary. See also O'Donovan's discussion of the distinction between natural authority and the authority of truth (ibid., 124-27).

cannot wisely fulfill their job responsibilities—unless they have gospel teachers teaching and giving oversight. The church *needs* elders to do their job, just as children need parents and teachers in order to grow into adulthood. In particular, the congregation needs elders to lead them in the exercise of the keys.

It is because elders and congregation have a different *kind* of authority, each within their respective jurisdictions, that any notion of "final authority" is somewhat relative, as I suggested in chapter three. In one sense, yes, final earthly authority rests with whomever possesses the keys, because the power of excommunication, like the power of the sword, means the ability to remove someone from membership and all activity in the body politic. And I am contending that the keys belong to the entire church, elders and members together. That said, Jesus alone is the final authority, and he commands the congregation to exercise its key-holding authority *in submission to* the elders. When the elders bring a motion to the congregation concerning, say, a matter of membership or discipline, the congregation should ordinarily follow. Involving them in guarding the *who* and the *what* of the gospel like this serves discipleship purposes. It apprentices them. It teaches them to spot false messages and discern hypocritical professors of faith. Only when the church believes that the elders' recommendation violates Scripture and that an action of disobedience to the elders will surely be vindicated on the last day by the One who truly possesses final authority should a congregation exercise the keys in defiance of the elders. In that sense, a congregation's "final authority" is a rarely used veto power or emergency brake to be pulled only when fidelity to the Bible or the gospel is at stake. Ordinarily, elders lead, and the church's authority is used to affirm and endorse this leadership.[183] Elder leadership plus congregational rule, most of the time, equals discipleship.

**Matthew 28 as deputization ceremony.** If you are a noncongregationalist who skipped the last section, thank you for tuning back in. There may be a bit more congregationalist-sounding language peppered throughout the ordinances discussion below, but the coast is mostly clear. With Matthew 28:18-20 and the Great Commission we come to something like a

---

[183]See Leeman, *Don't Fire Your Church Members*, chap. 5.

deputization ceremony for citizens of Christ's kingdom. Christians often seem to read Matthew 28 independently of Matthew 16 and 18, as if the Great Commission will be fulfilled by individuals. But an institutional reading would recommend reading these chapters together, particularly in light of the various textual links.[184] It's the ones who bind and loose on earth what's bound and loosed in heaven who would seem to take an especial interest in the One with all authority in heaven and on earth (Mt 28:18). It's the ones who gather in Christ's name who would seem to possess the authority to baptize in his name (Mt 28:19). And it's the ones with whom Christ promises to dwell when they gather who can expect him to dwell with them always, even to the end of the age (Mt 28:20).

If Matthew 16 and 18 establish the authority to publicly ratify those who belong to the new covenant, Matthew 28:18-20 explains what that covenant ratification or deputization ceremony looks like: baptism followed by teaching together with presence. (Matthew 26 could be said to do the same with the Lord's Supper, but we will not explore that here.) Here is how the new creation priest-kings are formally deputized:

"*All authority in heaven and on earth has been given to me.*" The rule of heaven and the rule of earth converge in Christ. The covenantal Lord of the church has authority in both domains.[185] His jurisdiction includes all things visible and invisible, all hearts and all bodies. He deserves the obedience of the nations and their kings.

"*Go therefore and make disciples of all nations . . .*" Christ has the authority to send his representatives into the territory of every other king without a visa, dismissive of any king's higher claim on them. The church is not "over" the state, but neither is it "under" it, existing by the state's permission. It does not let the state determine its terms of entry. Not only that, Christ tells his people to tell these other kings and their people that the real king is coming, that there is a warrant out for their arrest and that the real king promises a

---

[184]Pennington observes, "The authority given to Jesus in 28:18 likely echoes and grounds the authority given to the church by Jesus as found in 16:19 and 18:18, texts which famously use the same type of heaven and earth language." Pennington, *Heaven and Earth*, 205. Pennington credits Nolland, *Gospel of Matthew*, 1265. Wright also argues that Matthew 28:18 fulfills the promise of 16:18. N. T. Wright, *How God Became King: The Forgotten Story of the Gospels* (New York: HarperOne, 2012), 223-24.

[185]See Pennington, *Heaven and Earth*, 203-6.

covenantal release program. Through a new covenant he will restore them to upstanding citizenship if only they repent and believe.

"... *baptizing them in the name of the Father and of the Son and of the Holy Spirit*..." Jesus is not interested in sending out lone individuals or creating a voluntary society, where people come and go according to what suits their needs or desires. He means to establish a nation whose citizens are publicly and covenantally identified with the triune God. God places his name on them, and these people, in turn, wear God's name and gather in his name, being covenantally identified with one another. Heaven and earth converge in them, too. These are the ones who pray for it, store up treasures in it, seek it and, most remarkably, speak for it (Mt 6:10, 20, 33; 16:19; 18:18).

"... *teaching them to observe all that I have commanded you.*" If the rule of heaven and rule of earth converge in them, they must be taught to represent heaven's rule fully. Matthew 1:1 began, we saw, with the new genesis and the promise that God's political purpose for creation would be fulfilled. Matthew 28 ends with the first signs of that promise being fulfilled though the resurrected Son and these sons of the kingdom. Jesus, who we saw fulfilled Adam's political mandate, means to disciple, to teach, to train a people who will do the same by obeying everything that he commanded.

"*And behold, I am with you always, to the end of the age.*" Where Jesus earlier promised that he would identify himself and dwell in their gatherings, now he promises to identify with and dwell with these people until the end. His name will be upon them, his Spirit will lead them, his governance will guide them. Again, the nations of the earth will see heaven's rule among this national-border-crossing nation.

Through baptism people are formally and publicly reinstated to Adam's original political office and to the body politic of Jesus' church. The keys of the kingdom are exercised first *through* baptism. Baptism is the recognition of kingdom citizenship and covenant membership. It is the recognition that a person has been forgiven (or justified by faith alone)—covenantally united with Christ in his death and resurrection and all their benefits. It functions as the public badge or passport or identity papers among Christ's people and the nations now. When the nations come asking who belongs to Jesus and represents his rule on earth, the church points to everyone who has been baptized (and who continues to receive the Lord's Supper).

## A Church, Its Members, and the Ordinances

In light of all these texts, how should we think about church membership and its relationship to the ordinances? And what shall we say the local church is?

Earlier I observed that the local church is constituted in two moments. The first moment comes through the preaching of the gospel with salvation and one's inclusion into the universal church. But the church remains invisible at that point because faith dwells in the heart. The second moment comes when a group of Christians covenant together and affirm one another as fellow citizens and members of the body of Christ. This is the "two or three" gathering in Christ's name. By declaring one another members, they become members and so they become a church. A church *is* its members. And all of this is made visible through baptism and the Lord's Supper.

Let's unpack this a bit more.

***Church membership and the ordinances.*** What contemporary Christians programmatically call "joining a church" or "becoming a church member" is where and how a Christian formally assumes citizenship in Christ's kingdom, thereby making Christ's covenantal presence on earth public in a particular time and place. Not only that, church membership is the office that a believer assumes in exercising that same oversight of other believers, an office created by one's justification and formally authorized by Jesus' keys.[186] Excommunication or formal church discipline is the removal of a church's membership affirmation and from participation in the Lord's Table. It is a removal from office.

Church membership therefore depends upon the local church's *affirmation* and *oversight* of an individual believer's profession of faith, which it does through the ordinances of baptism and the Lord's Supper. O'Donovan again:

> This is the criterion of a church's membership. To recognize those who gather and to claim them for the community; to defy, where necessary, other

---

[186] "The identity of the church is given wholly and complexly in the relation of its members to the ascended Christ independently of church ministry and organization." O'Donovan, *Desire of the Nations*, 169. That is true insofar as a Christian's identity ultimately derives from Christ. Nonetheless, that identity is given public expression on earth through the local "church ministry and organization." I assume O'Donovan would agree with this.

communities which make rival claims on their allegiance; to rule out those who do not make the apostolic confession: this is the authority which the Spirit confers upon the gathering church.[187]

The body as a whole has an authority to formally affirm and oversee citizens of Christ's kingdom that the individual professor of faith does not possess. By analogy, I cannot formally affirm that I am a US citizen, even though I am one. Church membership, in the final analysis, is the formal recognition between church and individual of citizenship status, a recognition that must be ongoing in order for a congregation to give a credible testimony.

In contemporary parlance, Christians "join" churches. Perhaps it would be more theologically accurate to say that Christians should "submit" themselves to a church's affirmation and oversight. Submitting to a local church is one expression of how a Christian submits to Christ the king. It is the fruit of repentance. It is obedience to the one confessed as the Christ, the Son of the living God, and then it is the sharing of Christ's rule. It is, furthermore, *where* the believer submits and shares in kingdom rule.[188]

Baptism and the Lord's Supper, I said a moment ago, are the badge or passport of membership in Christ's body, a universal membership transacted or executed locally. They are how the new covenant gets publicly ratified. Oliver O'Donovan refers to the ordinances as the "abiding signs" and "marks of identification which will stamp a formal identity on the community." Faith comes first, he says, but a "certain structuring of the church's life is a given with that life," which the ordinances present. He sums up the work of the ordinances or sacraments:

> The sacraments provide the primary way in which the church is "knit together," that is, given institutional form and order. Without them the church could be a "visible" society, without doubt, but only a rather intangible one, melting indeterminately like a delicate mist as we stretched out our arms to embrace it. In these forms we know where the church is and can attach

---

[187]O'Donovan, *Desire of the Nations*, 176. Again, a (rare) difference with O'Donovan emerges in this last sentence regarding the Holy Spirit's authorization. I prefer to speak of Jesus' authorization and the Spirit's empowerment.

[188]Notice the apt title of Michael Horton's ecclesiology, *People and Place: A Covenant Ecclesiology* (Louisville, KY: Westminster John Knox, 2008).

ourselves to it. They are at once "signs" of the mystery of redemption wrought in Christ, and "effective signs" which give it a palpable presence in the participating church.[189]

Baptism, O'Donovan further observes, "marks the gathering community" and is the sign by which "each new believer accepts Jesus as his or her representative, and accepts Jesus' people as his or her people."[190] The Lord's Supper should not be individualistically viewed as a "'sacramental grace' which affects the believer in a different way from other kinds of grace"; rather, its work has to do with "the formation of the body. The 'one loaf' binds 'many' into 'one body' (1 Cor. 10:17). It determines the identity of this society by reference to the Passion: it is the community of those who have not only gathered to God's Christ, but have died with him."[191]

In fact, if the keys of the kingdom constitute the local church, and if the keys are exercised through the ordinances, it would seem that the local church is constituted as a public reality through the ordinances. While the gospel creates a people, the keys working through the ordinances create a body politic. Bobby Jamieson writes, "Without baptism, there may be self-proclaimed kingdom persons, but there is not kingdom *people*—no body politic."[192] The organized local church is the place on earth where faith goes public.[193]

As with the politician who gains office through a vote, so the decisive vote into kingdom office is cast in God's word of justification or forgiveness. But then comes the swearing-in ceremony and the television broadcast. That is what the local church does. The office here is not named "president" but "disciple," "new covenant priest-king," "kingdom citizen" or "church member." All four terms are different angles on the same thing. A *disciple* or follower of Jesus is a *new covenant priest-king* and *kingdom citizen*—a ruled ruler representing heaven. And a kingdom citizen is a *church member*, someone affirmed by the church as belonging to them.

---

[189] O'Donovan, *Desire of the Nations*, 172.
[190] Ibid., 177-78.
[191] Ibid., 180.
[192] Bobby Jamieson, *Going Public: Why Baptism Is Required for Church Membership* (Nashville: B&H Academic, 2015), 95.
[193] Jamieson, *Going Public*.

***What and where is a church?*** What then shall we say a local church is? To summarize all this in definitional form, we can say that a local church is *a group of Christians who regularly gather in Christ's name with the power of the keys to affirm the gospel and one another's citizenship in the gospel through the ordinances.* Individual Christians do not have the authority to exercise their key-carrying covenantal responsibility in isolation from one another or at whim; they use the keys whenever they are formally gathered "in his name."[194] The performative word of judgment of the keys of the kingdom, by declaring who is a citizen of the kingdom or a church member, formally constitutes the institutional church on earth—the local church. The constituting of members is the constituting of a church.

Or we can ask the question like the Reformers: where is the church? The local church exists *wherever Christians regularly gather in Christ's name to proclaim the gospel and to affirm one another as his disciples through the authority of the keys in the ordinances.* The gathering must be "regular" because occasional or one-off gatherings are generally incapable of performing the work of affirmation and oversight with any integrity. More significantly, a weekly gathering is the pattern set by the New Testament (e.g., Acts 20:7; 1 Cor 16:2; cf. Heb 10:25).

## A Heavenly and Eschatological Embassy and Signmaker on Earth

Having defined the essence of the local church and its institutional authority through the keys, we can pull the camera back and consider where the local church sits upon the landscape of the nations.

***A political assembly.*** For starters, it's worth summarizing why the local church, these people gathering in Christ's name, constitutes a political assembly. Recall that, at the conclusion of chapter four, I defined politics as the mediation of God's covenantal rule and then specified that definition in narrow and broad terms:

---

[194] O'Donovan: "To speak of a 'gathering' church . . . is to speak of a community which, for all the permeability of its skin, has a sharply defined core. To gather is to make a centripetal movement; it is altogether different from merely milling around or associating. The church that gathers must have defined the central point around which it gathers. The apostolic confession of Jesus, 'You are the Christ, the son of the living God,' St. Matthew would have us understand, is the confession that defines the church as such (16:16-19)." O'Donovan, *Desire of the Nations*, 176.

- *Politics narrowly conceived* implements God's sword-wielding covenantal rule invisibly through the justice mechanism of the Noahic covenant and visibly through the oaths and institutions of the special covenants.
- *Politics broadly conceived* is the acknowledgment that all of life exists within the jurisdiction of God's comprehensive rule or judgment, yet it awaits the visible performance of that judgment in the eschaton.

What makes the local church "political" in the narrow sense is not that it wields the sword, just as ambassadors don't wield swords and embassies don't wage war! But church members speak for one who does, and they implement his just and righteous rule in their life together. They commit themselves utterly to his law, his governance, his judgment. They come to Christ the king for harbor, safety, provision and protection, both now and eternally. They acknowledge that Christ possesses imperium.

Yet the political nature of the church extends to its relationship with outsiders as well. Its politics is not self-contained. The politics of its justice and righteousness sits inside of a much larger claim: that Christ is the King of kings and Lord of the nations. And because the nations have defied his justice and righteousness, they require his justification. This is the church's political message and how we might describe the church's life as political in the broader sense.

In other words, the church's political identity depends entirely upon the identity of its Lord and Judge and the fact that its Judge is the Judge of all. He is no metaphorical judge, and his kingdom is no metaphorical kingdom. His judgment over the nations is *visible* now in the fact that they are excluded from membership in the church and from the Lord's Table. And his judgment is *audible* now through the church's ambassadorial word.

**An embassy and signmaker.** Whether or not one agrees that the keys belong to every church member, this much might be agreed upon across Christian traditions: the keys, which are exercised through baptism and the Lord's Supper, *name* or deputize something as "Christian" or "Christ's." A church, as holder of the keys, has the authority to say, "This is Christ's authorized message" or "She is a Christian" or "He is not." Like ancient Israel, the church represents Christ's authority as a deputy, not just a delegate, to use Wolterstorff's distinction from chapter four. We *stand in* for Christ, like an ambassador or someone with power of attorney. And it's the local church's job to officially name who stands in this position.

Churches, we might say, are signmakers for the kingdom. They hang up signs over the *what* and the *who* of the gospel. They locate Christ's heavenly reputation and political rule on planet earth, which brings us back to chapter two's discussion of the inseparable connection between authority and institutional identity.[195] We prove our political identity, it was said, whenever we recognize a certain authority in the "basic sense of simply acknowledging that they are *there* and that they are *theirs*," to reuse O'Donovan words.[196] And an institution, again, is an identity- and behavior-shaping rule structure.

It is with all this once more in mind that we discover the inseparable connection between the *faith* and the *order* of the church. The Christian *faith* begins whenever someone acknowledges with heart and mouth that Jesus is Savior and Lord—the Lord to whom the nations and their governments will give an account (see Rom 10:9-10; Ps 2:10). This authoritative Lord then commands all such repentant professors to publicly identify with his name, as well as the name of the Father and the Spirit, through baptism. This public identification is nothing less than an institutional identification. It is an induction into an institutional *order*, however mere that order might be. And a local church is where that order gets housed. The inseparable connection between a church's faith and order, in other words, is located in the political nature of that faith. It is a faith whose essence involves submitting to a king, and submitting to a king necessitates a political order. Church polity foists itself into the conversation when Christians take the political metaphor of Christ's kingship seriously. Order and polity are an implication of the gospel, just like good deeds. Once believers formally identify with Jesus through baptism, they continue to gather "in the name" of Jesus (Mt 18:20; 1 Cor 5:4) and proclaim his death through the Lord's Supper (1 Cor 11:26), requirements which constitute formal gatherings of the church.

For all these reasons, I find that the metaphor of an embassy usefully captures many things about a local church institutionally considered,

---

[195]Perhaps the most striking picture of the political nature of the church and how this profoundly affects one's identity can be seen with the proclamation of a martyr, "I am a Christian." See Michael P. Jensen, *Martyrdom and Identity: The Self on Trial* (New York: T&T Clark, 2010).
[196]O'Donovan, *Desire of the Nations*, 47.

especially in contradistinction to the universal church, which I take to be a heavenly and eschtalogical community.[197] An embassy represents the authority, name, reputation, character and glory of one nation inside another nation. The local church does exactly this, only it represents a kingdom not across geographic space but accoss eschatological time. It represents the invisible spiritual realities of heaven, heaven's powers and heaven's battles against the cosmic powers of the present darkness and the spiritual forces of evil. A church is almost like a doorway to another dimension. Through the keys of the kingdom a group of Christians open this doorway to make the invisible visible. The keys comprise the saints' authority to establish themselves as a geographically and time-bound embassy of Christ's end-time and uncontested rule.

Before the days of Christian colleges, Christian political parties, Christian hospitals, Christian missions organizations, Christian bookstores, Christian celebrities, Christian rock bands, Christian radio and Christian dating websites, it was comparatively easy to ascertain who represented the Father, Son and Spirit on earth. Presumably it was even easier before the days of a Christian empire or nation. The keys exclusively belonged to the local church (or, other traditions would contend, its representative in the bishop or presbytery); and Christ's witness on planet earth, to a greater measure, was therefore tied to the accountability of churches. That accountability gets lost or at least diluted to whatever extent the name "Christian" is applied to institutions beyond the local church and its members. Certainly this presents an area for further consideration, and a place where much prudence is needed.

By giving the local church the keys of the kingdom, Jesus established it not only as a heavenly embassy on earth, representing heaven's rule, but as his eschatological embassy. The local church is an *eschatological* embassy in at least two respects. First, it is the in-history anticipation of God's end-time rule and end-time people, which means it is the beginning of the triune politics that we considered in chapter three: "[I ask] that they may all be one, just as you, Father, are in me, and I in you, that they also may be

---

[197]See also Peter O'Brien, "The Church as a Heavenly and Eschatological Entity," in *The Church in the Bible and the World: An International Study*, ed. D. A. Carson (Eugene, OR: Wipf & Stock, 1987), 88-119; Volf, *After Our Likeness*, 140-41; Brad Harper and Paul Louis Metzger, *Exploring Ecclesiology* (Grand Rapids: Brazos Press, 2009), 47-77; Ladd, *Theology of the New Testament*, 586-87; Beale, *New Testament Biblical Theology*, 614-772; Wright, *Paul*, 138-53.

in us" (Jn 17:21). This fellowship in the church is not just a hope for the church but a present (albeit imperfect) experience (1 Jn 1:1-4).[198] Second, it is a gathered or assembled in-history anticipation of God's end-time people in one place (see Mt 18:20; 1 Cor 5:4; 11:18; also Acts 2:46; 5:12; 6:2).[199] A church makes the heavenly and end-time union of God's people visible in the present as it gathers.

The church's eschatological nature means the local institution straddles present justification by faith alone and future justification or judgment in accordance with works. It admits members on account of a profession of faith in the triune God. But it keeps one eye always on the final justification according to works, requiring it to remove from fellowship anyone whose life is characterized by fealty to another lord. Hence, Paul borrows Old Testament cultic purity language to explicitly call these new covenant priest-kings to separate themselves, institutionally speaking, from the world:

> I will make my dwelling among them and walk among them,
>   and I will be their God,
>   and they shall be my people.
> Therefore go out from their midst,
>   and be separate from them, says the Lord,
> and touch no unclean thing;
>   then I will welcome you,
> and I will be a father to you,
>   and you shall be sons and daughters to me,
>   says the Lord Almighty. (2 Cor 6:16-18)[200]

The keys are to be used to draw a bright line between the church and the world, separating the holy from the unholy. Of course, this has been the pattern of God's covenant community throughout Scripture. The Garden of Eden had an inside and an outside, as did Noah's ark, the Israelites in Goshen, the night of the Passover, Israel's camp in the wilderness and the Promised Land itself. At every stage God marked off his covenant people by one visible sign or another, and God's priestly people have worked to separate clean

---

[198]See Volf, *After Our Likeness*, 128-29.
[199]Ibid., 135-58; contra Horton, *People and Place*, 182-84.
[200]See Wayne A. Meeks on the language of separation in Paul, in *The First Urban Christians: The Social World of the Apostle Paul* (New Haven, CT: Yale University Press, 1983), 94-96.

from unclean, holy from unholy. God's new covenant ecclesial people are marked off symbolically by baptism and the Lord's Supper. These signs of the covenant should help the world know where to go to witness the beginnings of true righteousness and justice.

Ironically, much Christian literature today, both academic and popular, encourages church leaders to blur or even erase that line between church and world, thinking it will make the church appear more accommodating and loving. As one academic author puts it, "The boundary between those who belong to the church and those who do not should not be drawn too sharply."[201] After all, "the establishment of clear boundaries is usually an act of violence."[202] Jesus, Peter and Paul had a different view. They argued that the church's very distinctness gives it evangelistic power (Mt 5:13-16; 1 Pet 2:9-11; 2 Cor 6:14-7:1).

***Religious tolerance—part two.*** Having established the fact that the local church is Christ's kingdom embassy on earth with the authority of the keys to name the *what* and the *who* of the gospel enables us to now insert the third and final plank in a biblical doctrine of religious tolerance. But first, the territory covered so far:

- *Plank 1*: We are not authorized to prosecute false religion or worship, at least until that false religion yields demonstrable harm to human beings. Genesis 9, we saw in chapter four, seems to guarantee what American lawyers call the free exercise of religion.

- *Plank 2*: God's universal lordship does not countenance dividing one part of human life from another part, such as the "religious" part and the "political" part, which is why I reject the "two kingdoms" or Enlightenment conception of religious freedom. Still, new covenant Christians recognize a "doctrine of two ages," which yields for the believer two whole planes of existence, the age of creation and the age of new creation, the latter of which comes by the Spirit and cannot be coerced.

These first two planks, however, leave open slightly the question of religious establishment. For instance, might a Christian prince or prime minister allow its citizens to worship whatever god they wished while also

---

[201] Volf, *After Our Image*, 148n84.
[202] Ibid., 151n97.

giving priority to one religion in particular—say, tax exemptions for churches but not mosques or synagogues?

The trouble with so many contemporary First Amendment–type discussions concerning the question of religious establishment is the lack of institutional specificity surrounding the concept of "religion" or "establishing religion." For instance, Representative James Madison kicked off the 1789 discussions in Congress about adding a bill of rights to the US Constitution by proposing the language, "The civil rights of none shall be abridged on account of religious belief, nor shall any national religion be established." Eventually, another representative offered, "Congress shall make no laws *touching* religion, or infringing the rights of conscience," an alternative that caused Madison to withdraw his motion and support this language instead. The House passed it. But several days later, they amended it again to "Congress shall make no law establishing religion, or to prevent the free exercise thereof, or to infringe the rights of conscience." When the discussion moved to the US Senate, more proposals and counter-proposals ensued until finally a House-Senate conference committee agreed on the language that stands to this day: "Congress shall make no laws respecting an establishment of religion, or prohibiting the free exercise thereof."[203] Ever since this language was decided upon, strict separationists and accomodationists have debated what exactly the original authors meant by "an establishment." The difficulty, journalist Steven Waldman has observed, is that neither Madison nor the other figures involved offered any explanation for what they meant by "religion" or "established." A separationist like Waldman argues that "clearly Madison . . . meant the word *establishment* to be quite broad and refer to any government involvement with, or even aid for, religion."[204] Yet what the 1789 Congress's conversation and the conversation ever since has generally lacked is an Augustininan perspective. As I have argued in the first five chapters of this book, it is impossible to divide religion and politics phenomenologically. Every law aids or has some "religious" worldview behind it, as does every lawmaker. There is no religiously neutral activity. We worship either God or something else. As such, it is impossible not to

---

[203]This narrative is recounted in Steven Waldman, *Founding Faith: Providence, Politics, and the Birth of Religious Freedom in America* (New York: Random House, 2008), 147-51.
[204]Ibid., 158.

establish religion, I argued in chapter one. Every law "establishes" some religion or religions.

Yet this chapter's discussion of the church's authority of the keys enables us to offer an institutionally precise statement concerning religious establishment, bringing us to the third plank:

- *Plank 3*: The institutional church, not the state, possesses the authority to formally distinguish true from false doctrine, and true believers from unbelievers. The church alone has the authority to formally name the things of God, whether doctrines or people.

The authority of the keys gives the church and only the church the power to hang signs: "This is a true church," "This is the true gospel," "This is a true gospel citizen." The church has an ambassadorial authority to speak for the king; a power-of-attorney authority to speak for his or her client.

It is on this third point of establishment that I rarely but crucially depart from the political theology of Oliver O'Donovan. O'Donovan gives the government the authority to say which bishop is a right bishop and which bishop is a wrong bishop—to hang signs over the doorways of their respective church buildings, as it were, indicating who is true and who is false. I fully agree that in governing leaders should pursue the path of justice and righteousness as prescribed by the right church. Again, there is no such thing as neutrality, and the state must govern following the teaching of *some* "bishop," whether a Christian, Muslim, Hindu or Rawlsian one. But at no point can the government require people to act rightly *in Jesus'* or *Allah's* or *Krishna's name*. It cannot declare on right doctrine or church membership. It cannot exclude one kind of bishop from offices in his government. And it cannot discriminate between one citizen and another based on their theological doctrine, church membership or lack thereof. One day every knee will bow and confess that Jesus is Lord (Phil 1:11), but Jesus does not mean for the state to enforce that day just yet. Indeed, as I have heard O'Donovan say in a lecture, the kingdom of Christ cannot be advanced by force. The church, again, has the power of naming or signmaking, not the state.

In other words, when it comes to the question of "establishing religion," we must make a distinction between writing laws and constitutions that depend upon the moral principles of religion and using the state's coercive authority to touch in any way the doctrines or membership of that religion—to participate in *organizing* a religion whether for all or even just some of the state's citizens. Scripture does not give the state the authority to do the latter, and avoiding the former is impossible. If the public square is a battleground of lords, as I have argued, any lawmaker or judge who forbids a so-called religious perspective in the writing of laws, calling it an establishment of religion, is doing nothing more than clearing a path for the imposition of his or her own religion. The establishment of religion in this broader sense is inevitable. Ideally, laws will represent the overlap of different religious perspectives. Often, they are simply an imposition. But those are the two possibilities—overlap or imposition. There is no neutrality. On the other hand, *the establishing of an establishment of religion*, such as a church, mosque or synagogue, is not inevitable. A government really can refuse to participate in organizing a religion, which it does whenever it refuses to adjudicate a religious society's doctrines or gives legal preference to the members of one religious society over another. For these reasons, I actually think the First Amendment's language concerning "no law respecting an establishment of religion" works decently well from a biblical perpective, if by "establishment of religion" one has in mind the authority of the keys (not that anyone ever has).

With this more precise understanding of the church's authority of the keys and the state's authority of the sword, we can sketch out a more institutionally specific picture of the relationship between church and state. The limits of government do not vaguely rest in epistemological skepticism, which is so often the argument from philosophical liberals, both Christian and non-Christian, as if we should not trust the government to be able to discern the difference between true and false doctrine.[205] James Madison's statement from one debate on religious assessments on this point is classic. His speech notes read, "What edition, Hebrew, Septuagint, or vulgate? What copy—what translation. . . . What books canonical, what apochryphal? The papists holding to be the former what protestants the latter, the Lutherans the latter

---

[205]For a Christian theorist who employs a measure of epistemic skepticism, see Greg Forster, *John Locke's Politics of Moral Consensus* (New York: Cambridge University Press, 2005), 28. For an example of a non-Christian who grounds his entire concept of justice in "partial skepticism," see Brian Barry, *Justice as Impartiality*, A Treatise on Social Justice 2 (Oxford: Clarendon Press, 1995), 168-83.

what other protestant & papists the former."[206] Madison's point was that politicians are not competent to answer such sensitive theological questions. He was right, but I would say for the wrong reasons. He was right that the government should stay out of these questions, but not because it's not competent. Presumably, a statesman or stateswoman can study these matters just as easily as a pastor and come to reasonable conclusions. Rather, the statesman or stateswoman should stay out simply because he or she does not have the authority to hang signs on behalf of Christ's kingdom. This is a prerogative reserved for the holder of the keys. Grounding the limits in skepticism, however, makes the boundary lines vague and may ultimately undermine the rule of law in other ways.

The grand mistake of Christendom was not that it "legislated morality." That is unavoidable. Its mistake was that the state and church jointly wielded the power of the keys by mutually affirming every citizen as a member of the church through infant baptism. It treated the membership in the church and state as two overlapping circles, thereby usurping the authority of the church, not to mention ignoring the new spiritual realities brought to bear by the new covenant. Likewise, the colonial Baptists were correct to contest religious assessments precisely because it put the keys of the kingdom into the hands of the church.

***An embassy on the international map.*** How then might we summarize where these heavenly and eschatological embassies called local churches lie upon the landscape of the nations? Several basic principles come to mind, drawing from discussions throughout this book, each of which requires further elaboration and integration. But that will have to await a future project.

*Two authorities, two ages, two mandates.* The local church and its members represent God's rule according to a "deputy model" of authorization. Christ has deputized it to wear his name and speak on his behalf on a limited range of matters. The state represents God's rule according to a "delegate model." Christ has delegated a measure of his authority to governments to fulfill a set of specific purposes according to his standards. But its decisions and actions do not bear his reputation as closely as does the church. The local

---

[206]Quoted in Waldman, *Founding Faith*, 116.

church possesses the power of eschatological declaration. The state posseses the power of temporal coercion. The local church is charged with declaring Christ's absolute, legitimate, comprehensive and authorizing rule over the nations and their leaders, pointing to the way of justification and justice, affirming who and what belongs to his kingdom, and exemplifying the just and righteous kingdom life. The state is charged with rendering judgment, a purpose enunciated most clearly in Genesis 9:5-6 and Romans 13:1-7.

*One king, one judge, one justice.* Christ is the King of kings. He promises to judge all governments and their peoples. Every person, institution and conception of justice is either for him or against him. There is no such thing as religious neutrality, even in the public square. People worship God or their false gods in all their political thinking and decision making. Scripture is clear about their accountability. The Father says to the Son, "You are my Son. . . . I will make the nations your heritage." And then to all governments: "Now therefore, O kings, be wise; be warned, O rulers of the earth" (Ps 2:7-12; also Rev 6:15-17). There is God's justice, and there is injustice, which means that all varieties of "justice" that "go forth" will be judged (Hab 1:7).

*A church's twofold jurisdiction.* The local church's jurisdiction extends in one respect to its own members and in another respect to the nations. It *disciples* the former and *evangelizes* the latter, using the words of King Jesus for both activities. Speaking God's Word from the pulpit and on the street is therefore political speech. It calls church members toward deeper repentance and the nations toward first-time repentance. The keys of the kingdom, put into use through baptism and the Lord's Supper, should keep the line between these two layers of jurisdiction clear.

*A model of true politics.* Through teaching and discipleship, the life of the local church should, little by little, increasingly picture a true politics and a true worship. In its confessions and corporate life together, the church should offer a contrast society or counter-culture of righteousness, justice and love (Mt 5:13-16; Jn 13:34-35; 1 Pet 2:9-12). The local church is where the nations join together as "one new man." It is where "little black boys and black girls will be able to join hands with little white boys and white girls as sisters and brothers," to borrow from Martin Luther King Jr.'s dream speech. Here in the assembly, enemies learn to love one another, turn the other cheek and walk the extra mile. The source of a church's politics and worship is nothing other than the gospel of justification, reconciliation and adoption.

*Evangelism as political engagement.* Likewise, the church's evangelism—its declaration of the gospel—is its first form of outward political engagement. The first political speech that the nations and their governors need to hear is that Jesus is their judge, who will one day judge their activities in the bedroom, in the boardroom, on the ballfield and in the ballot box. Yet not only is Jesus judge; he is also justifier, reconciler of the nations and risen Lord, before whom they must bow in contrition, fealty and honor. They must repent and trust in his work of atonement, by which he offers a political pardon. When church members leave the embassy building and scatter into the public square, marketplace and neighborhood, therefore, they go as ambassadors or prophets. Sometimes they go to bless and strengthen those economic and political structures that are necessary for a nation's livelihood and prosperity, as Joseph did in the face of an impending famine (Gen 41; see also Jer 29). Sometimes they go to call a nation to repentance for its many injustices, as many of the prophets did when confronted with the exploitation of the poor, widespread bribery and so forth. Prophets name the name of their God. They point to where the idols lie in each of those domains. They warn of judgment. And they explain the path of justification, reconciliation and repentance.

*Political engagement and representing Jesus as a delegate.* When a Christian steps into the public square, he or she does so as a *delegate*, in the specialized sense we have been using the term. His or her authorized task is to fulfill the Genesis 9/Romans 13 mandate that God gives to all humanity. As such, a Christian's job in the public square is no different than a non-Christian's: to render judgment, to establish order, arguably to facilitate prosperity and so forth. What's more, many of a nation's laws and much of a government's work will be in areas that are either morally insignificant or that do not divide Christians and non-Christians, and wise political engagement often requires certain nonmoral competencies in which certain individuals excel above others, whether Christian or non-Christian. No doubt, a Christian acting in a delegate capacity should still think through the various biblical principles that may or may not be at play in any given decision or debate. Further, he or she does not leave the "baptized person" behind, as it were. The publicly recognized Christian is still a publicly recognized Christian, such that one's activity and positions will bear upon the name of Christ, perhaps perceptibly, perhaps imperceptibly. That said, he or she is not there, generally speaking, to do the sign-hanging work of the church by fastening Jesus' name to this or that party, this or that policy, this or that constitution. One's constitutional or policy proposals generally belong to the loose-gripped, up-for-grabs category of wisdom. The movement from core Christian principles to public policies is seldom a straight line but often a "complex and jagged" path through layers of conditioning factors and prudential considerations over which Christians of good conscience might disagree.[207]

*Political engagement and representing Jesus as a deputy.* The more a Christian's activities in the public square become associated with Jesus Christ, however, the more we might say that that Christian's activities have been "deputized." Sometimes a Christian or church may not set out to pick a political fight, but the fight is foisted upon them anyway, as when the broader society's views evolve in a manner that put it at odds with historical Christian principles, and a group of Christians feel compelled to react to the new status quo. The deputization is a consequence of the fact that the broader public begins to associate *that* position with *those* Christians, something which most often occurs wherever a culture's idols seek to establish themselves in the marketplace or public square.

Yet deputization can occur not just when Christian individuals, churches, prominent leaders or institutions react, but also when they proactively and explicity designate some position, party, policy or candidate as "the Christian choice" or "a gospel mandate," or when they use any such language that effectively identifies it with Jesus, or when they somehow invoke the judgment of God for positions contrary to their own. To tie the name of Jesus Christ to some political position is, in a sense, to borrow or (as often as not) to usurp the keys of the kingdom. It can be a kind of binding and loosing on earth on behalf of heaven. It can effectively enshrine one's position on said party, policy or candidate as the *status confessionis*.

---

[207]Language of moving by straight line versus a jagged line between core Christian principles and policy applications is taken from Robert Benne, *Good and Bad Ways to Think About Religion and Politics* (Grand Rapids: Eerdmans, 2011), 39-80, esp. 71.

Admittedly, those who belong, say, to the "Christian Democratic" parties of Chile, Germany or Switzerland hardly intend to make membership in their party a test of faith, but that is only because the word *Christian* has been evacuated of meaning or significance, or because people don't think through all the implications of their language. An act of deputization can occur among groups of Christians on the Right or Left; it can occur among biblically faithful and institutionally recognized church leaders as well as among cynical and nominally Christian parliamentarians who have not set foot inside a church building for years.

I personally believe that some issues do rise to this level, but when they do, they should be the sort of thing in which the ethical issues at stake are so plain that the wrong position would be treated as grounds for discipline in the church. For instance, a faithful church might have reasonably decided that membership in the Nazi party was grounds for discipline. Whether or not one agrees with this example, the point is, identifying a political position with Jesus effectively means making it a condition of church membership. No doubt, the straighter the line is from core biblical principle to political application, the easier it is to identify such issues. The more jagged and complex the path, the more reluctant Christians should be to identify their position with Jesus' name but instead treat it as belonging to the category of wisdom.

*The limited utility of the "institutional/organic" distinction.* The inevitable fact of deputization—that is, that the political postures of Christians will be rightly or wrongly indentified with Jesus—points to the limitations of Abraham Kuyper's distinction between the "institutional church" and "organic church" for the purposes of separating a church's and an individual Christian's duties in society at large and the public square in particular.[208]

---

[208] Kuyper's discussion of these matters can be found in several places, including Abraham Kuyper, *Rooted and Grounded: The Church as Organism and Institution*, trans. Nelson D. Kloosterman (Grand Rapids: Christian's Library Press, 2013) and "Common Grace," in *Abraham Kuyper: A Centennial Reader*, ed. James Bratt (Carlisle: Paternoster, 1988). John Halsey Wood Jr., *Going Dutch in the Modern Age: Abraham Kuyper's Struggle for a Free Church in the Nineteenth-Century Netherlands* (New York: Oxford University Press, 2013) traces how Kuyper's formulation of the relationship between institutional and organic church evolved through three phases: from an early incarnational conception of the church heavily indebted to the Idealism and Romanticism of Schleiermacher, whereby the church constituted the ongoing life of the incarnate Christ with both internal and external aspects of the incarnation mimicked in the church's internal mystical life and its external doctrine, liturgy and governance (52-55); to church as institution and

I don't mean to say that this distinction is wholly without use for distinguishing between the authoritative relationships that comprise an organized local church and the elect, Spirit-filled body of Christ. It's a legitimate *theological* distinction because faith comes through hearing and not through membership or any sacrament in the local church. But it's an inadequate *political* or *public-oriented* distinction.

One of the purposes of the so-called institutional church is that it publicly identifies Christians as Christians. It deputizes them as Jesus Representatives. It gives an otherwise invisible Christian visibility—a Jesus nametag, if you will. Membership in the institutional local church, through baptism and the Lord's Supper, makes a person's whole life, public and private, "speak" about Jesus, almost like an *ichthus* (fish) decal on the car bumper makes one's driving reflect on the faith (for better or worse). For instance, two young single men sitting at my family dinner table learn what it means to be a *Christian* father and a *Christian* husband as they observe me interact with wife and children *because they know I'm a baptized, Lord's Supper-receiving member in good standing in my church*. Were I to abuse my family, this abuse would then characterize their impression of Christianity and Jesus, at least until the church removed me from membership as an act of discipline. The identity dynamic here is paralleled in matters of citizenship or family membership. What I personally do as an individual citizen abroad represents the USA, whether I mean for it to or not. Non-Americans will form impressions about America based on how I behave. The same relationship abides between my behavior and the name "Leeman." My behavior will affect the so-called family name. And so it is with the institutional church: the institutional church doesn't get left behind on the church steps

---

organism set in sacramental relationship, each essential and necessary to the other, like mind and body or river and banks, life flowing from the inner organism but expressed and channeled through the external institution (62-70); to the development of a third conceptual category in between invisible organic and visible institutional, namely, the visible organic, which consists of the fellowship of believers apart from any institutional structure and that constitutes the essence of the church on earth, meaning that the church's institutional form is necessary but not essential, *bene esse* not *esse*, like clothes to the body (85-91). See also James D. Bratt, *Abraham Kuyper: Modern Calvinist, Christian Democrat* (Grand Rapids: Eerdmans, 2013), 175-76, 183-85; Daniel Strange, "Rooted and Grounded? The Legitimacy of Abraham Kuyper's Distinction Between Church as *Institute* and Church as *Organism*, and Its Usefulness in Constructing an Evangelical Public Theology" (paper presented to the 66th Annual Meeting of the Evangelical Theological Society, San Diego, CA, November 2014); also published online at *Themelios*, Fall 2015.

on the way out of the building on Sunday. Like a citizenship or a family name, it "travels" with a Christian all week, identifying everything a person says and does to some extent with Jesus, whether in the bedroom, the boardroom or the voting booth.

Rooted at least partly in Idealism and Romanticism,[209] Kuyper's concept of the "organic church," on the other hand, tries to envision the Christian life and the church on earth *apart* from the saints' public institutional membership in a local church, *apart* from a church's authoritative affirmation, *apart* from a Christian's accountability to a church's oversight.[210] As a conceptual apparatus, it envisions a deputized Jesus Representative apart from any deputizing agency. Again, we can do that for *theological* purposes. But the very conversation we are having concerns the church's *public* posture, and for public purposes it makes no sense to talk about "Christians" apart from their deputizing agency since the activities of Christians will, in the public's eye, inevitably tie back to the agency.[211] When we come to talk about how Christians (as opposed to churches) should engage the public square, or what the mission of the church is, we cannot neatly divorce ourselves from the institutional church and simply speak about the organic church, again, because the institutional church always travels with us. A better distinction is needed than the institutional/organic one, at least for public and political purposes.

*Employing a joint/several distinction instead.* Nonetheless, one can understand why Kuyper and others have reached for some type of distinction for separating the institutional church's and the individual Christian's duties and obligations in relation to society broadly and the public square specifically. If there is to be any fixed institutional distinction between church and

---

[209]Strange, "Rooted and Grounded?," 17-18; Bratt, *Abraham Kuyper*, 183.

[210]Both Strange and Bratt have noted that Kuyper's distinction between the institutional and organic eventually evolved toward an institutional and organic opposition, such that "the organism is valorized to the detriment of the institute." Strange, "Rooted and Grounded?," 15; see also Bratt, *Abraham Kuyper*, 186. This in turn departed from the biblical pattern of consistently identifying the church with its gatherings, whether earthly or heavenly, and of "evacuating the word 'church' of any notion of 'the gathered' and of dislocating the visible organic church from any concrete congregation." Strange, "Rooted and Grounded?," 16.

[211]I think Daniel Strange is on point here when he writes, "Kuyper's distinction [between the institutional and organic] is overly neat and simplistic. Rather than describing two discreet conceptions of church, however inseparable, might it not be better conceptually to think of one reality that is the church that has been divinely revealed to us in many different metaphors all which qualify the other. What God has joined together let not Kuyper separate." Strange, "Rooted and Grounded?," 15.

state, we need some way to distinguish the church as a corporate actor from the church member as an individual actor. For instance, we would not say it's the mission or responsibility of the corporate actor to give a wife "her conjugal rights" (1 Cor 7:3); we would say it's the responsibility of the individual member. Is it the distinction between church gathered versus church scattered we want? Or church versus individual Christian? Or church local versus church universal? There are problems with each of these distinctions for our purposes, which I won't take the time to unpack. Instead, I propose we employ a Presbyterian distinction that goes back at least to the Scottish Second Book of Discipline (1578) between the church's joint and several power. In the Presbyterian conception, the congregation may possess this power, but the officers exercise it. The present-day Presbyterian Church of America's *Book of Order* therefore explains,

> Ecclesiastical power, which is wholly spiritual, is twofold. The officers exercise it sometimes severally, as in preaching the Gospel, administering the Sacraments, reproving the erring, visiting the sick, and comforting the afflicted, which is the power of order; and they exercise it sometimes jointly in Church courts, after the form of judgment, which is the power of jurisdiction.[212]

The elders' joint or jurisdictional power refers to that power they have when acting together or jointly. It binds consciences as representing the teaching of Scripture. The elders' several power, which can be exercised independently of one another, does not directly impact a person's jurisdictional relationship to the visible institutional church.[213]

Suppose we apply this distinction to the whole church. We could speak of the whole congregation acting corporately as a property of its joint authority, or we could speak of the individual members acting individually as a property of the church's several authority. In both cases we would be describing the local institutional church acting according to its biblical authorization. But we would say that the institutional local church *jointly* conceived possesses one set of authorizations or one kind of (narrow) mission: preach the gospel, celebrate the ordinances, make disciples and so forth.

---

[212] *Book of Church Order*, 6th ed. (Lawrenceville, GA: The Office of the Stated Clerk of the General Assembly of the Presbyterian Church in America, 2014), chap. 3, sec. 2.
[213] Preston G. Graham Jr., *A Kingdom Not of this World: Stuart Robinson's Struggle to Distinguish the Sacred from the Secular during the Civil War* (Macon, GA: Mercer University Press, 2002), 106-7.

And we would say that the institutional local church *severally* conceived possesses another set of authorizations and another kind of (broad) mission: obey everything Jesus commanded, love one's neighbor, do good, seek justice, glorify God in all of life and represent Jesus in all of this.

The church jointly exercises the keys. The church severally does not. The church severally has more freedom to engage in political dialogue in the public square. The church jointly has far less. Still, insofar as the church's several authority is intrinsically connected to the church's joint authority (unlike how the concept of the organic church eschews talk of authority altogether), particularly in the eyes of outsiders, we discover why church members must be very cautious in how they attach Jesus' name to their political advocacy. A Christian might be convinced that a flat tax is more just than a progressive tax and advocate accordingly. But since Scripture is silent on tax structures and since the issue is hardly a condition of church membership, the church member should take great care in making sure his or her advocacy does not pretend to speak for Jesus, the church or Scripture.

*The need for caution in deputizing one's political views.* In general, Christians (and the local churches behind them) must exercise especial care in deciding which matters to risk explicity associating with the name of Jesus. Here, indeed, is one place where the great reserve of two-kingdoms and spirituality-of-the-church writers is useful. Christians on the Right and Left can too quickly presume to speak on behalf of heaven by calling their pet political issues "gospel issues," whether the issue is immigration reform, debt relief, affordable housing, environmental care, balanced budgets or a particular legislative path on abortion. Several questions should be asked: First, does the issue at stake fall within the government's authorization to render justice (see Gen 9:5-6; Rom 13:1-7)? Not everything that the Bible calls sin falls within the government's jurisdiction. Second, does the law or practice in question explicitly contradict the rule of Christ (e.g., anti-conversion laws) or otherwise promise to earn the judgment of God by promoting injustice? Third, is the matter clear in Scripture, or an implication of an implication of an implication? Furthermore, it's worth noting that the laws of ancient Israel were uniquely given to Israel, just as Chinese law, strictly speaking, does not apply to the citizens of other nations. Some of the Mosaic laws reflect God's moral will for all nations, to be sure. But the nations are not bound by the Mosaic covenant as such.

*A church's primary deputized message to government.* Churches will have to confront different idols of culture and state in different times and places. But these kingdom embassies must constantly sound forth these deputized messages: (1) The government's authority comes from God, and it possesses this authority to render judgment between good and evil, justice and injustice. (2) The government's authority is temporary. It will pass. (3) The overnment must protect the survival of God's people, the church. (4) The occupants of government will be judged for a failure on any of these points, as well as for any idolatrous excesses and injustices.

To expand on the third point:

*Christians should pray for and work for government.* In order for the church to fulfill its duty as a signmaker, it needs the state to fulfill its work as a platform builder (Acts 17:26-27; 1 Tim 2:1-2). Churches should therefore work and pray for the state, just as Christians should work and pray for that other creation ordinance, the family.

*Churches are and are not a political threat.* Churches both are and are not a threat to the civic order. As we saw in chapter five, Festus determined that Paul committed no political crime worthy of death in Acts 25 and 26. At the same time, Christianity's disruption of the idolatry market in Ephesus led to rioting in Acts 19.[214] In other words, Jesus does not commission churches to wield the sword and challenge governments directly. But he does commission churches to challenge the idols and false gods that prop up every government and marketplace, whether the gods of the Roman Empire or the gods of the secular West. Since no government is free of idols, churches preaching the gospel will always pose a certain kind of threat. It's not the threat of an invader or insurrectionist; it's the threat of a virus, or termites, something that quietly works on the inside and chews away at the foundations until an idol collapses, along with the regime or economy sustained by that idol. In that sense, those regimes of history that have been unusually committed to their idolatry—from the early Roman Empire, to the fourteenth-century Mongol Empire under Tamerlane, to seventeenth-century Japan, to

---

[214] Again, see C. Kavin Rowe's excellent piece on this, "The Ecclesiology of Acts," *Interpretation* 66, no. 3 (July 2012): 259-69.

Nazi Germany, to even corporate America[215]—have been correct to fear Christian influence and have been consistent, from their standpoint of preserving their idolatries, in neutralizing the threat with persecution and punishment. Persecution has been the norm for Christians since the beginning (Jn 15:18-25) exactly because Jesus is a threat to the gods of the nations. Persecution is the logical consequence of idolatry.

*Religious tolerance.* From time to time, however, the church will find that its jurisdiction overlaps with the state's. When this occurs, the local church should (1) support the free exercise of other religions so long as demonstrable harm does not come to other humans and (2) oppose any attempt by the state to wield Christ's keys in establishing or regulating local churches. There is, in other words, a distinction to be made between establishing religion and establishing a church.

*Political success equals faithfulness.* As in evangelism specifically, so in political engagement broadly, the measure of success for Christians must not be victory but faithfulness. God will judge a church's faithfulness, not the outcome of its efforts. A church's confrontation of the nations and their leaders, whether in a bill on the legislative floor or in a gospel tract at the park, is sure to meet often with failure and strident opposition. But that does not change a church's task to speak faithfully as prophets and priests on behalf of Christ. Speak truly, and then expect the lions. Our witness will be vindicated over time, sometimes in this world, certainly in eternity.

*No such thing as a neutral legitimation for government, justice or religious freedom.* Christian political philosophers and theologians must know what they are capable of doing and not capable of doing. I believe we are capable of offering a *Christian* view of justice, but not capable of offering a neutral one without undermining our own. We are capable of providing a *Christian* defense of religious tolerance, but not a neutral one, again, without ultimately undermining our own. And so with theories of government legitimacy and political obligation: we can provide a *Christian* defense, but not a universally accessible one in a way that compels both believers and unbelievers at the level of first principles.

---

[215]See Patrick J. Deneen, "Corporatism and Gay Marriage: Natural Bedfellows," *American Conservative*, January 29, 2014, www.theamericanconservative.com/2014/01/29/corporatism-and-gay-marriage-natural-bedfellows/.

I don't think there is such an argument, because believers and unbelievers, on the whole, have incommensurate starting points. To assume we can provide a neutral political philosophy at a foundational level is to participate in the hubris of all rationalistic philosophy. To be sure, any reader familiar with Alasdair MacIntyre can perceive his influence on this point.

That said, with Christian conceptions of justice and government legitimacy in the background, Christians can offer pragmatic or wisdom-based arguments for various constitutional forms (such as a republican democracy) and for various policy proposals. Indeed, at the level of advocacy, I would argue that Christians should be methodological pragmatists, willing to employ whatever argument they can to be faithful and even win the debate in the public square. Love and justice, in fact, should impel Christians to want to win.

## Conclusion: The Unity of the Church

In the post-ascension era of the new covenant, God's political rule is publicly executed or manifested or "visible-ized" not just through the power of the sword, as it has been since Noah, but also through the keys of the kingdom. Wherever the keys are exercised through the Lord's Supper and baptism, we can expect to find God's rule on display, as well as the unity of the church made visible and institutional. This much, I believe, Baptists, Presbyterians, Anglicans and others can agree upon. To put it another way, every polity tradition is capable of agreeing with my claim that Jesus' rule is manifested on earth through the keys of the kingdom. The difference between various polity traditions comes down to who is holding the keys and, therefore, where the church's unity is made visible and institutional.

As a small-*c* congregationalist, I believe the congregation as a whole jointly holds the keys, which means the institutional unity of the church is evident in the gathered local or particular church. Indeed, I believe we should affirm that the very essence and sine qua non of a particular church as a *particular* church is this visible political unity. Surely all Christians are invisibly united in one faith, one hope, one remission of sins and one confession. Indeed, all Christians are united politically in one Lord. But this political unity is eschatologically manifested, exercised, visible-ized through preaching the gospel and the exercise of the keys in the ordinances. In preaching, the King calls upon subjects and citizens alike to repent and believe in the good news of the kingdom. With the keys of the kingdom, his authorized citizens employ the covenantal signs of the Lord's Supper and baptism in the binding and loosing acts of judgment that declare who and what on earth represents heaven. In other words, the kingdom of Christ becomes institutionally visible on planet earth in the local church. This, then, is the local church's essence *as* a local or particular church. And in a fallen world, all moral and spiritual accountability depends on visibility.[216] There is no accountability where people cannot see one another, which brings us to one last argument for congregationalism: the authority structures that aid the accountability of Christian discipleship rest comfortably inside the visibly gathered congregation and not in some geographically removed presbytery or bishop, which by definition would diminish the visible component of moral accountability.

To see that this institutionalized political unity is the sine qua non of the local church, it is worth comparing the relationship of two Christians who belong to the same church and the relationship of two Christians who do not. What is the difference? There is no difference in points of so-called spiritual unity (faith, hope, love, etc.). What makes these relationships different is that Christ's political authority is actually exercised "on earth" in the relationship of fellow church members, whereas it is not exercised between Christians who belong to different churches. Two fellow church members, insofar as they jointly hold the keys, can participate in one another's binding and loosing. For instance, each can participate in the decision to excommunicate the other. Two Christians in different churches cannot do this.

What then is a local church? It is a group of Christians who regularly gather in Christ's name to preach the gospel and to affirm and oversee one another's membership in Jesus Christ with the authority of the keys through baptism and the Lord's Supper. It is an embassy of Christ's kingdom on earth, whose corporate life embodies a rule that has been imported not across geographic space but from the end of time.

---

[216]Point heard from Os Guinness in personal conversation.

That means the church, in Stanley Hauerwas's words, "stands as a political alternative to every nation, witnessing to the kind of social life possible for those that have not been formed by the story of Christ"—"a 'contrast model' for all polities that know not God."[217] "It is from the life of the church . . . that we even come to understand the nature of politics and have a norm by which all other politics can be judged."[218] Salvation, whatever else it might mean, entails inclusion in a new people. It is, William Cavanaugh observes, "inherently social."[219] And Hauerwas again: "Jesus' salvation does not have social and political implications, but it is a politics that is meant as an alternative to all social life that does not reflect God's glory."[220] Hence, Bernd Wannenwetsch can observe that "the worshipping congregation can neither confine itself to the sphere of private religion, nor can it recognize the autonomy of political existence. . . . What has to be brought out is, rather, how the *reconciliation* between these forms of action and the spheres of life which belong to them comes to be experienced in worship."[221] "The kingly rule of Christ is God's own rule exercised over the whole world," says Oliver O'Donovan. What's more, this rule "is visible in the life of the church."[222]

Every candidate for president might promise "change," "justice," "relief" or "freedom," but Christians should look first to the members of their local *ekklēsia*. The state, after all, has been thrust into a peripheral role. God's Genesis 1:28 citizenship mandate has been fulfilled in Christ and will be accomplished in the church—in the place where people are baptized into the name of Father, Son and Spirit (Mt 28:19) and where mouths and hearts confess in worship that "Jesus is Lord" (Rom 10:9).

---

[217]Hauerwas, *Community of Character*, 12, 84.
[218]Ibid., 2.
[219]William T. Cavanaugh, *Migrations of the Holy: God, State, and the Political Meaning of the Church* (Grand Rapids: Eerdmans, 2011), 124.
[220]Hauerwas, *After Christendom? How the Church Is to Behave if Freedom, Justice, and a Christian Nation Are Bad Ideas* (Nashville: Abingdon, 1991), 58.
[221]Bernd Wannenwetsch, *Political Worship* (New York: Oxford University Press, 2004), 125.
[222]O'Donovan, *Desire of the Nations*, 146.

# Conclusion

This book set out to establish that Jesus grants Christians the authority to establish local churches as visible embassies of his end-time rule through the "keys of the kingdom" described in the Gospel of Matthew. By virtue of the keys, the local church exists as a political assembly that publicly represents King Jesus, displays the justice and righteousness of the triune God, and pronounces Jesus' claim upon the nations and their governments.

To that end, we considered the reigning liberal paradigm and how it is reinforced in Christian circles by a concept of the church's spirituality. The problem with both perspectives is that they treat the human being as divisible between a political part and a religious part, which humans are not. There is no such thing as spiritual neutrality in the public square and no such thing as political neutrality among the saints. In the biblical (and Augustinian) perspective, people either worship God or worship idols—on Sunday and every day.

Yet the fact that all of life can be viewed through both a religious lens and a political lens does not mean that God has not established different institutions for different purposes. Therefore, we began the project of building a broader political conceptuality that included God within its horizons by seeking a more precise understanding of political institutions. A political community, we saw, is a community of people united by a common governing authority possessing the power of life and death according to some conception of justice. And political membership, by extension, is a relationship in which an individual is subject to a governing authority and in which the authority affirms the individual. This institutional hermeneutic was then applied to the Bible's covenantal storyline, which showed us that politics is nothing more or less than the mediating of God's covenantal rule.

Life is broadly political in that it should be lived in accordance with the mandates of the Adamic and Noahic covenants to represent or image God in all the activities of human dominion. Yet life is narrowly political (politics as people typically conceive of it) through the Noahic covenant's provisions for a justice mechanism and the various institutions established by the line of special covenants.

We also saw that God intended to use a special people to model for the nations what a true politics looks like. When Israel failed at this task, it was handed to the divine Son, who came to do what Adam and Israel could not do. This second Adam, new Israel and Davidic son came to rule obediently by laying down his life for the sins of the nations and rising from the grave. In so doing, he offered a new covenant in his blood, so that all who would repent and believe might receive a pardon from sin and a share in his kingly authority. To that end, he granted them the keys of the kingdom, enabling them to fulfill their covenantal responsibilities to identify themselves with God and one another, distinguish themselves from the world, fend off any serpentine intruders and pursue together the life of righteousness and justice that rightly represent the Son, the Father and the Spirit.

As such, a local church publicly administers the office responsibilities of the new covenant. And a local church exists wherever a group of saints regularly gather to preach the gospel and exercise the keys by publicly affirming and submitting to one another through baptism and the Lord's Supper. The life of the church, among other things, is a citizen's life, whereby the saints share in kingdom rule together, jointly exercising the keys of the kingdom in one another's lives. By this token, a church's faith and order are linked through the gospel word and the power of the Spirit. The gospel word not only gives life to a people, it restores them to their covenantal job responsibilities, the ones that humanity possessed at creation but had forsaken. The keys of the kingdom authorize them to fulfill these job responsibilities individually and corporately.

In all this, the local church exists to display the righteousness, justice and love of the triune God. It is to exemplify for the nations what a true politics looks like. And in so doing it represents the King who possesses all authority on heaven and earth, and who therefore lays claim upon the nations. All humanity is called to repentance and faith, fealty and honor.

## The Political Hope of the Nations

Should political scientists like Robert Putnam classify churches as one more voluntary organization, like the Boy Scouts or a bird-watching society? I would prefer they did not. This is not because I believe that church membership should be compulsory. The state has no authority and no power to make it so. Still, the category of voluntary association does not adequately capture what the church is. The local church is a different kind of thing, and there is nothing else quite like it. Even the embassy metaphor is not fully sufficient. Living in the Washington, DC, area, I have attended functions in several foreign embassies. Never once have I heard their staffs refer to one another as "brother" and "sister," or as bricks in a temple, or as sheep in a flock, or as branches on a vine, all these being biblical metaphors for the church.

Still, to stick with the embassy metaphor a moment longer, there is something awe-inspiring about walking along DC's "Embassy Row," where nation after nation houses its ambassadorial staff in some grand old edifice, national flag flying out front. Each building represents another place and another people. Each makes one wonder what untold mysteries hide inside the diplomatic business of that nation.

Local churches, too, should make passersby wonder. People should see the flag of Christ raised high through the ordinances and find themselves intrigued by the strange ways of these people whose culture does not come from another place but from the power of a future age. Outsiders should discover a society of people who are not perfect but who know they are not perfect. Who still do regrettable and hurtful things but who then seek forgiveness, give forgiveness and pursue a new path together. In the life of the local church, the onlooking nations should discover a group of people who understand that their own sin merits condemnation, who recognize the need to depend utterly on a Savior and so who, in consequence, fight to turn the other cheek, love their enemies and forgive their debtors even as their own debts have been forgiven. That said, such personal meekness should not be mistaken for political weakness. Local churches will gather with or without the state's permission. They will declare their loyalty to their king even if it costs them their lives, because they know that their king owns not only them but their persecutors, and he will vindicate them on the last day as he judges the nations.

Abraham Lincoln, in his second inaugural address, famously exhorted a war-torn America to do everything it could to "achieve and cherish a just, and a lasting peace, among ourselves, and with all nations"—words now carved in marble inside the monument bearing his name. And, no doubt, those presidents and peoples who do pursue such justice and peace deserve a word of honor. For love's sake, Christians and non-Christians alike should employ the mechanisms of the state and the marketplace to do good to their neighbors by seeking justice.

Yet a Christian must also embrace this deep and inevitable tension: even while he or she, for love's sake, pursues justice and peace through the devices of the "age of creation," he or she must also recognize that everything eventually returns to dust (Eccles 3:20; 12:7). No constitution, no political campaign, no classroom lecture, no book of political theology will stop the inexorable march of death, heal the nations and produce a just and lasting peace. Might such activities provide space for the church to work toward this end? Yes. Might they point dimly in the right direction? Perhaps. But it is only the local church that has been authorized and equipped by the powers of the new covenant to taste such justice and peace.

The political hopes of the world should rest upon the local church—in its life together. Here the pardoning word of the gospel is spoken, and the obedience-giving power of the Spirit is applied. The warfare of the nations begins to end here. It's a different kind of politics, to be sure. It is the politics of aliens, strangers and unwelcome immigrants. It is a politics that expects, even embraces, persecution (Mt 5:10-12). Still, the hope of the nations is to be placed here—in this society gathered around a King who has laid down his life for the world. It is those who have submitted themselves to this crucified King who, in turn, lay down their lives for one another and beat their swords into plowshares and their spears into pruning hooks.

# Name Index

Anderson, Benedict, 118
Bannerman, James, 348, 353-54, 356-57
Barber, Nick, 109-10
Barclay, John M. G., 135n112, 271n90
Barth, Karl, 146, 148-51, 160n55, 254, 263, 267, 269-70n85, 284
Bauckham, Richard, 133-34, 137, 237, 298n5
Bayer, Oswald, 242
Beale, Gregory K., 50n100, 173n2, 213, 215n101, 220, 222, 237n148, 299, 300n10, 302, 304, 308n41, 309n42, 328-29, 330n89
Benn, S. I., 61n29, 213n97
Benne, Robert, 138
Berkowitz, Peter, 80
Berlin, Isaiah, 47, 164n66, 165n70, 327
Billings, J. Todd, 256n39, 256n41
Bonhoeffer, Dietrich, 120, 196
Bray, Gerald, 355
Brueggemann, Walter, 209-10, 211n90
Calvin, John, 292, 343, 353
Carson, D. A., 165-66, 268n82, 335n101, 339n122
Cavanaugh, William T., 28, 34, 36-37, 45n90, 76, 77n87, 78, 84, 102, 260, 387
Clowney, Edmund, 335n99, 336
Cohen, Stuart, 161n58, 189-90, 206-7, 230
Cotton, John, 338n119, 340n126, 349
Douglass, Stephen, 85
Dumbrell, William, 224
Durkheim, Emile, 76
Dworkin, Ronald, 78

Elazar, Daniel, 48-49, 161n58, 180n15, 182, 189-90, 206-7, 230, 236, 252
Elshtain, Jean Bethke, 29n22, 269n83
Ferguson, Sinclair, 302
Fish, Stanley, 268-69
France, R. T., 308n41, 311
Gathercole, Simon, 318, 322n68
Gellner, Ernest, 61
Gentry, Peter, 44, 50n100, 148n21, 185n28, 221-24, 227-28, 237n148, 247n15, 250n20
Gillespie, George, 354
Goodwin, Thomas, 337
Griffith, Benjamin, 343
Gunton, Colin, 103, 152, 153n34
Gutiérrez, Gustavo, 262-64
Hall, Peter A., 107n42
Hall, Stuart, 117
Hart, Darryl, 70-71, 85
Hauerwas, Stanley, 33-38, 41-42, 46, 88n125, 263n66, 266n74, 267, 269, 313n53, 316n57, 387
Heclo, Hugh, 98, 106, 140
Helwys, Thomas, 73
Hobbes, Thomas, 24n6, 28n18, 45n90, 57-58, 260
Hodge, Charles, 69
Horton, Michael, 40-42, 136, 323
Hood, Jason, 297n4
Jamieson, Bobby, 364
Jefferson, Thomas, 16, 73-74, 88, 90, 191, 194-95, 260
Jepperson, Ronald L., 107n39-40, 125
Johnson, James, 112n59, 113-14, 138
Kant, Immanuel, 64, 140, 281
Keach, Benjamin, 343

Keener, Craig, 336, 343n131
Knight, Jack, 112n59, 113-14, 138
Koppelman, Andrew, 72, 93, 95n136
Koyzis, David, 162n60, 315n55
Küng, Hans, 355-56, 356n178
Kuyper, Abraham, 26n11, 113, 134n110, 161, 176, 265, 378n208, 380
Ladd, George Eldon, 25-27, 109-10, 175
Letham, Robert, 151
Lewis, C. S., 283n120
Locke, John, 30-31, 38, 58, 62n31, 73-74, 88n124, 186-95, 198, 260
Luther, Martin, 29-31, 72, 78, 169-70, 176-77, 181n16, 242-43, 258-60, 274n96, 276, 331, 352-53
MacIntyre, Alasdair, 15, 28n20, 41-42
Madison, James, 29n22, 74, 199-200, 270, 371, 373-74
Mann, Thomas, 56, 83, 165
March, James, 107-8, 116, 127
McConville, J. Gordon, 43, 213n96, 215n101, 216, 219-20, 224-25, 230, 234, 239, 248, 254
McCormack, Bruce, 284n121
McDonagh, Edna, 269
McKnight, Scot, 313n52
Milbank, John, 33-35, 36n52, 45-46, 47n94
Miller, Nicholas P., 72
Mitchell, Joshua, 193n48
Moltman, Jürgen, 32, 37, 103, 259
Morris, Leon, 195n54, 343
Nicholls, David, 144
Novak, David, 121, 163
O'Donovan, Oliver, 24, 28, 33n36, 34, 39, 51, 108n47,

116, 154n36, 156n46, 166n75, 181n18, 197, 197n55, 199-200, 208, 208n80, 211, 262n59, 266, 274, 275n98, 277, 294-95, 304-5, 334n95, 358n182, 362-64, 365n194, 367, 372, 387
Olsen, Johan, 107-8, 116, 127
Palmer, Benjamin, 70, 85-86
Peck, Thomas, 354
Pennington, Jonathan T., 307nn36-37, 308n40, 311n49, 360n184
Peters, Guy, 59-60
Peters, R. S., 61n29, 213n97
Peterson, Robert A., 278n103
Pitkin, Hanna, 56n2, 59-60, 161-62
Pocock, J. G. A., 121-24
Putnam, Robert, 21, 36, 391
Rand, Ayn, 141, 326
Rawls, John, 29n22, 57, 57n7, 57n9, 58, 58n15, 63-65, 71-72, 75-76, 80, 109, 113, 113n62, 260
Ricoeur, Paul, 282, 282n137
Roberts, Simon, 61, 159

Robinson, Stuart, 68-69
Rowe, C. Kavin, 271
Sandel, Michael, 55, 80, 83, 85, 89n127
Schleiermacher, Friedrich, 99
Schwöbel, Christoph, 332-33
Scott, W. Richard, 61n26
Skinner, Quentin, 29n22, 31n29, 62, 62n30, 194n49
Stott, John, 284
Sweetman, Brendan, 78n91, 79-80
Taylor, Charles, 49, 91, 94, 139, 207, 328n82
Taylor, Rosemary C. R., 107n42
Tocqueville, Alexis de, 81
VanDrunen, David, 176n10, 176-80, 314n54
Vanhoozer, Kevin, 147n14, 148n18, 257n42, 282n114
Volf, Miroslav, 105n29, 149n22, 151nn28-29, 283n120, 301n15, 324n75, 346n129, 347n140
von Rad, Gerhard, 180n14
Waldman, Steven, 371

Waldron, Jeremy, 82, 201n65
Walzer, Michael, 79n93, 96-97, 97n141, 113n61
Wannenwetsch, Bernd, 166-67, 255, 387
Weber, Max, 60-61, 174n5
Webster, John, 142, 146n9, 148n20, 333
Wellum, Stephen, 44, 185n28, 221-24, 227-28, 237n148, 247n15, 250n20
Wolterstorff, Nicholas, 49n97, 59n19, 63n32, 66, 74, 161, 169, 169n80, 194n51, 199-200, 200n63, 205, 226, 229n136, 251n24, 260, 366
Wright, Christopher J. H., 130-31, 150
Wright, N. T., 27, 134, 135n112, 136, 155n42, 190, 203n68, 223, 229n136, 260, 299-300, 300n11, 318, 318n59, 320, 322-23, 330n89, 360n184
Yarnell, Malcolm, 303n20
Young, Iris Marion, 84n114, 112, 244
Zohar, Noam J., 97n141

# Subject Index

Adam's office, 16, 126, 158-68, 172-74, 184, 206, 208, 214, 215-16, 217-18, 220, 221, 222, 223-24, 228, 230, 240, 243, 244, 249, 275, 290-91, 296-301, 302-5, 305-6, 309, 321, 361
   See also Jesus: as new Adam; priest-king
authority, 24, 25, 30, 45, 48, 49-50, 51, 52, 58, 61, 66, 68, 73, 91, 95, 97, 99, 108, 125, 129-30, 139-41, 143, 152, 153-58, 161-62, 168-70, 172, 174, 224, 248, 256, 271, 303, 304-5, 308-9, 315-16, 326
   apostolic, 132, 309
   biblical, 41-43, 125, 128
   church, 132, 272, 277, 296, 309, 332, 334, 336-37, 339, 340-43, 345-59, 360, 363, 365, 368, 372, 380-82, 386, 389
   compared to power, 157
   delegated, 137, 181, 226-27, 374, 376
   deputized, 181, 226-27, 347, 359-61, 374, 377-78, 382-83
   elder, 132, 348-59
   to forgive, 279, 280, 281, 288, 313
   and freedom, 165
   God's, 144-45, 152, 153-59, 161-62, 168-70, 172, 201, 210, 211
   government (or state), 159, 161, 185-99, 204, 206-8, 272, 277, 372-74, 383
   and identity, 63, 116, 172, 240, 243, 303, 367
   of institutions, 111, 116, 117, 139-41, 270, 365

   joint and several, 380-82
   political, 112, 114-21, 125, 126, 144-45, 153-59, 161, 197, 211, 230, 240, 294, 386, 389
   *potentia absoluta*, 153-55
   *potentia ordinata*, 153-55
   source of political authority, 154-55, 161-62
   See also institution: hermeneutic; keys of the kingdom; political rebellion
baptism, 15, 81, 114, 116, 129, 166, 262, 295, 302, 334, 350, 352-53, 356, 360-64, 367, 370, 374, 376, 379, 385, 386
   See also ordinances
church
   centered-set vs. bounded-set, 104
   *communio* ecclesiology, 99-100
   as contrast model, 37, 277, 375, 387, cf. 225
   definition of local church, 365, 386
   discipline, 23, 52, 337, 339-41, 342, 345, 348
   as embassy, 13, 22, 24, 52, 272, 296, 366, 366-69, 374-85, 389, 391-92
   as household, 23, 301
   images for, 301
   institutional vs. organic, 378-80
   joint vs. several, 380-82
   made visible, 332-34, 385-87
   membership, 50, 52, 272-73, 362-65, 375, 386

   as people of the new covenant, 302, 305-7, 390
   as political institution, political nature, 13, 14, 21-22, 25, 32-38, 142, 275-76, 294-95, 365-66, 375-78, 382-85, 386, 390-92
   political message and engagement, 14, 376-78, 383-85
   political unity of, 23, 385-87
   as signmaker, 15, 50, 366-70
   as spiritual, 14, 31, 32, 51, 68-71, 84-86, 284, 285, 382, 389
   as voluntary organization, 22-23, 52-53, 391
   universal, 295, 301-5, 385
   See also authority; *ekklēsia*; keys of the kingdom
Church of England, South Africa, 14, 84-85
civil disobedience. See under political rebellion
citizen, citizenship. See under political membership
covenant, 48, 49
   Abrahamic, 177, 180, 181, 215-22, 295
   Adamic, 43, 181, 184, 214, 215, 216-17, 223, 230, 237, 238, 239, 390
   Davidic, 227-28, 249, 250, 254, 277, 306
   methodology, 40-44
   Mosaic, 181, 222-27, 241, 243, 277, 295, 308

new, 245-46, 247-54, 292-93, 311, 390
Noahic, 43, 51, 177, 180, 182-85, 204-5, 390
  as political, 49-50, 163, 164, 182, 221-22, 236-38, 248-49, 252-54, 254-55, 257-78
  relationship between special and common, 180-81, 216-22, 237, 277
doctrine of the two/two ages, 51, 246, 262, 274, 314, 374
ekklēsia, 27, 36-37, 350, 351, 387
epistemology, 35, 41-43, 255
evangelism, as political, 52, 136, 303, 376, cf. 130
forgiveness, 278-90, 311-15, 318
  political definition of, 284-86, 288-89
freedom of conscience, 13, 29-31, 55, 71-76, 87, 88, 89, 90-93, 169-70, 198, 200-205, 358, 371
  *See also* religious freedom/liberty; religious tolerance
gods. *See under* religion
gospel, 135, 140, 142, 278, 304, 317, 320, 325, 327, 332, 341-42, 353, 356, 357, 362, 364, 365, 376, 382, 390, 392
  holistic, 264, 265
  political, 32, 36, 151, 258, 267
  spiritual, 31, 32
  the "what" and the "who" of, 14, 50, 340, 342, 349, 357, 358-59, 367, 370
government (state), 13, 46, 49, 50, 60-62, 182, 268-69, 272, 275-76, 277-78, 373-74
  biblical foundation for, 185-99, 206-8
  form of, 189-91, 269-71
  as platform builder for true religion, 15, 50, 208
heaven, 307-9
hermeneutics, 43-45
  missional hermeneutic, 130-31
  political hermeneutic, 133-36

*See also* institution: hermeneutic
image of God, humankind as, 14, 82, 125, 149-53, 154, 158-59, 163-64, 165, 266, 168, 180, 183, 185, 187, 195, 200, 268, 291, 300, 304, 390
  *See also* Jesus: as true image of God
institution
  change of structure, 228-35
  conceptuality of, 25, 45-46, 48, 49, 105-11, 126-27, 139-41
  definition of, 25, 105-11
  hermeneutic, 27, 128-36, 138, 143, 389
  lack of institutional understanding, 25-26, 270
  new institutionalism, 27, 105-9, 126
  political, 112-14, 236-37, 247
  relational character of, 111
  salvation and judgment as institutional acts, 231-35, 237
  sin as institutional act, 172-75, 240-41
  *See also* authority: of institutions
Islam, 151-52
Jesus
  as new Adam, 160, 168, 296-97, 298-301, 302-3, 310, 315
  and new covenant, 245-46, 264-65, 302, 311, 390
  as offspring of Abraham, 299, 307
  as son of David, 229, 298-99, 306, 315, 390
  as true image of God, 154, 300
  as true Israel, 298-99, 306, 390
justice, 112-13, 114, 115, 117, 119-20, 125-26, 148, 152-53, 168, 172, 244, 375
  as inherent rights, 93, 199-201
  retributive, 280-84
  as right order, 93, 199-201

justification, 316-17
  anti-imperial, 133-34, 270-71
  as covenantal, 317-23
  by faith alone (*sola fide*), 14, 29, 46-47, 113, 243-46, 258-59, 287, 325-28, 330-31
  forensic, 323-35
  future according to works, 328-30
  New Perspective, 47, 241, 259, 318, 320
  as requiring institutional specification, 319-20, 322-23
  self-justification, 47, 240-46, 254, 261, 278, 290, 292-93, 298, 313, 317, 326-28, 330, 348
keys of Death and Hades, 136
keys of the kingdom, 14, 22, 23, 25, 50, 51, 52, 69, 95, 128, 129, 132, 140, 179, 275, 294, 295, 296, 317, 332-61, 362, 364-65, 366, 368, 369, 372, 373, 374, 375, 377, 382, 384, 385-86, 389, 390
  definition of, 340-42
  possessed by elders or congregation, 348-59
kingdom of Christ, 15, 23, 24, 52
kingdom of God, 28
Kuyperianism, 48, 95
liberalism, 28-31, 34, 35, 38, 39, 48-49, 55, 57-59, 72-76, 79-82, 87-88, 93, 94, 95, 113, 129-30, 165, 200-201, 389
  classical, 13, 57, 72-74, 87-90, 187-89, 260-61
  contemporary, 57, 62-67, 72, 75, 89
  critiques of, 33-38, 80-85, 191-97, 198-99, 200-201, 205, 207, 260-61
  public reason, 63-65, 209, 260
liberation theology, 32, 35, 144, 258, 262-64, 267
Lord's Supper, 15, 114, 127, 166, 295, 350, 356, 360, 361, 362-64, 366, 367, 370, 375, 379, 386, 390
  *See also* ordinances
nations, 24, 209-14
natural law, 88, 93-94

## Subject Index

ontology, 40-41
ordinances, 166-67, 337, 362-65, 381, 386, 391
  *See also* baptism; Lord's Supper
pacifism, 46, 267, 316
political community, 114, 117, 221, 125, 159-60, 173, 223-25, 262, 250, 289, 312-14, 389
  and territory, 117
political membership
  citizen, 23, 27, 64, 115-16, 119, 121-26, 154, 158-60, 163, 164, 167, 171, 173, 177, 178, 181, 184, 193, 206, 208, 212, 215, 216, 217, 219, 220, 221, 222, 225, 226, 227, 232-33, 236, 239, 243, 244, 247, 260, 262, 272, 273, 277, 287, 288, 290-91, 295, 296-97, 298, 300, 304, 305, 307, 310, 315, 317, 323, 324, 325, 330, 331, 333-34, 342, 344, 351, 360, 361, 362, 363, 364, 365, 372, 379, 386, 387, 389, 390
  definition of, 115, 121-26, 389
  subject, 115, 117, 118, 119, 121-26, 160, 163-64, 171, 177, 178, 184, 206, 208, 215, 216, 231-32, 236, 243, 247, 273, 277, 288, 295, 297, 304-5, 351, 386
political obligation, 31, 49, 81, 93-94, 140, 144, 168-70, 171, 187-88, 189, 192-97, 207, 209, 268, 384
  consent, 58, 73, 88, 130, 154, 156, 164, 174, 186, 189, 190, 191-96, 252, 352
political rebellion, 119-20, 170, 172-75
  civil disobedience, 24, 45, 170, 203
  revolution, 195-96

political theology, 15, 16, 25, 32-38, 40, 44, 47, 51, 120, 137, 143, 176, 211, 257-78
  Jewish, 48, 96-97, 120-21, 144, 161, 163, 180, 182, 189-90, 230, 232-33, 252
political unity, 117, 120-21, 325-28, 331
politics, definition of, 49-50, 56, 59-60, 82-84, 86, 182, 207, 237
post-liberalism, 33-38, 41, 48
preaching, 31, 52, 136, 294, 332, 333, 337, 338, 340, 353, 362, 381, 386, 390
priest-king, 16, 167-68, 183, 220, 223-24, 290-91, 296-97, 300-301, 303, 304, 305, 332, 334, 349, 351, 356, 357, 358, 360, 364
public/private divide, 13, 56-59
public square, 13, 14, 16, 26, 31, 33, 50, 52, 66, 68, 71, 72, 76, 79, 82, 83, 84, 90-94, 201-2, 204, 249, 260, 261, 268, 273, 373, 375, 376, 377, 378, 380, 382, 385, 389
  as battleground of gods/lords, 14, 50, 82, 90, 202, 373
Radical Orthodoxy, 33-35, 40-41, 45-47
relational turn, 99-105
religion, 13-14, 28, 81
  constructivist, 77-79
  establishing, 26, 371, 372-73, 384
  functional, 26-27, 76-79, 179
  gods, 14, 62, 73, 78, 79, 81, 87, 88, 90, 92, 199, 202, 203, 212, 213, 214, 258, 331, 375, 383, 384
  substantive, 26-27, 76-78, 179
religious freedom/liberty, 51, 71-76, 86-94, 199-200, 203

  *See also* freedom of conscience; religious tolerance
religious tolerance, 51, 52, 87, 199-205, 273, 370-74, 384
  *See also* religious freedom/liberty
representation, 161-62, 206, 226-27
  *See also* authority: delegated, deputized
Romanticism, 99-101
separation of the political and spiritual, 29, 36-38, 62-69, 76-86, 94-97, 143, 172, 179-80, 201-2, 209-14, 215, 238, 252-54, 258, 273, 371-72
sphere sovereignty, 45, 134, 176
state. *See* authority: government
Superman, 241
Supreme Court, 13, 64, 89
sword. *See* government
theonomy, 39, 48, 66-67, 94, 95, 152, 272
totalitarianism, 56, 62, 152, 157, 255-57, 258, 261, 314
Trinity, 40, 41, 79, 98, 102, 103, 143, 146-53, 154, 156, 158, 162, 171, 173, 256, 278, 284, 301, 302, 324, 368
two cities, 78, 176
two kingdoms, 29-31, 48-49, 68, 72-73, 86, 95, 135, 176-80, 181, 211, 258-60, 274-75, 370, 382
two swords, 31, 176, 262
wisdom, 39, 132, 134, 137-39, 190, 192, 193, 198, 274, 377, 378
worship, 34, 73-74, 78, 79, 91, 92, 95, 177, 179, 180-81, 200, 206, 208, 210, 215, 236, 292, 347, 371, 375-76, 387, 389
  false, 62, 86, 199, 202, 208, 213, 214, 266, 271, 273, 370
  freedom of, 202
  as political, 143, 165-68, 171, 172, 208, 214, 223, 238, 255, 375-76

# Scripture Index

**Old Testament**

**Genesis**
1, *102, 155, 156, 158, 159, 160, 162, 163, 183, 184, 217, 238*
1:1, *307, 308*
1:26, *160, 268, 304, 305*
1:27, *149, 183*
1:28, *125, 157, 158, 163, 183, 184, 216, 217, 219, 222, 299, 307, 387*
1:29, *130, 157*
1:31, *164, 243*
2, *127, 155, 158*
2:4, *305*
2:14, *125*
2:15, *167*
2:16, *130, 157, 158, 160, 163*
2:17, *158, 159*
2:18, *157*
2:22, *157, 158*
3, *103, 119, 175, 185, 196*
3–5, *228*
3:1, *255*
3:4, *173*
3:5, *78, 172, 240*
3:8, *174*
3:12, *174*
4, *127, 173, 186*
4:12, *188*
4:14, *186*
4:15, *186, 188*
5, *159, 173*
5:1, *306*
5:3, *159*
6:5, *202, 219*
6:11, *202*
7:1, *184*
8:20, *184*
8:21, *183, 185, 198*
9, *87, 179, 183, 184, 186, 189, 191, 192, 193, 196, 198, 199, 201, 204, 206, 370, 376*
9:1, *183, 184, 197, 217, 237*
9:5, *184, 186, 188, 189, 193, 195, 197, 201, 202, 237, 267, 277, 351, 375, 382*
9:6, *82, 137, 183, 196, 200*
9:7, *197*
9:9, *183*
12, *179, 216, 218, 221, 222*
12:2, *217, 221, 227*
12:3, *216*
15, *216, 222, 295*
15:6, *219*
15:18, *222*
15:31, *159*
17:2, *217, 222*
17:6, *217, 222*
17:7, *222*
17:8, *222*
18:17, *219*
18:19, *221*
18:23, *220*
18:25, *220*
20:9, *209*
22:16, *217*
22:17, *307, 309*
22:18, *218, 221*
26:3, *218*
26:4, *218*
26:5, *219*
26:24, *218*
28:3, *218*
35, *218*
35:11, *218, 221*
38:26, *220*
41, *376*
47:27, *222*
48:3, *222*

**Exodus**
1:7, *218, 222*
1:12, *222*
1:20, *222*
3:13, *226*
4:22, *306*
5:2, *209*
5:23, *226*
6, *223*
6:3, *226*
6:7, *223, 229, 231, 233*
9:16, *209, 226*
11:7, *223*
12:12, *214*
13:9, *268*
14:13, *235*
15:3, *234*
15:16, *235*
19:5, *224*
19:22, *167*
20:7, *226*
23:13, *226*
24, *295*
24:7, *224*
24:8, *311*
28:3, *137*
31:6, *137*

**Leviticus**
18:21, *226*
19: 2, *241*
19:12, *226*
20:3, *226*
21:6, *226*
22:2, *226*
22:32, *226*
24:20, *197*
26:9, *222*

**Numbers**
3:7, *167*
23:10, *222*
23:21, *175*

**Deuteronomy**
4: 6, *225*
4:8, *225*
4:10, *37*
4:30, *219*
5:31, *219*
6:5, *157, 255*
6:25, *225, 241*
7:13, *222*

10:16, *247, 253*
12:5, *226*
12:11, *226*
13, *199*
13:1, *225*
15:4, *222*
15:6, *222*
17:6, *346*
17:18-20, *227*
19:15, *346*
28:11, *222*
29, *247*
30:5, *290*
30:6, *247, 253*
30:9, *290*
32:39, *155*

**Ruth**
4:11, *26*

**1 Samuel**
2:6, *155*
8:5, *212*
8:7, *212*
24:11, *310*

**2 Samuel**
7:9, *227*
7:11, *227*
7:13, *228*
7:29, *222*
23:4, *158*

**1 Kings**
3:28, *274*
8:14, *37*
8:16, *226*
8:19, *228*
10:9, *228*

**2 Kings**
19:15, *175*

**1 Chronicles**
17:10, *227*
17:12, *26*

**Nehemiah**
8, *37*

**Job**
38:4, *155*
38:31, *338*
41:11, *155*

**Psalms**
2, *272*
2: 1, *214*
2:2, *306*
2:7, *228, 375*
2:10, *367*
8:5, *157, 223*
10:16, *231*
22:28, *175, 211*
24:1, *155*
28:5, *26*
29:9, *155*
29:10, *175*
47:2, *175*
47:7, *175*
47:8, *175*
72:1, *158*
89:3, *227*
91:11, *300*
96:10, *175, 210, 269*
96:13, *219*
99:1, *175*
103:19, *175*
107:37, *222*
110:1, *299*
115:3, *157*
118:22, *26*

**Proverbs**
1:7, *137*
7:3, *268*
14:34, *220*

**Ecclesiastes**
3:3, *138*
3:20, *392*
12:7, *392*

**Isaiah**
6: 5, *175*
9:1, *312*
9:6, *175*
11:1, *300*
11:6, *158*
13, *210*
21:9, *213*
22:15, *336*
22:22, *336, 338*
30:1, *213*
33:17, *234*
33:19, *234*
33:22, *211*
40:1, *312*
40:1-2, *235*
40:2, *155*
40:5, *235*
40:10, *155, 229, 235*
40:12, *155*
41:21, *175*
43:6, *155*
43:15, *175*
44:5, *268*
44:6, *175*
44:16, *77*
45:7, *155*
45:9, *155*
51:2, *222*
52:7, *229, 235*
52:8, *235*
52:10, *235*
52:13, *251*
53, *251, 283*
53:10, *283, 300*
53:11, *311*
54, *250, 251*
54:1, *223, 247*
54:9, *252, 283*
54:10, *250*
54:13, *251*
54:14, *251*
55, *251*
55:1, *247*
55:3, *251*
55:6, *251*
62:2, *235*

**Jeremiah**
1:10, *26*
3:16, *223*
3:18, *223*
8:19, *175*
9:23, *298*
10: 1, *155*
10:6, *210*
10:7, *175*
10:10, *175, 210*
13:23, *247*
21–36, *254*
23:3, *223*
24:6, *26*
29, *376*
30:3, *290*
30:4, *249*
31:4, *26, 290*
31:31, *247, 248, 311*
31:33, *268, 324*
31:34, *257, 278, 324, 357*
32:36, *247*
32:40, *249*
33:7, *26*
33:14, *249*
33:15, *249*
46, *210*
46:18, *175*

**Ezekiel**
1:3, *231*
11:18, *247*
25, *210*

## Scripture Index

28:1-19, *172*
34:11, *229*
34:20, *247*
36, *249, 250, 332*
36:9, *223*
36:10, *291*
36:22, *249*
36:23, *266*
36:25, *249*
36:27, *249, 254, 266, 332*
36:33, *249*
36:36, *266*
37, *250, 332*
37:15, *247*
37:21, *250*
37:24, *267*
39:21, *235*

### Daniel
3:14, *213*
3:18, *213*
3:28-29, *231*
3:29, *208*
4, *214*
4:34, *175*
4:35, *156*
7, *214, 291, 308, 309*
7:13, *223, 309*
7:18, *291*
7:22, *291*
7:27, *291*

### Hosea
1:1, *223*
1:10, *175*
2:23, *175*
11:1, *306*

### Amos
1, *210*
9:11, *26*

### Micah
4:6, *175*
7:16, *235*

### Habakkuk
1:7, *375*

### Zephaniah
2, *210*
2:11, *214*
3:15, *175*

### Zechariah
8:3, *229*
9:5, *235*
9:10, *229*

14:9, *175*
14:16, *175*

### Malachi
1:5, *235*
1:14, *175*
3:18, *235*

## NEW TESTAMENT

### Matthew
1-7, *306*
1: 1, *299, 305, 308, 361*
2:1, *306*
2:15, *299, 306*
3:1, *312*
3:2, *308*
3:7, *310, 314*
3:9, *300*
3:10, *315*
3:11, *315, 331*
3:15, *313*
3:17, *152, 308*
4:8, *308*
4:10, *308*
4:14, *312*
4:17, *308, 309, 344*
4:19, *309*
5:3, *293, 308, 313*
5:5, *308*
5:7, *313*
5:9, *309*
5:10, *392*
5:13, *370, 375*
5:16, *309*
5:17, *306, 315*
5:19, *338, 339*
5:20, *312*
5:21, *306, 314*
5:27, *314*
5:31, *314*
5:33, *314*
5:38, *133, 314*
5:44, *293, 314*
5:45, *309*
5:48, *309*
6:1, *309*
6:8, *309*
6:10, *175, 300, 308, 344, 361*
6:12, *313*
6:13, *313*
6:19, *308*
6:20, *361*
6:33, *361*
7:16, *331*
7:17, *315*
7:21, *314*

8-20, *307, 334, 336, 337, 339, 340, 342*
8:9, *126, 160*
8:10, *348*
8:11, *310*
8:12, *310*
9:12, *312*
9:33, *334*
10:1, *310*
10:20, *315*
10:32, *314*
11:18, *334*
11:23, *308*
11:25, *308*
11:27, *309*
12:8, *307*
12:28, *344*
12:29, *338*
12:50, *310*
13:11, *175, 309*
13:31, *175*
13:38, *310*
13:42, *312*
13:43, *310*
13:52, *306*
14-28, *336*
16, *110, 128, 129, 294, 307, 316, 334, 340, 342, 345, 348, 360*
16:1, *334*
16:13, *333*
16:14, *334*
16:16, *334*
16:17, *335*
16:18, *26, 294, 307, 316, 334, 335, 353*
16:19, *309, 336, 339, 340, 343, 361*
16:21, *313, 316*
17:24, *277*
18, *338, 339, 340, 342, 344, 347, 348, 349, 350*
18:1, *175*
18:15, *344, 345*
18:16, *345*
18:17, *345, 350, 353*
18:18, *309, 339, 345, 354, 361*
18:19, *345*
18:20, *116, 345, 346, 348, 350, 367, 369*
18:21, *293*
18:23, *314*
19:28, *304, 310*
20:25, *315*
21:2, *338*
21:31, *312*
21:32, *313*
21:33, *311*
21:43, *311*

22:20, *268*
22:30, *277*
22:44, *299*
23:9, *308*
23:13, *311*
23:27, *315*
24:35, *308*
26, *360*
26:27, *311*
27:25, *311*
27:42, *299*
28, *129, 359, 360, 361*
28:16, *308*
28:18, *157, 176, 304, 308, 359, 360*
28:19, *116, 360, 387*
28:20, *347, 360*

## Mark

1:13, *300*
1:15, *343*
3:27, *300*
7: 8, *139*
7:13, *139, 192*
10:42, *315*
12:28, *132*

## Luke

3:23, *299, 306*
3:38, *159*
4: 1, *299*
4:5, *168*
4:8, *168*
6:45, *203*
10:27, *157, 255*
11:52, *336*
18:9, *245*
18:14, *293*

## John

1:14, *147*
3: 3, *266*
3:18, *175*
4:34, *126*
5:19, *300*
5:30, *300*
8:28, *126, 300*
10:35, *319*
12:13, *299*
12:49, *300*
13:34, *375*
14:10, *300*
15:10, *126, 153*
15:12, *153*
15:18, *384*
15:23, *151*
17:5, *146, 147*
17:21, *369*

17:22, *153*
17:26, *153*
18:36, *23*
19:11, *269*
20:21, *135*
20:22, *343*
20:23, *280, 342, 353*

## Acts

2:34, *299*
2:46, *369*
5:12, *369*
6: 2, *369*
8:21, *358*
14:21, *350*
15, *341*
17:5, *122*
17:26, *208, 383*
17:28, *40*
19, *271, 383*
19:4, *343*
20:7, *365*
20:27, *44*
20:28, *353, 357*
24:15, *47*
25, *271, 383*

## Romans

2, *329*
2: 4, *208*
2:6, *236*
2:13, *328*
3:20, *242*
3:21, *322*
3:26, *245*
3:27, *327*
4:16, *216, 300*
5:12, *275, 299, 302, 324*
5:17, *300*
7:2, *338*
7:7, *242*
8:19, *265*
9:7, *300*
9:21, *157*
10:9, *367, 387*
10:17, *332*
13, *31, 46, 193, 214, 272, 277, 376*
13:1, *194, 206, 267, 375, 382*
13:4, *207*

## 1 Corinthians

3:21, *328*
4: 4, *328*
5:4, *116, 342, 347, 351, 367, 369*
5:5, *317, 331, 351, 358*
5:12, *317, 331, 351, 358*
6:1, *304*
7:3, *381*

7:4, *288*
7:27, *340*
7:39, *340*
10:6, *44*
10:31, *95, 166*
11:18, *347, 369*
11:26, *127, 367*
11:29, *317*
12:3, *270*
15:23, *300*
15:28, *175*
15:45, *299*
16:2, *365*

## 2 Corinthians

4:4, *301*
5:10, *328*
5:17, *303*
6:14, *370*
6:16, *369*
13:5, *331*

## Galatians

1: 6, *322, 351*
2, *320, 325*
2:14, *320*
2:16, *320, 327*
2:20, *79*
3, *320, 321, 322*
3:2, *321*
3:7, *321*
3:10, *321, 322*
3:12, *321*
3:16, *321*
3:19, *127*
3:21, *321*
3:24, *321*
3:26, *303, 321*
3:28, *321, 328*
3:29, *300, 322*
4, *322*
4:1, *322*
4:6, *303*
5, *325*
5:4, *325*
5:17, *325*
5:21, *328*
5:22, *325*
6:2, *325*
6:8, *328*

## Ephesians

1:21, *175, 176*
2, *324*
2: 1, *275*
2:2, *175*
2:14, *325*
2:16, *325*

2:19, *23, 325*
2:20, *335*
3:14, *145*
4, *358*
4:11, *357, 358*
4:15, *358*

**Philippians**
1:11, *372*
1:27, *304, 317*
2:1, *316*
2:2, *317*
2:3, *317*
2:5, *317*
2:12, *317*
3:9, *317*
3:20, *304, 317*

**Colossians**
1:15, *154, 301*
1:16, *301*
1:18, *158*
2:5, *295*
2:10, *175*
3:11, *328*

**1 Thessalonians**
1:5, *332*

**1 Timothy**
1:20, *358*

2:1, *273, 383*
3:1, *287*
3:15, *23*
5:7, *131*

**2 Timothy**
2:12, *125, 160, 304*

**Titus**
1:5, *350*

**Hebrews**
1:3, *301*
1:9, *152*
1:13, *299*
9:15, *167*
10:25, *365*
12:24, *167*
13:17, *353, 357*

**James**
4:1, *326, 328*
4:11, *173*

**1 Peter**
1:13, *257*
1:15, *257*
1:23, *332*
2:4, *356*
2:9, *356, 370, 375*
2:10, *324*

3:22, *175*
4:17, *23*
5:1, *353*

**2 Peter**
1:20, *42*
3:9, *185*

**1 John**
1:1, *369*
2:23, *151*

**2 John**
7, *331*
9, *151*

**Revelation**
1:6, *304*
1:18, *136, 336*
3:7, *336, 338*
5:10, *125, 304*
6:15, *268, 375*
9:1, *336*
11:15, *176*
13:1, *214*
20:1, *336*
20:6, *160, 304*
21:14, *335*
22:5, *125, 304*

# The Studies in Christian Doctrine and Scripture Series

Series Editors: Daniel J. Treier and Kevin J. Vanhoozer

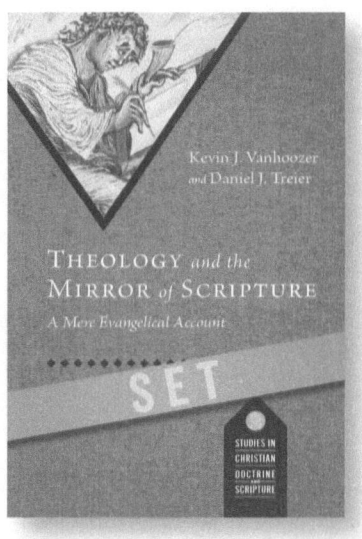

Studies in Christian Doctrine and Scripture promotes evangelical contributions to systematic theology, seeking fresh understanding of Christian doctrine through creatively faithful engagement with Scripture in dialogue with catholic tradition(s).

Thus: We aim to publish **contributions to systematic theology** rather than merely descriptive rehearsals of biblical theology, historical retrievals of classic or contemporary theologians, or hermeneutical reflections on theological method—volumes that are plentifully and expertly published elsewhere.

We aim to promote **evangelical** contributions, neither retreating from broader dialogue into a narrow version of this identity on the one hand, nor running away from the biblical preoccupation of our heritage on the other hand.

We seek fresh understanding of Christian doctrine **through creatively faithful engagement with Scripture.** To some fellow evangelicals and interested others today, we commend the classic evangelical commitment of engaging Scripture. To other fellow evangelicals today, we commend a contemporary aim to engage Scripture with creative fidelity. The church is to be always reforming—but always reforming according to the Word of God.

We seek **fresh understanding of Christian doctrine.** We do not promote a singular method; we welcome proposals appealing to biblical theology, the history of interpretation, theological interpretation of Scripture, or still other approaches. We welcome projects that engage in detailed exegesis as well as those that appropriate broader biblical themes and patterns. Ultimately, we hope to promote relating Scripture to doctrinal understanding in material, not just formal, ways.

We promote scriptural engagement **in dialogue with catholic tradition(s).** A periodic evangelical weakness is relative disinterest in the church's shared creedal heritage, in churches' particular confessions, and more generally in the history of dogmatic reflection. Beyond existing efforts to enhance understanding of themes and corpora in biblical theology, then, we hope to foster engagement with Scripture that bears upon and learns from loci, themes, or crucial questions in classic dogmatics and contemporary systematic theology.

## Finding the Textbook You Need

The IVP Academic Textbook Selector
is an online tool for instantly finding the IVP books
suitable for over 250 courses across 24 disciplines.

ivpacademic.com

www.ingramcontent.com/pod-product-compliance
Lightning Source LLC
Chambersburg PA
CBHW022226010526
44113CB00033B/510